'[*The Ideal of Manliness*] is a really splendid ⸏ ⸏evement; the expansion of a study of Thring to the wider scene is so well handled as are the deft, subtle but very significant category distinctions in public school theory and practice. I enjoyed it immensely (read at one go over a weekend).'
— Professor Christopher Tyerman, Oxford University, author, *A History of Harrow School 1324–1991*

'This magnificent book needs to be in the reference section of all university libraries.... It is truly a publication of great significance.... Historians will find it illuminating and social scientists need to be aware of the research methodology.'
— Robert Chappell, Fellow of Brunel University, in *Physical Education Matters*

'Thring, his legacy, his influence and his transformation of Uppingham School were all but pushed down my throat as sacred creeds during my time at Uppingham. His statue and portraits and name seemed to be everywhere. Malcolm Tozer shows us why. The man truly was as remarkable as Uppingham myth made him out to be. Edward Thring was one of those tireless and extraordinary reforming Victorians with an indomitable will, unquestioning sense of destiny and remarkable powers of persuasion. This marvellous book shows how they were combined with a genuinely pastoral sense of how education could benefit 'the whole boy' and thence the whole of society.'
— Stephen Fry

'Anyone interested in educational ideas and in the history of education will enjoy the book.... It is wonderfully researched, with detailed information on his resources, so that the reader follows a history of the theme of manliness through two centuries of schooling involving an analysis of the history of games, Christian worship and the influence of the Empire as it then was.'
— Ian Beer, former Headmaster of Harrow School, in *ASCL Associates News*

'In what can be ascribed as a seminal text . . . Malcolm Tozer has drawn from an extensive literature review of primary and secondary sources and in-depth research. . . . The book is worthy of "classic" status. Its scope and detail will have resonance for both specialists in the field as well as generalists.'

— Professor Ken Hardman, University of Worcester,
in *The International Journal of Physical Education*

'Thring is one of those historical figures who has been deeply influential but has now been largely forgotten, outside the rather small world of the public school historians. His notion of using a broad syllabus to find the particular talent of the particular child has echoes in today's thinking, for example. This book traces, with a scholarly and diligent eye, his impact on future generations. . . . I would even go so far as to say that serving school head teachers could learn a lot from this book.'

— David Turner, author, *The Old Boys: The
Decline and Rise of the Public School*

'Thring was years ahead in his educational thinking and pastoral work which benefitted not just Uppingham but the whole of the education sector. . . . Malcolm Tozer is to be congratulated on what is obviously a lifetime's work on his part and he can rest assured that he has done the man and the subject justice.'

— Paul Jackson, editor, *Prep School*

'*[The Ideal of Manliness:] The Legacy of Thring's Uppingham* is a well-informed, attractively written and handsomely presented study of a major nineteenth century educationalist. Some time ago I reviewed Michael McCrum's, *Thomas Arnold, Headmaster: A Re-assessment*. I remarked that . . . 'the re-working of well-thumbed secondary sources had gone on long enough.' Malcolm Tozer has more than met my challenge. I asked further for a contextual consideration of the remarkable nineteenth century evolution of the British public school from near insular nemesis to established international prominence following inter alia its espousal of the potent moralistic ideology of Athleticism in the wake of the wealth of industrialisation, the growth of middle class ambition and the spread of soft power imperialism. Again Malcolm Tozer has responded to the challenge. Edward Thring is there on the pantheon of great imperial educationalists. Malcolm Tozer has done him proud.'

— Professor J. A. Mangan, author, *Athleticism in the Victorian and
Edwardian Public School* and *The Games Ethic and Imperialism*

'The influence of Thring continues at Uppingham to this day. The basis of his approach equipped many old boys to be effective leaders of men in the First World War. Malcolm Tozer's book is an important account of how this came to be so.'

— Timothy Halstead, author, *A School in
Arms: Uppingham and the Great War*

'This important and far-ranging work . . . is the fruit of 40 years' experience and an immense amount of reading and research. . . . (The author) deploys a wealth of original documents . . . and his own prose carries the reader comfortably through this substantial book. . . . It is easy to see why Thring is still so highly regarded.'

– Tom Wheare, former Headmaster of Bryanston School,
in *Conference & Common Room*

'The mission of independent schools is far more ambitious than that found in most state schools; in addition to often excellent academic education, they frequently devote a third or more of their time to holistic all-round development, including sports and the arts. Opportunities to discover and nurture whatever talents each pupil has are seen as an entitlement; they are readily available, well taught and generously resourced. This, Malcolm Tozer asserts, is the legacy of Edward Thring's Uppingham. Music, art, gymnastics, cricket, crafts and drama flourished alongside the academic curriculum at this mid-Victorian school well before they were adopted elsewhere. What Thring termed 'the ideal of manliness' is the forerunner of today's 'wholeness'. The education of the whole man and the attention to the individual pupil are now the norm in all good schools, but it was not always so. This book traces that evolution.'

– Sir Anthony Seldon, Vice-Chancellor of the
University of Buckingham

'This book can be warmly welcomed as a more searching appraisal of Edward Thring than any previous account. . . . There is an impressive depth of documentation, drawn from Thring's diaries, as well as his better known sermons and published work. Tozer places Thring in the broadest possible frame. Detailed study of his headmastership is preceded by an analysis of the mentors past and present from whom he derived his educational ideas. The exceptionally long period of Thring's tenure at Uppingham is studied in depth. . . . The most original part of Tozer's book is his tracing of Thring's legacy long after his lifetime into the recent past.'

– Professor John Tosh, University of Roehampton,
in *History of Education*

'An excellent contribution to the literature on Muscular Christianity and manliness, which should be read by all serious students of the topics. The way the book provides evidence to challenge the received wisdom in a number of places is a particular strength.'

– Stuart Weir, in *Verité*

'Malcolm Tozer's substantial and well-contextualised study of changing values in the Victorian Public School and successor institutions . . . is a labour of love and a celebration, exploring the vision and the legacy of Edward Thring, headmaster of Uppingham from 1853 to 1887, one of the greatest nineteenth-century schoolmasters. . . . The heart of the book, and the longest section, is "True Manliness in Practice". The adjective "true" draws attention to the possibility of false or degenerate manliness as a constant threat. . . . Tozer faithfully and critically documents the growing tyranny of games and the descent into militarism in late-Victorian and Edwardian public schools . . . Tozer's last section carries the story forward into the twentieth century, claiming elements of Thringian manliness were revived in the work of John Royds, another visionary Uppingham Head, in the New School Movement, the Outward Bound Movement, and innovative new foundations such as J. H. Badley's Bedales and Kurt Hahn's Gordonstoun.'

– Professor Norman Vance, University of Sussex,
in *Paedagogica Historica*

George Christian and Edward Thring celebrating Holy Communion, from the Tercentenary windows in the Old School-room at Uppingham School. Designed by Charles Rossiter, art master 1873–97.

(photograph: author)

Education in Manliness

Education in Manliness explores the central educational ideal of the Victorian and Edwardian public school. The book traces the formulation of what Edward Thring, the most celebrated headmaster of the era, termed 'true manliness', noting the debt to the Platonic concept of the whole man and to Christian example, before examining the ideal's best holistic practice at Uppingham and other mid-Victorian schools.

The central chapters follow the tilting of manliness to the physical by the muscular Christians in the 1860s, its distortion to Spartanism by the games masters and sporting dons from the 1870s and its hijacking by the advocates of *esprit de corps* during the remainder of the century. The book lays bare the total perversion of the ideal by the military imperialists in the years up to the Great War and traces the lifeline of holistic education through the progressive school movement from the 1880s to the 1970s. It then brings this up to date by comparing true manliness with the 'wholeness' ideal of schools of the new millennium.

This book will be of great interest to scholars and students in the fields of history of education and the theory and practice of teaching, as well as school and university teachers, teacher trainers and trainee teachers.

Malcolm Tozer taught at Uppingham School from 1966 until 1989 and served as a housemaster for fourteen years. For six years from 1989 he was Northamptonshire Grammar School's first Headmaster and then Headmaster of Wellow House School for a further ten years. Since retiring in 2004, he has led inspections for the Independent Schools Inspectorate, served as a governor at Repton School and Foremarke Hall, and promoted partnerships in physical education and sport between state and independent schools.

Education in Manliness

The Legacy of Thring's Uppingham

Malcolm Tozer

Routledge
Taylor & Francis Group

LONDON AND NEW YORK

First published 2018
by Routledge

2 Park Square, Milton Park, Abingdon, Oxfordshire OX14 4RN
52 Vanderbilt Avenue, New York, NY 10017

Routledge is an imprint of the Taylor & Francis Group, an informa business

First issued in paperback 2020

British Library Cataloguing-in-Publication Data
A catalogue record for this book is available from the British
Library

Library of Congress Cataloging-in-Publication Data
A catalog record has been requested for this book

ISBN: 978-1-138-47934-0 (hbk)
ISBN: 978-0-367-48772-0 (pbk)

Typeset in Bembo
by Apex CoVantage, LLC

Visit the eResources: www.routledge.com/9781138479340

Ora et labora
Edward Thring's motto

Contents

Acknowledgements

This book is the culmination of waves of study spread over more than forty years. It was in the early 1970s, during the later stages of the writing of my master's thesis – later published as *Physical Education at Thring's Uppingham* – that I realised that Edward Thring saw physical education as a vital part, but only a part, of an education in manliness. Time and word restrictions allowed only a short chapter on the 'Ideal of Manliness' to be included and so it was left for me to find more time and more words to trace the evolution of the ideal – before, during and after Thring's headmastership. The result was my doctoral thesis, 'Manliness: the evolution of a Victorian ideal'; its research and writing occupied the late 1970s.

I was now a housemaster at Uppingham School: professional and family priorities demanded a break in study that lasted until the approach of the quatercentenary of the school's foundation in 1984 and the centenary of Thring's death in 1987. World-wide interest in Thring and his school encouraged me to publish a dozen essays, each needing more research on manliness.

My departure from Uppingham in 1989 for the first of my two headmasterships coincided with a sudden focus on 'masculinity' by scholars in several countries, in part to counterbalance the popularity of feminist studies. This made manliness a fashionable topic and over the next five years I received invitations to speak at international conferences and then to turn conference papers into essays. All this required more research.

The invitations dried up as I moved to my second headmastership in 1995, in part because interest in manliness as an educational ideal had waned as scholars turned their attention to broader issues of masculine power. All went quiet until my retirement in 2005 when the success of former pupils from independent schools in international sport and, in particular, at the summer Olympic Games from 2000 onwards, raised questions about the schooling they had received and the traditions on which that schooling was built. An introductory chapter in *Physical Education and Sport in Independent Schools* and an essay in *The International Journal of the History of Sport*, published in 2012 and 2013 respectively, sought to provide some answers.

My writings on manliness were now scattered over publications spanning four decades. Two events prompted me to gather them together, to bring their research up to date, and to publish them as a continuous and coherent story. The first was a request to review *'Manufactured' Masculinity: Making Imperial Manliness, Morality and Militarism* (2012), a swansong collection of essays by Tony Mangan that spans his forty-year career; the second was the publication of Nigel Richardson's *Thring of Uppingham: Victorian Educator* (2014), the modern biography that the headmaster has so long deserved. Tony and I sat together in the Uppingham Archives in the early 1970s and we have kept in touch as his international fame as a social historian has grown. If his forty-year story has a readership, so perhaps might mine. Nigel Richardson was an Uppingham colleague and we left for our first headmasterships at the same time. Now that he has published the full and rounded biography of the greatest British headmaster of the second half of the nineteenth century, there is likely to be interest in other facets of Thring's life and work. Nigel and I agree on the importance of manliness at Thring's Uppingham but its treatment necessarily formed only part of the biography and ignored what happened before and after Thring. Here is the complete story.

I owe thanks to many. It would have been impossible to contemplate this study without ease of access to the Uppingham Archives. I thank the Trustees and Headmasters of the school for granting it and for allowing me to publish what I found. The five Headmasters who span the forty years are John Royds (1965–74), Coll Macdonald (1975–82), Nick Bomford (1982–91), Stephen Winkley (1991–2006) and Richard Harman (2006+). I owe a huge debt of gratitude to Brian Belk and Jerry Rudman, successive archivists, for guiding me through their treasures.

I am grateful to past and present colleagues at Uppingham who have helped me over the years: Jeff Abbott, Peter Attenborough, James Barnett, Fiona Bettles, Geoff Frowde, Ben Goss, David Kirk, Bryan Matthews, Casey O'Hanrahan, Nigel Richardson, David Shipton and Neil Waddell. Beyond Uppingham, I have benefited from the advice of Richard Aldrich, Harry Armytage, Ian Beer, Gerald Bernbaum, Mary Byatt, Tim Chandler, Tim Clough, Ken Hardman, John Honey, Roy Lowe, Tony Mangan, David McNair, Gerald Murray, David Newsome, Mark Peel, Harold Perkin, Cormac Rigby, Brian Simon, Paul Stevens, John Tosh, Dale Vargas and Bob Wight. I must also thank the staff at the Bodleian Library, the British Library, the Cambridge University Library, Cornwall Libraries and the London Library.

My wife, Elizabeth, has lived with Thring for all those forty years. I thank her for her forbearance and support.

Malcolm Tozer
Portscatho, Cornwall
1 October 2015

I am very grateful to Aiyana Curtis, my editor at Routledge, for adding this book to her lists. It will now reach a wider market at home and abroad. The modification to the title is at her suggestion in order to capitalise on internet search engines.

The text has been shortened to match that of other history of education titles in the Routledge collection, mainly by reducing the length of quotations and by transferring the footnotes and bibliography to the Routledge website. They can be consulted at: www.routledge.com/9781138479340.

I have taken the opportunity provided by this new edition to invite Richard Maloney, Uppingham's headmaster since 2016, to have the final word in the Epilogue, and I thank him for granting me continued access to the Uppingham Archives.

Malcolm Tozer
Portscatho, Cornwall
1 December 2017

Prologue

On 27 April 1914, *The Times* published a short piece from its correspondent in Tokyo under the headline, 'Japanese Precepts for Boys'. The article was copied far and wide: it appeared in *The Singapore Free Press* on 27 May, in New Zealand's *Timaru Herald* on 11 June, in the *Milwaukee Journal* in America on 21 June, and in many other newspapers around the world. The Rev Harry Ward McKenzie, headmaster of Uppingham, spotted it as he read his copy of *The Times* at the end of the school's Easter holiday.[1] Headmasters of today collect and store anecdotes to use in sermons, speeches, and the like; perhaps this is what McKenzie did, for he used the story in his Speech Day address on Saturday 11 July, shortly before the end of the school year.

The article referred to the late General Count Nogi, a hero of the Russo-Japanese War of 1904–05 and well-known in Britain. On retirement from the army in 1908 he had been appointed President of the Gakushūin, a school for sons of noble families, and in 1912 he gave the boys his fourteen precepts. The report on McKenzie's speech in the school magazine suggests that he used some of them for comic effect and that the audience greeted each with laughter: 'Nothing makes a fool of a man so much as luxury. / Never use warm water in the winter. / It is a shame to wear torn clothes without mending them. / To wear the torn part patched is nothing to be ashamed of. / Never forget your coat of arms.'[2] Then McKenzie changed to a serious tone to close with the message he wanted his boys to remember.[3] It was the fourteenth and final precept: 'Be a man useful to your country. Whoever cannot be so is better dead.'[4]

News of the death of Count Nogi had been published in *The Times* on 14 September 1912.[5] He had committed suicide to coincide with the funeral procession for Mutsuhito, the Japanese Emperor. McKenzie and many of the adults in his audience would have known that Nogi's actions were in accordance with the *Bushidō* code of the *Samurai*: a warrior following his master in death. McKenzie's commendation of Nogi's final precept was an endorsement of its European equivalent, the Homeric code of honour, and of its legacy, the contemporary public-school ideal of manliness.[6] No-one at that Speech Day could have known that this ideal would soon be put to the test, even though the assassination of the Archduke Franz Ferdinand of Austria in distant Sarajevo a fortnight earlier had already set the course that would lead to the Great War.[7] It was not meant to be like this.

Wednesday 29 July was the last day at school for sixty-nine of the 430 boys who had heard their headmaster's valediction.[8] All were McKenzie's boys, joining Uppingham during his headmastership: the first in January 1909, the last in September 1912.[9] One, a master's son, was a day-boy; the rest were boarders spread across the thirteen houses. They were a successful year-group: only Oundle and Rossall had won more Higher Certificates with the examiners from Oxford and Cambridge; and fourteen boys would win places at the universities, three with exhibitions. Thirteen boys served as praepostors and twelve had won colours in sport. With 335 boys in the cadet corps, most of the sixty-nine would have taken part in Speech Day's ceremonial parade and marched before the inspecting eye of General Lord Luck.[10]

School was now over. Members of the cadet corps above the age of fifteen prepared for the annual camp, to be held in Hampshire. Along with hundreds of cadets from other public schools, the 134-strong Uppingham contingent assembled at the camping ground on Mytchett's Farm near Aldershot on Tuesday 28 July, expecting to be there until Thursday 6 August.[11] Events across Europe, however, had unfolded quickly in the wake of the assassination in Sarajevo and war suddenly seemed likely. The camp was disbanded on Monday 3 August to make way for reservists recalled to the colours; the boys went home. War was declared the following day.

All but two of the sixty-nine leavers of July 1914 served in the armed forces during the Great War. Nearly all joined the Army, with just three in the Royal Navy and two in the Royal Marines. Most were officers, for only three served in the ranks. Of the officers, fifteen were Second Lieutenants, thirty-one became Lieutenants, sixteen were promoted Captain and one reached the rank of Major.[12] They served well: eighteen were awarded medals for gallantry or were mentioned in dispatches.

Roland Garrod, a Second Lieutenant in the London Regiment, was the first to be killed, in France on 22 May 1915. A scholar and praepostor at school, he had won an exhibition to Clare College, Cambridge.[13] Three more of the group were killed that year; another six in 1916; then nine in 1917; and finally three in 1918. The twenty-second and last to die was Thomas Greenwell, a Lieutenant in the Northumberland Fusiliers, on 19 July 1918, also in France. Nearly a third of the leavers of July 1914 were killed in action or died of their wounds – twenty-two of the sixty-nine. It was not meant to be like this.

At least 2,129 Uppinghamians served in the armed forces during the Great War, more than five times the size of the school.[14] The roll of honour of those who died numbered 450 – nearly one in five. Most were junior officers and a third were aged under twenty-five.

News of the first death reached Uppingham in August.[15] Edward Cohan, a Second Lieutenant in the Royal Field Artillery, was killed in an accident on the second day of the war. The first death in combat occurred in Belgium on 24

August, the next just three days later. The first Uppinghamian to be named in the list of 'Fallen Officers' in *The Times* was John Caldecott, a Lieutenant serving with the Royal Garrison Artillery in Nyasaland; he died on 9 September.[16] The school's list of the fallen climbed to thirty by the year's end; ninety more names were added in 1915.[17] Five of the sixty-nine leavers of July 1914 had now been killed.

McKenzie must have felt a special association with boys who had joined Uppingham in his time. Of the 718 who had entered the school between January 1908 and September 1914, 144 were killed during the course of the war – one in five – with fourteen from his own house. Among the dead were eleven entrance scholars, one captain of school, fifteen school praepostors and seven who had won places at Oxford or Cambridge.

All fourteen boarding houses suffered.[18] The headmaster's house, School House, lost most boys – forty-three. The Lodge, the next oldest house, mourned thirty-seven deaths, including thirteen for boys who had spent all their years in the care of the current housemaster, Horace Puckle. Three of Puckle's boys were part of the cohort of sixty-nine who left school after Speech Day in 1914 – Edward Brittain, Roland Leighton and Victor Richardson. Their friendship formed the subject of Vera Brittain's *Testament of Youth*, published in 1933.[19]

McKenzie began his headmastership in January 1908 determined to raise pupil numbers, to lift academic standards, and to place Uppingham in the forefront of public schools. He succeeded on all three counts. Aged fifty-seven, three years older than the man he succeeded, Uppingham would be the prize at the end of a long career.[20]

The fifty-seven years of his life before Uppingham spanned the evolution of the ideal of manliness from its adoption in the 1850s by the new proprietary and raised grammar schools, through the muscular Christian years of the 1860s, onward to the hardiness of the 1870s and the games mania of the 1880s, through the imperial frenzy of the 1890s, and finally to the military manliness of the new century. McKenzie had been at some of the key schools at key times: as a boy at Guildford, a revived grammar school; two spells as an assistant master at Wellington College under its second headmaster, Edward Wickham; a short period in Scotland at H. H. Almond's pioneering school at Loretto; and then headmasterships at Lancing College and Durham School. He imbibed the ideal as a boy and transmitted its practice as a man. He was a brisk, breezy, efficient, popular, decent and athletic man but he was neither scholarly nor intellectual.[21] He was a thoroughly orthodox headmaster. It is unlikely that he ever questioned the ideal of manliness: he contributed nothing to its theory; he wrote nothing about it; he simply and unthinkingly conformed to conventional public-school practice. But by 1915 he must have had doubts. It was not meant to be like this.

McKenzie was approaching his sixty-fourth birthday when the war began and, under the terms of his appointment, he had three more years to run. Now, however, the stresses of leading a school in wartime began to take their toll.

So too did the strain from the constant news of the deaths of his boys – from Lancing, Durham and Uppingham. Matters came to a head when his own son, also called Harry, left Uppingham in July 1915 to enlist with the Argyll and Sutherland Highlanders. McKenzie's health broke soon after the school's return in September and at the end of the month he informed the trustees that he wished to resign at the end of term. He did.[22]

It was not meant to be like this – *dis aliter visum*.[23] In an age when cultured men and scholarly boys expressed their innermost thoughts and feelings through classical tags, this crucial Latin phrase would surely have come to mind – whether recalled from Virgil's *Aeneid* or remembered as the title of a poem by Robert Browning.[24] They would also recognise the poignancy of the original context. *Dis aliter visum* – literally: 'It seems otherwise to the gods' – comes from Aeneas's account of the Homeric legend of the Sack of Troy (*Aeneid* 2, 428). Ripheus, the most just and faithful of all the Trojans, was killed defending his city against the Greeks after the gods decided to withdraw their protection: his righteousness went unrewarded.[25]

*****

Thirty years earlier at Uppingham, Edward Thring, McKenzie's predecessor but one, delivered a sermon in chapel on a favourite theme. Near the end he told his listeners: 'I must think that to be known through England for true manliness is a better thing than to have a name for cricket.'[26]

This sentiment tells the reader much about the Victorian ideal of manliness. First, if there was a 'true manliness' then there must also be a mock manliness and that the two might be easily confused. Then we see that it is this mock manliness that is closely associated with prowess in sport, and we discover by implication that true manliness is not. Finally, and crucially, we are informed that Thring's purpose at Uppingham was to give each boy an education in true manliness.

By 1884 the words 'manly' and 'manliness' could have different meanings depending on whether or not the attendant ideal was true or mock. An examination of these same words from the year of Victoria's accession to the period after the Great War shows that there had been a steady evolution in their meaning. In 1837 'manly' is 'strong, robust, fearless; with the courage, dignity, fortitude of, or belonging to, man'.[27] In 1870 it is, in addition, 'not womanish; not childish',[28] and by 1891 'manly' has become synonymous with 'noble' and 'stately'.[29] At some stage it had also meant 'humane, charitable, generous' but by 1908 this definition was obsolete.[30] In the 1920s the idealistic qualities became less numerous and 'manly' was equated with 'masculine', 'grown up, adult, mature'.[31]

This evolution is important for it reflects what each generation thought the qualities of a man or, more correctly, a gentleman ought to be, and this in an age when the concept of a gentleman was of cardinal concern.[32]

Throughout our period, gentlemen dominated senior positions in the Church and charities, literature and print journalism, law and education, the Army and the Royal Navy, banking and City professions, commerce and industry, civic administration and the Civil Service, and politics and government. The ideal of manliness thus formed the leaders of Britain and her Empire. This interest in the qualities of a gentleman properly belonged to the public schools for, increasingly as the nineteenth century progressed, these schools became the main training ground for the sons of gentlemen and for the sons of aspiring gentlemen.[33] The education that a public-school boy received at his school mirrored the contemporary definitions of 'manly' and 'manliness' and, no matter how the needs of society changed from 'godliness and good learning' to 'Empire' or to 'service', so each generation was influenced by the current interpretation of this concept.[34]

Thring saw the communion and circulation of ideas, of thought and of feelings as a perpetual current, ebbing and flowing like water under the influence of external forces. The rain that begins the water cycle falls everywhere and then the terrain guides it into streams of steadily increasing power. It was thus with the ideal of manliness. This stream had its birth in antiquity but not until the end of the eighteenth century did it begin noticeably to affect the landscape; then, as the first half of the nineteenth century unfolded, so the stream raced to a vital torrent. It is at this time, in the years between 1850 and 1870, that the true ideal of manliness flourished and it owed its realisation to a generation of great headmasters. The foremost of these men – Edward White Benson, Frederick Temple, Frederic Farrar and Thring – sought to inculcate the ideal in their schools whilst Charles Kingsley strove to broaden its influence in other social spheres. These five men had much in common: most enjoyed a boisterous country childhood in which they adored the novels of Sir Water Scott and thrilled to the tales of Arthurian times. At school they read the same classics, notably Plato and Thucydides, and they carried similar prizes and comparable scholarship to their university colleges. Most went to Cambridge, for only Temple went to the older foundation, and there they came under the spell of Platonic-Romanticism as exemplified by the works of S. T. Coleridge and William Wordsworth, and then experienced its mission as advocated by Frederick Maurice. Maurice's influence was similarly felt at Oxford but here the sense of mission owed more to Thomas Arnold's zeal. A decade earlier Arnold had successfully combined the academic responsibility of a headmaster with the pastoral care of a school chaplain and from this pioneer work at Rugby School he brought a new dimension to education.

After gaining their degrees, each began his life's work: it could only be one of two vocations, schoolmastering or the Church, and in general it was both. Benson, Temple, Farrar and Thring took Holy Orders, went into the public schools, and in time became influential headmasters. Kingsley also entered the Church: he was never a schoolmaster but from his parish at Eversley he watched educational developments with great interest. These men now built on Arnold's foundation: education was not just self-determination and self-expression; it had a mission. Their model was the ideal of manliness.

The first chapter of this study follows that early stream of ideas and traces the formulation of the ideal, seeking to portray it through the words and actions of its chief exponents. As it was essentially an ideal of 'doing' rather than 'saying', the second chapter directs attention towards Thring's Uppingham for a contemporary picture of the ideal in practice. It is here during Thring's long reign at this rejuvenated Elizabethan grammar school that the ideal flourished longest and best. The Uppingham chapter ends with a biographical sketch of Hardwicke Drummond Rawnsley, one of its Old Boys, whose career exemplifies exactly what his headmaster wished to inculcate.[35]

Though the fullest realisation of the ideal of manliness was to be found at Thring's Uppingham, it was not the end of the evolution; water from the one wellspring can be diverted from its true course. Just as a river that slows may split into more than one branch, so the ideal of manliness started to meander off course. Even as Thring began his headmastership in 1853 the ideal was subjected to an athletic tilt and, as the mid-Victorian years receded, the allegiance to Sparta increased. The broad and increasingly sluggish river of athletic manliness is traced in the third chapter.

By the end of the nineteenth century the ideal of manliness had imperial and militaristic overtones added to its athletic ones and in the so-called Golden Age of the public schools the ideal reached a gaudy zenith. This fast moving cascade of white-water forms the substance of the fourth chapter. Then, during the crusades of the Great War, the ideal of manliness was thrown to a climax, thundering over a magnificent waterfall – but in the falling it died, quite suddenly, like the water that forms a stagnant pool.

This, on the surface, concludes the ideal of manliness: what was once a vital flow had by 1918 become a dead stillness. But it is not the end of the story. It is as if the true stream went underground, forming new springs that could be tapped if only one knew where to look. During the years of the hearty athletic back-slapping and through brash imperial pomp and show, the modest Thringian ideal lived on at smaller, less hearty and less brash schools. This lifeline is traced in the final chapter. When, in the years after the Second World War, the time was ripe, this ideal was seen to have as much value and validity as it once had at Thring's Uppingham.

Chapter 1

The making of true manliness

1 Plato: 'Truth, courage and self-control'

John Stuart Mill once remarked that the Greeks were the initiators of nearly everything, Christianity excepted, of importance in the world, and no history of nineteenth-century English education can ignore them.[1] Throughout the Victorian and Edwardian eras the two classical languages dominated the curriculum of the public schools, generally taking more than half the classroom time. Most schoolmasters and clergymen had read the classics at the universities and, as late as 1914, ninety-two of the 114 public-school headmasters were classicists.[2] Much earlier, Thomas Arnold, the headmaster of Rugby School from 1828 to 1842, had brought in two innovations to the teaching of classics that had increased their popularity: first, he shifted the balance away from Latin towards Greek; and secondly, he used a mix of classics and history to explain contemporary social and political problems.[3] Arnold's reforms soon extended to most public schools and after 1840 the classical pendulum stayed firmly in the Greek sector. Thus the ideas of ancient Greeks, suitably filtered for adolescent consumption, came to provide the philosophical grounding and mystical support for all shades of Victorian opinion. Although only a tiny minority of the nation might learn Greek, and a smaller fraction took their studies seriously, the influence of the reading men was soon most persuasive.

The Greeks, however, did not have just one school of thought on education; in Athens and Sparta, for example, we have two highly contrasted ideals, though both drew support from the same epics of Homeric times. The beauty of Greece is that every subsequent philosophy can find at least one Greek original to serve as a platform on which its own developments can be built. Thus, in the sixty-five years of Victoria's reign, Athens, Sparta and then Homeric Greece can each be shown to have its own Golden Age. The rise of the public schools and the emergence of athleticism from the 1860s owed much to Sparta, whilst the age of imperialism at the end of the century is decidedly Homeric; but both are distortions of the ever-pervading influence of Platonic Athens. It is a curiosity that as nineteenth-century public-school practice evolved, so it sought support from more primitive Greek models.[4]

Platonic influence on all our thinking about the conduct of life is incalculable. If we sometimes underestimate our debt in these matters to Plato, it is only because his ideas have become so completely part of our best traditions. Platonic impact often goes undetected for we are never really free from it. Platonism is a perennial philosophy but in the first half of the nineteenth century it dominated English thought. Early Victorians felt a kinship with the Athens of the last years of the fifth century BC and they looked to this past for the key to the problems of the present. There was great interest in classical history, and the era saw renewed attentions paid to excavations of the sites of antiquity.[5]

There are many similarities between the Athenian democracy and early Victorian England. Both were maritime nations and both had gained security after triumph in war: Trafalgar and Waterloo were to the Victorians as Salamis and Marathon were to the Athenians. Both had growing empires on which their commercial success was built. In name both societies were democracies, though in each case the democratic rights were shared by few: the slaves of Athens bear some similarity to the lower classes in pre-Reform Bill England. In both societies social unbalance was partly redressed by the political, educational and social service given to the state by the ruling aristocratic families. Both ruling classes were civilised and cultured, and paid considerable attention to the arts. Victorian England gleaned much support from Plato; he maintained that government should be by educated gentlemen rather than by technical experts. This inexpert intelligent ruler became the archetypal all-round, amateur administrator of world-wide fame. Plato was the gospel for most shades of Victorian opinion: Utilitarians and Radicals, Evangelicals and Tractarians, all drew on his educational thought as expounded in the *Republic*.[6]

The Platonic ideal of 'the beautiful and the good', though it was realised for less than eighty years, left behind it an imperishable memory. The well-born Charmides was the exemplar of this ideal: he combined modesty with pertness, and pride with sensitivity. He possessed all the desirable physical, intellectual, aesthetic and moral capacities and they were tuned in perfect harmony: he was the 'whole man'.[7] The revival of this philosophy as the basis of Hellenism occurred in Rome in Christian times under Plotinus. Platonism passed into the Western Church from Plotinus through Augustine, Boethius and Pseudo-Dionysius the Areopagite. Plato's social concern matched that of Christianity and his philosophy was easily absorbed by the Church.[8] Plato became the intellectual source for all Anglican theology from Richard Hooker onwards, through the Cambridge Platonists of the seventeenth century – Benjamin Whichcote, John Smith and Ralph Cudworth – and right through Victorian times.[9] This influence only underwent an eclipse under the Puritans but the interval was brief.[10]

At the beginning of the nineteenth century, Platonism, or rather the neo-Platonic philosophy of Plotinus, became the 'lifeblood of Romanticism'.[11]

Platonism and Romanticism were the dominant creeds at Cambridge in this period, whilst Oxford had Aristotelian and Tractarian leanings. To S. T. Coleridge:

> Every man is born an Aristotelian, or a Platonist. I do not think it is possible that anyone born an Aristotelian can become a Platonist; and I am sure no born Platonist can change into an Aristotelian. They are two classes of men, besides which it is next to impossible to conceive a third.
>
> (1830)[12]

These men, the subject of David Newsome's *Two Classes of Men*, dominated English thought throughout the century. F. D. Maurice, in doubting whether John Henry Newman was a Platonist, noted that 'the great evil of everything at Oxford (is) that there is nothing but Aristotelianism'. Maurice disagreed with Coleridge as to whether a Platonist could become an Aristotelian: 'all little children are Platonists, and it is their education which makes men Aristotelians' (1836).[13] A. E. Taylor took a step further: 'Aristotelianism itself, on close study, is steadily found to be only a rather half-hearted Platonism' (1925).[14] In concert with the Romantic sentiments of the period, Platonism was seen as the natural philosophy: only the sophistication of an Oxford education could deflect a man from the true path. R. M. Ogilvie, in his study *Latin and Greek*, noted the re-orientation of classics from Latin to Greek in this period, and especially towards Plato and Thucydides. At the universities the changeover occurred in the 1830s when William Sewell began to lecture at Cambridge on the *Republic*; Oxford followed suit in 1847 when Benjamin Jowett lectured on Plato. Thomas Arnold was responsible for much of the change in the schools. At Rugby, Arthur Stanley studied Plato and Thucydides above all others and the same picture emerges from Shrewsbury School under Samuel Butler and Benjamin Kennedy, and from James Prince Lee's King Edward's School, Birmingham.[15] Greek, and in particular Plato, became the staple diet in early Victorian public schools.

As the century progressed, so the Platonists came into dominance.[16] The poets William Wordsworth and Robert Browning were Platonists and Thomas Carlyle derived his Platonism second-hand from Christianity.[17] S. T. Coleridge was probably the greatest of the Platonic philosophers and he in turn inspired Frederick Maurice, Alfred Tennyson and Julius Hare, who at Cambridge formed a Platonist Club, the Apostles.[18] The *Republic* matched Maurice's dream of a universal Church.[19] For Charles Kingsley, Plato was the 'king' of philosophers, and John Ruskin would read something from the Bible and something from Plato each morning.[20] Of the later poets, William Cory and Matthew Arnold are two who glorified Platonism in their work.[21]

Plato was born in 428/7 BC and died at the age of eighty or eighty-one in 348/7. His whole thought was directed towards how society could be reshaped so that man might realise his full potential. This forms the theme of the *Republic*.

Plato was appalled by the sophistication of life in contemporary Athens and he sought to bring it back to a stricter Hellenic style: the *Republic* is a recall to simplicity. Plato's ideal city, the Republic, is but one manifestation of man's search for the ideal state, be it the City of the Perfect, Utopia, Civitas Dei or Heaven. His ideal citizen, or exemplar, combines the best of the legends of the past and all the hopes for the future. Each Republic has its own hero.[22]

Virtually all idealistic theories of education can be traced back to Plato: the aim is to produce ideal citizens to play their part in the ideal civic community. Service was the corner-stone: within an ordered society each citizen would disinterestedly concede his own preferment and loyally serve others.[23] Plato was convinced that happiness was the reward of virtue and that the virtuous life was the only pleasant one. It was not the having of strength, long life, health or wealth but the right use of them that made men happy.[24] In this aim the state's supreme function was education. Most importance was attached to the early years when the soul was plastic, and there was no distinction between the sexes. As Plato believed that the soul assimilated its environment, it was vital to surround the body with objects worthy of imitation. This was the basis of Plato's educational practice.[25]

The Greeks believed that the greatest work they had to create was Man and that the training of a noble personality was the prime aim. Before prescribing an education, Plato analysed the principles governing human life. There were three elements to a man's soul: appetitive, spirited, and philosophic. The appetitive was concerned with the pursuit of bodily desires – food, warmth and so on – and was not involved in education. The spirited was the source of courage and self-confidence, and was realised in ambition and self-assertion. The rational or philosophic element embraced the pursuit of intellect and all learning. The balance of the three elements was essential and this harmony Plato termed *arête*.

The term is hard to define exactly but Harold Nicolson's 'balanced achievement' is a fitting interpretation.[26] The soul was to aspire to three virtues: truth, courage and self-control.[27] It is from these virtues that the Victorian ideal of manliness stems so let us use contemporary sources to analyse their meaning. Truth – *aletheia* – implied all honest action, truth to oneself and truth to one's loyalties. Courage – *andreia* – had animal bravery as its base but rose to fortitude under affliction and in adversity; it was also the courage of men who are loyal to the principles which have been inculcated during their upbringing. Self-control – *enkrateia* – was obedience to authority, whether the authority of a ruler or to one's higher inner-self. Truth, courage and self-control are thus three aspects of the one Victorian ideal of manliness or, rather, they are the axes of a three-dimensional moral continuum: thus 'endurance' – of sorrow, pain, or illness – is the meeting point of courage and self-control.

The Greek conception of the education of the whole man is summed up in the term *paideia*. Plato defines this as 'the education in *arête* from youth onwards, which makes men passionately desire to become perfect citizens, knowing both how to rule and how to be ruled on a basis of justice'.[28] The word is derived from *pais* − a child − and originally referred to education of children, but in Hellenistic times the word came to signify 'culture'; thus the means became the end to be achieved. A man's *paideia* is his personal culture, the sum of his intellectual, physical, moral and aesthetic attributes that make him a whole man. Plato's educational practice to produce the whole man was based on music − *mousikē* − and gymnastic − *gymnastikē*. Music included literature, singing and playing instruments, and the plastic arts; it was central to Plato's philosophy that beauty in nature and art were but an outward sign of goodness. Gymnastic aimed at simplicity of life and diet, and the maintenance of good health. Music and gymnastic did not separately educate the philosophic and the spirited elements of the soul: a good body would not by itself make the soul excellent, but a good soul would render the body as perfect as possible. Music and gymnastic were thus finely tuned to produce the perfect harmony of the whole man.[29]

II Coleridge and Wordsworth: 'Let Nature be your Teacher'

Whenever society feels that its roots are undermined by the modern world, there is a tendency for it to become introspective. Lessons and legends of the past are reassessed, enriched by dreams of perfection, and refashioned yet again in the search for the ideal society. To S. T. Coleridge at the beginning of the nineteenth century, the age of mechanical improvement and empirical science was being undermined by 'talent without genius' and 'understanding without reason'. 'We have purchased a few brilliant inventions at the loss of all communion with life and the spirit of nature'.[1] Coleridge's aim, and the creed of all Romanticism, was to recover this communion and regain this spirit. He thus gave meaning to all who followed for whom Utilitarianism was the antithesis of life, and he became the spiritual source for all nineteenth-century moralists.

Thomas Arnold had a great reverence for Coleridge and many of his ideals gained support from the poet's *Aids to Reflection*. Through Frederick Maurice his influence was felt at Cambridge, Oxford and London: both Christian Socialism and the Broad Church Movement owed much to Coleridge's union of religion and morality. Arnold and Maurice in turn inspired others. At Cambridge, Frederic Farrar developed a 'boundless admiration' for Coleridge's work; at Oxford, Frederick Temple read him widely − 'I have been reading Coleridge a good deal lately', Temple wrote from Balliol, 'and I can hardly tell how much I admire him'.[2] Tennyson's *In Memoriam* is seen by some as one of the fullest expressions of Coleridge's religious thought.[3]

In effect there were two Coleridges. The early poet and critic was the fount of Romanticism; the later Highgate philosopher was best captured in *Table Talk*. The former was closely associated with William Wordsworth, for it was in their momentous partnership of the decade spanning the new century that two traditional currents of thought met. One was the Protestant line of Platonic humanism, the other the secular belief in Nature deriving from Jean-Jacques

Rousseau. In the combined creed that was to be the life-line of nineteenth-century Romantic thought, the former brought the message, whilst the latter provided the means: together they called for a simple life.

As Basil Willey explained in his study of *The English Moralists*, Coleridge's philosophy was descended from the sixteenth-century Christian Humanists and the Cambridge Platonists of the succeeding century. Richard Hooker, that 'God-centred Humanist', rooted English Protestantism in early Platonic traditions and steered it on a middle road between Papal Rome and Calvinist Geneva.[4] To the whole-man ideal of the Humanism of the Italian Renaissance, Hooker had added the search for a Christian society in which the desires for fellowship would be met.[5] Through John Smith of the Cambridge group, for whom 'purity shall be happy and vice miserable', and his successors, Christian-Platonism continued its middle path in religion between the Puritan and Prelatist extremes of Protestantism.[6]

'Wholeness' is one essence of Coleridge's thought. A man was a whole man and not an assemblage of parts: he was a living unity rooted in God. In the same way philosophy and theology were a single entity; and, further, religion and politics could not be separated. The main function of the Church as a human institution was the advancement of knowledge, the education of the people, and the civilising of the nation. Its spiritual role was based on the quest for virtue: in this respect he anticipated the later purge on the literalism of Biblical interpretation. Coleridge also foresaw the growth and danger of sectarianism: 'He, who begins by loving Christianity better than truth, will proceed by loving his own sect or church better than Christianity, and end in loving himself better than all.'[7]

It was through *Aids to Reflection* that Coleridge's influence was most directly felt by succeeding generations. These *Aids* aimed to present a rational groundwork for Christianity based on the fusion of reasoned philosophy and spiritual experience. They were prepared 'for all, who desirous of building up a manly character in the light of distinct consciousness, are content to study the principles of moral architecture on the grounds of prudence, morality and religion', but they were 'especially designed for the studious young at the close of their education or on their first entrance into the duties of manhood and the rights of self-government'.[8] The aim was to make the reader manlier; indeed the first edition was titled *Aids to Reflection in the Formation of a Manly Character*.[9] To Platonic *arête* and the whole-man concept of the Humanists, Coleridge added Christian moral duties: the result was the ideal of manliness.

> What the duties of morality are, the Apostle instructs the believer in full, comprising them under the two heads of negative and positive; negative, to keep himself pure from the world; and positive, beneficence from loving kindness, that is, love of his fellow men (his kind) as himself.[10]

The Greek ideal *arête*, it will be recalled, was the balanced harmony of the three elements of a man's soul and the three virtues to which the soul was to aspire were truth, courage and self-control. Platonic *arête* became Christian manliness when the moral virtues of goodness and service were added. Morality was a vital ingredient in Coleridge's whole man:

> Are not reason, discrimination, law, and deliberate choice, the distinguishing character of Humanity? . . . Can any thing manly, I say, proceed from those, who for law and light would substitute shapeless feelings, sentiments, impulses, which as far as they differ from the vital workings in the brute animals owe the difference to their former connexion with the proper virtues of humanity.[11]

This Platonic-Christian manliness was promoted by all parties within the early Victorian Church of England and the imitation of Christ became an all-encompassing ideal for each stage of every man's life.[12]

It is impossible to see the full relevance of Coleridge's teaching without an examination of his relationship with William Wordsworth. They complemented one another; the expression of Coleridge's ideas was greatly helped by the solvent powers of Wordsworth's poetry. Before their meeting in 1796, Coleridge and Wordsworth had each grown to love the countryside and to hanker after the simplicities of a rustic life.[13] Wordsworth brought to Coleridge the Rousseauian belief that man was by nature good and that civilisation produced the corrupting influence. Modern man could only be saved by *Emile*-like education in which the child should be brought up in the countryside and learn there solely from experience. Both Wordsworth and Coleridge felt that there was a bond between Nature and the soul of man, and that moral impressions were associated with enduring things, especially lakes and mountains:[14]

> Let Nature be your Teacher. . . .
> One impulse from a vernal wood
> May teach you more of man
> Of moral evil and of good
> Than all the sages can.
> (*The Table Turned*, 1798)

Thus the divinisation of Nature as a means of rehabilitating a man's spirit was passed into the mainstream of Victorian morality, and landscape became an inseparable element of nineteenth-century Englishness.[15] Soon art and craft-work were added as natural aids to learning. It was not necessary actually to live in an area such as the English Lakes, but it should exist as a place to escape to. Its healing power then fitted man with renewed vigour for life's struggle. From the 1820s the visitors and reading parties to the Lake District began to increase; in 1822 Wordsworth wrote his own *Guide to the Lakes*; by the 1840s a cottage in the Lakes became the realisation of a dream for many. Today the legacy is seen in the countless hikers and cyclists, and in the founding of the National Trust and the Campaign to Protect Rural England. The influence of the Lake District on the ideal of manliness was considerable. Many headmasters, including both Arnold and Thring, had cottages there, and Thring's pupil, Hardwicke Rawnsley, did his life's work from a Lake District parish. If the Lake District was not easily accessible, then any attractive countryside would do: the Bristol poor might go on picnics to the neighbouring downs, or the Working Men's College students might ramble in Epping Forest.

It is in *Tintern Abbey* that the fullest formulary of the Wordsworthian faith can perhaps be found:

> Therefore am I still
> A lover of the meadows and the woods,
> And mountains; and of all that we behold
> From this green earth; of all the mighty world
> Of eye, and ear, – both what they half create,
> And what perceive; well pleased to recognise
> In nature and the language of the sense,
> The anchor of my purest thoughts, the nurse,
> The guide, the guardian of my heart, and soul
> Of all my moral being.

III Scott and Tennyson: 'The spirit of chivalry'

Our present generation, wrote Basil Willey in 1950, is 'a generation which has so largely lost its sense of direction and of any distinct moral summons and yet it is anxious to recover both'.

> In our most unpleasant century we are mostly displaced persons, and many feel tempted to take flight into the nineteenth as into a promised land, and settle there like illegal immigrants for the rest of their lives. In that distant mountain country, all that we now lack seems present in abundance: not only peace, prosperity, plenty and freedom, but faith, purpose and buoyancy.[1]

The late Victorians may have felt confidence in the creed of progress, but the generations that came to manhood before 1870 were less assured. For many, the growing industrialism and materialism struck deep into the moral code. The philosophies expounded by Jeremy Bentham and the other Utilitarians were the opposite of their own concept of an ideal society. They in their turn looked back to the preceding centuries for guidance to 'direction' and 'moral summons'. The period adopted for assimilation was the Middle Ages.[2] In some respects the medieval revival became pretence: mock–Gothic castles and follies were constructed, and the stolid Prince Albert was even painted in full armour.[3] Here it was mere escapism. The interest in chivalry might at first also seem no more than fantasy but this inference would be mistaken; soon the knightly code would be important in art, architecture and literature. Moreover, it was used as a source of inspiration and of support for the present that would colour the mindset of all classes of society.[4] The knightly virtues of service and duty were seen as the synthesis of ennobling Platonic literature and Christian ethics, and their effect was to be felt right up until Rudyard Kipling's time.[5] But before 1850, three romances on chivalry helped to form the ideal of manliness: the *Waverley* novels of Sir Walter Scott, the epic *Song of Roland*, and the early writings of Tennyson on the Arthurian legends.

The enthusiasm for Scott was enormous.[6] 'He is my lost childhood', wrote William Cory, 'he is my first great friend'.[7] Frederic Farrar read *Ivanhoe* so many times that the characters were almost real; Thomas Hughes as a boy was an avid follower of these tales of romance.[8] The author of the *Waverley* novels was born in Edinburgh in 1771, and even at school his head was 'on fire for chivalry'.[9] It was to be a lifetime interest. Scott detested the selfishness of the new industrialism and he sought through his writings to hold to the morality of a day now passing rapidly away. His own code was drawn more from honour than from religious principle but, in sympathy with Coleridge, he disliked the intense pre-occupation of a man with his own soul. Though Scott and Wordsworth were to meet often, both at Abbotsford and Grasmere, there was little of a Wordsworthian in Scott but each had a respect for the different genius of the other. The spiritual world was not really within Scott's sphere and there was much substance in Carlyle's charge of 'worldliness'.[10] John Buchan saw Scott as Scotland's 'great liberator':

> He saved his land from the narrow rootless gentility and the barren utilitarianism of the illuminates; he gave her confidence by reopening her to the past; and he blended into one living tradition many things which the shallow had despised and the dull had forgotten. Gently he led her back to nature and the old simplicities.[11]

The appeal of Scott to his own age was immediate and his influence on his contemporaries and successors was great and enduring. He was translated into many languages and, with the exception of Shakespeare, no writer in English was so continuously reprinted in so many lands.[12]

The two *Waverley* novels that most draw on the age of chivalry are *Ivanhoe* (1819) and *Quentin Durward* (1823). *Ivanhoe* was immediately popular: it is hard now to recapture the atmosphere in which the novel won its resounding success, but the fortunes of the Disinherited Knight were avidly followed by generations of boys. Scott chose as his stage the Merrie England of Richard Coeur de Lion and his theme the hostility between Norman and Saxon. To the forests of the English Midlands he added a romantic blend of Robin Hood, Saxon legend and medieval chivalry. The customs of three centuries may be confused, but the glittering pageantry cannot fail to catch the imagination. Excitement is poured on excitement: the tournament at Ashby; the revels of the Black Knight and Friar Tuck; the adventures of Locksley; and so on to the end of the tale. Richard, 'the first in honour as in arms, in renown as in place' is the epitome of manliness: 'English chivalry were second to NONE who ever drew sword in defence of the Holy Land.'[13] One incident from the tournament at Ashby serves to illustrate the ideal in practice:

> In his fourth combat with De Grantmesnil, the Disinherited Knight showed as much courtesy as he had hitherto evinced courage and dexterity. De Grantmesnil's horse, which was young and violent, reared and plunged in the course of the career so as to disturb the rider's aim, and the stranger, declining to take the advantage which this accident afforded him, raised his lance, and passing his antagonist without touching him, wheeled his horse and rode back again to his own end of the lists, offering his antagonist, by a herald, the chance of a second encounter. This De Grantmesnil declined, avowing himself vanquished as much by the courtesy as by the address of his opponent.[14]

Quentin Durward is rated by many a better novel than *Ivanhoe*. The setting in fifteenth-century France, when the feudal system and the chivalric code were beginning to break down, made its appeal in that country immediate; in England its acceptance was slower. Quentin is one of the best of Scott's heroes because the author was content to make him only young, chivalrous and heroic, and he burdened him with no oppressive moralities. The story rests in the hero's attempts to halt the erosion of the chivalric ideal. As Scott wrote in the 1831 introduction to the tale:

> The spirit of chivalry had in it this point of excellence, that, however overstrained and fantastic many of its doctrines may appear to us, they were all founded on generosity and self-denial, of which if the earth were deprived, it would be difficult to conceive the existence of virtue among the human race.[15]
>
> But (he continued) like other old fashions, it began to fall out of repute, and the weapons of raillery could be employed against it, without exciting the disgust and horror with which they would have been rejected at an earlier period, as a species of blasphemy.... In like manner, the principles of chivalry were cast aside, and their aid supplied by baser stimulants. Instead of the high spirit which pressed every man forward in defence of his country, Louis XI substituted the exertions of the ever-ready mercenary soldier, and persuaded his subjects, among whom the mercantile class began to make a figure, that it was better to leave to mercenaries the risks and labours of war ... [16]

The message to the nineteenth century was clear.

At the close of the eleventh century an unknown poet composed the work we now call the *Song of Roland*. Although the legend was well known in medieval times, it was not until the publication in 1837 by Francisque Michel of the earliest and most complete manuscript that more modern interest was satisfied.[17] This one great French national epic, much sung at the time of the Crusades, is centred on the death of Roland, Lord of the Breton Marches, at Roncesvalles in 778.[18] The battle portrayed was in fact no more than a skirmish between a detachment of Charlemagne's army and some Basque raiders but the legend embroiders this into a crusade against twelve Saracen chieftains and their army of 400,000 men.[19] In the story, Roland, 'courteous, knightly, noble and brave', bears the burden of being a legend in his own lifetime. He has the conflict of endeavouring to perform the impossible yet still remaining true to his ideals of humility, concern for fellows, and the general good. It was a conflict with which mid-Victorian headmasters, notably Edward Thring, were much in sympathy.[20] The presence of Oliver, Roland's companion, who is more concerned with commonsense survival, makes the contrast vivid.

The poem opens with Charlemagne contemplating the complete conquest of the Saracen-held old Christian kingdoms of Spain. A council of peace however prevails and Roland, a nephew of Charlemagne, is named ambassador to the Saracen king. Betrayal is at hand, for Roland and his small band are set upon by a vast army of Saracens at Roncesvalles in the Pyrenees. Roland refuses to sound his horn and call for reinforcements: 'That would be mad, insane! / For I would lose renown throughout sweet France.'[21] Roland's small band holds its ground heroically. 'Towards the pagans, Roland's gaze is proud; humble and fond each glance back at the French.'[22] Before the final overwhelming onslaught, Roland consents to Oliver's call to sound the horn and the Saracens flee the battlefield. The dying Roland thus claims victory, a victory that is made real by the arrival of Charlemagne's army. The moral drawn is that the defeat now can be the victory later on.[23]

One of the enigmas of the Victorian age is the evolution of the poetry of Alfred Tennyson. There are, in effect, two Tennysons with *In Memoriam* as the divide. The later civic bard belongs more to the age of imperialism; here we are concerned with the Tennyson of the early lyrics. This is the poet who for William Cory was 'the light and charm of my poor life'.[24] It was this Tennyson that Charles Kingsley sketched when he visited Eversley, and the one John Ruskin greatly admired.[25] The 1842 collection of Tennyson's work is seen by many to be the crown of his genius.[26] In his years at Cambridge from 1828–31, he was drawn into the Apostles and they imbued him with the modest yet deep conviction that it was his duty to serve England through his poetry.[27] His respect for their spiritual leader, Maurice, was life-long and in 1851 Tennyson asked him to be the godfather of his first child.[28] The poet possessed that distinctive nineteenth-century excellence, the habit of accurate observation of nature and the power to produce definitive renderings. This love of nature, which stemmed from his boyhood in Lincolnshire, developed into a religious respect. His vision of England was distinguished primarily through the character of the landscape rather than by place, language or race.[29] Nature was God's handiwork, his symbol language, and to study it was not aesthetic indulgence but a solemn duty.[30]

The fusion of Tennyson's reverence for nature, love of England and the ethos of service was realised in his idylls on Arthurian legends which were to form a nineteenth-century extension of Edmund Spenser's *Faerie Queen* and Thomas Malory's *Morte d'Arthur*. These myths were to haunt Tennyson's whole career, and indeed he hinted that their culmination in the 1872 publication of *Idylls of the King* was his most important work.[31] The writing of the *Idylls* spanned many years but most had been composed before 1850. Arthur, his 'blameless King', was to be the perfect personification of English character and he, as well as the other protagonists, acted in their medieval guise as role-models for nineteenth-century men and women.[32] The theme of the *Idylls* matched Scott's *Quentin Durward*, for as A. C. Benson wrote:

> Arthur's object is to establish law and order, civilisation in the highest sense, a high standard of unselfish and noble life. The attempt fails: his knights were meant to set a noble example of manliness, devotion and purity; but the court teems with scandal, and finally the evil and seditious elements are triumphant.[33]

Tennyson's message was as transparent as Scott's but Tennyson was less despondent and his *In Memoriam* ended with trust in a better world and in a loftier race:

> A soul shall draw out from the vast
> And strike his being into bounds,
> And, moved thro' life of lower phase,
> Result in man, be born and think,
> And act and love, a closer link
> Betwixt us and the crowning race
> Of those that, eye to eye, shall look
> On knowledge; under whose command
> Is Earth and Earth's, and in their hand
> Is Nature like an open book;
> No longer half-akin to brute,
> For all we thought and loved and did,
> And hoped, and suffer'd, is but seed
> Of what in them is flower and fruit;
> Whereof the man, that with me trod
> This planet, was a nobler type
> Appearing ere the times were ripe,
> That friend of mine who lives in God,
> That God, which ever lives and loves,
> One God, one law, one element,
> And one far-off divine event,
> To which the whole creation moves.

IV Arnold: 'A thorough English gentleman – Christian, manly, and enlightened'

Thomas Arnold played an important role in the evolution of manliness for he was the first headmaster who sought to inculcate the ideal in his charges. As the *Quarterly Review* of 1860 noted: 'Dr. Arnold was the first who laid down the doctrine, now generally recognised, that the headship of a school is a cure of souls.'[1] Religion and education had been closely associated for centuries but until Arnold's time the link had largely been in name only. To Arnold they were inseparable. He believed in an absolute identity between Church and State, and there was no contradiction between things spiritual and things secular.[2] Within this fundamental truth, as Arnold saw it, education and religion became equivalent. Education was moral training for children, whereas religion was its application to all ages.[3]

Arnold's synthesis of social and religious problems did not agree with the accepted Evangelical and Tractarian standpoints; he was too practical for the Evangelicals. He also believed that the eighteen-hundred years of progress since St Paul meant that literal interpretation of the Bible was untenable: it was the generous reading of the spirit that was important.[4] The Tractarians, on the other hand, Arnold regarded as idolaters who placed the affairs of the Church even above reverence for Christ. To Arnold, the Church ought to be rooted firmly on earth and all its social problems; the Tractarian appeal to the ideal of a divinely-inspired Church only divorced it from reality.[5] Arnold, after S. T. Coleridge, and with Julius Hare and Frederick Maurice, thus became a founder of the Latitudinarian or Broad Church Movement which stood between the extremes of Evangelicalism and Tractarianism.[6] This took social problems as its sphere of interest and steadily evolved into the Christian Socialist Movement associated with Maurice, Charles Kingsley and Thomas Hughes.

Arnold's immediate concern was his own social world at Rugby. Here he was the first headmaster to make religion an integral part of school life. His earliest aim was to get himself appointed chaplain; this was essential for his conception of the role of pastoral responsibility between a headmaster and his boys.[7] Gradually the chapel became the centre of school organisation and his sermons were used to explain the purpose of life and the role that the school should play. In this respect Arnold was supremely successful: no subsequent public school was without its chapel and the headmasterly sermon became an essential ingredient of public-school life.[8]

Thomas Arnold was born in 1795. He first went to school at Warminster and his letters home indicate that he possessed normal boyish spirits. He then moved on to Winchester College and it is from his experiences there, Norman Wymer believes, that Arnold drew his insight into the contribution each boy could make in the communal life of a school.[9] Certainly the bullying he received his first night as he knelt to pray gave support to his later theories on the wickedness of childhood.[10] Though precocious, Arnold seems to have had his share of schoolboy interests: he was keen on swimming and running; he even seems to have got into mischief. This love of a healthy vigorous life persisted when he went up to Oxford University. Bathing, running, rowing and nature expeditions were popular recreations.[11] Arnold was an outstanding scholar: he obtained a first in *Literae Humaniores* in 1814 at the age of nineteen and the Chancellor's medal for both English and Latin Essays in 1815 and 1817 respectively.

On leaving Oxford he opened a private school with his brother-in-law at Laleham: this was to be his home for the next ten years. It was at this leafy site by the Thames that Arnold developed the practices he was later to use at Rugby. The core of Arnold's approach rested on a warm relationship between master and pupils, a relationship unusual for the time; several of his later pupils at Rugby saw him as a 'second father'.[12] Physical activity and rambles in the countryside helped in this intercourse. Looking back on Laleham, Arnold wrote to a fellow teacher:

> I should say, have your pupils a good deal with you, and be as familiar with them as you possibly can. I did this continually more and more before I left Laleham, going to bathe with them, leaping and all other gymnastic exercises within my capacity, and sometimes sailing and rowing with them. They I believe always liked it, and I enjoyed myself like a boy, and found myself constantly better for it.[13]

A 'gallows' and a 'pole' were constructed in the grounds to further the gymnastic exercise.[14] This early inclusion of gymnastics within a school is perhaps unique and stems from Arnold's German studies. Even as he took up his appointment at Rugby, gymnastic considerations were important:

> The Rugby prospect I contemplate with a very strong interest: the work I am not afraid of, if I can get my proper exercise; but I want absolute play, like a boy, and neither riding nor walking will make up for my leaping pole and my gallows, and bathing, when the youths used to go with me, and I felt completely for a time a boy as they were.[15]

He need not have worried. He gained his gallows at Rugby; he swam, and he had his daily vigorous walk. To Arnold this daily exercise was an important relaxation, and the strengthening of the body helped strengthen the mind.

> It is this entire relaxation, I think, at intervals . . . that gives me so keen an appetite for my work at other times, and has enabled me to go through it not only with no fatigue, but with a sense of absolute pleasure.[16]

Arnold fell under the spell of the Lake District in 1824, before his appointment to Rugby. The combination of the proximity of Wordsworth

– they met that year for the second time – and the magnificence of the scenery determined that Arnold should own a cottage there.[17] Soon Fox How, not far from Wordsworth's home, was purchased. After 1828 it was Fox How and not Rugby that became the Arnold home; the family would leave for the Lakes on the first day of the school holiday and then return at the latest possible moment. The rush away from the materialism and industrialism of the Midlands to the hearth of Romanticism grew ever more important: eventually Arnold gained an almost physical craving for beautiful country and a phobic loathing of the Midlands. Boys would be taken to Fox How 'to refresh their health when they get knocked up by the work'. The whole sixth-form went there with Arnold in 1841 when a typhoid epidemic had closed the school.[18]

Arnold was the first headmaster who saw his school as a microcosm of the ideal Christian society, a nineteenth-century version of Plato's Republic, and through its influence he led the moral rearmament of the governing classes.[19] Anglican Christianity, the classics and moral education would now become tightly interwoven at Rugby and they would remain so at all public schools throughout the Victorian era.[20] Three lasting influences resulted from Arnold's Rugby: a more relevant classical curriculum; a viable prefectorial system; and the chapel sermon.

Arnold redefined the teaching of classics, making it acceptable to all shades of religious opinion despite its pagan content.[21] He directed attention towards the attainment of social and individual perfection through an emphasis on Plato and Thucydides,

He also devised a structured school society based on the subjugated authority of the sixth-form; in the opinion of Charles Vaughan, one of Arnold's pupils and later headmaster of Harrow, this was 'the distinguishing feature of Public as contrasted with Private Schools'.[22] Within this society Arnold extolled a sense of mission: Bonamy Price imbibed this spirit:

> Every pupil was made to feel that there was work for him to do – that his happiness as well as his duty lay in doing that work well. Hence an indescribable zest was communicated to a young man's feeling about life; a strange joy came over him on discovering that he had the means of being useful and thus of being happy.[23]

Arnold had turned the prefectorial system into a missionary organisation.[24] The third lasting influence was the headmasterly sermon from the chapel pulpit. To Vaughan each sermon was 'brief, manly, original, often heart-searching'.[25] Thomas Hughes recalled his first sermon in *Tom Brown's Schooldays*:

> The oak pulpit standing out by itself above the School seats. The tall gallant form, the kindling eye, the voice, now soft as the low notes of a flute, now clear and stirring as the call of the Light Brigade bugle, of him who stood there Sunday after Sunday, witnessing, and pleading for his Lord, the King

of righteousness and love and glory, and with whose spirit he was filled, and in whose power he spoke . . . we listened . . . to a man who we felt to be with all his heart and soul and strength striving against whatever was mean and unmanly and unrighteous in our little world. It was not the cold clear voice of one giving advice and warning from serene heights, to those who were struggling and sinning below, but the warm living voice of one who was fighting for us and by our sides, and calling on us to help him and ourselves and one another.[26]

'Is this a Christian school?' Arnold would ask: 'It is not necessary that this should be a school of three hundred, or one hundred, or fifty boys; but it is necessary that it should be a school of Christian gentlemen.'[27] The school was 'God's temple', 'to which the sons of Christian parents, and no other, are sent to receive a Christian education'. All boys had a role to play; even the youngest boy had influence over others:

> every one of you has a duty to perform towards the school, and that over and above the sin of his own particular faults, he incurs a sin, I think even greater, by encouraging faults or discouraging good in others, and farther still, that he incurs a sin, less I grant in the last case, but still considerable, by being altogether indifferent to the conduct of others, by doing nothing to discourage evil, nothing to encourage good.[28]

Arnold believed in 'original sin' and he had an obsessive pre-occupation with the denunciation of evil.[29] He listed six moral vices: sensual wickedness, lying, bullying, disobedience, idleness and 'a spirit combination in evil and of companionship'. Lying as a moral offence was particularly oppressive for young boys but the general feeling grew up that it was a shame to tell Arnold a lie for he would always believe it.[30] The sixth vice, 'a bond of wickedness', was the subject of a whole sermon: it was the vice 'by which a boy would regard himself as more bound to his companions in ties of wickedness than to God or his neighbours in any ties of good'.[31] This shot deeply into the code of schoolboy loyalty.

The virtues which Arnold extolled were adult rather than adolescent. Childhood comprised the elements of manhood but in chaotic disarray: the faults of youth were the retention too long of ignorance, selfishness and thoughtlessness, when manhood implied wisdom, unselfishness and thoughtfulness. Childhood was an inferior but necessary prefatory state to manhood: manliness was thus the exact opposite of childishness and, the quicker it could be attained, the better was Arnold pleased.[32] It is curious that a man who enjoyed the society of boys as much as Arnold undoubtedly did should yet have held such a low opinion of their intrinsic moral capacity. Arnold even saw childishness as a growing vice, fostered by the new novels on Pickwick and Nickleby.[33] Yet at the same time the virtues he wished to inculcate in young boys were so adult: self-denial and charity were professed as the highest of Christian graces.[34] Manliness was thus the adult state reached when all moral weakness had been conquered and it was independent of intellectual capacity: it was possible for a clever boy to be childish and a not so clever boy to be exceedingly manly.

Arnold's aim was to produce 'a thorough English gentleman – Christian, manly, and enlightened', but the demands he made were so great that he was almost doomed to failure and disappointment:

> I will tell you what seems to be wanting (he once preached in chapel) – a spirit of manly, and much more of Christian thoughtfulness. There is a quickness and cleverness; much pleasure, perhaps in distinction, but little in improvement; there is no desire of knowledge for its own sake, whether human, or divine. There is, therefore, but little power of combining and digesting what is read; and, consequently, what is read passes away, and takes no root in the mind. The same character shows itself in matters of conduct; it will adopt, without scruple, the most foolish, common-place notions of boys, about what is right and wrong; it will not, and cannot, from lightness of its mind, concern itself seriously about what is evil in the conduct of others, because it takes no regular care of its own, with reference to pleasing God; it will not do anything low or wicked, but it will sometimes laugh at those who do; and it will by no means take pains to encourage, nay, it will sometimes thwart and oppose any thing that breathes a higher spirit, and asserts a more manly and Christian standard of duty.[35]

It is perhaps hard to say that Arnold failed as a headmaster but, in many vital ways, he did. Had it not been for Arthur Stanley's influence, both as a senior pupil and through his celebrated biography, Arnold's impact at Rugby during his reign and nationally after his death would have been less. Frances Woodward, in her study *The Doctor's Disciples*, maintains that much of the boys' reverence for Arnold was largely due to Stanley and certainly his *Life and Letters of Thomas Arnold* built Arnold's posthumous reputation.[36] When *Tom Brown's Schooldays* was published in 1857, the school portrayed was an 'absolute revelation' to Stanley, opening up 'a world of which, though so near to me, I was utterly ignorant', and the arguments on how rough Arnold found Rugby and how pure he left it have raged ever since.[37] Michael Sadler, in the preface to Arnold Whitridge's *Dr Arnold of Rugby*, gave examples to illustrate that life at Rugby in Arnold's day was still barbaric, whilst in Norman Wymer's *Dr Arnold of Rugby* such practices had clearly been stamped out.[38] Of the modern appraisers, Terence Copley cited examples of heavy-handedness that do Arnold no credit; Christopher Tyerman found him an arrogant and bad-tempered bully; and Michael McCrum judged some of Arnold's treatment of parents to be most unpleasant, but overall their re-assessments of his achievements and legacy were sympathetic.[39]

Arnold's failure stemmed from his lack of understanding of boys. Few at Rugby had any real communication with him, and his own boys in School

House reported that Arnold did not even remember their names. He mingled as a friend with the inner circle of the sixth-form but he was awkward in his dealings with the younger boys. He was too involved with his repressive and adult ideal of manliness to be relaxed with the part-moulded product.[40]

This attitude brought three sad results. First, only boys who reached the sixth-form had any real communication with Arnold.[41] Secondly, boys who did not come up to standard were summarily expelled; 'the first, second, and third duty of a schoolmaster is to get rid of unpromising subjects'.[42] And thirdly, the strain placed on the loyal praepostors in the sixth-form sapped their individuality. Arnold recognised this problem: 'by their whole training they (the praepostors) fit the character for manly duties at an age when under another system such duties would be impracticable', but when a praepostor failed in his duty, as Thomas Hughes's brother George did, he was immediately expelled.[43] The difficulties remained when these disciples left Rugby; to Stanley a world without Arnold became a world without a sun.[44] This is a legacy of failure and it is due in part to the lack of any organisational system: Rugby was a world centred solely on Arnold. Other headmasters would attempt to use his methods in other schools, but their ends were their own and not his. The result was Arnoldianism – a philosophy claiming Thomas Arnold as its spiritual leader but following principles only marginally drawn from his practice.[45]

Despite these shortcomings, Arnold is important in the evolution of the ideal of manliness. He brought the ideal into the schools; he rooted it in Platonic Athens; he was the first who sought to foster the ideal in (at least some of) his pupils; and he was the first to appreciate the power and the influence of the headmasterly sermon. The practical sense of mission that he inspired in others as the public-school system expanded enabled much of what followed to come to fruition in mid-Victorian England.[46]

V Maurice: 'A fellowship in Christ'

The ideal Christian society that Thomas Arnold strove towards at Rugby gained wider meaning in the years between 1848 and 1852 through the efforts of the Christian Socialists. This social creed was the practical synthesis of a half-century of philosophical exaltation: Coleridge supplied the base with his blend of religion and politics; Carlyle directed the attention towards the advancement of the poor; Julius Hare, from Coleridge, revived the interest in Platonism; Wordsworth, with Coleridge, associated God's will with the beauty of nature; and Arnold had sketched a blue-print of this nineteenth-century Republic at Rugby. The man who instilled this Christian Socialist philosophy in his contemporaries in such a positive way was Frederick Denison Maurice.

Maurice, the son of a Unitarian minister, was born near Lowestoft in 1805. He received his elementary education at home before entering Trinity College, Cambridge. Hare was Maurice's tutor and it was from him that Maurice imbibed his love of Plato:'I have never taken up any dialogue of Plato without getting more from it than from any book not in the Bible.'[1] Hare was also a member of Coleridge's Highgate circle and he would seem to have instilled the Romantic spirit in his pupil: certainly Maurice was greatly struck by the beauty of the Lake District and he would later often holiday there.[2] In his second year at Cambridge, Maurice and John Sterling founded the Apostles, 'a gallant band of Platonic-Wordsworthian-Coleridgian anti-Utilitarians'.[3] The Cambridge of the period was more progressive than Oxford and, from a standpoint between infidel radicalism and the Oxford Movement, the Apostles would discuss the leading questions of the day. Tennyson was also a member of the group and Coleridge was soon brought in by Sterling.

Maurice joined the Inns of Court in London on leaving Cambridge but only a few years were necessary however to show him his real vocation, for in 1830 he transferred to Exeter College, Oxford to read for Holy Orders. Four years later, at the age of twenty-nine, Maurice was ordained and shortly afterwards he was appointed chaplain to Guy's Hospital in London. Maurice now became closely associated with the newly-founded London University: in 1841 he was appointed professor of English literature and modern history at King's College, and in 1846 he transferred to the chair in theology. His concern for the education of women was rewarded in 1848 with the creation of Queen's College; later he was appointed its first Principal.

In 1846 Maurice relinquished his chaplaincy at Guy's Hospital and took on a similar role at Lincoln's Inn. This new post had no parochial responsibilities thus giving him more time for his educational work; the freedom also permitted the evolution of Christian Socialism. Since the beginning of the nineteenth century Evangelicalism had been the dominant philosophy within the Church of England. Evangelical theology was, however, so other-worldly and ultra-saintly that it had little relevance to the lower classes. The Evangelicals were only interested in saving souls; their missionary zeal at home and abroad was entirely directed towards individual conversions and they turned a blind eye to the environment of their converts and to its causes. The poor were encouraged to accept their state with resignation and humility. It was the Evangelicals who were to become the fiercest opponents of Christian Socialism.[4]

If the Evangelicals were individualistic in their concern for conversion and Puritanical strictness, the Tractarians were no less so in their involvement with personal discipline and sacramental ritual. This traditionalist wing of the Church of England had evolved in the 1830s from the old-world cloistered virtues of the Oxford Movement. As true conservatives, the Tractarians were opposed to progress and liberalism, and they sought to direct attention away from the social needs of the present to questions on the religious archaeology of the past. Their aim was to make Christianity deeper and spiritually larger, and each Christian a model of exclusive personal piety. The Tractarians, like the Evangelicals, were openly hostile to Christian Socialism.

Maurice had a dream of a universal Church which matched the highest aspects of Plato's Republic; this striving for the salvation of the whole race, and not just personal salvation, became the gospel of the Christian Socialists:

> I was sent into the world that I might persuade men to recognise Christ as the centre of their fellowship with each other, that so they might be united in their families, their countries, and as men, not in schools and factions.[5]

To Maurice, man was not composed of two entities, 'one called religious, the other secular'; he was an integrated whole.[6] The Church therefore had a role to play in the social and educational advancement of humanity. Maurice saw Christian Socialism as a movement, and not a political party, which would serve as a link between the unsocial Christians and the unchristian Socialists: 'Our greatest desire is to Christianise Socialism'.[7]

It was Daniel Macmillan, the Cambridge publisher, who in 1842 first drew Maurice's attention to the social conditions of the poor. Macmillan asked Maurice to prepare some religious writings for the use of the artisan classes.[8] Later Macmillan was to introduce many Cambridge undergraduates to the Christian Socialist Movement. Meanwhile, from his base at Lincoln's Inn, Maurice had taken charge of a small poor district in the parish and had set a number of young men, chiefly from the Inns of Court, to work in it. These men, soon to include Charles Kingsley and Thomas Hughes, had been attracted by the reports of Maurice's weekly preaching. The initial impetus for the social work seems to have come from one of the students at Lincoln's Inn, J. M. Ludlow. He had received part of his education in Paris and, from his experiences there with *La Société des Amis des Pauvres*, Ludlow brought the socialist experience into the movement.[9] Gradually other young men were drawn in by Maurice's magnetism: Arthur Stanley, John Llewellyn Davies (the co-translator of Plato's *Republic*), John Ruskin, Leslie Stephen and William Cory. Most came from Cambridge, and especially from Trinity College. All agreed that if Christianity was to be a universal religion it needed a human heart.

The year 1848 saw the true founding of Christian Socialism. It was the year of revolution in Europe: in Ireland there was famine, and civil strife was only checked by armed force; in February there was revolution in several continental cities; in March there were riots in London, Glasgow, Edinburgh and Liverpool. The London disturbances culminated in a Chartist rally on 10 April that year but, in the face of the military, the demonstration collapsed. After the abortive rally, Kingsley and Maurice met and that evening Christian Socialism was born.[10] Together they drew up a broadsheet to the 'workingmen of England' – 'the first manifesto of the Church of England, her first public act of atonement for a half-century of apostasy, of class prejudice and political sycophancy'.[11]

The first practical act of Christian Socialism was the formation of a night school in London's Little Ormond Yard in September 1848. Bible classes under Maurice's tuition and day-trips to Epping Forest soon became vital ingredients.[12] The ideal of a 'brotherhood of workers' was then extended with the formation of Working Associations: Charles Kingsley vividly portrays a tailoring cooperative in his novel on Christian Socialism, *Alton Locke*. But this aspect of Christian Socialism was not a success and by 1854 only the Working Men's College remained as the concrete outgrowth of the movement.

Perhaps Christian Socialism was doomed to failure, for in the strictest sense Christianity and socialism are irreconcilable; the very name Christian Socialism is a contradiction in terms. Contributory factors in its demise were certainly the distraction of the Church from social problems by the threats of Roman Catholic aggression and by the Tractarians, the personal attacks on Maurice by the Evangelicals, and the re-direction of the nation's energies and attention to the Crimean War.[13] But the time was not yet ripe. The moral demands made by the Christian Socialists were too great and the workers were not fit for association; they had not been educated to the Platonic-Christian ideal of service.[14] The concentration of resources on the Working Men's College thus became the investment of Christian Socialism for the future. This may be the movement's one lasting monument but its creed that charity was an obligation for the well-off had far-reaching legacies and, individually, much more was done: Ludlow and Friendly Societies; Kingsley and sanitary reform; Maurice and education; Octavia Hill and housing for the poor. These all owed their inspiration to the failed Christian Socialism.[15]

VI Ruskin: 'The beautiful in all things'

Accuse me not
Of arrogance, unknown Wanderer as I am,
If, having walked with Nature threescore years,
And offered, far as frailty would allow,
My heart a daily sacrifice to Truth,
I now affirm of Nature and of Truth,
Whom I have served, that their DIVINITY
Revolts, offended at the ways of men
Swayed by such motives, to such ends employed;
Philosophers, who, though the human soul
Be of a thousand faculties composed,
And twice ten thousand interests, do yet prize
This soul, and the transcendent universe,
No more than as a mirror that reflects
To proud Self-love her own intelligence;
That one, poor, finite object, in the abyss
Of infinite Being, twinkling restlessly![1]

These lines from Wordsworth's *Excursion* were placed by John Ruskin on the title page of each volume of his *Modern Painters*. The first volume was published in 1843 when the author was only twenty-four; it and the subsequent volumes were immediately regarded as one of the greatest expositions of truth of the age. The lines from Wordsworth were well chosen, for here in the middle years of the century Ruskin reaffirmed a confidence in Nature as a teacher and beauty as a moral agent, beliefs that Coleridge and Wordsworth had expounded fifty years earlier.[2] Ruskin was a true Platonist and he noted the intersection of the Platonic and Biblical messages. He had experienced the full force of the Romantic revival, including a reverence for the past and a love of Scott's novels.[3] To Ruskin, a gentleman justified his social position by extending chivalric qualities to those beneath him.[4] Ruskin was also concerned with the effect of industrial work on moral consciousness.[5] In his support for the Pre-Raphaelite Brotherhood and its aim 'to encourage and enforce an entire adherence to the simplicity of nature' and in his services to the Working Men's College, Ruskin was true to his predecessors.[6] It is from his years with the college and the Oxford-undergraduate road-builders at Hinksey that Ruskin developed his commitment to social reform, a fervour first expressed in *Unto This Last*.[7]

Though many of Ruskin's direct educational ideas were fanciful – he would have every public-school boy learn to plough – his indirect influence carried great force.[8] His overall aim was to make 'the beautiful in all things that God has made' more universal in the service of education.[9] To this end he wanted beautiful classrooms, with much decoration, relics of antiquity and engravings of historic sites; like Plato he believed in the educational powers of assimilation of the environment. He also wanted every boy to learn a manual craft and to take nature study so that the communion with Nature would be the greater.[10] Natural physical activities – riding, swimming, running and the like – were important: children should be as 'active as hares' and the 'body must be made as beautiful and perfect in its youth as it can be, wholly irrespective of the ulterior purpose'.[11]

Another indirect influence on education came from Herbert Spencer, though from the diametrically opposite standpoint. Whereas the idealist Ruskin wanted education in the laws of health and physical activities to produce a beautiful and perfect body, the realist Spencer sought by the same means to prepare for 'the survival of the fittest'; a phrase, first coined by Spencer which echoed the current Darwinian theories on evolution.[12] To Spencer, the physical development of children was in the national interest. He thought it strange that 'while the raising of first-rate bullocks is an occupation on which educated men willingly bestow much time and thought, the bringing up of fine human beings is an occupation tacitly voted unworthy of their attention'.[13] Spencer advocated a cold and scientific approach to the production of a better race; manliness had no place in his theory of morality.[14]

VII   Kingsley: 'The prerogative of a man is to be bold against himself'

The man who in the years from 1848 to 1859 did most to bring the ideal of manliness to the attention of his countrymen was undoubtedly Charles

Kingsley. Through his pamphlets, sermons and lectures, and by means of his best-selling novels, Kingsley was able to spread the gospel of the Romantics and the principles of Thomas Arnold and Frederick Maurice, and then bring them to bear on the religious, social and educational problems of his time. Kingsley's influence was to be far-reaching for he was the greatest all-rounder of his era: as a churchman he became a Canon of Westminster; as a propagandist he was the thorn that provoked John Henry Newman's *Apologia*; as a scientist he corresponded with Charles Darwin concerning evolution; as a historian he held the post of Regius Professor at Cambridge for nine years; as an educationalist he tutored the Prince of Wales; and as an author he gave Macmillans their first best-seller in *Westward Ho!*. But most of the accomplishments listed above came to fruition after 1859, the year when 'Parson Lot' of the Christian Socialist movement stepped back, and Canon Kingsley, Chaplain to the Queen, stepped forward.[1] The essential Kingsley – the Kingsley of the ideal of manliness – was the one of whom W. R. Grey wrote: 'the dust of combat is to him the breath of life.'[2]

As is fitting for a man so closely associated with the Victorian era, Kingsley was born in the same year as his Queen, 1819. That his birth place was at Holne, between Dartmoor and the river Dart, was particularly satisfying to Kingsley for, despite innumerable moves around England, he always regarded himself as a Devon man.[3] His mother's passion for the county was so great that she walked about it constantly during her pregnancy so that it might be communicated to the unborn Charles.[4] Her son grew up amidst the legends of Drake and Grenville and the tales of the Spanish Main. He was sent to Helston Grammar School in Cornwall to receive his senior schooling. It was a happy choice for at Helston he came under the wings of two sympathetic teachers. Derwent Coleridge, the second son of S. T. Coleridge, was the headmaster and the school presumably owed much to the Romantic influence. From C. A. Johns, the other master of this small school, Kingsley derived his love of natural history: many boyhood hours were spent roaming the moors and shore about the Lizard peninsula.[5] On his father's translation to a London parish, Kingsley attended the newly-founded King's College and used it as a cramming establishment for entry to Cambridge; Ruskin and Farrar also proceeded to university in this way. During three pleasant and boisterous years at Magdalene College, Kingsley met his future wife and also took Holy Orders.

Kingsley was the true Romantic. In 1852 he wrote, 'I confess myself a Platonist; and my aim is to draw men, by showing them that the absolute "God the Father", whom no man hath seen, is beyond all possible intellectual notions of ours.'[6] From boyhood he knew much of Coleridge by heart and in manhood he was 'delighted' with *Aids to Reflection*.[7] Wordsworth and a love of nature were ever-present influences. From childhood reading, Malory's *Morte d'Arthur* and Spenser's *Faerie Queen* – 'perhaps the most beautiful poem that has ever been penned by mortal man' – brought the Platonic-Christian ideal of chivalry.[8] Roland too was a Kingsley hero, and in 1851, whilst on a visit to Germany, he stopped at Roland's castle at Rolandseck.[9] At Cambridge,

Kingsley found Tennyson's works 'the most beautiful poetry of the last fifteen years' and the later *In Memoriam* he felt to be 'the noblest Christian poem which England had produced in two centuries'.[10] Ruskin's *Modern Painters* completed the spectrum: 'it was a noble, manful, godly book, a blessed dawn too.'[11]

'Nature was to him . . . the voice of God' was how Stanley summed up Kingsley's reverence.[12] But with Kingsley the love was not solely reserved for mountains and lakes: all nature was beautiful. 'Beauty is God's handwriting – a wayside sacrament; welcome in every fair face, every fair sky, every fair flower, and thank for it Him, the fountain of all loveliness.'[13] His children would accompany him on his walks about the parish, and on the journey they would examine the wayside. 'Study nature – not scientifically, that would take eternity. Try to extract every line of beauty, every association, every moral reflection, every inexpressible feeling from it.'[14] Nature was an educator and to study it was to commune with God: such study was an integral part of the training in manliness:

> Let no one think that this same Natural History is a pursuit fitted only for effeminate or pedantic men. I should say, rather, that the qualities required for a perfect naturalist are as many and as lofty as were required, by old chivalrous writers, for the perfect knight-errant of the Middle Ages: for . . . our perfect naturalist should be strong in body; able to haul a dredge, climb a rock, turn a boulder, walk all day, uncertain where he shall eat or rest; ready to face sun and rain, wind and frost, and to eat and drink thankfully anything, however coarse or meagre; he should know how to swim for his life, to pull an oar, sail a boat, and ride the first horse that comes to hand; and, finally, he should be a thoroughly good shot, and a skilful fisherman; and, if he go far abroad, be able on occasion to fight for his life.[15]

The naturalist would also need to be gentle and courteous, sympathetic to the poor, brave and enterprising. In short he would aspire to the ideal of chivalry.[16]

It was in 1842 as a young curate at Eversley in Hampshire, the parish from which he did his life's work, that Kingsley became acquainted with the philosophy of Maurice: Fanny, soon to be Mrs Kingsley, sent him a copy of the recently published *The Kingdom of Christ* and Kingsley later saw this as a turning point of his life.[17] *The Kingdom of Christ* gave Kingsley the fundamental philosophy for his own beliefs. Two years later, Kingsley and Maurice met in London and as 'Prophet' and 'Master' respectively they became the hub of the Christian Socialist movement. Kingsley and Maurice were very close: their beliefs coincided exactly but their personalities differed.[18] Whereas Maurice was the philosophic, retiring listener, Kingsley was the exuberant, active talker: what Maurice preached, Kingsley did. It was as a doer, not as a thinker, that he brought Christianity into the lives of the ordinary people; he was the forceful embodiment of Maurice's ideas.[19] In Kingsley the clerical function was never divorced from his everyday life; he was a layman in the guise of a clergyman. And, above all, he made Christianity alive and happy, and he put an end to the belief that to be religious you had to be ascetic or gloomy or censorious.[20]

Kingsley's main contribution to the ideal of manliness was certainly as a propagandist but his interest in science brought with it a new dimension. His model society was based not only on Greek philosophy and Christian principles but also on modern knowledge, for science could enable the body to serve God more fully.[21] To Kingsley 'healthy bodies are the only trustworthy organs for healthy minds', and he believed that the ascetic neglect of health was no more than sheer laziness and untidiness. Kingsley had always been active: besides the shooting, hunting, rowing and fishing, he was an avid tree-climber (like many another mid-Victorian) and an enthusiastic walker (once walking the fifty-two miles from Cambridge to London in a day). 'You', he wrote as a young man to Fanny in 1841, 'cannot understand the excitement of animal exercise from the mere act of cutting wood or playing cricket to the manias of hunting or shooting or fishing.'[22] Exercise strengthened his health so that he might give greater service – and Kingsley's health was never sound. He must have found the 'muscular Christian' jibes particularly unkind. In 1859 he wrote to Thomas Hughes: 'This is my fortieth birthday. What a long life I have lived and silly fellows that review me say that I can never have known ill-health or sorrow. I have known enough to make me feel very old.'[23] In the case of the poor, mere exercise was not enough: their food was putrid, the environment was filthy, and their health was neglected. Kingsley thus became a leader of the hygienic movement, an influence which was to have a large effect on the social conditions and education of Britain's working classes for the remainder of the century.

Kingsley's ideal of manliness owed much to the age of chivalry, an era that he saw as a synthesis of high-minded Greek literature, Plato in particular, and the Christian faith. It was 'a very fair ideal of manhood: that of "the gentle, very perfect knight", loyal to his King and to his God, bound to defend the weak, succour the opprest, and put down the wrong doer'.[24] To be manly implied being active, whereas womanliness was essentially passive; Kingsley's manliness included feminine aspects, such as tenderness and tears, but it was decidedly anti-effeminate.[25] Effeminacy by his definition was far-ranging, including anything smacking of individualism, be it Puritanism and Evangelicalism on the one hand, or Tractarianism and Roman Catholicism on the other.[26] Thus manliness implied male virtues.[27] These were the Platonic virtues of truth, self-control and courage. True courage was not brute or animal courage, but a courage linked to duty.[28] Heroism was courage 'beyond the limits of duty', and never 'out of the path of strict duty'. Platonic θυμός, which Kingsley translated as 'rage' or 'pluck', was the particularly masculine element that distinguished manly behaviour from the effeminate.[29] Health and strength were to be encouraged for then the commitments to service could be more fully realised.

It was in about 1857 that the term 'muscular Christianity' became attached to Kingsley's concept of manliness; it probably owed its invention to T. C. Sandars, one of those 'silly fellows' who reviewed him.[30] At first he found the phrase offensive, but the label stuck. 'I have to preach the divineness of the whole manhood', he wrote to Maurice, 'and am content to be called a Muscular Christian, or any other impertinent name, by men who little dream of the weakness of character, sickness of body, and misery of mind, by which I have brought what little I know of the human heart.' Later he was to regard it as 'a clever expression, spoken in jest', and he would even throw it into his own sermons for effect. If it were to mean a 'healthful and manful Christianity' that did not exalt feminine virtues to the exclusion of masculine ones, then he might even accept it.[31] That this same expression acquired a different slant under zealous and eloquent men owed little to Kingsley, and he was by no means the prop and stay of muscular Christianity.

In common with the other Christian Socialists, Kingsley saw education as the key to the future. He believed that his own views 'coincided warmly' with Thomas Arnold's: 'Oh! Why did that noblest of men die?'[32] It was Arnold who had made education truly Christian:

> Till the better method of education which the great Arnold inaugurated shall have expelled the last remnants of that brutal mediaeval one, unknown to free Greece and Rome, but invented by monks cut off from all the softening influences of family, who looked on self-respect as a sin, and on human nature as a foul and savage brute and therefore, accustomed to self-torture and self-contempt, thought it no sin to degrade and scourge other people's innocent children.[33]

Kingsley went further than Arnold and permitted no corporal punishment in his house, feeling that much lying resulted from fear of such reprimand. It is perhaps ironic that the advocate of flogging in *Westward Ho!*, regarded so much as a gospel of muscular Christianity, did not carry his own theory into practice.[34] Kingsley's educational aims matched those of many later headmasters: 'In my eyes the question is not what to teach, but how to educate; how to train not scholars, but men; bold, energetic, methodic; liberal-minded; magnanimous.'[35]

On the founding of nearby Wellington College in 1859, Kingsley developed a keen friendship with its headmaster, Edward Benson and his interest in schools extended to Thring's Uppingham. Kingsley became a keen advocate of natural history and physical education in these schools as he saw that they were essential to the ideal of manliness. At Wellington, Kingsley lectured to the boys in natural history and helped in the founding of a museum. He also instituted a steeplechase, a fine mixture of his natural history and sporting aims. In the movement that brought education to the children of the poorer classes, Kingsley was an enthusiast for physical education as well as for hygiene, and girls were not to be neglected.[36] Such activities brought physical and moral health, and educated the whole man. Games brought out virtues that no book could give:

> daring and endurance, but, better still, temper, self-restraint, fairness, honour, unenvious approbation of another's success, and all that "give and take" of life which stands a man in such good stead when he goes forth in the world, and without which, indeed, his success is always maimed and partial.[37]

As David Newsome noted in *Godliness and Good Learning*:

> If Kingsley had been a headmaster, he would have taught his boys to jump five-barred gates, to climb trees, to run like hares over difficult country; and there would have been nature rambles, a school museum stocked with specimens collected by the boys, science lessons and occasional lectures on hygiene and drains.[38]

Kingsley never had the opportunity, but other men did, and in essence this is what they put into practice in their schools.

Although Kingsley had no direct impact as a headmaster, his influence as a novelist, poet, propagandist and popular scientist was both broad and pervading. It is in his novels in particular that Kingsley's ideal of manliness is best conveyed: 'I am going to take a sermon of Maurice's and turn it into language understanded by the people.'[39] Though his books now read somewhat long-windedly, one is constantly struck by the keen eye for nature and the Victorian gift for word-painting.[40] Most of Kingsley's heroes are indeed manly men but never are they mere animals and never are softer qualities such as tenderness and geniality overlooked.[41] It is perhaps in *Westward Ho!* that Kingsley most fully portrayed his own ideal of manliness. The novel was written in 1854 during the Crimean War and it has been seen as a propagandist recruiting novel.[42] This may be so yet, more concretely, the novel portrayed the virtues of Protestant manliness against the vices of Roman effeminacy. When Kingsley wrote to Thomas Hughes that it 'is a sanguinary book, but perhaps containing doctrine profitable for these times', the reference is just as likely to be to the Papal Aggression of the early 1850s as to the Crimean War.[43] It was a Protestant nationalism that Kingsley preached.[44]

The novel is a tale of the Spanish Main set in Elizabethan times. The Spaniards are of course effeminate: 'they pray to a woman, the idolatrous rascals! and no wonder they fight like women', whilst the Devonians from Bideford are manly Protestants.[45] The hero, Amyas Leigh, is a sixteenth-century Charmides: 'broad limbs, keen blue eyes, curling golden locks, and round honest face'. He is of the best Devon blood and is brave, courteous and truly noble.[46] Though not highly educated, he knows the names of every bird, fish and fly, and can read the meaning of every drift of cloud.

> It is a question, however, on the whole, whether, though grossly ignorant (according to our modern notions) in science and religion he was altogether untrained in manhood, virtue, and godliness; and whether the barbaric narrowness of his information was not somewhat counterbalanced, both in him and the rest of his generation, by the depth, and breadth, and healthiness of his Education.[47]

But manliness needed more than this:

> "I should like to be a brave adventurer, like Mr Oxenham." (Amyas asks Sir Richard Grenville.) "God grant you become a braver man than he! for as I think, to be bold against the enemy is common to the brutes; but the prerogative of a man is to be bold against himself."
>
> "How, Sir?"
>
> "To conquer our own fancies, Amyas, and our own lusts, and our ambition, in the sacred name of duty; this is to be brave, and truly strong; for he who cannot rule himself, how can he rule his crew or his fortunes?"[48]

It is this ideal that embodied all that many a public-school headmaster wished to promote in his school.

VIII Farrar: 'Now, Eric, now or never!'

Westward Ho! was not the only novel that sought to inculcate the ideal of manliness in its readers, for the late 1850s saw the birth of the public-school novel and its enlistment in the battle for hearts and minds.[1] Chronologically, Thomas Hughes's *Tom Brown's Schooldays* of 1857 came first but a comparison with the novels of Frederic Farrar shows that the latter represented an earlier ideal. Farrar in quick succession wrote three public-school novels in the years between 1858 and 1862: *Eric, or Little by Little* (1858), *Julian Home* (1859) and *St Winifred's or The World of School* (1862). All three sold widely throughout the remainder of the century. The books were, however, probably bought for boys rather than by boys, for each appears mawkish and stuffy when compared to the vigour of *Westward Ho!* and *Tom Brown's Schooldays*. In later and more cynical times, Farrar's stories were greatly ridiculed and the term 'Ericin" might then be applied to any pious behaviour by schoolboys.[2] *Eric* and its two brother novels were probably presented to boys as they were about to go for the first time to their public school, for each would serve as a warning of what might happen to an unsuspecting adolescent. The never-named vice is, of course, masturbation.[3] Parents and god-parents would have been in sympathy with Farrar's preface to the 24th edition of *Eric*:

> The story of 'Eric' was written with but one single object – the vivid inculcation of inward purity and moral purpose, by the history of a boy

who, in spite of the inherent nobleness of his disposition, falls into all folly and wickedness, until he has learnt to seek help from above.

Farrar's own background bears many similarities to Charles Kingsley's. After schooling at King William's College on the Isle of Man, he attended King's College in London. There he became a devotee of Frederick Maurice.[4] In 1856 he went up to Trinity College, Cambridge, the home of many Christian Socialists, and there joined the Apostles.[5] On leaving Cambridge and having taken Holy Orders, Farrar became a schoolmaster, first at Marlborough College and then from 1855 to 1870 at Harrow. He then returned to Marlborough as headmaster. Farrar was an excellent teacher of the scholarly but he was reluctant to think well of the less able boy. Everything and everyone, a Harrow Old Boy recalled, was either all black or all white in his eyes and a boy was 'altogether an angel or something far lower'.[6] Pastoral care was important and lessons in manliness were to be learnt in the classroom where, under Ruskin's influence, decorations were to include antique casts and Fra Angelico prints.[7] A natural history society was also founded by Farrar and he sought to teach all that was 'beautiful in literature, arts and nature'.[8] No games-player, Farrar did not appreciate mere physical energy but swimming he did encourage. He determined that every boy in his class should swim and when they all succeeded he would reward them with a morning off school. Farrar the preacher was very like the author, 'all flowers and figures' as a former pupil recalled, and it is probable that his sermons were more appreciated at Westminster Abbey in his later role as Dean than they were as delivered at Harrow and Marlborough.[9]

The three school novels – *Eric, Julian Home* and *St Winifred's* – have much in common. All were largely autobiographical: the first two based on his own days at King William's and Trinity College respectively, whilst the third referred to his time as a housemaster at Harrow.[10] Farrar admitted that all the settings and most of the characters and events were based on real life.[11] All three stories contain mountain-rescue and sea-rescue episodes in which devotion and courage are displayed. Each allows the death of a selfless and virtuous friend – a 'gentle, holy, pure spirit' – to serve as inspiration to the hero. These schoolboy equivalents of Coventry Patmore's contemporary 'angel in the house' played a key role in each story to allow the adolescent readers to come to terms with their own social, spiritual and sexual development.[12] The three heroes, Eric, Julian and Walter, separately wend the same path. Each is reared in beautiful countryside with 'nature as his wise and tender teacher', and each possesses a 'manly bearing' and an 'honest look'. Lessons in manliness are learned in the quiet bearing of unjust punishment and in the penitent struggle if it had been just. Self-denial, the refusal to tell lies and use cribs and the chivalrous defence of the weakling against the bully, are also exalted. Each hero succeeds in fending off the mock manliness of low stories, smoking and drinking, and of being 'taken up' by older boys through misapplied hero-worship.

Eric was written early in Farrar's Harrow career in an attempt to improve the moral tone in the school. He was shocked by what he found: good-looking young boys had female nicknames; many were recruited as older boys' 'bitches';

and boys openly sported naked in bed together. A year after the publication of the book, 1859, the headmaster, Charles Vaughan, resigned when his romantic relationship with a boy was discovered.[13]

The school in *Eric* is thirty years out of date and belongs to the pre–Arnoldian era. There is negligible pastoral care, no prefectorial system and no organised games. Manliness comes from Eric's own inner struggle; the school is nothing, the individual is everything. The tone of the story is best illustrated by an example:

> "Russell, let me always call you Edwin, and call me Eric." "Very gladly, Eric. Your coming here has made me so happy." And the two boys squeezed each other's hands, and looked into each other's faces, and silently promised that they would be loving friends for ever.[14]

It is just possible that boys might behave in this way but to later public-school boys it was certainly improbable. In a famous passage Eric's manliness is on trial:

> Now, Eric, now or never! Life and death, ruin and salvation, corruption and purity, are perhaps in the balance together, and the scale of your destiny may hang on a single word of yours. Speak out, boy! Tell those fellows that unseemly words wound your conscience; tell them that they are ruinous, sinful, damnable – speak out and save yourself and the rest. Virtue is strong and beautiful, Eric, and vice is downcast in her awful presence. Lose your purity of heart, Eric, and you have lost a jewel which the whole world, if it were "one entire and perfect chrysolite", cannot replace.[15]

Farrar returned to the attack at the end of the chapter in case the message had been overlooked by the reader:

> Oh, young boys, if your eyes ever read these pages, pause and beware. The knowledge of evil is ruin, and the continuance in it is moral death. That little matter – that beginning of evil – it will be like the snow-flake detached by the breath of air from the mountain-top, which, as it rushes down, gains size and strength and impetus, till it has swollen to the mighty and irresistible avalanche that overwhelms garden and field and village in a chaos of undistinguishable death.[16]

Julian Home opens with the hero about to leave a school based on Farrar's contemporary Harrow. The hero is a fair cricketer but he cannot bear the months of talking cricket 'shop' which, with few boys interested in intellectual pursuits, proves the staple conversation.[17] But the story quickly moves on to Cambridge and includes a portrait of a don reminiscent of Leslie Stephen: a type who would not display an interest in anything more important than a boat race or a game of bowls to save their lives.[18] At the university Julian steadily gains in manliness, and by his graduation he

> had grown in calmness, in strength, in wisdom; he had learnt many practical lessons of life; he had gained new friends, without losing the old. He had learnt to honour all men, and to be fearless for the truth. His mind had become a well-managed instrument, which he could apply to all purposes of discovery, research, and thought; he was wiser, better, braver, nearer the light. In a word, he had learnt the great purpose of life – sympathy and love to further man's interest, faith and prayer to live for God's glory.[19]

'To the sacred memory of one in Heaven, these pages which faintly strive to inculcate the courage, the virtue, and the tenderness of which that life was so shining an example, are dedicated with affection too strong for words, with regret too deep for tears!' So reads Farrar's dedication in *St Winifred's*, a tale that sought to guide the boy-reader through his school life. The ideal of manliness is even more explicit than it was in *Eric*, indeed 'manly' may well be the most frequent adjective in the book. St Winifred's is a contemporary school modelled on Harrow. There is a prefectorial system and games are an important feature of school life. Unlike Roslyn School in *Eric*, St Winifred's positively aids the education of the individual and promotes the ideal of manliness. Even here though, in a 'bad time' there could be a 'bad house', and the reader is shown that even the youngest boy can turn the tide:

> Even the character of the Noelites was beginning to improve; in that bad house a single little new boy had successfully braved an organised antagonism to all that was good, and by his victories, virtuous courage had brought over the others to the side of right, triumphing, by the mere force of good principle, over a banded multitude of boys far older, abler, and stronger than himself.[20]

Individual example was still important: 'There were many boys at St Winifred's gentle-hearted, right-minded, of kindly and manly impulses; but all of them except Walter, lost their golden opportunity of conferring pure happiness by disinterested good deeds.'[21]

Despite the sales of his novels, Farrar probably felt, as the 1860s slipped by, that he was clinging to virtues of a day passing rapidly away.[22] Certainly *St Winifred's* contains a *cri de coeur*:

> If, in popular papers or magazines, boys are to read that, in a boy, lying is natural and venial; that courtesy to, and love for, a master, is impossible and hypocritical; that swearing and corrupt communication are peccadilloes which none but the preacher and pedagogues regard as discreditable, how

can we expect success to the labours of those who toil all their lives, amid neglect and ingratitude, to elevate the boys of England to a higher and holier view?[23]

IX The Titans: 'The union of piety, energy, and cheerfulness'

Manliness existed as a word long before the Victorian period but, as no ideal was attached, it was of no concern to the educationalist. Traditional manliness was primarily associated with the lewd and lecherous, high-living and hard-drinking, horse-and-hound variety of country squire. Although his days were not yet to be numbered by the evangelical zeal of the early nineteenth century, his example did become the model of what the new manliness would replace.[1] Soon schoolmasters would no longer tolerate an upbringing of fighting, rat-catching, poaching and other forms of general lawlessness.

As we have seen, what Edward Thring was to term 'true manliness' grew from roots that tapped many sources of nourishment. Much came from the Romantic Movement associated with Coleridge, Wordsworth and Scott, which in turn looked to Plato and Christianity for its ideal. Platonic manliness sought to produce that balanced all-rounder, the whole man, and it advocated the three virtues of truth, courage and self-control. Christian ethics and a reverence for Nature were welded to this Platonic base and a Rousseauian, child-centred education was adopted as the most effective means of inculcating the ideal. Here manliness is the earthly foundation of godliness.[2]

Arnold at Rugby was the first headmaster who determined to mould his pupils to this manliness. Decisive leadership, strong pastoral care, a morally-earnest classical curriculum, the prefectorial system and a chapel-centred school life, these were his means, and his purpose was to convert evil children into saintly adults as quickly as possible. Childishness was a prefatory state to manliness, much inferior but sadly necessary. The ancient ideal of the whole man now became Athenian manliness: it sought to civilise boys and had brutishness as its target.

The idealised societies created by Arnold and his disciples gained wider recognition through the efforts of the Christian Socialists. Under the leadership of Maurice and Kingsley, many young men were drawn to a movement that determined to improve the lives and working conditions of the nation's poor: now Platonic service was extended beyond school cloisters and college quadrangles. Evening schools, Bible classes, country outings, boxing and football, all became common-place and many of the men who organised these activities would become the headmasters of the next generation. Kingsley and Ruskin did not enter the classroom but, by their efforts at Eversley and Hinksey and through their popular writings, they spread the manly message far and wide. A robust and sporty coating of sugar made the Christian pill easier to swallow: all this was muscular Christian manliness. Its advocates fought against exclusivity.[3]

Kingsley's strain of manliness owed much to the age of chivalry. The ideal of 'the gentle, very perfect knight' found its Victorian counterpart in chivalric manliness. Effeminacy was the despised opposite but manliness did not preclude gentle acts and displays of emotion. Boys and men might walk arm-in-arm; hugs and pats on the back were normal; and crying, whether out of joy or sorrow, was acceptable.[4] Family life and parental responsibility were important too, with Prince Albert and Queen Victoria portrayed as the model partnership of husband and wife, father and mother.

The late-Georgian gentleman was now a relic of an age passing rapidly away; meanwhile his mid-Victorian successor was being remodelled to be the instrument of a brand new moral authority.[5] True manliness was now ready to be put into practice. The public schools became the prime means of its promotion and by the end of the 1850s it was essential that sons of respectable families should attend these schools. The number of public schools increased three-fold by 1860 to meet this demand.[6]

*****

'Of all decades in our history,' wrote G. M. Young, 'a wise man would choose the eighteen-fifties to be young in.'[7] Here was an era of great men – Kingsley, Maurice, Ruskin and Matthew Arnold were the 'prophets' of the new age, with Spencer, Darwin and Tennyson not far behind – and able men became great headmasters.[8] It is probable that no other period of history saw so many intellectually gifted, morally earnest and spiritually convinced men choose schoolmastering for their careers. As David Newsome concluded:

> The nineteenth-century headmaster is now almost a legend: . . . he was a Titan in an age of Titans: undisputed monarch of his kingdom, spiritual leader of his flock, mentor and chastiser of his charges, feared and respected by Governors, parents, masters and boys alike.[9]

The foremost Titans of this group numbered three: Edward Benson, Frederick Temple and Edward Thring. Benson was the headmaster of Wellington from its founding in 1859 until 1873 and was later Bishop of Truro and Archbishop of Canterbury; Temple was headmaster at Rugby from 1858 to 1869 and, later, Bishop of Exeter and Archbishop of Canterbury; Thring was headmaster at Uppingham from 1853 until his death in 1887. These men fostered the ideal of true manliness in their schools.

Benson was a headmaster of the Arnoldian mould and, given the chance of building a new school, he endeavoured to found it on the lines of Arnold's Rugby. Arnold's influence reached Benson second-hand through his own headmaster, James Prince Lee of King Edward's, Birmingham. Lee had been one of Arnold's first appointments at Rugby and the first to leave to become a headmaster.[10] Benson had a deep attachment to Lee and from him felt the full flow of the

Romantic movement. In 1848 he entered Trinity College, Cambridge and there gained a first in the Classical Tripos. During his Cambridge years Benson was much impressed by Harvey Goodwin who was doing Christian Socialist work in the city. The Romantic influence remained strong; in 1881 he went on a reading party to the Lake District and there visited Arnold's house and sites associated with Wordsworth. Benson had determined to be a schoolmaster ever since he had read Stanley's life of Arnold and in 1852 he was delighted to accept Edward Goulburn's offer of a mastership at Rugby. In 1857 Temple succeeded Goulburn as headmaster and from this date a strong friendship built on mutual admiration developed between the two future archbishops.[11]

Benson's chance of a headmastership came in 1859 with the founding of Wellington College as a national memorial to the Iron Duke, and on Temple's advice he took the post. Prince Albert was Chairman of the Governors and the driving force behind the venture. He sought to create a Germanic military academy in which the barbarism of fagging and flogging of the old public schools would have no place. The prince sent Benson on a tour of German and Prussian schools and, though the headmaster was far from impressed by what he found, he sought to impose many ideas culled from German practice: numbers were to be limited to 250; boys would sleep in cubicles to increase privacy; a uniform would be worn; and the curriculum was to be broadened to include modern languages, music, science, art and gymnastics.[12] On Prince Albert's death in 1861, however, Benson steered the school away from the ideals of its founder and closer to those of Arnold. Wellington now came to the forefront as a public school and strove to lose its image as a military academy for orphans.

Of all headmasters it is perhaps Benson who is nearest as a disciple of Arnold but through a lack of understanding of boys and, above all, a want of sympathy, he was a figure held in great terror.[13] The school was maintained in an iron discipline by 'an indiscriminate use of the cane'.[14] Benson could not be popular: to many boys he was a headmaster for grand occasions; he would preach in chapel on virtues that only a saint could attain; and he could exercise thundering judgement.[15] Benson's Broad Churchmanship, his respect for 'manliness and chivalry', and his friendship with his near neighbour, Charles Kingsley, indicate that he believed in the ideal of manliness but he was unable to nurture it to any large extent in his school.[16] There were, though, to be no overtures to the cult of games. Prefects were always picked from the intellectual elite, and Benson could write light-heartedly about school matches and not feel any obligation to go and watch them.[17] If Benson had been able to relax more – as for instance when Temple visited Wellington and led headmaster and boys in a game jumping over piles of heather – he might have been better able to communicate the ideal of manliness to his charges.[18] But physical activity meant little to Benson:

> in his last summer half at school he actually managed to bowl someone out, and was standing complacently receiving the plaudits of his friends when

he fell unconscious on the ground, having been struck on the top of his head by the ball which had been thrown high into the air in triumph.[19]

Frederick Temple had all Benson's virtues and none of his vices, and he was considered by some of his contemporaries to personify manliness by his rugged appearance.[20] A wise man in the 1860s with the gift of foresight would have sent his son to Temple's Rugby, assuming that he had not heard of Thring's Uppingham. Temple, like Thring, had that rare ability to communicate easily with his pupils. Temple was born in the same year as Thring, 1821, in the Ionian Islands where his middle-class father was serving as an army officer. On return to England, Temple attended Blundell's School in Devon and there won the Balliol scholarship at the age of sixteen. At Oxford he continued his studies brilliantly, gaining firsts in both classics and mathematics. He became part of the Broad Church Movement through his tutor A. C. Tait, who was appointed Archbishop of Canterbury in 1868.[21] On graduation he took Holy Orders and was elected a fellow of his college.[22] Temple's academic ability was matched by his physical vigour: as a boy he had been used to hard manual labour on the farm, unlike Benson who had an urban childhood, and he would delight in the pleasures of the countryside. At Oxford he was fond of country walks and he would join in college sports with enthusiasm. A love of the works of Wordsworth, Coleridge and Tennyson followed naturally.[23] After a few years as principal of a teachers' training college at Kneller Hall, Temple was appointed headmaster of Rugby in November 1857. Three of Temple's testimonials came from influential Old Rugbeians – Arthur Stanley, Arthur Clough, and Matthew Arnold – and these presumably carried weight with the trustees.

The Temple era saw all that was best come to Rugby. Goulburn's headmastership had not been a success and the trustees regretted their decision to move away from Arnold's liberalism; academic standards and the moral tone had fallen, so too had pupil numbers.[24] The trustees now wanted another Arnoldite headmaster, though some worried that Temple was not a proper gentleman. Their concerns seemed justified when he scandalised the town by walking from the railway station to the school, and carrying his own luggage.[25] They need not have worried: the school roll rose again and stayed high; pomp and ceremony were reduced; a huge rebuilding programme was undertaken; the curriculum was overhauled to include science; and art and music gained enthusiastic encouragement.[26] Temple saw education as the cultivation of moral qualities and mental discipline, and each teacher should be a role model of how to be both moral and learned.[27] Masters joined the boys in their games and boys might even come to chapel off the playing-field still in their games kit.[28] The chapel became the mainspring of his influence but there were no moral exhortations: example was the operative method.

Much of Temple's success came from the fact that, unlike Benson, he was a boy at heart. Physical activity was important to him. Rumour had it that he told his first new boys that he could run a hundred yards, climb a tree, or jump a brook with the best of them: at first this was accounted bragging but that impression was dispelled when it was heard that he had climbed all the elms in the school's grounds to ensure that they were safe for boys to tackle.[29] Physical activity not only enabled Temple to mix with the boys but it also formed a valuable educational tool in that it was a 'potent factor in his hands for the moulding of human character'. Games allowed the praepostor, who was always a member of the sixth-form, to relax from the strain of responsibility and be a boy again.[30] And it was not work or games, but both. In his evidence to the Public Schools Commission, Temple commented that boys were not excused games through academic pressures: 'It is certainly the general custom for boys most distinguished for their progress in intellectual studies to take interest in all the games.' But the athletic ethos was not encouraged:

> A boy athlete, not high up in the school, was reported to Temple for neglected work; he was sent for by the chief to his study, the time fixed apparently accidently being just as an interesting match was about to begin. The boy went, but he found Dr Temple immersed in correspondence; he stood watching the Headmaster's pen and gazing furtively at the match out of the window. A silent hour passed, and "no side" was called in the Close. "Now you may go", said the Headmaster without looking up. There was no need to enforce the moral further.[31]

It was, however, at Uppingham in the years between 1853 and 1870, where Edward Thring was 'arguably the most influential figure in public-school history since Arnold', that the ideal of true manliness was most completely put into practice.[32]

Chapter 2

True manliness in practice

I Thring and Uppingham: 'Education for True Life'

> Whose life was work, whose language rife
> With rugged maxims hewn from life;[1]

Tennyson wrote these words of the Duke of Wellington; he might have written the same words of Edward Thring who began his headmastership at Uppingham School in 1853 and died in harness in 1887. Thring's life was his work. When he came to Uppingham in the East Midlands' county of Rutland, he found a country grammar school of some twenty-five boys; by his death the number had been steady at 300 for more than twenty years and both Thring and Uppingham had gained national renown.[2] Tennyson's words are particularly apposite for Thring, for the word 'life' was his watchword. To Thring, life or, in particular, 'true life' was a principle of action, thought and speech. The words appear in countless addresses, over half his sermons, and they punctuate the text of his books. If the boys wanted to mimic Thring, they would most certainly choose a phrase that contained the word 'life'. Thring was adamant: education was training for 'true life';[3] and true education was

> nothing less than bringing everything that men have learnt from God, or from experience, to bear first upon the moral and spiritual being by means of a well-governed society and healthy discipline, so that it should love and hate aright, and through this, secondly, making the body and intellect perfect, as instruments necessary for carrying on the work of earthly progress; training the character, the intellect, the body, each through the means adapted to each. This is the object of education.[4]

This was the ethos of Uppingham and 'true life' meant doing the work for Christ. To examine Thring's educational thought, one has to study what he sought to achieve at Uppingham and then relate the product to the ideal. We shall find that Tennyson's second line is also applicable to Thring, for he was a great coiner of maxims. One of his favourites was 'Honour the work, and the work will honour you'; an examination will indeed show that his work honours Thring.[5]

Thring began his headmastership on 10 September 1853 with the innovation of a holiday and a cricket match with his few pupils, a match in which Thring later recalled he got '15 by some good swinging hits'.[6] No doubt the innings did delight his pupils but the first years were not to be as idyllic as that first day. Thring was determined to work the foundation more efficiently and to begin at once his 'great educational experiment'.[7] However, the experiment nearly failed on several occasions: the boys did not take to his ideas of honour and schoolboy loyalty; the newly-appointed masters did not readily comply with Thring's wishes; and, almost to a man, the Governors of the foundation took no interest in the advancement of the school.[8] Despite these obstacles, success came: by mid-summer 1857 the school was bigger than it had ever been before and was doubling every two years. Trusted masters, including Robert Hodgkinson and John Baverstock, were at Thring's side and by Christmas he had won over William Earle – Earle had been usher, or under-master, on Thring's arrival.[9] Thring was now firmly in command and his 'great educational experiment' was in full swing. It was a unique experiment and one that would have lasting influence on education in England and further afield. 'No school has ever impressed me like Uppingham', Thring was told by a visiting headmistress in 1887: 'Other schools may be bodies corporate, but Uppingham has a soul.'[10]

As Cormac Rigby argued, there is no evidence that Thring had a blueprint for a school as he took up his headmastership.[11] He only gave serious thought to his career when he became engaged to be married in the autumn of 1852 and, before he obtained the Uppingham vacancy, he had applied for two other posts.[12] Bryan Matthews, however, believed that when Thring did turn his thoughts to headmastering, Uppingham was the sort of school he would have looked for: it was small and ready for an enterprising headmaster. It was also isolated, a good quality for an experimental site, but accessible. Railways were approaching Uppingham from several directions and these would be vital for the school to grow beyond its local resources.[13] Thring might thus have chosen 'an Uppingham' but he did not have a blueprint for a school. His career shows Thring to be a pragmatist: if a new idea suggested itself and was seen to contribute to the overall plan, then it was adopted and absorbed into the system. It is in this way that Thring's philosophy can be traced, thus we must turn to the thirty-two years before he came to Uppingham. It was in these early years that he absorbed the ideal of true manliness; it was after 1853 that he put the ideal into practice.

Edward Thring was born at Alford in Somerset on 29 November 1821. His father, John Gale Thring, was rector and squire of the parish; his mother, Sarah, was the daughter of the vicar of a neighbouring parish. Edward was the fifth of seven surviving children.[14] His father, who had been educated at Winchester and St John's College, Cambridge, was a sound scholar and all his sons were to receive their preliminary classical training from him. Sarah Thring, an intelligent and gentle woman, had scholarly connections in her own family but for Edward her strongest influence came through a sincere sense of Christian duty. The Thring brothers shared a boisterous boyhood on the Alford estate, in the pools of the Brue at the bottom of the garden, and in the surrounding countryside. Edward was remembered as always out of doors and his own memories recalled the freedom of life there. It amused Thring greatly when he returned to Alford that he was still remembered by the gamekeeper as 'Young Squire'.[15]

Nature was one of Thring's first teachers and she maintained her role throughout his life. At Uppingham he 'really enjoyed' his outdoor communion and his diary noted the appearance of each year's first crocus, hyacinth, swallow, and so on.[16] Whether rambling in the countryside with his collie at his heels, or visiting his 'rural friends' in the aviary, or holidaying in the Lake District, Thring always held a spiritual regard for nature: 'But what consoles me is the sight of *life* everywhere: the rush of life in the tree and the grass. That is a wonderful comfort, that thought.'[17] Thring regarded nature not as an aesthetic experience but as a mystical one: 'Beauty is the expression of the mind of God seen through a material medium.'[18] It was through flowers and trees, animals and birds, sky and clouds that God spoke to man: 'Sky and earth combine to compose the message.'[19] Whilst at Grasmere in 1874, Thring preached on the theme that 'He made the earth speak a new language to all men'. This is the creed of the Romantics and expressed at the Lake District heart of Romanticism. Back at Uppingham, Thring preached a similar sermon to his pupils.[20]

Poetry to Thring was an extension of nature and his Cambridge jotting books contain much Wordsworth, Coleridge and Tennyson.[21] He shared this enthusiasm with his younger brother, Godfrey, later a celebrated hymn-writer.[22] Wordsworth was Thring's greatest love and all his works were much read; the poet was a great source of spiritual uplift to the schoolmaster; and overtones of Wordsworth are present in Thring's own sonnets.[23] The headmaster would often talk on Wordsworth to the boys and he would lend them his own volumes. One day he complained that he had incomplete sets for the borrowed copies were not always returned.[24]

Wordsworth may have taught Thring to look around him but it was Ruskin who encouraged him to look to the skies. The publication of the initial volume of *Modern Painters* promoted awareness of the sky with its chapter 'Of the Open Sky'. Here Ruskin asserted that much of nature's moral message had been ignored by previous generations. Thring did not miss it for he had read Ruskin at Cambridge and later he wrote that he owed 'to Mr Ruskin's *Modern Painters* more of thought and fruitful power than to any other book, or any other living man'.[25] This is one of two of Ruskin's works that Thring knew well – the other was *Fors Clavigera* – and, on the one occasion that they met, he was able to thank the author for them.[26] J. M. W. Turner was the great exponent in painting of the moral worth of the sky, and Thring was a keen admirer of the artist's renderings of sunrise and sunset, and of different types of cloud formations.[27] Thring often visited art galleries: he admired Italian art, adored Giotto's Arena Chapel in Padua, and was impressed by Dürer, but no art contained the great moral and spiritual force that he found in Turner's paintings.[28] Ruskin's thought was to colour much of Thring's educational practice; five months before own his death, Thring gave his treasured Ruskin volumes to his three daughters.[29]

Just as Turner follows naturally from Ruskin so, in the true spirit of Romanticism, Thring had a cottage in the Lake District. It was in 1863 that he first leased Ben Place and it became the family holiday home for fifteen summers. Only when Borth in Mid Wales presented a stronger attraction did the Lakes lose their hold. Ben Place is at the heart of the Romantic's paradise for the area is littered with Wordsworthian memories: Fairfield towers behind the cottage, Grasmere is a mile away, and Wordsworth's cottage is at the other end of the small lake. Thring would often invite boys to Ben Place and together they would stand at Wordsworth's grave, walk the poet's favourite Easedale, or go to Thring's treasured spot at Tongue Ghyll waterfall. Ben Place became Thring's 'Dreamland Home'. There he would be his most relaxed and carefree self; there he wrote most of his books and his poetry; there that he gained strength for the coming term. 'Yes', Thring wrote to Hardwicke Rawnsley, an Old Boy who lived and worked in the Lake District,

> rejoice in your sight of beauty, and your hearing of the creature voice of the hills, and your reading of the inaudible word of God in lake and mountain; it is a great privilege. . . . I find that the having seen and enjoyed gives me strength and not weakness in harder hours and sadder scenes.[30]

Alford, Thring's birthplace, is situated in legendary countryside: five miles away is Cadbury Hill and, after Alford, the Brue flows to Glastonbury. It is a region rich in myth and legend for Cadbury is believed to be the site of King Arthur's castle, the nearby mere is where Arthur is reputed to have thrown his sword, Excalibur, and the history of Glastonbury Abbey is finely interwoven with the search for the Holy Grail. Thring knew his Arthurian tales well and, when his friend Juliana Ewing visited Alford in 1884, he was disappointed that he could not be there to conduct her to the Cadbury site.[31] History through legend and heroic exploits was the way Thring would introduce children to learning: 'Give them to read Poetry, the Lives of Good Men, narratives of noble deeds, Historical Stories, and Historical Novels, Books of Travel, and all the fascinating literature of discovery and adventure.'[32] Many years later Thring remembered how all history had been a 'shadowy ghostland' until, when on holiday in France at the age of twenty, he had seen Richard Coeur de Lion's mark at Rouen.[33] At Uppingham Thring endeavoured to enliven the shadowy ghostland through pictures and artefacts, and the library – the library in 1867 containing much Tennyson, seven volumes of Wordsworth, all of Scott, and much of Kingsley.[34]

Sir Walter Scott was an early favourite and everything from the beauty of the *Waverley* novels, the charm of the ballads, the music of the lyric poetry to the glory of the romances, all brought pleasure and delight. In 1885, when he addressed the Education Society as its President, Thring told of his love of Scott:

> Here let me record my own deep obligations to Sir Walter Scott, the noblest of writers. Many of his novels I have read over and over again. The glorious lesson to honour, and paint with honour, antagonists and their beliefs, can be learnt nowhere so well as in him. . . . How manly his spirit, like the air of his own mountains, full of gallantry and truth! . . . He gave me an acquaintance with words, and a freedom in using them, for which I am, and ever shall be, grateful. . . . Health and honour flow forth from every word he wrote, an heir-loom to us all for ever. I rejoice in confessing my great debt to him, and others may get from similar reading the happy gains I got from him.[35]

Tennyson was another Thring favourite and his Cambridge jotting books and *Education and School*, first published in 1864, contain many Tennyson extracts. Thring was himself an enthusiastic poet and there is an Arthurian flavour about much of his own work.[36] *A Wanderer* and its related poems were written at Ben Place and later remodelled into *The Dreamland*.[37] These poems exude Thring's passion for the Lake District and express his belief that God speaks to men through nature: as Hardwicke Rawnsley wrote in *Literary Associations of the English Lakes*, 'he never tired of translating the life of man into the life of Nature, and of making the trees and rocks and streams and waterfalls speak with human knowledge.'[38]

A second recurring theme in Thring's poetry is the *Song of Roland*. The first mention of Roland comes in a letter to Lewis Nettleship, a favourite Old Boy then at Oxford. Thring wrote that he had been reading the Roland legend and that he had composed his own poem on the theme.[39] The poems in the *A Wanderer* collection contain four which absorb the Roland legend and the theme was to haunt Thring for most of his life.[40] The last verse of *Dream of A Life* from the early collection embodies the crucial message:

> And so he died and hither came to be
> The king of hopes that live again, the king
> Of battles lost, just in the early spring
> Of a good cause which dies not in the loss,
> But won when summer ripens, and brings on
> The harvest, and the dreams become the life.[41]

Roland's heroic death at Roncevalles, where he claimed victory in defeat as the Saracens dispersed when the trumpet sounded to call Charlemagne's army, clearly held great attraction for Thring, and especially the concept of the 'lost battle won'.[42] This message occurs in many of his poems and in much of Thring's other writings. Thring explained the message in a letter to Nettleship:

> As to the lost battle, it seems to me that all true working life is to the worker of the nature of the lost battle: day by day there is such a pouring out of seemingly wasted blood; and success, as it is called, is such a mockery, that the feeling of the lost battle is always at hand the more one succeeds. Men praise the things one does not fight for, and mock the things one does, and their praise does not please, and their sneers do wound.[43]

The theme of the *Song of Roland* is clearly the pilgrimage of Thring's own spirit. His life at Uppingham was always a battle – with masters, with trustees, with inspectors – and when fame came it was not the fame he sought. To this day Thring is remembered most for the formation of the Headmasters' Conference, and even in his lifetime Uppingham's prominence came first through sporting prowess. Both are distortions of Thring's central purpose. Though often despondent for the present, Thring was always hopeful for the future and he believed that his ideals would eventually come to fruition beyond the confines of Uppingham. The 'lost battle won' is thus a cry from the heart: 'To bring up the rear of the lost battle in a good cause is the greatest thing in the world. For the lost battle is always the victory of life later on.'[44]

In 1863 Sarah Thring sent her grand-daughter Margaret a book edited by Mrs Gatty. Thring avidly read it himself and discovered 'one of those refreshing little story books which from time to time keep my feelings clear and simple and nerve me for life'.[45] The book was probably a volume of the hugely popular *Aunt Judy's Tales*, with stories contributed by Mrs Gatty's daughter, Mrs Ewing. Thring's daughters subsequently subscribed to the tales and he used a quotation from them in his 1864 *Education and School*.[46] Margaret Gatty was also the author of a long series of stories, *Parables from Nature*; copies were bought for the Uppingham library.[47] The *Parables* were allegorical tales taken from nature in which Christian morals were charmingly drawn. A love of nature filled the tales and behind the 'innocent masks' of animals Mrs Gatty gently pressed her message.[48] The *Parables* formed part of the Romantic inheritance: Tennyson and Kingsley were her heroes and they in turn admired her work.[49] Thring felt that *Parables from Nature* was 'the most beautiful book in its way in the English language. The mother and daughter have opened a new world of higher life and thought and feeling for mankind.'[50] When Thring's middle daughter, Margaret, complained that an issue of *Aunt Judy's Tales* contained no story by Mrs Ewing, Thring helped her to write a letter to the author.[51] She replied with a short story composed especially for Margaret, which in turn led to correspondence between headmaster and author that lasted over fifteen years.[52]

In the 1870s the news that a loyal African prince had been killed in a skirmish with Zulus, whilst some accompanying Englishmen had escaped, gave Juliana Horatia Ewing the idea for a story. In the tale Mrs Ewing, the wife of a serving soldier, wanted to bring home to the civilian population the military concept of selfless honour that was at odds with civilian indifference.[53] She took as her theme that it was better to die trying to save a stricken comrade than not to risk one's life at all. Thring seems to have heard of the story from its earliest days and was an enthusiastic admirer even before its publication.[54] The story, *Jackanapes*, appeared in *Aunt Judy's Magazine* in 1879 with a frontispiece painting by Randolph Caldecott. In 1883 it was published as a shilling edition by S. P. C. K. and became a best-seller.[55] The story, the 'favourite child' of Mrs Ewing's imagination, related in simple language how Jackanapes risked his life in battle to save his fallen comrade.[56] As a result of this 'heroic example and noble obligation' he is fatally wounded; he dies with pride felt for his 'gallantry and devotion'. At Jackanapes's funeral, the text taken was 'Whosoever will save his life shall lose it, and whosoever shall lose his life for My sake shall find it'. Grey Goose, the personification of civilian life, fails to see any point in Jackanapes's brief life.[57]

Thring wrote enthusiastically to Mrs Ewing: 'I love *Jackanapes*, it is perfect.' He told her that he was going to lecture to the school on it and that he had insisted that Hawthorn's, the local bookseller, ordered fifty copies for display in his window.[58] To Thring, 'Life touches life' in the tale; it was the most direct appeal of heart to heart, exquisite for its simplicity and for its purity of spirit.[59]

> I, for my part, agree with the old General, who is said to have locked himself in his room every Sunday to read Mrs Ewing's story of "Jackanapes" unseen. I could not trust myself to read it in public.[60]

Thring and Mrs Ewing corresponded for many years, and her nephew was to come to Uppingham, but they were only to meet in 1885 when Mrs Ewing lay dying.[61] Thring returned a few days later to preach the funeral address and then, back at Uppingham, he wrote *In Memoriam – Mrs Ewing*.

> The bugles, like the silver call
> Of God's own trumpets, rang;
> The very dust to diamonds turned,
> And forth her heroes sprang.
>
> Then changed she to a twilight strain,
> So sad, so softly bright;
> Sweet death, sweet life, dissolved in tears,
> Each tear an orb of life.[62]

Mrs Ewing's last story was published posthumously in 1885. *Laetus Sorte Mea* told the story of a boy who knew he was to die young but who nevertheless wanted to live and die a soldier. Thring took *Laetus Sorte Mea* to his heart.[63]

> I have been reading *Laetus*. My whole world has altered, and I am in a nobler, higher, purer, and more unselfish world. . . . But above all things

I am striving to be *Laetus sorte mea*, and to have no more repining or unsettled wishes, and plans or fear or disappointment. Airs of Paradise are nearer than ever before. I am *Laetus*.[64]

After Mrs Ewing's death in May, soon followed by publication of *Laetus Sorte Mea*, Thring's life changed. No longer was there despair of the present; no longer was he despondent. Roland's 'lost battle won' gave way to *Laetus Sorte Mea* – 'happy with my lot' – and he removed all mention of Roland and lost battles as he prepared his poems for publication in *Poems and Translations*.[65] His friendship with Mrs Ewing provided Thring with an understanding that made his last years almost golden, soon finding their fullest realisation in the Conference of the Headmistresses, held at Uppingham in June 1887.[66] As he confided to his diary: 'It is curious how Mrs Ewing's life and meaning has set me going on all this woman's work.'[67]

II Ilminster, Eton and Cambridge: 'Greek sunshine versus London fog'

Thring's childhood at Alford was a happy one and it was in the secure environment of the home that the Christian, Romantic and Chivalric foundation of the ideal of manliness was laid. Life at school had its influence too but the effects were negative rather than positive, and their result was seen in the realities of life at Uppingham rather than in moral precepts. Thring was eight when he went away to a preparatory school in the nearby town of Ilminster. It had a reputation for 'ability and severity': Thring remembered the severity more than the ability and even in his last years he could still contrast the freedom of home with the prison-like nature of school.[1] In his 1885 address to the Education Society, Thring told of his Ilminster years.

> My first acquaintance with school began at eight years old, in an old-fashioned private school of the flog-flog, milk-and-water-at-breakfast type. All my life long the good and evil of that place has been on me. It is even now one of my strongest impressions, with its prim misery, the misery of a clipped hedge, with every clip through flesh, and blood and fresh young feelings; its snatches of joy, its painful but honest work, grim, but firmly in earnest, and its prison morality of discipline. The most lasting lesson of my life was the failure of suspicion and severity to get inside the boy-world, however much it troubled our outsides.[2]

The harshness of Ilminster helped to produce Uppingham: 'it was my memories of that school and its severities that first made me so long to try if I could not make the life of small boys at school happier and brighter.'[3]

In 1832 Thring went up to Eton for nine years, first as an Oppidan and then as a Colleger – 'Those nine years, with all their chequered feeling, did not leave me in ignorance of the good and evil of a great public school.'[4] John Keate was Headmaster and the term before Thring's arrival witnessed the flogging of eighty randomly chosen boys to quell an incipient rebellion. Keate's severity of rule was in sympathy with fellow headmasters trying to reform undesirable public-school traditions; little emphasis was placed on religious and moral education.[5] On his appointment Keate was in sole charge of a class of 170 and in Thring's time there were just nine masters to 570 boys in the upper school. Only the clever and willing had opportunities to learn; the rest were left to fend for themselves. Thring was in Chapman's house for his first three years. James Chapman was a sensitive teacher who approached his work with evangelical zeal. He and fellow housemaster George Selwyn used to hold special evening services in Windsor which Thring and his friend John Mackarness, later Bishop of Oxford, would attend.[6] Chapman's reports spoke well of Thring – the 'little fellow' progressing steadily on all fronts. Many years later Thring was still to correspond with Chapman, who may have been his model housemaster. Certainly Thring would have approved Chapman's declaration that 'Education I believe to be the great hope, as well as the great work of our day'.[7]

In 1835 Thring went into residence as a Colleger. A Colleger's life was severe: at eight o'clock each evening the seventy boys were locked in the Long Chamber, a large and bare room infested with rats, completely without supervision. Beds were in short supply so younger boys slept on the floor; older boys monopolised the few wash-basins.[8] Boy government ruled, with the younger boys at the mercy of their elders. Thring was later to write:

> Who can ever forget that knew it, the wild, rough, rollicking freedom, the frolic and the fun of that land of misrule, with its strange code of traditional boy laws, which really worked rather well as long as the sixth form were well disposed or sober?[9]

At Ilminster there had been no freedom, now it was there in abundance. In between there must be a happy medium. In 1860 Thring contrasted Uppingham with his own schooldays: 'Surely this leading the school in all their life, without destroying their freedom at all, must have a great effect.'[10] At home Thring was accustomed to an outdoor life and at Eton he developed his love of physical activity. Thring was remembered as a 'great runner long before the days of the "athletic" sports'.[11] He played cricket and football, and he was prominent for the Collegers in the match 'at the Wall' with the Oppidans, but fives was the real love.[12] A contemporary remembered Thring as 'a capital fives player . . . he used to make a good fight on the fives court with the captain of the cricket club who had more reach. . . . His pluck and muscle were peerless'.[13]

In 1841 Thring left Eton as senior Colleger and Captain of School, and he was Captain of 'Montem' on the last but one occasion on which this Eton festival was celebrated.[14] What did Thring take with him to Uppingham? Certainly Chapman's influence and recollections of the horrors of Long Chamber; so too a belief that you cannot educate herds, and that a school should be designed so that all might learn; and then too, a love of games, and especially of the brand of fives peculiar to Eton. In addition, two Eton contemporaries came – John Baverstock in 1857, and William 'Daddy' Witts in 1861, and both were true 'fellow-workers'. Eton was not however the only public school to contribute to Uppingham practice, for by 1853 Thring had further insight into the established system. Three of his brothers were educated at Shrewsbury when that school was celebrated for the best scholarship in England. Benjamin Kennedy was Headmaster at this time and when in 1866 Kennedy congratulated Thring on some of his Latin grammar works, he was delighted. 'Kennedy's name is to me quite historical, . . . and as a wielder of classical languages he is unrivalled.'[15] In his years between Cambridge and Uppingham Thring served as an examiner at Eton and Rugby. Although Thring believed that Thomas Arnold was a great idealist, he was not so sure about his qualities as a schoolmaster.[16] 'What personal influence could do, he did. What wise and thoughtful application of means should have done, he did not.'[17] Thring regarded *Tom Brown's Schooldays* as the 'bitterest satire' ever written on education.[18] It showed a school resting entirely on Arnold's personality and not on any concrete system that Arnold could hand on to a successor – 'and my own experience more than supports its truth'.[19] Thring was determined not to make Arnold's mistake, for he would aim to build an Uppingham that would flourish on the lines he would set until well after his death. 'A man must build his ship, as well as be able to command her' was Thring's maxim.[20]

Thring went up to King's College, Cambridge in the autumn of 1841; he was in residence as scholar and fellow for five years. These 'very quiet, powerful years' he later treasured as one of the best periods of his life.[21] He read much and worked hard, 'now heavy with labour, now buoyant with hope, bringing great searching of heart, and much balancing of right and wrong, much anxious weighing of the value of education and life, and their true use'.[22] Under the system operating for King's Scholars at that time, Thring took his degree without examination. Proof of his scholarship comes in his winning of the University's Porson Prize for Greek Iambics as well as various College prizes. He also won the College Cooke Prize for scholarship and good behaviour, surely a forerunner of the Uppingham medal 'For good work and unblemished character'.

Thring's studies at Cambridge in the 1840s were dominated by the classics. Aeschylus was undoubtedly Thring's favourite, and the translation of the *Agamemnon* was a labour of love that stretched over many years; it was published posthumously.[23] Old Boys remembered Caesar and Tacitus as other Thring preferences, and his choice of subjects to be portrayed on the walls of the school-room indicates that Homer, Herodotus, Plato, Demosthenes, Euclid, Pindar, Cicero, Virgil, Horace and Livy were similarly in favour.[24] True to the Cambridge Platonic tradition, there is no mention of the Oxonian Aristotle; moreover, Thring could be carping on Oxford scholarship and character. 'I have a mean opinion of Oxford scholarship', he wrote in 1860; to be followed in 1863 with 'I am sick of Oxford men with their flimsy pretty ways, like weedy racehorses at best.'[25] It comes as no surprise that most Uppingham masters of the early years graduated from Cambridge.[26]

The Platonic influence was strong at Uppingham. Thring was much in agreement with Plato's ideas on education as expressed in the *Republic* and he sought to put the philosopher's ideals into practice. Thring thought that something must have radically gone wrong in the intervening centuries for the process that had turned out Plato's young Athenians to be distorted into the schooling the average English schoolboy now experienced, a contrast he would equate with 'Greek sunshine versus London fog'.[27] Thring was a warm recipient of the Platonic principle that the soul absorbs its environment and, whether of buildings or classroom decoration, the countryside or art, Thring always sought perfect surroundings. It was a principle applicable in learning too: 'Nature prescribes . . . that the first business of the young is to collect material. . . . This determines . . . the first great axiom of early teaching; open Fairyland.'[28] Whether in art and crafts, gymnastics and music, or the education of girls, the Platonic influence is ever-present. Always education was directed towards moral excellence, and the aim of true-life was service:

> True life-science . . . accepts as a self-evident fact the necessity that, in any world which is not a bungling mistake, every individual has a sufficient share always, and at all times, in the main objects of life and the true progress of the race to which he belongs.[29]

III Holy Orders: 'One of the surest ways of doing good'

The quiet years at Cambridge were not spent solely in academic study, for it was there that Thring determined to take Holy Orders: in 1846 he was ordained a deacon, then the following year he became a priest in Gloucester. Bernard Darwin regarded Thring as 'the most Christian man of his generation'.[1] Deep humility was the corner-stone of his philosophy: 'the great secret of my own life has been the doing patiently and correctly the thing in hand, and waiting till God changed it, not striving to carve out my own way, but to watch and find what way He willed.'[2]

Christianity, life and education were equivalent to Thring and it was impossible to separate one from the others. Yet, though he was so ardent a Christian, it is not possible to chain Thring to any party of Christian thought and doctrine. At Cambridge he was exposed to theological argument between various Church parties but he dismissed their 'controversial bickerings' as 'gladiatorial shows'.[3] From a review of Thring's sermons it is impossible to tell to which religious, philosophical or even political camp he belonged.[4] In 1873 Thring told of his own stand in a letter to the Rev Edward White: 'I strive in a straightforward way to do the right without parade of party, and simply as right.'[5] There was thus no pushing of a particular religious doctrine at Uppingham and, as a result, the school gained support from parents who were 'bitter dissenters' as well as from 'moderate men'.[6] As Thring told a candidate for a mastership at the school: 'My own beliefs are decided Church, but I am *broad* towards other people who are religious, but no irreligious man can be appointed by me.'[7] There was an air of tolerance at Uppingham: Thring had his own religious philosophy but he was not going to force it on others. In a letter to an Old-Boy clergyman, written in 1885, Thring advised that it was a clergyman's duty not to align himself politically.[8] The same might well be said of Thring and his religious beliefs.

Thring seems to have been as much a pragmatist in religion as he was in education. At Cambridge he could be a member of the High Church Camden Society yet at Uppingham a bust of the Low Church hero Martin Luther stood in his study and he would readily quote the first Protestant.[9] Corporate worship was to be important at Uppingham, and active participation was vital, but the services contained no ritual.[10] Thring resisted the introduction of the Athanasian Creed; the chapel was never consecrated, thus allowing the headmaster to stay aloof of ecclesiastical disputes; Thring never fasted in Lent; and, unlike Thomas Arnold, he believed in 'original righteousness' rather than in 'original sin'.[11] He was bitterly opposed to celibacy: 'I know why men turned ascetics, they were too cowardly to face the world as Christian men moving in it.'[12] 'Rather a divine life than a divine knowledge', Thring wrote in his jotting book at Cambridge, for theology held no fascination.[13] 'Theological bigotry knows no laws, human or divine' was a phrase that he used in a letter on the question of the consecration of the chapel.[14] Willingham Rawnsley, a master at the school, recalled that religion to Thring was not theology but life:

> He hated cant, he hated gush, he hated unreality, he hated morbid developments of any kind. None of the great parties in the Church could possibly have claimed him as an adherent. The phrase "religious world" to him had no meaning. By religion he understood serving God and doing good to men. Of theological shibboleths, of pious phraseology, which appeared to him to embody no divine truth, he sometimes spoke in language of profound contempt. Matters of ecclesiastical ceremony, of procedure, of posture, and the like, were to him quite unimportant. But in essentials no man was more reverent.... In a word, religion was to him not a thing to be criticised, dissected, formulated, nor to be overmuch talked about – but a thing to be practised and made the rule of life.[15]

Practise religion rather than preach it was to be Thring's rule. 'We must dare to act for ourselves', he wrote at Cambridge, 'and break through the religious etiquette which prescribes sixpences where pounds ought to be given.'[16] In the same period Thring wrote this of poverty: 'He that oppresseth the poor reproacheth his Master, but he that honoreth him hath mercy on the poor.'[17]

This became Thring's message throughout his years at Uppingham and he never equated poverty with wickedness.[18] Thring cannot be labelled other than just Christian but, nonetheless, this aspect of his Christian practice coincides with the Christian Socialist work of Frederick Maurice and Charles Kingsley.

Thring met Maurice once, in 1862, when the latter took over a Leicestershire parish for part of the summer. Thring found Maurice thoughtful-looking and not at all gladiatorial. 'He talked pleasantly, but not very much, gave me the impression of observing men rather than displaying himself, withal gentle in manner and quiet, a man seemingly who had rather teach than fight, and rather fight than give way.'[19] Thring, then, was by no means an ardent disciple of Maurice and, when the FDM Club was founded in 1882, the original members did include Harvey Goodwin and Alexander Macmillan but Thring was not among them.[20]

Thring did however have indirect contact with Charles Kingsley. He had corresponded with Mrs Kingsley since 1870 and letters talk of Charles Kingsley's 'strong feeling for Uppingham and the work here'.[21] She sent Thring an autographed copy of Kingsley's *Brave Words to Brave Soldiers*: Thring prized it and in reply wrote: 'It cheers me much to find myself, as life goes on, associated, however far off, with those who have worked for righteousness and striven for the good cause, as he did, a real pioneer.'[22] Mrs Kingsley was now living in Leamington Spa where, with her daughter Rose, she became closely associated with the High School – today the Kingsley School. In 1886 Thring was invited to the school's Speech Day where he presented the prizes and gave an address.[23]

A point on which Thring and the Christian Socialists would not have seen eye to eye was the question of evolution. Maurice and Kingsley readily accepted the scientific evidence but Thring was not so sure. 'Nursery babble', Thring would label it, and its protagonist Herbert Spencer was dismissed as 'a most consummate donkey'.[24] Thring's *Life-Science* was directed against the moral pretensions of science, whilst a letter of about 1880 states Thring's position: 'Science is making great and real discoveries, but many of its theories are in direct contradiction to the facts of the human world and sound reason.'[25] Once again, Thring stands aloof as far as religion is concerned.

Thring followed his own advice that clergymen should not publicly be involved in politics. Oswald Powell, an Old Boy, remembered Thring in 1886 prohibiting 'until further notice any political subjects being discussed' in the school.[26] He applied the same veto to himself: 'I have long determined not to go out of my own line in public, and not to be tempted to platform work or writing for the press.'[27] William Gladstone, the Liberal prime minister, might be thought a 'wicked man', and a Radical could be defined as either a 'clever fool' or an 'ignorant fool', but always a 'fool', but Thring kept these thoughts to his diary.[28] He once told Thomas Powell, another Old Boy: 'I am a Radical Conservative – that is, I want quietly to change everything that is, but to change them slowly and on the old principles, reforming everything.'[29] He was fearful of socialism and he distrusted government intervention, but he was never indifferent to the plight of the poor. His great law was 'Help – never give' for he agreed with Octavia Hill's observation that 'it was far easier to supply the poor with proper dwellings than to teach them to dwell in them properly'.[30] Help the poor to help themselves was Thring's advice, for if they are given everything they will not learn to be self-sufficient.

In 1846 Thring agitated for reform of examinations at Cambridge, a campaign that took him into print with *A Few Remarks on the Present System of Degrees at King's College Cambridge*.[31] This was published by Macmillans and led to a long chain of friendship with the family. In 1868 Alexander Macmillan recalled:

> It was nearly a quarter of century since I first knew you, and since my dear brother and I used to speculate on the line in which you were to become eminent, for you were among the first of Cambridge men whom his clear eye determined as fitted to do world work in one line or another.[32]

Daniel and Alexander Macmillan's publishing house in Trinity Street became the meeting place for many undergraduates and fellows. It was Daniel who in 1842 first drew Maurice's attention to the plight of the poor and asked him to prepare some religious tracts for them. Later the Macmillans were to introduce many undergraduates to the Christian Socialist Movement. Thring was a regular visitor to Trinity Street and in later life he remembered fondly 'those early days, so vivid in my memory', and he would speak of his good fortune in being 'thrown in' with the Macmillans at that time.[33] Daniel Macmillan saw his publishing business as a means of spreading God's word to the lower classes and it was a cause that found a sympathetic admirer in Thring.

Daniel Macmillan was delighted when Thring informed him that he was taking the Uppingham appointment:

> It seems to me one of the surest ways of doing good. While a man is giving life and strength to his country in that way he does not proclaim himself either patriot or prophet, but merely seems to be working for wife and family. It has the great advantage of making no fuss.[34]

It was through Daniel Macmillan that Thring saw the quiet certainty of letting God plan his path. When he died in 1857, Thring continued the friendship with his brother, Alexander.[35] Macmillans published most of Thring's works, beginning with *The Elements of Grammar Taught in English* (1851) and *The Child's Grammar* (1852), both published before Thring went to Uppingham. The Thring and Macmillan families became very close: the Macmillans visited Uppingham on at least two occasions, in 1861 and 1864; the Thrings returned the visits to Cambridge in 1862; and they were invited to the new London home in 1867.[36] Thring would write enthusiastically about developments at

Uppingham and on the early years of the Headmasters' Conference, and he found a matron's job in the school for a friend of the Macmillan family.[37] The Macmillans recommended Uppingham to their friends and several sets of boys came; then in 1861 Alexander asked if Thring could take his sons and the sons of Daniel.[38] They came: Daniel's eldest son Frederick entered Uppingham the following April and his younger brother Maurice, the father of Harold Macmillan, the future prime minister, followed in 1866. Thring found great sympathy in his friendship with the Macmillans; they were all 'fellow sufferers' trying hard to improve the lot of the world.

The Macmillan friendship was not the only one to last well beyond the Cambridge days for in these years Thring cemented his relationship with William Witts and through him met Harvey Goodwin. Witts left Eton ahead of Thring and was a fellow of King's College before Thring took his degree. In his early years at Uppingham Thring twice asked Witts to join the staff, but without success, and then in 1861, quite out of the blue, Witts asked if he might still come. Thring was delighted and said yes at once.

> How wonderfully things are brought about. (Thring wrote in his diary.) Of all living men I had rather have him as a colleague, and now he asks me when I thought it was all over, and if he comes will build a house and set himself up. I am exceedingly cheered and strengthened by this . . . I know no more conscientious, hardworking, nice-minded fellow than Witts is, full of information and with a great connection.[39]

The saintly Witts did more than just build a house and wholeheartedly join in the Uppingham experiment for, more concretely, he donated £1000 to start the chapel fund. Four years later, and years before Thring's wildest dreams, the school had its own place of worship. The inaugural sermon was preached by Harvey Goodwin, then Dean of Ely, soon Bishop of Carlisle, and a regular visitor to the school.

Witts and Goodwin were close friends at Cambridge and Thring met Goodwin through Witts.[40] During his Cambridge years Goodwin was Vicar of St Giles where Witts served as his curate for seven years.[41] Goodwin was an ardent Mauricean and a keen Romantic: as a boy he had been brought up an Evangelical but Maurice's *The Kingdom of Christ* and Coleridge's *Aids to Reflection* modified his viewpoint.[42] In 1847 Goodwin and Witts founded an institution in Cambridge for 'youthful offenders', their aim being to reform these boys rather than to punish them.[43] Later, in 1853, this grew into a Cambridge branch of the Working Men's College and was run on the lines of the London original. Alexander Macmillan and some Trinity College men initiated this expansion and they invited Goodwin to be the college's first principal.[44] When Witts moved to Uppingham, Goodwin entered his two boys for the school and, from that time until Thring's death in 1887, no Uppingham festival was complete without a sermon or a speech from him. His 'spirit of manly, practical

Christianity for everyday life' was much in sympathy with the headmaster's: 'Go and do' would be his message to the Uppingham boys.[45] Goodwin's sermon at the 1882 Founder's Day was particularly Thringian in context:

> it is quite certain that a boy's character is formed quite as much out of school as in it, that is the free and honourable intercourse with his peers quite as much as the direct teaching which he receives from his masters, that makes the boy what he ultimately becomes. Nay, even in the case of the master himself, it is not mere scholarship or technical skill that will make a man successful in his profession, unless also he possesses and cultivates other qualities which boys respect, and which give a tone to the school, and affect in a hundred indefinable ways a boy's conduct and heart.[46]

IV Gloucester: 'If these fellows don't learn, it's my fault'

When in 1869 Lewis Nettleship was nearing graduation at Oxford, he wrote to Thring to ask what he ought to do on coming down. Thring's advice to his former captain of school was immediate: he should work with a mission to the poor, for it would be the best corrective to the impractical tendencies learnt at university:

> There is an absolute necessity, if you are to carry out your great work worthily, that you should lay your foundations deep in the great realities of life, and that can only be by learning the sufferings and glories of the poor. This is the antidote, too, for the feeling of "vanity of vanities, all is vanity" which you speak of. . . . Curiously enough, and it may be a help to you, the school is just founding an East End Mission.[1]

Here Thring commends to Nettleship his own experience after Cambridge for he was to be ever-thankful for his years in the slums of Gloucester.

Shortly after he had been ordained a deacon, Thring decided early in 1847 to accept the curacy at St James's Church in Gloucester. It was a new parish of mean houses where most of the inhabitants were dockers or labourers on the nearby railway. It was a depressing area, an unhealthy one, and the infant mortality rate was high.[2] Thomas Hedley was appointed vicar on the formation of the parish in 1842. Like many graduates of Cambridge's Trinity College, he was a firm believer in such a mission to the poor yet, sadly, it eventually claimed his life at the early age of forty-two.[3] Thring was ever grateful to Hedley's influence and he related to his own biographer, George Parkin, how it was through Hedley's example that he experienced the intense religious conviction that he should consecrate all of his powers to God's service.[4] Thring later told Hedley's daughter that her father 'was the most single-minded Christian I ever met, and wise and intellectual withal. He stamped himself deep on me; much of my life here is indebted to him, how much I cannot tell.'[5] On Hedley's death, two of his sons came to Uppingham as some of Thring's first pupils.

Hedley built a school alongside the church, and it was there that Thring gained his first insight into teaching. It was a rude shock:

> Never shall I forget those schools in the suburbs of Gloucester, and their little class-room with its solemn problem, no more difficult one in the world; how on earth the Cambridge Honour man, with his success and his brain-world, was to get at the minds of those little labourers' sons, with their unfurnished heads, and no time to give.[6]

It was this experience that laid the foundation of his methods at Uppingham, and these children gave Thring some of his powerful axioms:

> They gave me the great axiom, "The worse the material, the greater the skill of the worker".
>
> They called out the useful dictum with which I ever stepped silently over the threshold – "If these fellows don't learn, it's my fault".
>
> They disentangled all the loose threads of knowledge in my brain, and forced me to wind each separately in its place, with its beginning and its end.
>
> They bred in me a supreme contempt for knowledge-lumps, or emptying out knowledge-lumps in a heap, like stones at a roadside, and calling it teaching.
>
> They made me hate the long array of fine words, which lesson-hearers ask, and pupils answer, and neither really knows the meaning of.
>
> They taught me how different knowing is from being able to make others know.
>
> Nay, they taught me the more valuable lesson still, how different knowledge which can be produced to an Examiner is from knowledge which knows itself, and understands its own life and growth.[7]

It was glorious work at Gloucester, but it took its toll on Thring's health, and in the spring of 1848 he was forced to leave. For the next two years he convalesced at Great Marlow: during this period he read with private pupils and served as an Examiner for Eton, Rugby and Cambridge. In 1851 he took a curacy at nearby Cookham Dean, where he again taught in National Schools, and in this same period he prepared his first two texts for the Macmillan brothers.

In the years before Uppingham Thring made several long journeys across Europe; one year he travelled through France, and in another he followed the course of the Rhine from Switzerland to the sea.[8] Cities in central and eastern Germany were visited in the company of his brother Henry and a friend.[9] In the autumn of 1852 Thring embarked on the planned climax of his European travels, the traditional English gentleman's Grand Tour through Belgium, Germany, Bohemia, Austria and Italy, and then onwards through Greece and Turkey to reach the Holy Land. His diary for this tour is largely a record of the sites and galleries he visited: there is no reference to visits to schools and universities, nor is there any contact with continental educationalists. There is nothing to suggest that the German influences later to be found in Thring's educational thought and practice were formulated in these visits abroad. He was simply another tourist.[10]

Nonetheless, the German influences are there. In Italy that November fate played its hand when Thring hurried to Rome at his parents' bidding. His brother Godfrey was set to make a fool of himself by proposing marriage to the daughter of a Prussian customs official, a match that they clearly thought unsuitable. Thring, ever the opportunist, solved the problem in the surest way by proposing to Fräulein Koch himself. To his delight, Marie accepted his offer.[11] Thring immediately cancelled his plans to visit the Holy Land and returned to England. He needed a job.

Marie brought the German influences to Uppingham as part of her dowry and they were then adopted by her husband. Her role at the school was a vital one for Thring was certain of the innate 'purity and goodness' that a woman would bring to any venture.[12] The marriage was to be most happy – 'I can only say I found my marriage the most perfect earthly blessing', Thring wrote to a friend, 'beyond my lover's hopes even, and worth all.'[13] Marie, with her sister Anna who came to live in Uppingham and served as Thring's secretary until his death, not only supported her husband but also contributed her own part: no school function was complete without her presence.[14] Her drawing room concerts were the foundation of music at Uppingham. She substituted German-style student caps for the boys' mortarboards; she encouraged the teaching of German in addition to French, and the appointment of Germans to teach it; and it is probable that she had some say in the inclusion of science teaching, once again taught by Germans.[15] She opened the gymnasium, the first at an English school, on her birthday in 1859 and she was always present at the anniversary gymnastic competitions.[16] It seems probable that she, rather than her husband, first recognised the role that a gymnasium and a gymnastics master could play at Uppingham for the gymnastic system so commonly adopted in German schools was almost unknown in England. Marie's influence on the life of the school was always strong: the second and subsequent editions of Thring's *Theory and Practice of Teaching* were dedicated 'To my wife, and partner in school life; to whose courage and help I owe so much of life, and of work done.'[17]

The German links were steadily strengthened in the first years of their marriage. The Thrings occasionally holidayed in Germany, and German and Swiss governesses were brought over for their daughters.[18] German-speaking masters first arrived in 1855: a total of 18 were appointed in Thring's headmastership.[19] Most were musicians but others taught science, art, gymnastics and modern languages. Some of the early men remained in England only a few years but later ones, including Georg Beisiegel and Paul David, became influential colleagues and were still at the school long after Thring's death.[20] Thring read deeply in German literature and he translated many German hymns, songs and poems into English. Then too, there was the bust of Luther in his study.

V Uppingham: 'The great educational experiment'

Thring's own education in manliness was now complete. In 1853 he applied for the headmastership of Durham School and was granted an interview. The Durham governors chose Henry Holden, then headmaster of Uppingham Grammar School. Thring in turn applied for the Uppingham vacancy, secured it, and was appointed on 1 September. From that day until his death in 1887, Thring's life and Uppingham's rebirth are one story. After his first look at the school he told a friend: 'I think I have found my life-work today.'[1] That life-work was to put the ideal of manliness into practice.

Thring may not have had a blueprint when he took up his headmastership but he did have an idea for a school. Early in 1854 he began his reforms and then, at the end of 1858, he paused to take stock. These expanded notes on his 'great educational experiment' were logged in the front of his diary on 20 December. They were later re-organised in a *Statement* to the trustees, for Thring wished to expand the school further but could not do so without their consent and financial backing – the first was only grudgingly given and the second never came. The introduction to the *Statement* sets the scene:

> The first necessities of schools are too often glaringly violated by those in best repute, and the public having had no true standard to refer to, have learnt to look upon these blemishes as necessary conditions of great schools, whereas they are no more necessary than perpetual typhus fever is necessary.
>
> There is a large percentage of temptation, criminality, and idleness in the great schools – a moral miasma – generated by known causes, and as certainly to be got rid of even by more mechanical improvements – a little moral drainage – as the average sickness of a squalid district. This is the task which the School at Uppingham has set itself to carry out.
>
> The excellence of a School, over a series of years, depends, first, on its machinery for education; by which is meant appliances, whether material or otherwise, for conducting the work: the ship, and officers, and crew taken numerically. And, secondly, on the manner in which this machinery is worked: the discipline, knowledge and navigation of the vessel.[2]

Thring's first step was to appoint a good staff. He inherited Earle and two assistants; Earle took some years before he accepted the innovations, but when he did it was done wholeheartedly. Thring turned to Cambridge in his search for new blood, and he was determined to find a permanent team. The men appointed had to be prepared to sink their own funds into the venture as the trust only paid for existing staff. They would receive their income from the boarding houses that Thring would ask them to build. That Thring actually attracted such men gives some measure of his personal magnetism, for at this stage there was no guarantee of success.

Thring needed a team of masters with different strengths: 'to teach an upper class requires more knowledge, a lower more skill as a teacher.'[3] Boarding was arranged on a house basis but teaching was done in forms: a housemaster superintended his own house but taught a form of boys from all houses. To ensure that each boy obtained individual attention, Thring limited the size of each class to 30. The masters were further expected to be with the boys in their out-of-school activities; the reminiscences of two, Sam Haslam and Willingham Rawnsley, record much playing of football, cricket and fives with the boys.[4] A parent of one boy gave warm praise for this practice:

> The masters at Uppingham, generally speaking, take part with the boys in their games; thus indicating much good sense as well as kindly feeling. Many are the important results of such a coming together out of school, as admirably adapted to develop character and increase knowledge, as to invigorate health.[5]

Some of the early appointments were dreadful mistakes but gradually Thring built up his team.[6] By the early 1860s it was complete and once a week the housemasters met in Thring's study to discuss school questions. Although he allowed his colleagues to air their opinions, Thring would often claim 'absolute powers'.[7] He demanded unswerving devotion from his staff and for the most part he got it. One repeated bone of contention with the housemasters, however, rested on the size of houses. A housemaster's income depended on the number of boys in his house so Thring was often pressed to allow them to take more. He never consented and, in addition to his class-size decree, he applied two other vetoes with regard to numbers: a house should have no more than 30 boarders and the school should be limited to 300.[8] Thring's reasoning on the second point was that 'A headmaster is only headmaster of boys he knows. If he does not know the boys the master who does is their headmaster and his also.'[9] In addition to the housemasters, Thring appointed masters for the 'extra' subjects; music, gymnastics, modern languages and the like. These men, who were almost all German in the early years, were equally 'superior men' to the housemasters but they did not contribute vast sums to the venture. Their incomes came from the 'extra' fees.

Once Thring had started to appoint masters, the next step was to see that the material appliances of the school were adequate. In 1853 the school comprised the headmaster's house, a school-room, some studies and a few ball courts. By 1884, the tercentenary of the school's foundation, the staff claimed to have invested £91,000 in the school and Thring had accumulated hefty overdrafts and mortgages.[10] First priority was given to boarding houses: between 1856 and 1862 four new houses were built and others were converted from existing buildings. Three further houses were added between 1866 and 1872. Many schools had boarding houses before Uppingham but in general these were no more than hostels only marginally part of the educational system; at Uppingham they were central. As Canon Robinson noted to Thring's delight during the later Schools Inquiry Commission, 'at Rugby the school made the houses, and at Uppingham the houses made the school.'[11] Thring favoured free-standing boarding houses over dormitories grouped around quadrangles; the latter might look more impressive but they offered boys no difference between life in lessons and life out of school.[12] Each Uppingham house was 'a little commonwealth' ruled by its housemaster as *paterfamilias*, housing his family and up to 30 boys. Almost all housemasters were in Holy Orders and most were Cambridge men.[13] They created a happy school community: taking walks together, hosting parties for their children, visiting each other's homes, organising concerts and so on.[14] The influence of the housemaster, his wife and their children was vital for this added 'home feeling'.[15] Hardwicke Rawnsley certainly appreciated it:

> I had always felt strongly that we enjoyed a great advantage at Uppingham under Thring, where the home life of the masters was made to touch the whole school. The daughters of the masters moved like sisters among us, and one was never without a kind of sense that the atmosphere of home had followed one to school . . . the presence of purity as one finds it in a good home affected the whole school.[16]

An examination of the town's census returns for 1861, 1871 and 1881 shows that only one of the twenty-two housemasters was a bachelor, and he had married before the following census.[17] The homely feel would have been especially strong when newly-wed housemasters and their wives were bringing up large families of young children: in 1861, for example, there was an average of three under-sevens in each house.[18] This domesticity of boarding-school life was unusual, perhaps unique, and at odds with the arrangements in the schools described by John Tosh in his study, *A Man's Place*.[19] Sophia Haslam, the newly-married wife of the housemaster of The Lodge, kept a diary for the period 1870–73. Boys are named throughout as she records conversations, details of illnesses, triumphs in sports, and much more.[20] Thring was an avid letter-writer and much of his correspondence was with the parents of his boys in School House; no doubt he insisted that each housemaster maintained similar contact *in loco parentis*.[21]

Each boy had a partitioned sleeping cubicle within a dormitory, and his own study. Both were to be Uppingham hall-marks. Thring believed that 'a large dormitory introduces far too great opportunity for undetected evil' and that 'the single room cannot be so healthy'.[22] These 'tishes' gave the boys privacy at night for, as Thring wrote mockingly of Frederic Farrar's *Eric*, 'do not suppose, whatever words may assert, that little Christian confessors say their prayers, and kneel, and at last win respect of their more hardened companions in doing so.'[23] Thring on arrival found some small studies adjacent to his own house; he greatly expanded the system so that each boy should have his 'castle'. E. W. Hornung recalled these studies in the Uppingham novel, *Fathers of Men*:

> They were undeniably cosy and attractive, as compact as a captain's cabin, as private as a friar's cell, but far more comfortable than either . . . with a table and two chairs, a square of carpet as big as a bath sheet, a bookshelf and pictures, and photographs and ornaments to taste, fretwork and plush to heart's content, a flower box for the summer term, hot water pipes for the other two, and above all a door of (one's) own to shut at will against the world.[24]

The housemasters taught in their own house halls whilst the non-housemasters worked in cottages about the town, so at first there was no pressure to build proper teaching accommodation. The numbers in the school, however, quickly swelled: there were just twenty-five boarders on Thring's arrival; thereafter the total doubled every two years through the 1850s. A whole day's holiday celebrated the 200 mark in May 1863; then, two years later in September 1865, Thring's self-imposed limit of 300 was reached. The school was full and the need for more room was now pressing. The purpose of Thring's *Statement* was to urge the trust to provide more facilities but in the end it was left to Thring and the masters to dig deeper into their own pockets. G. E. Street was appointed in 1861 as architect for a new school-room, and two years later it was opened.[25] Then, thanks to Witts's generosity, came Street's chapel: this began life with Goodwin's sermon at the inaugural service in the summer of 1865. Now, with the chapel directly built onto the school-room, both in the Gothic Revival style, Thring rejoiced in the concrete reality of godliness and good learning: 'twin fortress homes, the one of holy worship, the other of work made holy'.[26] Other facilities also came in these early years: a gymnasium in 1859, a carpentry shop in 1863, and a cricket pavilion in 1864. Thring was working towards his target that every school ought to provide 'a School Library, Museum, Workshop, Gymnasiums, Swimming Baths, Fives Courts, or any other pursuits that conduce to a healthy life'.[27]

'Machinery, machinery, machinery should be the motto of every good school.' By machinery Thring meant all those factors that would promote excellence so that the system did not solely rest on the personality of the headmaster or the talented teacher: the educational equipment; the buildings, also referred to as 'The Almighty Wall'; the ratio of staff to boys; and the arrangements in the houses.

> As little as possible should be left to the personal merit in the teacher or chance; as much as possible ought to rest on the system and appliances, on every side checking vice and fostering good, quietly and unostentatiously, under the commonest guidance.[28]

Once the machinery had been constructed, the next point was to put it to work, and at Uppingham, as at any school, academic study was the core of the system.

Thring's curriculum was firmly based on the traditional Latin and Greek, but mathematics and English as well were compulsory. Music, modern languages, gymnastics, art, carpentry and natural sciences were brought in to 'restore balance'.[29] Scholarship was important and in 1860 Thring secured agreement from his housemasters for each to take one boy free so that there could be a 'stream of intellect' in the school.[30] It was however the business of the school to teach and train every boy, and not just to offer knowledge to the clever and the hard-working: 'everyone has to be dealt with; racing stables and a crack winner or two will not do.'[31] Thring's insistence that the school should take boys of all abilities led to the reputation that Uppingham was best suited to the average boy or the dullard rather than to the scholar.[32] This slight against the school's academic standing was undeserved, as Tony Mangan found when he examined the entrants for Jesus College, Cambridge for the period 1849–85: here the number of Uppinghamians ranked third behind boys from Eton and Harrow, both much larger schools with greater metropolitan and aristocratic intakes.[33]

Thring was convinced that the best education of the mind came through a classical and literary training, and so these subjects were given greatest emphasis in the curriculum. These, he believed, made the mind 'strong and ready' and did not confine it to 'narrower ranges'.

> Let the mind be exercised in one noble subject – a subject, if such can be found, capable of calling into play reasoning powers, fancy, imagination, strength, activity and endurance, and be sure that in the intervals of work, there will be plenty of time for less exhaustive pursuits.[34]

There was such a subject: the classics. In his *Education and School*, first published in 1864, Thring stated the case for the central role of classics in the Uppingham curriculum:

> They are the perfection of mere humanity, as distinct from the living power breathed in all modern life, literature, and artist-work by Christianity.
>
> They are the means by which the history of the early world, its facts, its wars, its treaties, its social life, became known to us.
>
> They are the perfection of art, the perfection of the shaping of the human mind . . . the classics are the perfection of languages in mere word-power and form.
>
> They are the fittest training to show how thought should be expressed, calling into play every power of the human mind.
>
> They are as languages the foundation of our own.[35]

R. M. Ogilvie has shown how Arnold had slanted the classics towards the study of Plato and Thucydides, and indeed these were the foremost authors studied at Thring's Uppingham.[36] In his Greek lessons, the headmaster would link moral issues in Plato with passages in the Bible. Other authors listed in the schedule of work compiled for the Schools Inquiry Commissioners included Herodotus, Aeschylus (Thring's favourite), Sophocles, Homer and Cicero.[37] Thring was critical of current methods of classical teaching and he complained to Alexander Macmillan on the dearth of good classics teaching aids. In 1855 he wrote a little 'construing book' for the publisher; then in 1863 he produced a sequel in an attempt to make the study of classics more relevant to modern needs.[38] The second book was the one praised by Benjamin Kennedy.[39]

Spenser's *Fairie Queene*, Shakespeare's *Macbeth* and *Hamlet*, Scott's novels, Chaucer, Milton and Johnson were all studied in English lessons, with Keble's *The Christian Year* reserved for the younger boys.[40] History texts were chosen for their moral worth: 'The Great Romans, The Great Dutchmen, the type of Englishman that built our Indian Empire, appealed to Thring.'[41] Books included Mommsen's *Rome*, Motley's *Netherlands* and Kaye's *Indian Officers*. The teaching of English grammar was fundamental, especially for the younger boys. 'You might just as well feed and clothe an Indian like an Esquimaux as generalise rules for English, from the Latin or Greek languages.'[42] Thring had already produced two books on English grammar in the years before Uppingham; further texts were added in the 1860s.[43] All were used at the school. French and German had a place in the curriculum, though as 'extra' subjects. Thring believed that French was merely suitable for 'conversational purpose', so more emphasis was placed on German with its 'complete structure' that made it more valuable as an intellectual training.[44]

VI A physical education: 'The racer's spirit'

When Thring came to Uppingham the boys had the use of two ball courts, an indoor play area and a cricket field for their recreation. Cricket was the most popular game and there had been a 'properly constituted Eleven' since the 1830s. William Earle joined the staff in 1850 and quickly took an interest in the game. Hockey was a popular winter recreation, even transferring to the ice in severe years, whilst bat-fives were played in the ball courts. On the long half-holidays the boys were accustomed to roam freely, to sledge and skate in winter, and in summer to trek to Stockerston brook or to the Welland for a swim.[1]

Thring maintained the liberty of the relaxed school bounds and the freedom to roam. Before the introduction of the athletic sports in 1859, cross-country runs involving much jumping of hedges, fences and streams, were common, as were 10–15 mile paper-chases, with the whole school and some masters taking part. Competitions at jumping the toll-bars on the roads leading into the town proved great entertainment.[2] Thring's boys inherited the two bathing places. The brook at Stockerston, two miles to the south-west of the town, was nearer, but the pits in the stream were continually silting up until the occasionally levied subscriptions once again put them in 'tolerable order'. In general it was reckoned better to make the longer walk to the Welland.[3]

The cricket match on the first day of Thring's appointment heralded a new interest in games. Both Thring and Earle regularly played cricket with the boys: Thring remained dressed in his clerical costume, having handed his black wide-awake hat to the umpire. His batting might have been somewhat rustic in style but his under-arm bowling would often surprise the unsuspecting batsman.[4] Fives was Thring's real love at Eton and Cambridge, and a court to the Eton specifications was soon constructed within the indoor play area.[5] He introduced football that first winter, a curious mixture of the Eton Field Game and the early Rugby code, and it soon came to be called 'Uppingham Football'. The jollity and the amateurism of these early years are well recorded in Thring's games songs – two for cricket and one each for fives and football.[6] The 'Football Song' suggests that the game was more an epic free fight than a contrast of skills: the whole school used to play together and Thring and some of his masters joined in.[7] In 1862, when he had given up playing regularly, he was asked to play in a match between the sixth-form and the rest of the school. That evening he wrote in his diary: 'I could not help thinking with some pride what Headmaster of a great school ever played a match at football before. Would either dignity or shins suffer it?' He played again the following week.[8]

In 1857 the first boys' Committee of Games was formed, probably on Thring's initiative. He wrote out many of the rules and instructed the committee to the effect that all boys who played cricket should help with the spring rolling of the pitch.[9] During these early years the committee was an extension of Thring's own authority, with trusted praepostors applying his policies. As the numbers in the school increased, a long search began for additional playing-fields, a search logged in Thring's diary for 1859 to 1861.[10] The school was divided into two clubs for games; the various XIs and XVs were distinguished by coloured caps and ribbons. Cricket matches were maintained with local sides and the boys tried to arrange a match with Rugby School, but nothing materialised. 'All in good time', Thring noted.[11] Within the school various pick-up games were played – Tall v Short, Cambridge v the World – but if a boy did not wish to play he could just as easily go off for a swim.[12] Problems with the owners of the land adjacent to the Stockerston brook had forced the school to look elsewhere for a bathing place. Eventually a tar-pit near the cricket field was acquired and adapted into a suitable pool.[13] New Eton fives courts were steadily being built and a school pairs competition was instituted in 1864. Thring regularly played the game and, with Witts as his partner, would challenge the competition champions; invariably headmaster and chaplain would win.[14]

The athletic sports were introduced in 1859.[15] The heats and finals of the various events were spread out over two or three weeks in March and seem designed to fill the gap between the end of the football in January and the start of the cricket season. In February the boys were encouraged to train for the sports; nothing however was allowed 'beyond normal exercise and abstinence from pudding'. Thring, of course, joined in the competitions, one year recording 4' 5" in the high jump and 16' 1" in the long jump. His diary notes the boys' pleasure in the sports and his delight in his own performances; the following year he wrote that through the sports 'one feels one with the boys'.[16] In the first years the steeplechases were the blue-riband events: the early ones were long and arduous, but an accident to a boy in 1860 persuaded Thring to make them shorter and less difficult. The races tested a boy's manliness and brought out what Thring termed the 'racer's spirit'.[17]

In September 1859 two of Thring's masters, the Swiss-born Dr Gerold Benguerel and the Old Etonian George Mathias proposed that a gymnasium be built.[18] Thring readily agreed. The construction of 'a plain cheap building' began immediately and was opened on 24 November that year by Marie Thring on her birthday. The boys 'crowded in to great glee'.[19] The following January Thring appointed twenty-two-year-old Georg Beisiegel as gymnastics and music master, and he was to serve Uppingham loyally until his retirement in 1902. It is probable that he had trained at the Royal Central School of Gymnastics in Berlin.[20] It was the innovation of the gymnastics classes as part of the curriculum that warranted Beisiegel's appointment, for they were on the same footing as the other 'extra' subjects. In 1865 about a quarter of the school were receiving gymnastic tuition, whilst other boys could use the gymnasium in their free time. In the German gymnastics tradition, exercises using fixed and portable apparatus – Indian clubs, vaulting horses, parallel bars, rings and the like – were tailor-made to improve each boy's strength and agility.[21] The climax of the year for the gymnastic pupils was the gymnastic competition, always held on the anniversary of the opening of the gymnasium. Each class was examined in turn, with the results published alongside those for the academic subjects in the Christmas examination lists. It was part of Marie's birthday routine to present the gymnastics prizes, the nature of which puzzled generations of Uppinghamians: first prize was a goose, second a large pork pie and third a pot of jam. Willingham Rawnsley recalled that they were chosen 'according to a fancy of the Head-Master's that prizes for Gymnastics should be things that perished in the using'.[22] Beisiegel's pioneer work was quickly recognised beyond the school; he became acquainted with leading authorities, including Archibald Maclaren at the Oxford Gymnasium; and in time he became vice-president of the National Physical Recreation Society and president of the National Society of Physical Education.[23]

W. S. Patterson, the author of *Sixty Years of Uppingham Cricket*, reckoned that a new chapter of Uppingham cricket began in 1863; but the changes affected much more than the game. The *Uppingham School Magazine* made its first appearance in April. House matches and athletics championships for the various sports and games were adopted, and silver trophies were presented to the winners. House matches lead naturally to school matches and 1863 witnessed Uppingham's first 'public-school match'. The cricketers gained a new pavilion and soon clamoured for a cricket professional to coach them, while the footballers tried to steer their game towards one of the newly-accepted national codes. These changes coincided with a gradual loosening of the reins by Thring and the emergence of greater participation by the boys in the government of the school. Up to 1863 all changes in the school can be directly linked to Thring; after this date certain powers connected with the day-to-day life of the boys were entrusted to the praepostors, although Thring always kept, and often used, a headmasterly veto. It is no chance coincidence that this period saw the last use of the title 'Uppingham Grammar-School' and an increased use of the term 'a public school'.[24]

From 1863 the boys took a greater part in the organisation of sport. The power of the Committee of Games increased; compulsion in games operated once a week and fines were imposed for non-attendance. The individual athletics Champion Cup was introduced in 1864 with athletics, gymnastics, fives, swimming and cricket averages all contributing marks on a weighted scale. House challenge cups in football and cricket appeared the same year, and both contributed with the individual sports to a house Athletics Championship. House matches in fives came in 1869. In this period the boys examined all their games to see if they were of public-school standing. The praepostors felt that hop-scotch, peg-top and marbles were unsuitable activities so the younger boys were deterred from playing them. Gymnastics too was attacked, especially for its preferential position in the weighted scale of marks for the Champion Cup, but its position was secure.[25]

Editorials in the new school magazine explained the value of athletics to the school. These statements probably duplicated the text of Thring's own speeches at the annual sports prize-giving ceremony. 'Now the object of all our games', the 1866 editor reported,

> but of the sports in particular, is to produce the manly spirit of competition, and the love of training the body, for training's sake; whilst the prizes won by the successful competitors are but a secondary, and, as it were, incidental result. For not only are "all who do their best equally honoured", but the unsuccessful do in effect win a prize equally with their victors, since we cannot doubt that the lessons learned on the racing ground will have their practical application in any field of active life.[26]

Football and cricket were by far the most popular games. Thring's younger brother, Charles, joined the staff in 1859 and from his experiences of football at Shrewsbury and Cambridge he gradually steered the rules of the Uppingham game towards those of the 'Cambridge Rules', soon to be embodied in the code of the Football Association on its foundation in 1863.[27] House matches brought 'more spirit' to the play and an Old Boys' match was introduced in 1865. Because of the various school codes in existence at this time, a public-school match at football was impossible but in cricket there was no such problem. Thring would seem to have initiated the 1863 match with distant Rossall School, a match that needed a four-day excursion by coach and train. The result of the Uppingham victory was telegraphed back to an excited school and great enthusiasm greeted the victors on their return. It was however to be the only Rossall match; in 1865 geographically nearer Repton School issued a challenge to Uppingham and this match became a regular fixture.[28] The cricket success gave rise to another cry for a professional coach. Thring eventually consented to such an appointment for two or three weeks at the beginning of the season on alternate years.[29]

Physical education thus had an important part to play in the Uppingham curriculum, and it was there by Thring's design.[30] One aim was the maintenance of good health; and a second was, in the Ruskinian sense, to make 'the body . . . as beautiful and perfect in its youth as it can be, wholly irrespective of the ulterior motive'. To Thring:

> the one pre-eminent mark of the highbred man is the simple play of the limbs that move with perfect ease, and, as they move, throw off a sense of liberty, and grace, and unconstrained command of strength, able at any moment to do anything that courage may demand of activity, or duty impose on endurance.[31]

This, then, was the role of gymnastics. Here the whole body could be developed and exercised 'irrespective of ulterior motive', and the repertoire of skills learned in the gymnasium would ensure that the gymnast was 'the master of strength, and trained movement'. Gymnastics was 'the only representative we have of pure exercise of the natural body, combining strength and skill, and stands quite apart in its character from either the races or the games'.

Athletics was essentially competitive, but always voluntary. The purpose of the sports was to push the individual boy to the limits of speed, endurance and strength. Numerous heats were arranged in the various events to provide measured competition for as many boys as possible, but to realise Thring's aim the sports had to be voluntary. The object was to inculcate that 'racer's spirit':

> the world is so constituted that there is competition everywhere, and everywhere the weaker goes to the wall; all are certain at some time to be defeated, and if our Athletics teach us here at school to bear to be beaten with good grace and to look upon victory as by no means assuring us against future defeat, they will have been of real use to us in after life.[32]

Athletics thus gave boys experience of victory without pride and defeat without depression; indeed they were instituted to form 'that manliness of character'.

The country pursuits of running with hounds, rambling, swimming, skating, sledging and so on are the timeless pursuits of the English countryside, and it was in this recreational light that they were encouraged by Thring. The country-born headmaster inevitably joined in. These activities were delightful, spontaneous and uninhibited; they allowed time for conversation and they led to a communion with nature. What is of particular significance is that Thring continued to encourage them even when games, at Uppingham and elsewhere, began to play a more time-consuming role in the boys' lives.

'Games are wondrous vital powers,' wrote Thring, 'and a true school will deal with them as of the highest educational value.'[33] Games fulfilled a threefold role. First they presented a situation in which boys and their masters could mix:

> We mix much with the boys in games . . . many a boy whom we must put at a low level in school redeems his self-respect by the praise bestowed on him as a games player, and the balance of manliness and intellect is more impartially kept.[34]

When the Schools Inquiry Commissioners interviewed Thring, they were surprised that he counted games as educational, and they were amazed that he and his colleagues joined the boys at their play.[35]

Second, games also provided a healthy competitive environment: there was no choice between 'manly games, or learning'; the choice was both. One could

> escape (from the classroom) to a thorough good game, and restore the balance of human nature by a hearty game on both sides (boys and masters), of both understanding a good drive or cut, of both admiring a stinging catch, which sends mutual respect into the tips of the fingers.[36]

Third, character was trained in games; 'Never cheat, never funk, never lose temper, never brag' were unwritten rules that promoted manliness.

> For games represent the right actions of bodily life, and all right action is pleasure. But the very games they play are full of pain, possible disagreeables, blows, defeat, disappointment, mortified pride, trials of temper, trials of courage, trials of honesty.[37]

It should be noted that team spirit, or what came to be called *esprit de corps*, was not listed as one of the qualities instilled by games. Thring had been reprimanded over this blind-spot by John Mitchinson, the headmaster of King's School, Canterbury, in his review of *Education and School*, but to no effect.[38]

Physical education was an integral part of Thring's curriculum, and the boys were encouraged to approach it 'on the same basis as our other school work'.[39] If a boy was good at athletics and games it did not necessitate that he be poor at Latin and Greek, and *vice versa*. The purpose of games was to arouse the quality of manliness and for this to work the games need not be treated as a 'science'. Thring was uneasy about the school's cricket success as he did not wish athletic prowess to be praised for its own sake. From his earliest days at Uppingham he was wary of 'mock heroics' in games, for he knew full well that 'strength is the school-boy's idol'.[40] Thring viewed any games coaching with suspicion as it might shift the emphasis from the average boy to the talented athlete. He watched school matches with mixed feelings: if the school won easily he was 'sorry for it'; if they were surprisingly beaten it would 'do them a great deal of good'; if they played without spirit he was annoyed.[41]

As games became more important to the boys, so Thring applied a number of vetoes to keep the movement in check. Although he regarded the spring rolling of the cricket pitch as a school duty, in all other games fagging was forbidden: 'If fagging enters into school-games, it taints them with a sort of curse of slavery for little boys.'[42] The appointment of all games officers had to meet with Thring's approval and all were chosen from the sixth-form. To play in any match a boy had to have 'leave' from his form-master, his housemaster and the headmaster, and such permission could be withheld for poor work or bad behaviour. Similarly, the acceptance of the cricket professional's services at such a limited level was at Thring's insistence.[43]

VII Nature, art and music: 'All can get the loving eye'

> The woods from Wakerley to Wardley Chase
> Are filled with schoolboy rangers, and once more
> The Bathers gleam white-armed by Welland's shore;
> The Runners ply the old accustomed race –
> These track the fox, and those the badgers trace
> Up to his woodland dwelling known of yore [1]

Memories of Uppingham throughout Thring's headmastership speak of the freedom to roam the countryside. John Skrine, at school in the 1860s, remembered the 'large liberty to ramble where we liked', and his memories were shared by the Rawnsley brothers and Charles Cornish; J. P. Graham's recollections of the 1880s were similar.[2] A journalist visiting the school once commented on the absence of 'high fences and notices to trespassers', a feature he commonly found at other schools.[3] Thring maintained friendly links with local farmers and an annual donation to the Rutland Agricultural Show undoubtedly helped. Boys who broke Thring's countryside rules were restricted to the main roads for their walks.[4] Half-holiday excursions were common; Thring and his masters would ramble with the boys.

'All can get the loving eye', Thring wrote. Every season had its own character, its own birds, flowers and trees: everything varied with the season.[5] The boys were encouraged to observe every happening, and then to note them:

> Not a bird should fly unnoticed; the note of the chiff-chaff should be heard. Not a song should sound, not a wing be moved, without appealing to seeing eyes and hearing ears.
> Look at the clouds, what a difference it makes in mind-power to one who loves the beauty of clouds.[6]

This was Thring's way of teaching natural history; in the field rather than through text-books, but then the aim was for a moral experience and not mere factual learning.[7] Many of Thring's boys maintained a love of nature throughout their lives. Willingham Rawnsley, who later wrote *Highways and Byways of Lincolnshire*, was one: 'a good walk in the country can do more in some ways for a boy with eyes than twenty games of cricket or football.'[8] Nature was also brought into the school. A museum was started to house the boys' collection of grasses, stones and sea-shells and a large aviary was constructed in the gardens of Fairfield; Thring would write enthusiastically of the latest addition.[9] Before the building of the gymnasium in 1859, the site was used for 9' × 3' garden patches for the boys. The Thrings were keen gardeners and they would give small plants to the boys, together with prizes of larger ones for the best gardeners. Later, in 1871, forty-two garden plots were allocated in Fairfield.[10]

Beauty was not to be restricted to the natural world for all art, the 'expression of high thought, whether music, or poetry, or sculpture, painting', was brought into the heart of the school.[11] Architecture had long been one of Thring's interests and he was determined that the new buildings, especially the school-room and the chapel, should be the best that money could buy. G. E. Street's long connection with the school was expensive, but his allegiance to the Gothic Revival and its strong Christian associations matched Thring's rejection of styles inspired by pagan Greece and Rome.[12] A. E. Street, the architect's son, designed the reredos mosaic in chapel in the style of the Pre-Raphaelite Brotherhood.[13] Lectures with slides were given on architecture as early as 1860, and Thring was delighted when a master formed an Architectural Society: a visit to Peterborough Cathedral was its first outing.[14]

Thring thought that architecture was a language, a means of communication; similarly 'pictures and sculptures speak through the eye'.[15] Christian Reimers, a German, was appointed as his first art-master in 1856 and soon Thring determined that every boy in the upper classes had to learn some drawing. Here, as in other areas of the curriculum, Uppingham was well ahead of current public-school practice. Pictures were also important teaching aids − give 'honour to lessons', Thring would say, with the addition of paintings of birds and animals; Livy should be read against a background of the Alps or modern Rome.[16] Thring aimed to have classrooms decorated to meet different educational needs − a Roman room, a Greek room, an English room, and so on − and, in the decorations of the School House hall, the photographs in his classroom and the murals in the school-room, he gave ample evidence of his belief in the Platonic principle that a soul absorbs its environment.[17] The murals, including portraits of Thring's heroes, were painted by a later art-master − Charles Rossiter.[18]

Rossiter had trained at Leigh's School of Art in London and by 1873, when he joined Thring's staff, he was a leading painter of the day. His works were exhibited at the Royal Academy, and he contributed the design for the mosaic portrait of Bernardino Luini for the South Court of the Kensington Museum.[19] Rossiter also created much stained-glass for the school that reflects his enthusiasm for the style of the Pre-Raphaelite Brotherhood. Architecture, murals, stained-glass and mosaics were all in harmony. Several of Rossiter's pupils later exhibited their own work at the Royal Academy.[20]

Craft-work too was important. In 1869 Thring invented a slow combustion stove and nearly suffocated whilst experimenting with it in his greenhouse.[21] More successful was the founding of a carpentry school in 1863; Thring became a pupil and in time produced a casket decorated in relief with portraits of his children.[22] Later a metalwork shop with a forge was installed; the boys made their own scientific instruments whilst their headmaster worked alongside them designing and making a 'Drop-Gate' for the cricket field.[23] Thring ensured that arts and crafts contributed valuably to the curriculum – 'So get rid, for ever, of the idea that Painting, Music, Architecture, Sculpture are less noble as mind-power, because we may not put them, possibly, into our hard-work time.'[24]

Shakespeare was included in the school-room murals and *Macbeth* and *Hamlet* were certainly studied by the boys, but other evidence of drama on the curriculum is slim. In another letter to Edward White, Thring wrote about 'that great power "acting" and the stage', revealing that his family performed 'theatricals' at Christmas, and how he wanted his children and the boys of the school to appreciate drama: 'I don't want to leave acting to the devil a bit more than dancing. Good acting is the most literary thing in the world, the most living instiller of new thought and bright brain power possible.'[25] Thring recorded that plays and 'acted readings' were staged; Rossiter oversaw scenery production, and one of the art master's daughters designed and made costumes; but no other information has come to light.[26]

Neither Reimers nor Beisiegel was the first of Thring's appointments to teach music for Herr Schäfer had joined the school in 1855 to become the fifth member of the initial teaching team.[27] This was surprising in several ways: first, England at this time was notorious as 'the country without music', with only William Sterndale Bennett as a contemporary English composer known to foreigners; secondly, other than the provision of chapel choirs, the English public schools had no musical tradition – indeed music was considered 'rather unmanly' and more fitting as a feminine accomplishment; and thirdly, and most remarkably, Thring was himself quite unmusical and tone deaf. 'He did not know one tune from another', his daughter Margaret remembered, 'except perhaps the National Anthem'.[28] As Thring later explained in a third letter to White: 'though I support music zealously from a sincere belief in it, I am an ignorant, careless savage, and know nothing about it'.[29] That Thring recognised the power of music was undoubtedly due to Marie, and once more the German influence was to be felt in a succession of music masters. Uppingham music began in her musical evenings with a small choir of six or so boys; soon it was to expand to congregational singing in chapel, when the practice at most schools was for only the choristers to sing, and to two or three concerts a term given by a choir of over a hundred voices.[30]

Reimers succeeded Schäfer in 1856; he was immediately commissioned by Thring to set to music the words for the first Uppingham school songs. Robert Sterndale Bennett, the grandson of William and a twentieth-century director of music at the school, believed that these were probably the first songs with English lyrics to be used at an English school; they were certainly published some years before John Farmer went to Harrow and Joseph Barnby arrived at Eton.[31] Three songs stem from the partnership: *The Uppingham Chorus*, *The Cricket Song* and *The Fives Song* were published in 1856. Christopher Cowan, one of Sterndale Bennett's successors, believed that it is a mistake to approach these songs with any solemnity for they are 'real entertainment music' in the tradition of German student songs.[32] A verse from *The Fives Song* gives a taste of the genre:

Oh the spirit in the ball
Dancing round about the wall,
In your eye and out again
Ere there's time to feel the pain,
Hands and fingers all alive,
Doing duty each for five.
Oh the spirit in the ball
Dancing round about the wall.[33]

In 1857 Heinrich Riccius succeeded Reimers and soon received assistance from Beisiegel, the gymnastics master. Two more Thring songs were set to music by Riccius and, with the three from Reimers, were published in 1858 by Macmillans as a volume of *School Songs*. Thring added a preface:

There is a tendency in schools to stereotype the forms of life. Any genial solvent is valuable. Games do much; but games do not penetrate to domestic life, and are much limited by age. Music supplies the want.

Echoes of Uppingham now displaced *The Uppingham Chorus* whilst *The Rockingham Match* described the popular annual visit to a nearby castle for a game of cricket. The lyrics for two other games songs, *The Old Boys' Match* and *The Football Song*, date from these early years but were not set to music until later.

These early teachers had worked wonders with the boys yet their frequent replacement as they returned home to Germany proved frustrating. Thus in 1865 Thring consulted William Sterndale Bennett, who was about to travel to Leipzig, and asked him to find a suitable man for a permanent appointment. The composer had regularly attended Mendelssohn's Conservatorium in that city since he was first acclaimed by its academy in 1837. He asked his friend Ferdinand David, the principal violin teacher, if he could recommend anyone for the Uppingham position, and David suggested his own son Paul, aged twenty-five. Thring then wrote to Paul David: 'It has long been a matter of great interest to me to make music take a proper place in English education.'[34]

How Sterndale Bennett charmed David, a pupil of Liszt and a member of the Mendelssohn and Schumann circle, to accept Thring's invitation is not known; what is certain is that David sacrificed personal renown in his own country to give Uppingham a distinction and excellence in music above any other school in England. The composer continued to be interested in David's work and he would visit the school twice a year as an examiner; the performances by the boys, especially the instrumentalists, never ceased to amaze him.[35] In November 1873 Thring asked the composer 'to give us a tune, to be a memorial of his connection with us, and he promised to do so, and seemed pleased, as I hoped he would'.[36] Sadly, the composer died in 1875 before the promise was kept.

Thring was obviously pleased with his catch for he declared Monday 13 March 1865 'a half holiday in honour of Herr David's arrival'.[37] Under David's direction music was soon 'an essential part of school life': it became a timetabled subject in the 1870s; more than a third of the school was now learning a musical instrument; and the atmosphere was such that one year the school's best violinist was also its cricket captain.[38] David appointed additional teachers, almost all German, to form a team of six to meet the school's expanding needs. He created an orchestral tradition 'without parallel in any school in the world' and the symphonies of Haydn, Mozart and Beethoven became standard fare.[39] Chamber works were also played, and a large choral society performed a regular cycle of oratorios by Handel and Mendelssohn.[40] The orchestra rehearsed on Sunday evenings, with many boys dropping in to listen. David was thrilled when he heard some whistling tunes from Beethoven's 5th Symphony as they walked about the school.[41] As Bernarr Rainbow writes, 'Paul David was indisputably the first to bring public school boys into regular contact with musical performances.'[42] Uppingham set the pattern for school music at its best that others would strive to follow.

Thring and David were to collaborate on many songs, including in 1873 a new school song, *Ho! Boys, Ho!* 'What may not come of School Songs', Thring wrote enthusiastically in his diary. May that year witnessed the first all-Uppingham concert: 'The boys encored the School song again and again, and all rose and stood whilst it was being sung. . . . The zeal of the boys was wonderful.'[43] David had travelled to England in the company of Joseph Joachim, also one of his father's pupils and soon the leading violinist of the time. David and Joachim maintained their friendship and the violinist visited the school every spring, joining the orchestra in its rehearsals and delighting in the boys' singing of the Uppingham songs. Joachim also attracted other eminent musicians to support David's pioneering efforts – including the trumpeter Julius Kosleck, the 'cellist Julius Klengel and the violinist Josef Ludwig – and he gave the Uppingham boys the encores that no other audience was permitted.[44] How magnificent it must have been to hear him play with the school orchestra, perhaps the Mendelssohn concerto dedicated by the composer to Paul David's father.

David taught at the school for a total of forty-three years and served under one of Thring's successors.[45] On his retirement in 1908, the University of Cambridge awarded him the first honorary degree of its type. The citation read: 'In the enthusiastic and successful teaching of the art of music in the schools of today no-one has set a more auspicious example for a longer time than Mr Paul David, our first Master of Music.'[46]

VIII Right and wrong:
'Safer to trust much than to trust little'

After he had been at Uppingham only a few months, Thring noted in his diary: 'Boys mean well on the whole. . . . May we have large liberal forgiving hearts all our lives.'[1] In his 1859 *Statement* to the trustees, Thring outlined the weaknesses of the traditional public-school system:

> Bullying is fostered by harshness in the masters and by forcing boys to herd together in promiscuous masses.
>
> Lying is fostered by general class rules, which take no cognizance of the ability of the individual to keep them; and they cannot do so when each boy is not sufficiently well known for his master to understand, sympathise with, and feel for him.
>
> Idleness is fostered, when there are so many boys to each master, that it becomes a chance when it will be detected, and a certainty that no special intelligent teaching and help will be given, or indeed can be given, to the individual when in difficulty.
>
> Rebellion and insubordination are fostered, when from the same causes many boys who are either backward or want ability, find no care bestowed on them, are obnoxious to arbitrary punishments, have nothing to interest them or give them self-respect, and learn in consequence to look upon their masters as natural enemies.
>
> Sensuality is fostered when these and like boys, from the same causes, are launched into an ungoverned society without any healthy interest, anything higher than the body to care for (the mental part being unmixed bitterness), thrown on their own resources, or want of resources, often exposed to scorn in school, whilst the numbers and confusion give every hope of escaping detection.
>
> The atmosphere of schools is, in consequence, in all their out of the way regions thick with falsehood and wrong; no more necessary, however, than a fog on an undrained field when the country round is clear; but considered necessary by the old-fashioned farmer because it has always been so.

Thring concluded his *Statement* with a *cri de coeur* that was to have immense influence on the English educational system:

> The young must be trusted, but not trusted in situations which would ruin their elders: this is at the root of the public school evils.
>
> The young must be trusted, but then the system must be truthful as well as trustful. It does not do to work a slave driver's whip, or a slave master's rations, side by side with the licentious freedom of the backwoods.
>
> In accordance with these principles, early in 1854, the School at Uppingham began to be remodeled.[2]

Thring was an autocrat, and his character was often seen as 'downright, fearless, uncompromising and intolerant of show and pretension' but this is only one side of the coin.[3] With his family, or with the sixth-formers whom he taught daily, he was completely at ease. His daughter Margaret recalled the homely side of his character – he was 'essentially genial, buoyant and optimistic'.[4] John Skrine, a boy at the school in Thring's early years and later on the teaching staff, called him 'The King of Boys'.[5] Thring's pleasures were simple: staging parties for the children of masters; leaping in the garden with his children; spending two hours building a snow woman for his daughters; delighting in children dancing at a party; charades with the boys in School House; and he would even look forward 'with childish enjoyment to a lie-a-bed, and a quiet Sunday'.[6] Uppingham boys were treated not as schoolboys but something between sons and pupils, 'as affectionate and confiding as sons ought to be, and as full of affectionate reverence as pupils'.[7] And there was to be no false dignity: in September 1862 another headmaster visited the school wearing the top hat accorded to a doctor of divinity:

> I was much amused by sundry masters and masters' wives insisting on the necessity of my never wearing a doctor's hat as utterly uncongenial with the spirit of this place. I too felt the anomaly. In our true, honest, every-day life-work here a mock dignity would be singularly out of place.[8]

Thring's most important precept was that education must be centred on the child, and this was the very cornerstone of Uppingham's foundation. In his first months as headmaster he wrote in his diary:

> It is better to draw out the feelings of children even if growth of a careless eye be somewhat too luxuriant, than to chill them back into a more precise culture, losing their hearts in the process. It is better to let children find experience in their own little world and roam in it with them, than to lift them up into your castle though it be a castle of truth and enclose them in its stone walls.[9]

Uppingham was a boy-world where it was 'safer to trust much than to trust little': a school must either be a 'complete prison rule' or 'a wise trust'. Prison rule would be effective and it would give little trouble but it was not founded on trust. It took Thring some years to break down the barrier of mistrust between boys and masters but gradually he won their 'allegiance to a good cause'.[10] Thring's ambition was to make Uppingham 'the most trustworthy school on English ground', and educational observers as eminent as J. G. Fitch believed that he realised his target.[11] Obeying his own notion, 'Remember if you have children, not to treat them as children after they are grown up', Thring gradually loosened the reins, and allowed the boys more privileges as the system began to work.[12]

The government of the school was conducted through the body of praepostors. Each praepostor was chosen from the sixth-form, thus preserving a sanity of outlook about athletic prowess, and each was expected to be 'thoroughly trustworthy as a helper of the helpless, a doer of justice, and having the spirit of order and true open life'.[13] Hardwicke Rawnsley recalled how the system worked during a 'school row':

> As was Thring's way, the matter of bringing the offender to book rested largely with the elder boys who were pledged by their position as "Praepostors" and members of the Sixth form, to safeguard the honour and welfare of the school; so the boys assembled in the big School and there was a great silence. Then Nettleship, as head boy, rose and, fearlessly fronting the whole school, asked the lads to remember they were trusted and called on them to be worthy of the trust. He ended with his appeal to their sense of honour, "Uppingham is a little place, and I dare say you fellows think it doesn't matter how we treat our masters or one another, but at least it shall never be said, if I can help it, that Uppingham boys are either liars or cowards!" Ever after one seemed to look at Nettleship as a kind of impersonation of truth and bravery.[14]

As the praepostorial system began to take hold, so the boys took on more responsibility: first came the Committee of Games (1857), then the library and a debating society were put in the boys' charge (1860), and a few years later the *Uppingham School Magazine* was born (1863).[15] Thring's influence was always there of course and he would often be asked to sort out 'controversies' or to unravel 'tangles'; he regarded his role as 'arbiter and legal adviser'. In 1860 Thring published a set of essays, *School Delusions*, ostensibly written by members of the sixth-form; the essays, not surprisingly, expressed Thring's own ideas. He addressed the essays to the school 'not only as explaining much of our life here, but as a genuine expression of feeling from amongst yourselves'. To his diary he confided, 'Their own companions' words may perhaps have some effect'.[16]

There was, of course, still schoolboy crime at Uppingham and Thring would launch out at one of his 'jaws' to the boys on the evils of 'thieves' honour'. Smoking and drinking were 'put down with a strong hand' and boys found with catapults and pistols were banned from all teams.[17] In 1859 the cricket captain and some friends were caught smoking and drinking by the praepostors; Thring removed their titles and privileges.[18] Thring gained something of a reputation as a 'flogger' but, on investigation of this legend, Cormac Rigby found that there were more memories of friends of Old Boys being beaten by Thring than actual recollections of having been beaten themselves. John Wolfenden, a twentieth-century headmaster at the school, recalled at the Thring centenary celebrations in 1953 one of the famous legends:

> You remember how he found one day posted in the Colonnade the names of two teams listed for a cricket match under the headings "Those who have been beaten by Mr Thring" versus "Those who have not". "Ha!" said he, in that rather gasping, guttural voice "if that game is played again all the players will be in the same side!"[19]

Boys were beaten at Thring's Uppingham but only by Thring and not by masters nor by praepostors. In 1885 Thring, in a letter to his chaplain, mentioned that he kept a book of all canings and sixteen boys had been beaten in that term. Such chastisement was used for disciplinary offences and never for 'the punishment of sins'; its advantages were that it was certain, quick, much feared, and soon over. Public expulsion or quiet removal of a boy only happened when Thring felt the cause had been lost and the boy was beyond the influence of school power.[20] Generally this was for 'sins', meaning moral offences. Each year Thring would warn the school that any boy found corrupting another or behaving indecently would immediately be expelled; those committing less grievous offences would silently be withdrawn.[21]

Thring intended that a sound morality should be fostered by the homely life in the boarding houses – here the ladies of the school played a vital role – and through the broad range of extra-curricular activities provided for a boy's leisure, but he did not propose to allow any boy to 'sin blindly' when it came to sex. No boy was to be left in ignorance. Thring did not believe in individual questioning and probing – 'I earnestly deprecate a perpetual pulling up by the roots to see how the plant is growing' – but in Bible lessons he would speak 'with perfect plainness on lust, and its devil worship'.[22] Thring's notes for his school addresses and the texts of his speeches to the 1884 Carlisle Church Congress and to public-school Old Boys in London the following year, both on the plight of the poor, indicate that the approach was identical. 'Curiosity, ignorance, and lies form a hot bed of impurity.' For curiosity Thring had no remedy to propose but ignorance and lies were on a different footing. He denounced the current fashion of wrapping sex and womanhood in a veil of mystery: 'I suppose every one is acquainted with some of the current lies', he told his Carlisle audience.[23] There were to be no delusions and no exaggerations in Thring's approach; facts were facts. Purity was life from God; sexual intercourse, and Thring used these actual words, was the most sacred of acts; voluptuousness was heathen; 'Sex is not a curse' – 'Lust is a curse.'[24] Any indecency at school was thus 'sham manhood' and, like the leper cast out, anyone found corrupting others would go.[25] Thring saw the subservient position in society of woman to man, when she was either slave or mistress, as the root cause of immorality for in this state woman became the object of lust. Equality of the sexes would abolish lust: 'it is one of the great hopes of our time that woman's work is largely recognised.' It is against this background that Thring became the champion of education for girls.[26]

IX North Woolwich:
'The rich boys must learn to help the poor boys'

Thring was determined that his boys should be aware of their social obligations. One oft-repeated part of that message was: 'Give not; lend, help, support, but give not.'[1] The first Uppingham schoolboy efforts were, however, restricted to donation to the parish church.[2] 'The rich boys must learn to help the poor boys' was Thring's war-cry, and to this end he instituted Saturday evening lectures to bring in glimpses of the outside world. Scattered amongst the illustrated addresses and lantern-slide guides were talks from visiting missionaries and clergymen. It was from such occasions that George Bell, the founder of the Regent's Park Boys' Home, gained support for his destitute lads; a college for the blind in Worcester received funds; and the Bishop of Brisbane secured financial promises for the building of a church in Queensland. Missionaries working abroad and Old Boys setting out on charitable ventures at home received tangible assistance from the boys after visiting the school and telling of their hopes and plans: in this way the school was linked with missionary work in Japan and Honolulu, with native educational scholarships in South Africa and India, and with church building in the Australian outback.[3]

Old Uppinghamians could help and give, and each leaver was left in no doubt by the message from Thring's sermons that he should not remain 'in his own station', thus creating a gulf between the rich and the poor, but that he should do some work in the 'lost places of the Kingdom', in the 'bare and dirty streets', and in the 'outcast settlements that skirt our great cities'.[4] Rarely were Thring's boys religious romantics, carrying prayer-book and Bible to darkest Africa or purveying middle-class values in untamed slums: they were far more likely to be involved with missionary responsibilities than trying to increase church membership, with being and living rather than with sending and preaching.[5]

But the problem of how boys still at school could help as well as give remained unsolved until the spring of 1869. Two entries from Thring's diary record the events:

> April 17th An excellent lecture last night from Mr Foy for the Additional Curates' Society; one of the best I ever heard.

> April 25th The school has determined to start an East London mission in consequence of Mr Foy's lecture. We think we shall get £100 a year, and it will interest the boys. I am very pleased with the idea. We had £17:18:3d for our special offertory today.[6]

Clearly the Reverend John Foy had presented a vivid account of his missionary work in the East End of London and no doubt he had thrown out some sort of challenge to his audience. It is probable too that sensible caution dictated that Foy had cleared his script with the headmaster but, nonetheless, all the evidence suggests that it was the boys who brought the idea of the mission to Thring, and not *vice versa*. A few days after Foy's talk, a delegation of boys came to Thring to ask if they might do something towards assisting the home mission work; in response the headmaster charged them to draw up plans to show what they hoped to achieve. The main points in the boys' prospectus were that they resolved to establish an Uppingham Home Mission somewhere in the East End of London, and that they hoped to support its work through special offertories from their own chapel collections and by promises of annual subscriptions from the masters. The ever-loyal masters agreed immediately to donate £40 a year and, with the amounts gleaned from the chapel collections, a sum large enough to cover a curate's stipend was quickly assembled.[7]

News of the venture was announced in the school magazine and soon the Old-Boy community was keenly involved with the project.[8] Thring may or may not have produced the actual idea but he was certainly quick to see its possibilities. Ever the opportunist, here was the innovation he had sought, a means by which the school could both help and give. He confided his hopes to his diary:

> It is a great thing to get the idea into the boys of giving personal help to the poor. I admit, too, I am proud, I hope not in a self-glorious way, of once more being the first to start a thing likely to be imitated and to bear good fruit.[9]

Once the Additional Curates' Society saw that the school was in earnest, the suggestion was made that it should maintain a curate in Bethnal Green. The Bishop of London was also consulted: he was asked to identify the parish most in need of assistance and he produced the name of North Woolwich. An Uppingham committee then set off to examine the claims of the various candidates, reporting back to the school on its return. The bishop's proposal was endorsed, and Uppingham settled on North Woolwich.

Thring now turned his attention to the appointment of the missionary curate. It is likely that he wrote round to all suitable Old Uppinghamian candidates – those in, or contemplating, Holy Orders – each probably receiving a letter similar to that sent to Nettleship with its throw-away broad hint.[10] The trawl produced an excellent catch when Wynford Alington accepted the challenge, so becoming the first missionary curate at North Woolwich. Alington had joined the school in Thring's first year, the eighth pupil added to the roll.[11] He was the foremost pupil; leading the cricket XI, serving as captain of school and gaining Uppingham's first open scholarship to university. On winning a first at Magdalen College, Oxford, Alington proceeded to Holy Orders and was ordained by the Bishop of Gloucester and Bristol to the curacy of St James's in Gloucester, the same parish where Thring had begun his professional life. Early in 1870, Alington began his mission work in North Woolwich.

Henry Boyd, later principal of Hertford College, Oxford, had recently been appointed vicar to an area at long last receiving attention from the Church of England; Alington was to be his curate. The parish of St Mark's, Victoria Docks, in North Woolwich was a huge stretch of marsh country situated to the east of London, bounded to the south by the Thames and to the north by a four-station length of the Fenchurch Street to North Woolwich railway. The population along the riverside was dense and rapidly increasing, with more than eight people sharing each low house. What particularly struck the visiting Uppingham master Willingham Rawnsley was the want of order and the disregard of all appearances: 'plenty of dirt, plenty of children, plenty of pigs: all three to be found for the most part in the astounding ruts of the main thoroughfare'.[12] The area was a moral and physical no man's land; not yet part of the London borderland, so without the modern civic amenities, but no longer truly rural. It was the worst of both worlds. The new works along the Thames – a cable factory, the gas works, an iron works and a rubber manufacturer – attracted a large number of single men to the parish and these formed a hard colony more than usually dead to the call of religion.[13] These men became the first target of Alington's ministry. As they spilled from the factory gates each midday – bound for the local public houses, racing to the notorious pleasure gardens, or just loitering about the roads – he set out to meet them and to win them. Braving their coarse jokes and their self-satisfied independence, he sought an audience where he could, conversing with some, reading to others. Gradually he was accepted and soon the work bore fruit.[14]

The Uppingham mission began in a school-room and a mission-room: the former also served as the parish church, whilst the latter housed the various mission meetings. Among the regular events staged in the mission-room were a mothers' meeting, where between twelve and twenty mothers met and made use of the clothing club, and a working men's club, which flourished with the financial support of local employers. Evening classes proved popular with the men, provided they were related to engineering or art-work; the basics of literacy were far less attractive. Work with the children brought the quickest results and the greatest satisfaction. The weekday National School had nearly 400 pupils on its roll, though with a school-room capacity of about 200, these had to be taught in two shifts. Visiting inspectors found plenty of fault with the facilities, whereas they had nothing but praise for the teaching: one assumes that Thring's influence had yet to be felt in the former but was already there in the latter. Twelve volunteers helped with the teaching of the Sunday school, which had 240 children on its books, and saw more than half of them attend regularly each week.[15] Alington returned to Uppingham periodically to inform the school of the progress that was being made, return visits were made by Uppinghamians past and present to support him at North Woolwich, and developments were carefully logged in the school magazine.

By the end of 1870 Alington was able to report that, as a result of Uppingham's contributions, a new school building was just about ready for use and that the foundations of the mission church were soon to be laid. The additional school-room caused few anxieties but the same could not be said for the church of St John's. The marshland of North Woolwich provided poor foundations and even a search twenty feet below the surface failed to reveal solid rock. Eventually the architect decided to lay a one-foot sheet of concrete as the building's base, though Boyd advised impishly that the bishop should be sent in haste to consecrate the finished church for delay might mean that he would only have the chance to bestow a parting benediction on the vanishing gable.[16]

Two years later, in September 1872, Alington's new church was completed and there was great excitement at Uppingham in anticipation of the journey down to the consecration ceremony. Thring, five masters, some ladies, forty-eight boys and fifteen Old Boys – a party of seventy-four in all – joined the congregation of 600 'mainly well-dressed middle-class people'; the Bishop of Rochester delivered a suitably 'manly straightforward' sermon; the Uppingham choristers remembered Thring's advice that they should follow the lead of the local singers, helping rather than showing off; all the boys who were eligible stayed on for the communion, to the delight of the bishop and the headmaster; and the church behaved by not sinking a single inch.[17] All then adjourned to the adjacent school-room for lunch, a round of speeches and a series of toasts, and hopes were expressed that further churches would soon be built elsewhere in the sprawling parish. The Uppingham boys were dispatched to catch the afternoon train from Euston whilst Thring remained to preach at the evening service. He delighted in the fact that most of his Old Boys had stayed on to hear him and he expressed to them the hope that North Woolwich would become a regular 'school-meeting ground' for them as well as for the boys of the school.

Once back at Uppingham, Thring gave the whole school an account of the day's events, telling them:

> England has never before had this fastening of a school on to real life work in the world outside. May it increase and spread. Alington must have felt his loneliness swept greatly away as he looked on the goodly array of his school-fellows, past and present, who met to join helping hands in his work. I trust to see this mission a great central pivot of Uppingham life, as much Uppingham as Uppingham itself to our best blood, even more so, as being a more tangible idea of living work to the ordinary mind. Thank God for this. Thank God.[18]

The next week Alington informed the school that in its first Sunday of services the church had a '*grand* congregation', whilst at Uppingham Thring confided to his diary: 'Back from North Woolwich after one of the most remarkable days of my life, and one that I verily believe will mark an epoch in England.'[19] The mission events came at a time when Thring was much under pressure from the threatening Schools Inquiry Commissioners and much committed to the responding agency, his brain-child, the Headmasters' Conference, and his spirits were somewhat at a low ebb.[20] But despair for Uppingham and the present was swamped by optimism for North Woolwich and the future it represented.

> The more I think of North Woolwich the more my heart rests on it. There is such a taste of life in it. Who can tell in these days what may become of buildings. Even now here in these buildings how much can I see of possible decay in the spirit within – how much of the hostility in the world outside … But the living hearts they cannot take away from us; they cannot quell the spirit which united us at North Woolwich, and made school and parish meet on common ground. That is real. . . . The boys seem to have been greatly struck with their visits.[21]

The school and parish continued to meet on common ground, with Uppinghamians past and present dropping in at North Woolwich, and posted reports for the magazine and Saturday evening talks keeping the school abreast of developments. Then in 1875 there was a second and similar happy visit by a large party from the school to the parish for the consecration of a second mission church.[22]

The Uppingham and North Woolwich connection came to a formal end in 1878 when Alington was appointed Commissary and Vicar-General of the Metropolitan of South Africa, and set out for Zululand; informal contact, however, was still maintained. The Uppingham mission lived on, transferring to St Saviour's in Poplar where the Bishop of London determined there was now greatest need. Here another Old Uppinghamian, Vivian Skrine, was in charge

and the methods used were much as at North Woolwich. Uppingham's pride
at Alington's appointment to South Africa turned to grief within the year on
receipt of the news of his death through typhoid. Thring felt the loss of this
most manly of his earliest boys keenly: 'Our first-fruits in the truest sense have
now been taken.'[23] The mosaic reredos in the school chapel was erected in
Alington's memory, and the decorated south window of the adjacent school-
room was dedicated as the memorial to Uppingham's missionary first fruits at
North Woolwich.[24]

Thring did not intend that Uppingham should relax its efforts on the founding
of the East End mission and he was ever alert to new opportunities and changing
circumstances. In 1877, Thring re-vitalised the Mutual Improvement Society
to strengthen the relationship between the school and the town.[25] The school
community – masters, their families and boys – joined with their neighbours
in Christmas jollities and Feast Week fun and games, provided a sports field and
helped with the levelling of the ground, and formed clubs for cricket, football
and tennis to encourage organised physical recreation. The local girls were not to
be forgotten, for the ladies of the school presided over the 'Grasshoppers', a tennis
club to complement the male 'Locusts'; an Old Boy of the period later recalled
with glee his vision of Thring demonstrating the strokes of this new-fangled
game to a row of daughters of Uppingham tradesmen.[26] All was in sympathy
with Thring's maxim: 'Merriment unlocks the heart and removes constraint.'[27]

Ever since his earliest days as a curate in Gloucester Thring had realised that
the effectiveness of any ministry to the urban poor was necessarily limited by the
squalor in which the unfortunates lived. Now, as the fame of Uppingham and its
missionary efforts at North Woolwich and elsewhere spread, so it brought invitations
to the headmaster to speak from national religious and charitable platforms. In
1884 he was charged by his old Cambridge friend, Harvey Goodwin, now Bishop
of Carlisle, to address the Church Congress on 'The Best Means of Raising the
Standard of Public Morality'. His message to the assembled churchmen was blunt:

> Foul air kills animal life, foul surroundings kills higher life. Whole families
> pigging it in one room cannot in a civilised country be chaste. We have
> talked too much, and done too little. We are too religious, we talk of divine
> truths and build churches, when we ought in God's name, and for Christ's
> sake, to be going round with a scavenger's cart, and a navvy's pickaxe,
> carting off filth and making sewers. I believe in a Gospel which builds
> sewers first, and Churches afterwards.[28]

There was a similar call the following year for less humbug about purity and
for more help with provision when Thring addressed a London conference of
public-school Old Boys:

> We have talked religion long enough, suppose we obey God's voice in
> Creation, and Christ's practice, and begin with happier life in Christ's

name first . . . Let mission rooms, and attractive teaching, and attractive amusements, and life, buy them. Get your demoniac clothed and in his right mind, then preach to him. Do as you would be done by, give him pleasure as well as work, touch him with higher life ('The Charter of Life').[29]

The title of this conference held at St Paul's Church, Knightsbridge, was 'The School of Life' and its purpose was to advertise, to co-ordinate and to propagate the work of the public-school missions. Thring's and Uppingham's pioneering efforts were recognised and acknowledged by the organisers and by the six other serving or former public-school headmasters on the platform, and together they stood as one in their call for greater involvement by public-school men in the plight of the poor, for greater awareness amongst boys still at the schools of the conditions in which the majority of the urban masses lived, and for renewed efforts by all to found more public-school missions in the numberless needy areas in the nation's cities. The conference call to show 'the readiest hand and the most open heart' was both heard and answered, for soon the public-school mission, and its university college counterpart, was to be a common feature of urban life throughout the land. Such was the Uppingham legacy.

X Chapel: 'The regiment of the brave and the true'

'I see Thring plainest in the pulpit' recalled E. W. Hornung, 'no longer a little old man, but majestic noble and austere.'[1] It was in his sermons, 'the true organ of his thought', that Thring would explain to the boys the purpose of 'True Life' and the role that Uppingham was to play.[2] The 'Almighty Wall' might be the body of the school, and the 'machinery' its life-blood, but the spirit came through in the headmaster's sermons.[3] For the first few years of Thring's headmastership the boys attended services in the parish church and Thring was denied access to the pulpit, yet on each Sunday evening he would deliver his sermon in the School House hall. In September 1860 Thring moved the services to the school-room adjacent to the parish church and now made his sermon an integral part of the pattern of worship.[4] Thring long felt the need of a chapel of his own, free from 'party opinions', and after the arrival of Witts his dream came true.[5]

In 1858 Thring published a volume of the School House sermons to serve as a prospectus for the school and to assure prospective parents that he was trustworthy on religious matters. It was dedicated to the masters – 'true fellow-workers and friends' – and prefaced in characteristic style:

These sermons are sent into the world as part of a system, and as exponents, in some degree of the experience of working men, that it is possible to have a free and manly school life, complete in all its parts, neither lost in a crowd, nor shut up in a prison, nor reared in a hot-bed.[6]

Nearly 400 manuscripts of other Thring sermons are held in the Uppingham Archives, and of these about a third were published in 1886 in the two-volume *Sermons Preached at Uppingham School*. Some of these had already been printed for private circulation at the request of boys and masters. Reading these sermons more than a century later, one is struck by the simple sincerity: they read as parables. They were neither intellectual nor theological, nor did Thring speak down to the boys. Each sermon would seem to have been written out in one attempt; Thring might make a few amendments on reading over the manuscript, but here the main purpose was to insert the pause marks needed for his delivery. That delivery contained 'no art, no dexterity of phrase or of articulation'; he merely would speak straight from the heart, with rarely a movement except to turn the leaves. Each sermon had a biblical text and most a title: the length, in an era notorious for prolixity, was no more than ten minutes. Thring stood as a 'prophet' of God, and in his sermons he spoke as Moses to a 'chosen people'.[7] Over half the sermons are directed towards the explanation of 'True Life'.

'What is truth?', Thring would ask, for this was the premier virtue. It was 'the knowledge of ourselves, and the humility springing from such a knowledge', it was 'the doing of what we know to be right each moment that a thing we know to be right has to be done'.[8]

> Truth claims that your amusements shall be manly, and hearty, and honourable, that there shall be no cheating; neither the cheating which steals time and cheats God's working day of works nor the cheating which in the game itself takes more than is right.[9]

The boys were encouraged to 'take delight in all truly manly unselfish work, in every thing that demands patience and strength of mind'. 'It is a manly choice that will not, can not, see in living for self anything to compare with the service of Christ.'[10]

True bravery was the second virtue. 'It is strange', Thring argued, 'considering the admiration men have for courage, how very little as yet the manliness of Christ's service has been set up as the ideal of the young man.' But 'let us not confound bravery with strength, as fools do' for 'the lowest kind of bravery is animal bravery'.[11] 'True bravery wants no strength but its own life'; it was more likely to be the virtue of the poor, the weak and the oppressed than of the strong, for it enlisted the power of the steadfast soul to withstand sneers and mockery and long periods of personal trial.[12]

> The truly brave strong man will face any danger that ought to be faced; the truly brave strong man will master any fear, fear of shame, and fear of ruin, as well as fear of danger; the truly brave strong man will not give way to mean temptations and fearful lusts.[13]

Self-mastery was an essential for 'true manliness'; it completes the Platonic ideal. 'Manliness means the cheerful bearing heat and cold, hunger and thirst, work and hardship, pain and weariness.'[14]

> If we train ourselves to be perfectly ready, to bear hunger and cold then we have got rid of the main temptation. If we are able to have the hardy elastic feeling of not caring for hardship then is our own spirit strong within us, then are we beginning to be free indeed.[15]

Thring gave a detailed review of this 'self-denial' in one of his earliest sermons:

> You are called upon to war against the flesh; that is, to learn not to care for any mere bodily feeling in comparison with higher things. If you bear hunger without ill-temper, that is being Christ's soldier; if you give up dainties and nice things to eat or drink, that is learning to be Christ's soldier; if you can work on when tired, or begin work when tempted to indulge the body in rest or play, that is learning to subdue the flesh. See, then, how well adapted our life here is to give this self-command, and how much that may perhaps have seemed tiresome, or want of freedom even, is in reality Christ's service and perfect freedom. . . . Our set times, then, are most valuable assistances to freedom, training you not to care for your own fancies, but at any moment, what ever you are about, to be able to turn to what is right. . . . And again, in their proper degree, how our very games and exercises strengthen the body and will do it right, and make the mere sitting idling by the fire, or lounging in the sun, childish and contemptible; or again, furnish opportunities for self-denial, by being given up readily at the calls of higher duties. All these things, then, are to make you free – and are freedom – breaking off from your necks, if rightly done, the slavery of selfish fleshy appetites.[16]

To aid the process there was early morning school to throw boys out into the cold on a winter's morning, and an hour of work before breakfast to make the stomach the servant of the mind.[17]

The cheerful bearing of pain, whether physical or emotional, was another important ingredient of self-mastery, 'the thing for a man to face with high heart, and rejoice in having faced'.

> We have to strengthen and fashion the inward life into a state of fearless excellence; and to refer everything to this. And every day brings its contribution; every act, done or undone, plays its part. Difficulties become tests of willingness and strength; the character that can face a hard task is learning much beside the task itself. Pain is a teacher; the character that does not flinch from pain is being moulded for high work. Sorrow teaches; the patient spirit is learning the peace of God.[18]

The self-mastery of the 'manly effort of purity and truth' would both prevent corruption and jealously guard the morality of the school. 'Brethren', Thring called, 'be watchful, watch and cherish in holiness purity, and true righteousness, that seed of life to come, that present seed of immortality, – your body.'[19]

The 'joy of strength and movement' is evident in many sermons and 'the blessing of health' that came from games was often praised; but always games were regarded as of secondary importance compared to the ideal of manliness, and warnings against making games a 'science' span Thring's whole life at Uppingham – as the following excerpts illustrate.[20]

> Another making excellence in games his object and being put out by anything which interferes with that, because he is working for himself and not for Christ.
>
> (1853)

> And in yourselves, what scope for doing the right and giving up hand and foot and eye, the love of power in games, the love of skill in lessons, for the sake of just doing at the time the distasteful task with friendly welcome.
>
> (1875)

> I must think that to be known through England for true manliness is a better thing than to have a name for cricket.
>
> (1884)[21]

Denouncements on the 'idolatry of strength' were just as likely to be directed at the intellect as at the body. There were two worlds, 'the world of knowledge and the world of character and feeling', or 'power worship' and 'True Life': you must choose to follow Caesar or Christ. 'Instruments are not life', and 'man . . . is judged by the use he made of the powers not by the powers he had.'[22]

> I would draw your attention to the barefaced heathenism which a school can, and does hold. The shameless way in which, as a matter of course, the strong body, or strong in brain, take advantage of the weak in common life. . . . Never do a thing because you are strong.[23]

The tone throughout Thring's sermons is one of encouragement to greater endeavours, yet of forgiveness if the progress was not always maintained. Life 'was a battle of good against evil' and each boy had to fight his own way, not blindly like 'the slave heart' but with eyes open and using his own talents. The sermons are messages of exhortation and hope; little time is wasted condemning sin and there is hardly any mention of hell.[24] The parable of the sower and the seed was a Thring favourite:

> A life made up of love of Christ and manly honest feeling, which may be tempted, which may fall, which may make many mistakes, but nevertheless

whether tempted, or fallen, or making mistakes, like a plant never leaves off the upward push.[25]

The Sower, sowing his seed of life in an Uppingham field, was depicted for all to see in the stained-glass of the most prominent window in the school-room.[26]

Earth was a training ground for the Kingdom of Heaven and man was only put on it so that the whole business of his life could be 'active manly work and training and nothing else'. School was that training ground in a life's first years:[27]

> A school can realise in a way that is seldom found elsewhere, the bond of common life, of being, like the Israelites, a small yet a most highly endowed band in a great world, a brotherhood, able to act together, and throughout all our earthly life to feel the tie of brotherhood, to feel that the good of one is the good of all, the evil of one is the evil of all, to feel that all we do is not private, but part of a common honour, as I, at all events feel daily, hourly, with a ceaseless sense of peace at not working save for common good. What might you not do if every heart beat high for the common cause? . . . A life of manly power, of liberty, of strength, as was set before the Israelites.[28]

As 'was set before the Israelites', the Book of Exodus was thus 'The Architect's Plan', for here could be found all the doctrine, all the facts, of the great Christian tradition. Here could be found the true spirit of holiness: 'Holiness is the giving life to what has to be done, it is an everlasting present, a quiet spirit of daily, silent, patient, enduring work.'[29]

Jacob and Abram were two of Thring's heroes. How similar in many ways was the modern schoolboy's life to that of Abram, taken away from home to face lessons in manliness:

> The manliness of the hardy body, and free heart was the aim of God's first schooling. City power, knowledge power, luxury, and inventions were rejected in this first schooling, in favour of *manliness*; not mere bravery, but true manliness, the pure heart of the hardy shepherd life, the liberty of the wide pastures, the fields and the hills, the incessant care day and night of the flocks, gentleness to animals, simple food, the bearing heat and cold, the readiness to risk life against wild beasts in order to save their flocks, in a quiet righteous way, without the excitement in gain of war, and with no one looking in.[30]

The boys' work at school, as much as that at North Woolwich or in strange lands, was true holiness. If the chapel was the heart of the ideal of manliness, the Uppingham 'machinery' was its life blood.[31]

> Your daily life here is just planned out on such a plan as to try your courage in little things every day; to try your courage in good whether

you have the life in you that can readily resist temptation in this way and be brave; to try your courage in body, in games and outdoor life whether you have the life in you to overcome weariness, laziness and pain and be brave in body; to try your courage in your main work, whether you have the life in you which can overcome the dislike of tasks, resist idleness, feel the brave spirit that hour after hour can do its work lovingly in spite of the pain of hard reading and the allurements of amusement, and be brave intellectually.[32]

The school, like the ideal of chivalry, was 'rough and imperfect' for 'some few are manly and true, the great majority perhaps mean well, but in a cowardly weak way; and there is simply little or no trace of the gallant united effort to do good work unflinchingly.' Thring challenged his boys to make that extra effort: 'When you have acknowledged God as King you will feel with thankful sober trust the gain of having done honest work, the happiness of manly life, the joy of brave and patient endurance.'[33]

A number of sermons refer to the school's mission in North Woolwich, for Thring knew 'no more glorious gain than being able to understand the lives of the poor, of the great army of God's poor, and all the power of weakness that is life and truth'.[34] One Sunday he talked of his own year at Gloucester and of Thomas Hedley:

> I remember the great man, for he was a great man, the quiet clergyman, under who I begun parish work, said in words I have never forgotten, said "I never see a particularly disagreeable little boy come into my parish school without thinking here is some one I have to learn to love for Christ's sake."[35]

Education was for 'True Life', and the purpose of schooling at Uppingham was to enable each boy to make the fullest realisation of his abilities so that the life pledged to God's service was as valuable as possible.[36] Thring's message was clear, so too was the portrayal of the true exemplar of the ideal of manliness:

> There is no more striking character stamped upon Christ's Gospel than the thorough manliness of its earthly practice. It is *the* character, in point of fact, – yea, *the* character of Christ Himself, as Pilate unconsciously proclaimed, "Behold the Man." The spiritual Adam, the second Father of this human race, who in His own person set forth all that was heroic, enduring, and brave; the *manliest* character that this earth has ever seen, who transmitted to His spiritual children the power of being truly men, – men in heart and not merely in outward form, gallant, brave, and wise; in its best sense, *manly*, – not like the brutes, in bodily lusts and unrestrained appetites, looking to bodily powers as manhood, instead of

to the glorious exercise of the pure and strengthened spirit. For there is a growth of body which is in no sense true manhood; and there is a growth of the spirit which in its truest sense is so, though it be a child's body.[37]

Thring's last sermon was never preached for he was taken with a fatal illness on the day it was to have been delivered. His text was 'knowing good from evil' (Gen III, 4–5):

I need not point out how completely God's plan is carried out in the plan of a School like this. What opportunities for manliness and self-denial there are in the work and the games, in the in-door life and the out-door life. How much of the joy of manliness is here as well as its trials. What room there is for obedience. How your life together calls for gentleness and forbearance with one another.[38]

After writing these words Thring turned to his diary, and closed the day's entry almost in prophecy – 'And now to bed, Sermon finished, and a blessed feeling of Sunday coming' [39]

XI Confirmation: 'A perfect pattern of manly power'

The dreams of childhood and of youth
Were pleasant dreams I wot
But they are gone forever gone
And I lament them not.
Who would not change his dimless hopes
For manhood's stirring strife?
For those who like it nursery milk,
Give me the wine of life.[1]

The whole of Thring's efforts were directed towards making a boy 'manly, earnest and true'.[2] The school years were the crucial phase of a boy's life; not a preparation for life, but the most important stage of a life. Each pupil arrived a boy, each left a man, and 'nursery milk' was exchanged at Uppingham for 'the wine of life'. The evolution was gradual but the process accelerated for each boy at about the age of fourteen as he prepared to confirm his Christian baptismal vows and assume adult membership of the Church of England. Each would then be ready for service in the 'Christian Knighthood'. The whole school took part in the annual ceremonies associated with confirmation and, as year succeeded year, so every boy took this rite of passage to manhood. As Thring's manuscript notes held at the back of the first volume of his three-volume Bible state, 'Every one must be a communicant.'[3]

Each March or April, Thring would inaugurate the confirmation week with a sermon at Sunday's service. Then on successive weekday evenings, at a time when Thring believed that boys were at their most receptive, he would speak to separate groups assembled in the chapel. First he would address the youngest boys about the confirmation process, and then on the next evening he would concentrate on the boys who were that year's confirmation candidates. A visiting bishop, and usually a close friend, led the actual confirmation service on the third day, and on that evening Thring would address all the older boys as communicants. The confirmation week was formally closed on the following Sunday with a second sermon delivered by Thring to the whole school.[4]

Thring's sermon at the beginning of the confirmation week had two purposes: to remind the boys of their membership of a distinctive community and to warn them of the sexual dangers associated with 'mock manliness'. Thring often compared the boys to the Israelites on their flight from Egypt to their new home on the banks of the Jordan; the much-annotated text of *Exodus* in his Bible became 'The Architect's Plan' for their moral training. He believed that the rigours and deprivations of the Israelites' captivity had bred a hardiness of character, whilst the rescue at the parting of the Red Sea had inspired a single-mindedness of purity. Thring saw Moses and his followers as:

> young, and brave, and strong, ranks clear of traitors, clear of sensual lust, limbs hardy and obedient from the hardy wilderness marches, spirits burning with high hopes, feet standing at the boundary line between preparation and victory, eyes fixed on the hills of their future homes.[5]

He urged the boys to identify with the Israelites and to view the confirmation service as the boundary line in their own lives between preparation for battle and eventual victory.

Then there was Thring's second purpose, the warnings on 'mock manliness'. The Israelites had been clear of sensual lust, and so too should Uppinghamians. The boys were encouraged to 'manage' their thoughts on such matters and to beware those who were sexually self-indulgent. The warnings were explicit:

> Who is that crawling along, pale and tottering, with his face full of pox and death even already claiming on his brow? Can this be he, the young, the handsome, the strong, who some eight or ten years ago was the envied champion of his school or college? Yes, it is he. Can it be the little boy who so few years ago was playing with idleness, and laughing merrily over his petty tricks, tricks alas often praised or made a joke of by those who ought to know better?[6]

A few evenings after the Sunday sermon, Thring addressed the hundred or so junior boys. He told them that they had outgrown the involuntary demands of mewling childhood and he likened them to the Israelites who had escaped from slavery in Egypt. The crossing of the Red Sea had its parallel in their initiation to the Christian Church at the time of their baptism. They had been freed of original sin and they now walked at liberty as the sons of God. No responsibilities would be placed on them until they had grown in power, purity and manliness, and they should use this interval to learn to become 'soldiers of Christ'. The folly of the 'mock manliness' of homoerotic habits, whether performed alone or with others, was starkly stated, and, in the manner of the period, the likely downhill path to lunacy or death was clearly signposted. The boys were thus encouraged to manage their thoughts by avoiding idleness, to harness their energies by being busy in their leisure time, and to strengthen their willpower daily by reading at least ten verses of their Bibles. Should they however fail to heed the moral warnings, they would be spared no mercy. 'Secret poisoners', he assured them, would meet instant dismissal from the school.[7]

It was the turn of the fifty or so confirmation candidates to be addressed by Thring on the following evening. He developed his Israelite theme, for their lives moved from a childlike baseness to an enlightenment that he associated with adulthood. The dependency of childhood matched the Israelites' call for food in the wilderness and God's answering provision of manna and water. Daily bread was provided for God's people to sustain their power for living and, in return, they would serve God's purpose in the way that they led their lives. The Israelites now stood overlooking their Promised Land, happy to honour the promise they had made to God for their safe deliverance. In the same way, the confirmation candidates were at the boundary between boyhood and manhood, and they should be ready to use all their talents and powers for the good of their fellow people.[8]

Each boy in the school had talents that could be used for good or for ill – like the money that might relieve the long-term sufferings of the poor or bring temporary happiness to the drunkard – and each had it within him to use his own unique gifts, to perform his own miracles, and to strive for his own Promised Land.[9] To do this 'true courage' was needed. This was not to be confused with the strength, energy and hardiness of the body, though one could not have 'true courage' without those animal qualities. 'True manliness' rose above these by the addition of quiet endurance, righteousness and gentleness, and through a patient willingness to bear reproach, shame, obscurity, pain and misunderstanding when on active service in a good cause.[10] Thring repeated his warning on the consequences of indecency and he spoke too of the letter of advice on the matter given to him in his youth by his father: 'A quiet, simple statement . . . and a few of the plain texts from St Paul saved me.' He also drew on the happiness of his own marriage, expressing the hope that all boys would in time become happy husbands and fathers, and he invited them to join him in a confirmation pledge – 'never to harm a woman in thought, word, or deed'.[11] And, as ever, the exhortations were accompanied by a warning, for failure in this respect would mean instant dismissal.

After the following day's confirmation service, Thring turned his attention in the evening to the one hundred and fifty or so senior boys who were already communicant members of the Church. Here was the opportunity to remind them of their promises. The school was a 'regiment for Christ' and anyone found guilty of gross indecency or of corrupting another would leave it at once. The 'purity of good women' was recalled and the boys were asked to 'reverence it' by keeping their own bodies pure for eventual marriage.[12]

Thring could not resist the urge to remind the senior boys of the need to read those ten verses of the Bible each day and to complain that their attendance at the twice-weekly communion services was not as regular as he would have wished. He ended with an exhortation: 'A great school is an army in the regiment of the brave and the true' where the boys were to live 'the high and happy Christian life, the honour and the power of being a Christian, the wisdom, the bravery, the true nobility of being enrolled in the army of Truth and of Christ'. He would ask if 'the idea of Christian knighthood was beginning a new life? . . . May it not begin here – even here'?[13] This army would win 'victory' on the battlefield of life, and each enlisted soldier would be God's hero:

> God's hero, the man who bears and does all things easily, gently, lovingly – the hero, who may die without glory, but who has been felt to be a perfect pattern of manly power by every living being with the heart of life, whose life has been touched by the life. For life touches life, and passes on in silence, invisible, into other lives, even as rain that falls gently on the earth, and seems to pass away, till the harvest comes, and speaks of a hidden, wonderful spread of unseen goodness.[14]

Thring brought the confirmation week to a close with his sermon to the whole school during the next Sunday's chapel service. After the exhortations and warnings introduced in the previous Sunday's sermon, and developed in the separate evening addresses to the three groups of boys, the second Sunday sermon usually found Thring in cheerful mood. His last confirmation sermon, delivered in March 1887, saw him on particularly happy form. Taking as his text, 'Sin, that it might appear sin, working death in me by that which is good, that sin by the commandment might become exceedingly sinful,' (Rom VIII 13), Thring confided that his chief worry as headmaster was that even in a good school sin could gain a toehold:

> [I]t is in a school that all the little beginnings of corruption are thought so lightly of by those who do them, it is in a school that the Apostle's warning is most neglected, and uncleanness is named filthiness, and foolish talking and jesting in an unseemly way go on.[15]

It was for that reason, he reported, that he had to be so vigilant:

> Today, once more, I can look on this school, and speak to you as one regiment in the army of Christ, one in Confirmation Week, one on this

Commemorative Sunday, one as marching under our Lord, one as having thrown in your lot with life and honour and truth, loyal and faithful soldiers and subjects of Christ your king. It is a glorious feeling to feel we are one body in Christ. I do not mean that evil has gone, or that no traitor is here, but I do mean that we can feel that as one body we are bounded together to do holy service. I do mean that we can feel a happy confidence in the truth and desire to be true of the school as a whole. I do mean that we can feel that we have a common cause and are ready to work together for it. I do mean that the battle against sin in this place is a real battle, and the Holy Spirit of God is dwelling with us here.[16]

Thring's confidence that his boys could lead the 'True Life' was high for he believed even the young could be valiant soldiers in that regiment – 'The spirit that does right, because it is right, is as strong in the little child as in the old.' His closing rallying call saw the promise of 'Victory':

Brethren, in this Confirmation and Holy Communion, let one spirit breathe through our ranks. Let us stand today shoulder to shoulder as one regiment on the battlefield, resolute, with one voice, and one power to cast out from this place the unclean spirits and their lies.[17]

*****

The whole Uppingham 'machinery' was geared to the training of 'True Life': it was essentially a moral education. Thring would speak often to the boys on the twin aims of the school: first, 'the winning a character for truth and true honour'; second, 'the winning a character for scholarship'. The order of preference was vital; material success was the very antithesis of 'True Life', a life that made all its abilities, whether of body or intellect, as perfect as possible and 'guided by right love and right hate' submitted them to the service of God.[18]

Thring was especially suspicious of mere intellect and at Cambridge he noted: 'An overgrown intellect is as much a disease in human nature as an enlarged liver in the body.' Much later, in a paper entitled 'Education, or Idolatry', he continued: 'Many learned men are mere human maggots, crawling lengths of masticated books, swollen out to an unwieldy size which is much glorified in the kingdom of the lean where the fat man is king.' Knowledge was like a guinea, being part of the owner: it could have power in its own right but it ought to serve its master. Men who lived for the intellect alone were doing work for the devil; men who submitted their intellect to the guidance of a moral purpose did God's work.[19]

Bodily strength was the second power that could be used for good or ill. The body, like the intellect, had to be the servant of God's will. It was to be trained to resist the temptations of too much or too luxuriant food; it should be able to bear exercise, weariness, cold, heat and pain; it should work efficiently and skilfully; and it should be master of its own physical temptations.[20] Thring, a true squarson's son, was used to a rough life. Not all boys came from a similar background: 'the more I see of the middle classes the more their self-indulgent presumptuous folly fills me with fears for the future of this country.' Life at Uppingham was designed to build the best bodies but there was to be no luxury in all this genial life, not the faintest approach to it. 'The dog in the kennel barks at the fleas, the dog who is hunting does not feel them' was Thring's own maxim. Each year, at the prize-giving after the sports, he would speak 'on pluck and fair play and the value of wide sympathies, and the difference between a strong body and a plucky heart, that the one is as dead without the other'.[21] The legend on the back of a photograph of the winners of the final heat of the quarter-mile race in 1865 describes the ideal in practice:

> Mitchell, leading, collapsed within 2 yards of the tape; a boy – Gordon – passed him and won the race, but C Childs, running 3rd, pushed him over the line in front of himself, thus giving him the 2nd prize – a Quart Pewter – which he still prizes.[22]

Neither intellectual strength nor bodily strength was to be lauded at Uppingham: what was sought was a Platonic harmony, in school and out of school, in work and in play, in body, intellect and soul.[23] When a favourite pupil failed to secure the expected first at Oxford, he could write to his headmaster: 'No doubt harder reading might have made a First sure. But I feel I have got more from other sources, rowing even included, much that no mere reading could give.' Thring, in reply, agreed.[24]

'Leisure hours most affect character and are the hinge on which true education turns.' Boys were to be free in their out of school hours but not cast adrift; higher tastes, objects and occupations were to be cultivated in these hours and by this means 'animalism' could be checked and 'manliness' aroused. To Thring – 'Training means, *everybody learning how to use time well*.'[25]

> Boys or men become brave, and hardy, and true, not by being told to do so, but by being nurtured in a brave, and hardy, and true way, surrounded by objects likely to excite these feelings, exercised in a manner calculated to draw them out unconsciously.[26]

At the time of the Thring centenary celebrations, Oswald Powell recalled how he had often heard Thring end a school speech with the hope that whenever boys went out into the world from Uppingham they would carry with them such rules for conduct, and such determination always to live the 'true life', that they should get in all lands and among all ranks a character for manliness. This, Powell continued, he cared for more than any number of honours, and he knew Thring to be absolutely sincere on this, and every other principle.[27] Two entries from Thring's diary illustrate the principle in action:

> Took leave of (a pupil) tonight. Am greatly pleased with him; he has been an honest, manly fellow, and I am proud of his taking those feelings from the school. He said that he could not do much in classics and work, but he hoped to represent the truth and manliness of the school, which was the great thing. I told him that indeed it was, and that I had as great an affection and respect for him on that account as if he could get the Balliol.

> Had a very cheering letter forwarded me this morning by the guardian of one of the boys who wants to subscribe £5 (to the chapel fund) on account of the good the school has done him, and quotes with pride my declaration that to have been at Uppingham must be a passport for honour, integrity, and manliness. He is a heavy, ill-educated fellow too. If he has felt this strongly the leaven has been working. God be praised for this.[28]

XII Hardie Rawnsley: 'A son of the School that reared him'

Were Thring's boys true to the ideal of manliness? To follow their careers after leaving Uppingham and to lay their triumphs at Thring's feet does not really answer the question; nor would it be in accordance with the principle of 'True Life'. Yet the question still needs to be answered – was the ideal put into practice? If what the boys chose as their future careers is an acceptable criterion, then the answer is a most definite yes. Taking the first half of the Thring years as reference, 1853–70, the careers of Uppinghamians are decidedly at odds with those of boys from other public schools. T. W. Bamford noted how Rugby in this period produced twice as many boys who followed careers in law or in the armed forces as those who entered the Church, and at Harrow the Church ranked fifth a long way behind the armed forces, administration, politics, and law. At all the schools in Bamford's survey, there had been a steady decline in the number of boys taking Holy Orders since 1835, and this included Rugby part way through Arnold's headmastership. At Uppingham from 1853–70 the Church was clearly the most chosen career, well ahead of law and the armed forces. Two clergymen were produced for every soldier, and throughout Thring's headmastership the percentage of boys entering the Church was higher than at the schools cited by Bamford. In the years after 1870 the armed forces and business came to the top in agreement with the trend at the other schools, yet even here the growth in business as a career was much below that seen elsewhere. As a career choice in the whole of Thring's headmastership, the Church ranked third.[1]

W. P. James proclaimed that Thring's boys were too straight for the 'crooked game' of politics and, indeed, no Members of Parliament figure in the lists before 1871. Thring was always against the army as a career, reckoning it to be a 'monotonous and unsatisfactory life', and instead he directed the boys towards the professions and, especially in the early years, to the Church. If we are to choose an average boy, then we must take a future clergyman. If the following of his career is an acceptable test of the ideals–into–practice question, what other qualifications should the average boy have? Certainly he should come in the first half of Thring's headmastership, for then the ideal of manliness was at its strongest. Cormac Rigby has shown how an average parent of the first years chose to send his son 'to be under Thring' rather than 'to be at Uppingham', and the parent probably had some personal or professional connection with the headmaster or with the Thring family at Alford.[2] The average boy, therefore, should come from such a family. Several boys meet these criteria but only two have left sufficient record of their lives for a biography to be traced. One, John Skrine, served later as a master at Uppingham and then as Warden of Glenalmond, but he was too much a mystic to be an example of the ideal in practice. My choice then falls on Hardwicke Drummond Rawnsley.

Rawnsley was born in 1851 at Shiplake-on-Thames, and Thring was his godfather. His father, Canon Drummond Rawnsley, was a man of letters as well as a clergyman. When Thring published *Education and School* in 1864 it was dedicated to Drummond Rawnsley – 'The first personal friend who trusted me in his professional life'. Thring never forgot that here was the first associate to entrust a son to his care.[3] At the time of Hardwicke's birth, Thring was also working in the Thames valley and it was presumably then that the friendship began. Shiplake was the Rawnsley family home. At some stage in the 1850s the family moved to Halton Holgate in Lincolnshire, where Canon Rawnsley took on a larger parish.[4]

Willingham was the first son to go to Uppingham, in 1855 at the age of ten. Hardwicke followed at the age of eleven in October 1862 and, in all, five of the six Rawnsley brothers came to the school. Hardwicke was under the care of Edward and Marie Thring in School House for eight years, during which he imbibed the ideal of manliness from its very fount. In lessons he was remembered best for his power in answering divinity questions; his intellect was such that he had secured a school scholarship in 1865.[5] On the games field and in the gymnasium he was plucky rather than talented: Willingham had been school champion but Hardwicke, despite enormous endeavours, had to be content with runner–up. A love of nature was naturally absorbed and from his years of roaming the Rutland countryside, and through his collection of stuffed birds and animals, Rawnsley developed into a talented naturalist. School House boys, however, would complain at the perpetual smell of animal skins emanating from his study. Thring taught him to use his eyes in the countryside and made him 'see some beauty in the least of God's creatures'. Back at school these impressions were 'knocked into rough verse'. In 1869 he won the school's prize for English verse, and in these years he absorbed Thring's love of Wordsworth's poetry.[6] Rawnsley completed his Uppingham career as captain of School House, surely an exemplary position, and in 1870 he left for Balliol College, Oxford.

Lewis Nettleship had gained the top Balliol Scholarship from Uppingham in 1864. Now Rawnsley came as his tutee and the Thringian influence continued. Benjamin Jowett had just begun his mastership of the college and it was already gaining in reputation for both scholarship and social conscience. John Ruskin was Slade Professor of Fine Art at this time and Rawnsley joined the famed band of Ruskin's road-makers who did much good for the Hinksey poor.[7] Sporting activity was maintained: Rawnsley won the high jump in the Freshman's Sports of 1870, and later came third in the 1872 University Championship. Many contemporaries remembered him best as the Balliol troubadour, composing songs and ballads by the yard and singing them at any celebration which required musical entertainment.[8]

On gaining his degree in 1874, Rawnsley impetuously jumped from one career possibility to another: chemistry, medicine and missionary work were all considered. Thring was consulted and sent Rawnsley a typical reply:

> You must learn to feel that this world and this life of ours is really, thoroughly and completely governed by a very present God. . . . Don't get into the habit of thinking God cuts out the world with a pair of scissors and that you hold the handle of them, as so many do, or act as if they did. "His judgements are like the great deep". Your father's letter is a good and wise letter. God's work wants every power we can bring into play, and remember when once we begin the ceaseless conflict of modern working life there is no more storing up of material to work from; empty or full, one has to put out something. Your whole inside may feel like a scraped wall before whitewashing, so bare and empty and hopeless, and yet something must be produced. Well it is then if there is stock and stuff enough of old habit and old fulness to make it possible for the used-up powers to still do good work. Again, a knowledge of medicine is a wonderful gain to a missionary, and so far from the climate being more injurious as you get older, the more settled time of life is the best for endurance of that as for other things. But this is of small account, what is real is God's will, and it is God's will that you should have some more training first. Follow that will honestly however it may pain, and be sure you will live to bless it.[9]

Rawnsley became a lay-chaplain in the Soho district of London for the period of 'more training' and gradually 'God's will' was seen. He volunteered for missionary work in Madagascar but was turned down on the advice of doctors;

the interest in chemistry waned, and then he decided against medicine. The choice had to be social work in Britain.

Rawnsley had fallen in love with the Lake District when he stayed at Ben Place with the Thrings during a university vacation.[10] He met Ruskin there and maintained contact with him on return to Oxford. Through Ruskin he was introduced in Soho to Octavia Hill. She had been an ardent campaigner for many years for better social conditions for the poor, and in Rawnsley she found a keen fellow-campaigner. Their friendship and collaboration lasted until the end of her life and, when she died, Rawnsley preached the sermon at her memorial service.[11]

In December 1875 Rawnsley was ordained a deacon in Gloucester Cathedral, and then early in the following year he was appointed by John Percival to run the Clifton College Mission. Percival had heard of the Uppingham Mission and the idea obviously impressed him. In 1875 he formed a mission committee in the school and then this in turn gave birth to the first mission to follow Uppingham's lead. Rawnsley was appointed curate and some rooms in a cottage and the upper-floor of a carpenter's shed were provided in the Newfoundland Road district of Bristol.[12] The mission was situated in the heart of the docklands. Rawnsley arrived to find

> muck-heaps and farm refuse, on which jerry builders had set up rows of houses, which periodically got flooded and sucked up fever and death from chill for the poor folk who lived there. No lamps. Streets only wadeable through. A few public-houses of the worst sort'.[13]

He spent two long hard years in Bristol and his success can be traced in his reports to *The Cliftonian*: a night school was started; various clubs and activities were inaugurated; games and swimming were eagerly followed; and there were weekend expeditions to the surrounding countryside. But, as the *Dictionary of National Biography* records enigmatically, not everything went smoothly: 'His success in winning the confidence of the people in one of Bristol's poorest areas, through his unconventional approach to the priestly ministry, paradoxically led to his dismissal.' No more is known.

In December 1877 Rawnsley was ordained a priest in Carlisle Cathedral and took the living at the village of Wray. No decision as to why the Lake District was chosen is recorded but the ordination in Carlisle may provide a clue. Thring's friend Harvey Goodwin was now Bishop of Carlisle and it is possible that Thring may have sung his godson's praise when the bishop was seeking to inject new blood into the diocese. Certainly Rawnsley and Goodwin were to be close friends; on Goodwin's death Rawnsley was chosen to write his biography.[14] One month after taking the Wray living, Rawnsley married Edith Fletcher in Brathay's church: both his father and Thring performed the service and Lewis Nettleship was best man.[15] His future mother-in-law had previously written to Thring for a character reference on the young man. He replied:

> If H. had asked me for my daughter I should have given my consent – that is the best answer. I have a very high opinion of him from the most intimate knowledge.... He is so far from commonplace, so original, so full of strange power.... I have never known anything wrong or mean about him.... I believe he is sincerely desirous of doing the right always.[16]

The couple stayed at Wray vicarage for five years, where their son Noel was born in 1880, and then Goodwin presented Rawnsley to the living at Crosthwaite, north of Keswick. Here many old friends were frequent visitors to the happy family home: the Thrings, the Skrines, the Davids, Nettleship; and new friends too including Frederick Temple, now Bishop of London.[17] Rawnsley made Crosthwaite his life's work until his retirement in 1917; by then he had been appointed a Canon of Carlisle Cathedral and he was a Chaplain to the King. Rawnsley was a well-loved parish priest and a forceful orator from the pulpit. He once sought Thring's advice on the composition and delivery of sermons:

> I don't believe with your pitching into your congregation. The only power in the spiritual world is οικοδομή – orderly building. The glory and happiness of doing good ought to be the preacher's sole theme, with a dash of how to do it. To paint a thrilling and touching heart-picture is a hard thing – so to draw a clear and striking path of holiness is a hard thing, but to knock a fellow on the head is easy; it merely wants a fist, the other wants heart and head. If clergymen spoke of the Heavenly Father's gift of love, and the happiness of the sons who receive and act, we should not have so much evil; but people get frightened at God, and repelled instead of attracted.[18]

The apprenticeship at Thring's Uppingham, with Ruskin in the Hinksey digging days, with Octavia Hill in Soho, and at the Clifton Mission, came to fruition in the Crosthwaite years. Rawnsley was now ready for his life's work:

> I believe strongly that the law of Christ and the love of Christ should embrace and govern the whole round of practical life – the social as well as the intellectual; the commercial as well as the practical; the life of action as well as the life devotional; the hours of recreation as well as the hours of labour.[19]

Rawnsley took a keen interest in the schools in his parish and he visited them frequently; singing, dancing, gardening and gymnastics were all encouraged. He talked to the children about exhibits in Keswick museum and he wrote them several school songs. He was closely involved with the foundation of Keswick Grammar School, and was keenly in favour of co-education. The temperance cause found him an ally, not through mere preaching but in encouragement for the provision of recreational and educational counter-attractions. He was closely involved with the National Home Reading Union and with a holiday association that gave trips to the Lake District for the working classes of the industrial North. The Cumberland Nature Club elected him its president in 1904. He was the founding father of the Keswick School of Industrial Arts, an innovation that gained considerable backing from Ruskin. This began as a night school in the parish room, and quickly expanded to buildings of its own with a full-time staff of teachers of arts and crafts.[20]

Rawnsley believed that a communion with nature would help to lead the poor to Christianity, and he was deeply opposed to the practice of restricting access to beautiful places to the rich and the educated.[21] In 1883 the beauty of the Lake District was threatened by a proposed railway from Buttermere to Braithwaite; Rawnsley leapt to the defence of the countryside and quickly gained the tag, Champion of the Lakes. At the annual meeting of the Wordsworth's Society, Rawnsley proposed that a Lake District Defence Society be formed 'to protect the Lake District from those injurious encroachments upon its scenery which are from time to time attempted from purely commercial or speculative motives, without regard to its claims as a natural recreation ground'.[22] Ruskin wrote sympathetically but despairing: 'It's all of no use – You will soon have a Cook's tourist railway up Scawfell, and another up Helwellyn, and another up Skiddaw, and then a connecting line all round.'[23] The satirical magazine *Punch* joined the defence:

> What ho, my merry Philistines here's news and no mistake,
> They're going to run a railway round and spoil each pretty lake,
> And hear the famous cataract that Southey song of yore
> The locomotive's noise shall drown the murmur of Lodore.

In 1879 Octavia Hill and Richard Hunter had formed the Commons Preservation Society; now they joined forces with Rawnsley. Defence funds were launched, articles were published in journals, footpaths were forcibly kept open and the rallying cry – 'The Lake District is in danger' – sounded round the country.[24] Then in 1893 the Falls of Lodore, the island on Grasmere, came on the market and Rawnsley proposed that it be bought for the nation. He took the idea to Octavia Hill and Robert Hunter, and together they launched the National Trust for Places of Historic Interest and Natural Beauty, a movement known today simply as the National Trust.[25] For the next twenty years he served as the society's honorary treasurer and leading 'advocate'. Whenever a piece of the Lake District was threatened, the tactics were the same: Rawnsley would thunder, the public would be stirred and the money would be found to buy the land for the National Trust.[26] John Bailey of the Trust could only gaze in wonder: 'you are the hardest unpaid worker in these islands.' Rawnsley's main influence was in the Borrowdale region; here over eighty properties were purchased.[27]

There were quieter sides to the man too. Guide-books on the Lake District were written and innumerable sonnets were composed on commission for periodicals and newspapers. The flow from the pen was exhaustive and eventually *Punch* could stand it no longer: 'Today is the thirtieth anniversary of the day on which Canon Rawnsley wrote his first sonnet; he has since written 30,000!'[28] Yet even here there were causes to fight. In 1886 he proposed to the Wordsworth Society that a reading room be built as a permanent memorial to the Lake poets; then, on Rawnsley's initiative, Wordsworth's first home, Dove Cottage in Grasmere, was bought by public subscription and adapted as a Wordsworth museum. In 1900 Beatrix Potter was having difficulty in convincing publishers of the merits of her illustrated *The Tale of Peter Rabbit*. Rawnsley joined the attack, encouraging her to print it privately; he even turned the whole story into verse in case that was more attractive.[29] It was not, and eventually Frederick Warne published the original.[30] Rawnsley opening verses went as follows:

There were four little bunnies
– no bunnies were sweeter
Mopsy and Cotton-tail
Flopsy and Peter

They lived in a sand-bank
as here you may see
At the foot of a fir
– a magnificent tree.

Just like his Uppingham headmaster, Rawnsley was impulsive, dynamic, tireless, eloquent, irascible and of a mercurial temperament, with a stocky figure and piercing blue eyes. In Keswick he was known as 'The Volcano': there was always something to erupt into – a memorial on Helwellyn to a faithful dog; crusades against the massacre of birds for plumage; rights for persecuted Armenians; subscriptions for paintings for the National Gallery; the construction of Jubilee bonfires; vulgar comic postcards and low station literature; bleached white bread and Cumberland butter; pornography and screen violence in the cinema; nationwide pyrotechnic displays in celebration of the Armistice in 1918; and much, much more.[31]

On his death in June 1920, his memorial in Crosthwaite church was inscribed with the words: 'Who battled for the true, the just'. The National

Trust dedicated Friar's Crag, Lord's Island and part of Great Wood on the shore of Derwentwater to his memory and a plaque records:

> In honoured memory of Hardwicke Drummond Rawnsley, 1851–1920, who greatly loving the fair things of nature and of art set all his life to the service of God and man.

It is a memorial to the ideal of manliness.

John Skrine wrote Rawnsley's obituary for the *Uppingham School Magazine*: he had no doubt at all that here was an exemplar of everything Thring stood for –

> He was in the fullest sense a son of the School that reared him. In his character and career he carried the Uppingham "legend", which is not legendary but is living fact. His godfather, Edward Thring, was very truly father in God to this godson. That word which was ever on his great teacher's lips, "true life", a mystic word and more clearly realised perhaps in the soul that in the mind of its speaker, has been nobly and luminously interpreted by the vivid career of generous social helpfulness which is the story of Hardie Rawnsley. In that life of vital service the master will have seen an answer to his prayer for a pupil that he should "here or elsewhere still continue the living life which Christ has given us here".[32]

Hardie Rawnsley lived Thring's ideal of true manliness.

Chapter 3

Athletic manliness

I Games:
'The means of innocent amusement and exercise'

Well before 1800, games were played in public schools. Cricket, boating and fives were popular at Eton in the 1760s and instructors were on hand to teach boxing, fencing and dancing.[1] The state of sport was much the same at Harrow and other schools.[2] Cricket had long been a popular pastime and there are numerous records of its play at public schools. Rowing, bathing and fives were also activities of long-standing and all sports were organised by the boys for their own recreation. Less formal but seemingly more popular pastimes included fighting, poaching and other forms of general lawlessness.

Aristocrats spent long periods on their rural estates where an important part of life was sport. Riding, hunting, shooting and fishing were all enjoyed. Sports of a different nature were also firmly established: the Jockey Club had controlled racing since about 1750; the Royal and Ancient Golf Club at St Andrews was formed in 1754; and the Marylebone Cricket Club, the ruling body for the game, was founded in 1788.[3]

The 'barbarian' country sports claimed most attention in the public schools in the early nineteenth century but already 'ridiculous stress', in the view of Sidney Smith, was being placed on 'philistine' games.[4] Lord Byron talked his way in to the Harrow XI for the inaugural cricket match against Eton at Lord's in 1805, although he was keener to indulge in the post-match drunken festivities than to make his mark in the game.[5] Cricket, football and rowing were introduced at Westminster School in London from 1808 when the headmaster, William Carey, curtailed the boys' freedom to roam and restricted them to the school's grounds.[6] Boys arranged all their own games at Shrewsbury during the long headmastership of Samuel Butler from 1798 to 1836; Butler saw no educational value in them.[7] Some observers attached the ideal of manliness to these pursuits, though to Smith it was 'as seductive to the imagination as it is utterly unimportant in itself'.[8] But as the years passed, so the position of games strengthened.

The lawless recreations of the boys came under attack during the reforms of the public schools in the second quarter of the century. George Butler, headmaster of Harrow in Byron's time, was probably quickest off the mark; by the time of his retirement in 1829, games had effectively been compulsory for many years. The boys controlled everything but the licence to impose compulsion on a school of over 200 came from Butler.[9] One of the earliest actions of Benjamin Kennedy when he succeeded the other Butler at Shrewsbury was to provide a playing-field for cricket so that the boys might have 'the means of innocent amusement and exercise in their leisure hours', but he allowed the boys' hunt to remain.[10] Thomas Arnold thought otherwise on his appointment at Rugby in 1828, for he banned hunting and poaching, and disbanded the boys' pack of hounds. The check on these pursuits led to an increase in other forms of recreation on the school site. Cricket had long been popular and football had an ancestry older than 1822 when William Webb Ellis 'with a fine disregard for the rules' picked up the ball for the legendary birth of Rugby football. Organised games were firmly entrenched at Eton in the 1830s when the future Bishop Patteson, and Thring's contemporary, threatened to leave the field unless the use of bad language ceased.[11] Charles Wordsworth, then second-master at Winchester, used games as a means of inculcating desirable social qualities:

> My habit of mixing with the boys in play-time and of taking part in at least some of their games, such as cricket and bat fives, not unfrequently enabled me to acquire over them in such matters an influence which I could not otherwise have gained, and which I endeavoured to employ so as to correct whatever I observed of undue harshness and want of consideration toward those whose position in the school made them liable to be fagged.[12]

Wordsworth sought to limit this fagging in games, a practice of long-standing in which younger boys were ordered by their elders to retrieve 'kicked-out' footballs or, in these days before the invention of cricket nets, to field for the batsmen.[13]

By 1850 cricket, football, rowing and various racket games were all common at public schools. The boys were responsible for the organisation of the games, though sometimes they had the aid of masters. Masters too would occasionally join the boys in play. The first headmaster to use games as an element of school management, Tony Mangan suggests, was probably Charles Vaughan at Harrow. When this favourite pupil of Thomas Arnold was appointed in 1844 at the age of twenty-eight, with no experience as a schoolmaster, he had to tackle both ill-discipline and falling pupil numbers.[14] His response was to introduce methods used by his own headmaster plus much playing of games, the latter despite the fact that Vaughan was no sportsman. With disciplinary rather than educational aims, there was no need for masters to be involved. Vaughan worked through the senior boys, and by early 1853 they had formed the Harrow Philathletic Club 'with the view of promoting among the members of the school an increased interest in games and other manly exercises'.[15]

The first headmaster to go a step further and impose games on a school where the boys did not play them was George Cotton, reputedly the young master in *Tom Brown's Schooldays*. Cotton was appointed from Rugby to be Master of Marlborough in 1852. He inherited a chaotic, barbarian school in which fighting, bird-nesting and squirrel-hunting were the main recreations.[16] In a speech to the assembled school Cotton outlined his policy:

> The Council informed me on my appointment that the school was in a bad state of discipline, and they hoped that I would allow no boy to go out except in pairs with a master. I told them that I could not accept office on such terms, that the school I hoped to govern was a public school, not a private one, and I would try and make it govern itself by means of prefects. The school now knows how matters stand. They must either submit to the prefects or be reduced to the level of a private school and have their freedom ignominiously curtailed.[17]

With the introduction of prefects, bounds were tightened, drinking and other forms of lawlessness diminished, and the school day became more organised. Cotton imported Rugby football and cricket to replace the country pursuits; these not only acted as an antidote to mischief and trouble but also enabled Cotton's influence to be diffused more effectively through the active participation of young men newly appointed to the staff.[18] Soon Cotton had introduced matches with other schools, including Cheltenham College and Rugby.[19]

In 1860 a letter to the *Cornhill Magazine* from a parent, writing under the pseudonym 'Paterfamilias', opened a controversy on the quality of education at the public schools that led eventually to the creation of the Public Schools Commission under Lord Clarendon. Nine schools were inspected: seven boarding schools – Eton, Charterhouse, Harrow, Rugby, Shrewsbury, Westminster and Winchester; and two day schools – Merchant Taylors' and St Paul's. Paterfamilias complained that although the schools, and Eton in particular, provided a fair intellectual education, there was a complete absence of moral training. In the writer's view, gentlemen became gentlemen at Eton not through the education they received there, but because they were the sons of gentlemen.[20] By the time of the publication of the Clarendon report in 1864, a remedy had been found: games would provide the moral training for they inculcated 'some of the most valuable school qualities and manly virtues'.[21] The report expressed worry at the poor teaching and philistine nature of the education at public schools, but it wholeheartedly rejected Paterfamilias's claim of moral laxity.[22]

> Boys from public schools have decidedly improved in point of moral training and character within the last twenty years. The old grossness and

brutality have disappeared, and the use of coarse language is, at the larger schools, confined to a few.[23]

Several reviewers of a few years earlier had welcomed *Tom Brown's Schooldays* for its athletic outlook and the games it advocated were even seen as 'the most important branch' of education.[24] 'It is in these sports that the character of the boys is formed. It is from them that the readiness, pluck, and self-dependence of the English gentleman are principally caught.'[25] 'They bind the different generations of the school together, they promote the attainment of skill in the game, and they prevent intellectual superiority from being the only one formally recognised in our education.' The *Edinburgh Review* was not so sure:

> A boy might readily infer from 'Tom Brown' that he was only sent to school to play at football, and that lessons were quite a secondary consideration.[26]

The *National Review* agreed:

> Whatever novels may say to the contrary the mere athletic training produces a feeble, gregarious, helpless, cast of character, dependent for vigour that it has upon accidental circumstances, and unfit for the real work of life.[27]

But the warnings were generally ignored. Vaughan and Cotton had shown how games could be used to impose discipline in schools; the Public Schools Commissioners welcomed the role they played in moral training; Darwin's evolutionary ideas and Spencer's philosophical writings warned of the survival of the fittest; and the spirit of competition inherent in all games matched the feelings of the age. The flood-gates opened: all schools would play games.

In this era of the most rapid expansion of the public-school system, with many new schools founded and still more raised from old grammar schools, the basic formula for a public school was derived. Such a school should be a self-contained society, partly self-governing and partly ruled by an autocratic headmaster. The aim of its education was less in intellectual qualities and more in terms of leadership and the arts of social ascendancy: it was in this latter aspect that games would contribute their part. The end-product was the Christian gentleman personified in Tom Brown. As each new school came about, so the games ethos was more readily accepted and soon the older foundations followed suit. 'Private school' games were summarily abolished, sometimes by the boys, sometimes by the headmaster. Marbles, peg-top, skipping, tip-cat, hop-scotch and the like were quickly replaced by football, generally the Rugby variety, cricket and rowing. Clifton under John Percival was typical of the newer schools which felt this distorted influence of Arnold: Rugby football was played on the 'Close', and cricket 'reflected the headmaster's influence quite as faithfully as the rest of school life'.[28] At the mother-school, Rugby, the years after Temple witnessed the rise of the athletic 'swell' to usurp the power of the prefects and saw a growing glorification of things muscular.[29]

Games however are essentially a boy-culture and, as Tony Mangan noted, the emulation of Vaughan and Cotton by other headmasters had unforeseen results. Soon the tail was wagging the dog as boys at all schools clamoured for cups and colours, house competitions and school matches, resident professional coaches and better facilities. Within a few years games alone determined the status of a boy within his school, and the position of that school in the rank–order of public schools.[30]

II Hughes: 'What would life be without fighting?'

It was the publication in 1857 of Thomas Hughes's *Tom Brown's Schooldays* that was partly responsible for the tilting of the ideal of manliness towards the physical. With William Cory and Leslie Stephen, Hughes orchestrated the emergent cult of athleticism.[1] That Hughes had distorted the Maurice/Kingsley ideal of manliness was probably done in all innocence; he did not comprehend the full ideal, for only the physical aspect, with which he was most familiar, was within his understanding. When a few years later Hughes saw that manliness was becoming muscularity and that the physical means to the earlier ideal had in their turn become the athletic ends, he tried to close the stable door. By then the horse had bolted, for Tom Brown had run off with the ideal of manliness.

Hughes was born in 1822 at Uffington in the White Horse Vale of Berkshire. There the earliest influences were a strong squire for a father, a boisterous country upbringing, and a delight in the novels of Scott. He attended a preparatory school near Winchester before going to Rugby in 1833. Hughes arrived at Rugby in Arthur Stanley's last term. Stanley, 'the embodiment of Arnold's deepest wishes', had just won the Balliol scholarship, whilst Charles Vaughan had gained the Trinity: it was Arnold's most prized year.[2] Hughes however was no scholar, and he never reached the exalted inner circle of Arnold's sixth-form. Nonetheless he developed an admiration and respect for Arnold's moral purpose, although the headmaster would not have always agreed with his pupil's interpretation. Hughes's own success came on the playing-fields. He captained 'Bigside' at football and played in the game requested on Queen Adelaide's visit to the school. He was also captain of cricket and a member of the Rugby XI first to play at Lord's in 1840.[3] It was in these games and through the pranks and escapades of this relatively unreformed Rugby that Hughes developed self-reliance, courage and sportsmanship: but this was hardly Arnold's ideal of manliness.[4] In 1842 Hughes went up to Oriel College, Oxford – in this period a home of strenuous athletes rather than serious scholars. There he took to rowing but still found time to play as a freshman in the 'Varsity cricket match'.[5]

Oxford may not have had much intellectual influence on Hughes but it did affect him politically: he became a Radical. On coming down he determined to be a lawyer and it was during his time at Lincoln's Inn in 1846 that Hughes first heard Maurice preach. He was immediately infected by the spirit of service and the sense of fellowship that Maurice espoused, and for the next fifty years he was to be one of the most ardent disciples. Two years later Hughes became a founder member of Christian Socialism. Here, as very much the odd man out amongst Maurice, Ludlow and Kingsley, it was hard to find a role for this boisterous athlete. At first it was merely the 'donkey-work', but gradually he became the support on whom the others could lean.[6] He was immediately likeable; a cheery, slangy language developed between Kingsley and Hughes, and they would often holiday together in the mountains of Wales.[7] When the Working Men's College was formed in 1854, Maurice announced to the founding members that Hughes was joining them; there was great laughter as someone called out, 'We are not going to start a cricket club!'[8] Thus Hughes was little in demand as a lecturer but he was very popular as an athlete or pugilist. Later there came clubs for cricket and rowing together with day trips to the countryside. In the *Working Men's College Magazine* for May 1859, Hughes wrote of the need for a healthy body: 'Round shoulders, narrow chests, stiff limbs, are as bad as defective grammar and arithmetic.'[9] The culmination of the effects of the Crimean War and the Indian Mutiny, the Napoleon III scare of 1858–59, and Lord Elcho's call for action, saw Hughes forming two companies of the Working Men's College Corps as part of the 19th Middlesex Volunteers.[10] Major-Commandant Thomas Hughes, 'a kind of John Bull regenerate', was in his element.[11] The association of manliness and patriotism had begun.

In 1856 Hughes wrote *Tom Brown's Schooldays*. The aim at first was to bring out what he wanted in a school for his son, but gradually it evolved into a memorial to Thomas Arnold. He showed some of the early chapters to Ludlow and Kingsley, and they encouraged him to continue; Kingsley admired the emphasis on a standard of manliness based on hard work and service to others.[12] In September of that year Hughes wrote triumphantly to Daniel and Alexander Macmillan, the Cambridge publishers: 'my chief reason for writing is, as I always told you, I'm going to make your fortune.'[13] He did. In seven months Hughes received royalties of £1250, and by January 1858 over 11,000 copies had been sold.[14] Most of the reviews were enthusiastic, though there were some complaints on the sentimentality and on the moral standpoint. Kingsley thought it a 'noble book': he had been asked to write on it for the *Saturday Review*, but under special orders 'not to lay it on too strong'.[15] He later penned some thoughts to Hughes:

> I have often been minded to write to you about "Tom Brown", so here goes. I have puffed it everywhere I went, but I soon found how true the adage is that a good wine needs no bush, for everyone had read it already, and from everyone, from the fine lady on her throne, to the red-coat on his cock-horse, and the school-boy on his forrum (as our Irish brethren call it), I have heard but one word, and that is, that it is the jolliest book they ever read.'[16]

The appeal of this convincing, vigorous and moving school novel was immediate: the successful formula that Hughes had found was applied by others in every school novel to the end of the century and perhaps beyond. Its influence in schools was to be far-reaching.

The story of *Tom Brown's Schooldays* is simple. Rugby is the setting in which Tom discovers himself and builds his character. Tom is an ordinary true-blooded English boy:

> It's very odd how almost all English boys love danger; you can get ten to join a game, or climb a tree, or swim a stream, when there's a chance of breaking their limbs or getting drowned, for one who'll stay on level ground, or in his depth, or play quoits or bowls.[17]

His father sends him to Rugby not to become a scholar:

> Well, but he isn't sent to school for that – at any rate not for that mainly. I don't care a straw for Greek particles, or the diagamma, no more does his mother. What is he sent to school for? Well, partly because he wanted to go. If he'll only turn out a brave, helpful, truth-telling Englishman, and a gentleman, and a Christian, that's all I want.[18]

To be 'brave, helpful, truth-telling', these were almost the three Platonic virtues of manliness – courage, self-control and truth.

Tom is soon proud to be a Rugby boy and, after hearing his first Arnold sermon, he resolved 'to stand by and follow the Doctor'. The heart of the tale rests in the conflict between those boys who wished to maintain 'the good old days' and those who have accepted the Doctor's morality. Tom is pulled back and forth between the two factions, but in the end of course good prevails over evil. Tom cemented his own manliness through his catalytic friendship with Arthur, who is weak in physical power but leonine in moral courage.[19] Arthur's transformative effect on Tom, in the manner of the 'angel in the house', persuaded many early readers to view him as the real hero of the story.[20] The message to be drawn from the actions of both Tom and Arthur was that a true Christian manfully cooperates with others in the fight for right. Hughes's manliness was defined as the fusion of high spirits, self-reliance and courage in the service of all good works, and it was the basic, and virtually sole, Christian virtue. This is an ideal drawn more from Charles Kingsley than Thomas Arnold.[21]

In accepting the Tom Brown stereotype, the new public schools also took on the love of physical activity that is explicit throughout the story. To fight with one's fists was seen as manly:

> After all, what would life be without fighting, I should like to know? From the cradle to the grave, fighting, rightly understood, is the business, the real, highest, honestest business of every son of man. Every one who is worth his

salt has his enemies, who must be beaten, be they evil thoughts and habits in himself, or spiritual wickedness in high places, or Russians, or Border-ruffians, or Bill, Tom or Harry, who will not let him live in quiet till he has thrashed them.[22]

How Arnold would have shuddered at the prospect of Tom Brown taking on 'Slogger' Williams in his name. Boxing and football, the Rugby variety of course, were encouraged as replacements for 'private school' games that were now seen to be unmanly.

The novel was possibly the first writing to advocate team spirit at school as training in patriotism. After the School-house football victory Brooke, the captain, asks,

but why did we beat 'em? answer me that — (shouts of "your play"). Nonsense. 'Twasn't the wind and kick-off either, that wouldn't do it. . . . Why is it then? I'll tell you what I think. It's because we have more reliance upon one another, more of a house feeling, more fellowship than the school can have. Each of us knows and can depend on his next hand man better — that's why we beat 'em to-day. We've union, they've division — there's the secret — (cheer). . . . I know I'd sooner win two School-house matches running than get the Balliol scholarship any day — (frantic cheers).[23]

Here then was ready-made team spirit; but not all games fostered it. Cricket did:

"What a noble game it is too." (said the master)

"Isn't it? But it's more than a game. It's an institution", said Tom.

"Yes", said Arthur, "the birthright of British boys old and young, as *habeas corpus* and trial by jury are of British men."

"The discipline and reliance on one another which it teaches is so valuable I think," went on the master, "it ought to be such an unselfish game. It merges the individual in the eleven; he doesn't play that he may win, but that his side may."

"That's very true," said Tom, "and that's why football and cricket, now one comes to think of it, are such much better games than fives or hare-and-hounds, or any others where the object is to come in first or win for oneself, and not that one's side may win."[24]

Thus we have the Tom Brown formula; self-reliance came through fighting and boxing, and team games produced *esprit de corps*. It was a philosophy that could rule the Empire, but the distortion of the ideal of manliness was complete.

Macmillans invited Hughes to write a sequel and he immediately seized the opportunity to redefine manliness.[25] *Tom Brown at Oxford*, dedicated to Frederick Maurice, was published in 1862; alas it was a novel written from the head and not from the heart and it did not have the success of the original. In the period between leaving Rugby and going up to Oxford, Tom had led a sporting life. He was now a 'better horseman and shot' but, so Hughes emphasised, the 'whole man had not grown'.[26] Though college life was to be both philistine and athletic, Tom gradually grew to realise that there were more important matters and he enrols in the noble brotherhood of 'muscular Christians'. Here Hughes carefully distinguished between the 'hail-brother well-met' musclemen and the genuine article:

> the least of the muscular Christians has hold of the old Christian and chivalrous belief, that a man's body is given him to be trained and brought into subjection, and then used for the protection of the weak, the advancement of all righteous causes, and the subduing of the earth which God has given to the children of men. He does not hold that more strength or activity are in themselves worthy of respect or worship.[27]

But the appeal of the sequel largely went unheard.

As the years passed, so Hughes became more depressed and disillusioned; disheartened at the change from Christian Socialism to trade unionism, and disappointed at the evolution of the ideal of manliness into a cult of masculinity. In a series of lectures delivered to the Working Men's College in 1876 he attempted to redefine manliness in line with the Kingsley model. In particular, he now located Christ's manliness in self-control and the quiet acceptance of his fate. Hughes also noted that 'athleticism is a good thing if kept in its place, but it has come to be much over-praised'.[28] These lectures were subsequently published as *The Manliness of Christ*. Manliness now served as an envelope for courage, tenderness and thoughtfulness for others. Courage, whether of persistency, determination to have one's way, or contempt for one's own ease and safety, only rose to manliness when the component 'duty' was added. Hughes cited Nelson as an example of true manliness because of his extreme devotion to duty.[29] Now true manliness was as likely to be found in a weak body as in a strong one; whilst proficiency in games was not even a test of animal courage, let alone of manliness: 'a great athlete may be a brute or a coward, while a truly manly man can be neither.' The possession of the Royal Humane Society's medal for saving life was 'prima-facie' evidence of manliness.[30]

As he withdrew from socialism, so Hughes spent more time on writing, including a succession of biographies for Macmillans on manly heroes such as Alfred the Great and David Livingstone. But the England of the late 1870s was not Thomas Hughes's England. The slump caused by the rise of Germany and the United States in world markets, the mounting secular feeling of the nation, the growing luxury at public schools, and the ever-increasing professionalism of their sport, combined to see the end of Tom Brown's world.[31] It was a saddened Hughes who turned his back on England and sought a new world in America. There he helped plan a pioneer settlement in Tennessee where grown-up Tom Browns would prove that they were not anachronisms.[32] The name of the colony was Rugby, but sadly the dream did not come true.

III Cory and Stephen: 'My brethren and my home are there'

Thomas Hughes's role in the conversion of moral manliness to hearty masculinity may have been unintentional but with William Cory and Leslie Stephen the consolidation of this new ideal was deliberate. More importantly, Hughes was a Christian of simple faith whereas both Cory and Stephen became influential agnostics of the new age. It is to Cory and Stephen, and not to Hughes, that Edward Bowen at Harrow, Edmond Warre at Eton and Henry Newbolt, the poet of imperialism, all owed their lineage.

William Cory had a pedigree similar to that of the titanic headmasters; in particular, he was an exact contemporary of Edward Thring at Eton and Cambridge.[1] He shared in their delight in Scott and Tennyson, and there was enough of a Romantic in Cory to value *Jane Eyre* greatly and to inspire him to make a pilgrimage to Charlotte Brontë's Haworth on the Yorkshire moors.[2] After gaining the prized Newcastle Scholarship at Eton in 1841, Cory went on to shine intellectually at Cambridge. He became a scholar of King's in 1842; the following year he won the Chancellor's English medal with a poem on Plato; and in 1844 he gained the Craven Scholarship. On graduation, he first thought of taking Holy Orders but, with some relief, he accepted an invitation to return to Eton. London was near enough for Cory to be involved with the Christian Socialist Movement and by 1852 he was a member of the council for the Society for Promoting Working Men's Associations.[3] Of the leaders of Christian Socialism, it was to Hughes rather than Maurice that Cory was drawn.[4] After the failure of Christian Socialism in 1854, Cory ceased to be involved with social reform and soon too his Christian faith was to evaporate.[5]

It is probably from Hughes that Cory saw the latent potential of athleticism. He was no sportsman at Eton and Cambridge, if only because of his very weak eyesight, but the mid-Victorian boost in games-playing at his old school owed much to Cory's influence. By 1860 he had instituted house matches for cricket and that year he presented a championship cup. One of his rules for the competition hinted at future developments: ordinary dress was not to be worn and all players had to wear white cricket shoes. His attentions were also felt on the river and reached their culmination in the now famous *Eton Boating Song*, written for the Fourth of June celebrations of 1863.[6]

> Jolly boating weather,
> And a hay harvest breeze,
> Blade on the feather,
> Shade off the trees,

Swing, swing together,
With your bodies between your knees,
Swing, swing together,
With your bodies between your knees.[7]

Cory was an effective and influential teacher but he also displayed a partiality for good-looking boys and a weakness for pupils from aristocratic families. He 'adored' athletes as long as they had a mind, and he thought bookish scholars 'incomplete people'.[8] Cory found a supply of his Charmides-like ideal, ready to relish his intellectual Hellenism, in the eight sporting and intelligent sons of Lord Lyttelton, one of the Public Schools Commissioners.[9] But Charmides had to be a soldier:

> His pupil-room at Eton . . . was close to the street, and the passage of the Guards through Eton, to and from their Windsor quarters, is an incident of constant occurrence. When the stately military music was heard far off, in gusty splendor, in the little town, or the pipes and drums of some detachment swept blithely past, he would throw down his pen and go down the little staircase to the road, the boys crowding round him. "Brats, the British Army!" he would say, and stand, looking and listening, his eyes filled with gathering tears, and his heart full of proud memories, while the rhythmical beat of the footsteps went briskly echoing by.[10]

He was 'a patriot to the marrow of his bones': deeds of military heroism, the sight of the Royal Navy off Spithead, and the Eton shooting VIII winning both the Ashburton Shield and the Spencer Cup at Wimbledon in 1868, these were the things most likely to thrill his heart.[11]

Cory's lasting influence beyond Eton came through his poetry; *Ionica* was published in stages between 1858 and 1877. Whether on the romance of the river and the cricket field, or on the glory of battle and the hopes of the patriot, the poems always reflected a Platonic agnosticism with never a gleam of Christian hope. His 1863 *A Retrospect of School Life* gives perhaps the fullest intimation of his philosophy:

> There courteous strivings with my peers,
> And duties not bound up in books,
> And courage fanned by stormy cheers
> And wisdom writ in pleasant looks,
> And hardship buoyed with hope, and pain
> Encountered for the common weal,
> And glories void of vulgar gain,
> Were mine to take, were mine to feel.
> And to myself in games I said,
> "What mean the books? Can I win fame?

> I would be like the faithful dead
> A fearless man, and pure of blame.
> I may have failed, my School may fail;
> I tremble, but this much I dare;
> I love her. Let the critics rail,
> My brethren and my home are there."[12]

The immense popularity of *Tom Brown's Schooldays* had inspired admiration, even adoration, of Arnold's Rugby; other public schools were quick to be associated with the collective glory; now Cory expressed through *Ionica* and the *Eton Boating Song* the sentiment that no earlier generation had felt. The cult of 'the old school' was born.

Technology encouraged its growth, especially the railway and the telegraph that ran alongside. Public-school Old Boys could communicate swiftly with each other and with their schools; reunions and sports matches against the boys were arranged at short notice; frequent trains made weekend travelling from Oxford, Cambridge and London to the schools both cheap and swift; Old-Boy cricket and football tours might fill the long university vacations; and London would play host to Old-Boys' dinners. All these exploits were lovingly recorded in school magazines.

The universities of Oxford and Cambridge followed the lead of the schools. Boys who had enjoyed sport at their public schools generally wished to continue their participation once at university; some on graduation three or four years later became the schoolmasters of the next generation, taking their love of games with them to complete the circle.[13] In this way Charles Thring (Shrewsbury and St John's), William Witts (Eton and King's) and Sam Haslam (Rugby and St John's) moved from public school to Cambridge and on to Uppingham; many more young men made similar journeys to other schools. The universities were also the cradles for the organisation of competition and the codification of rules. Distances for athletic sports and rowing races had to be agreed; numbers playing in matches at football and other team sports had to be settled; and rules for the different versions of football played at the schools had to be blended. The last, no easy task, led to the creation of two national codes: that played by the Football Association from 1863 and its rival, the Rugby Football Union, in 1871.

Until the following decade, dons at the universities who wished to marry had to relinquish their fellowships so there was a steady turn-over of young men; nearly half of all dons were in their twenties, and many were athletic.[14] Matthew Arnold complained that 'the real studies of Oxford are its games' as these men took a leading role in university sport; the Rev Leslie Stephen, an enigmatic character at Cambridge, was one.[15] Stephen could be appreciative of Kingsley's work but he loathed Maurice. The only consistent factor noted by Noel Annan in his two biographical studies was a subtle contempt for all culture and the world of ideas.[16] It is after his rejection by the Apostles that Stephen, a tutor at Trinity Hall from 1854, shunned the company of intellectuals and became the leader of the athletic set. He encouraged long-distance walking to guard against 'idleness and effeminacy' and became president of its club, the Boa Constrictors.[17] The Athletics Sports, founded in 1860, and the first University Athletics Match with Oxford in 1864, both owed their inception to Stephen.[18] He competed against Oxford too, winning the mile and the two miles in 1860, and the latter again in 1861.[19] He coached the college's rowing VIII, prizing the sport as the epitome of team spirit, and he led Trinity Hall to head of the river in 1859 and again in 1862.[20] He also formed a college militia in answer to Tennyson's call for riflemen to meet the threat of Napoleon III.[21]

Stephen became the very personification of a muscular Christian and his approval of boys being flogged at school as 'a sacred initiatory rite' and 'a sort of strange chivalry' went down well with many schoolmasters.[22] According to Annan, it is he and not Kingsley who ought to be regarded as the founder of that movement.[23] Soon, however, Stephen lost his own Christian faith; he resigned his fellowship and veered towards agnosticism.[24] Only the Spartan masculinity of the muscular Christian ideal remained.

IV Almond: 'The consecration of the body'

Sparta gained more followers at a school that revelled in Scotland's brisker climate. The *Public School Magazine* for 1902 noted that those who sought the unique in public-school education should, since Thring was now dead, no longer consider Uppingham but instead turn their attention north of the border to Almond's Loretto.[1] It is at this school, more than at any other in the second half on the nineteenth century, that the ideal of manliness became the central purpose of the educational system and its legacy was to be far-reaching, both within Scotland and further afield.

Hely Hutchinson Almond, a Scot, was a product of Glasgow University who then proceeded as Snell Exhibitioner to Balliol College, Oxford in 1850. On his return to Scotland he took a post as assistant master at Merchiston Castle near Edinburgh. Rugby football and cricket had been newly imported to Scottish schools at this time and Almond became keenly involved in their development at Merchiston. In 1862 a nearby private school came up for sale and Almond sank his funds in the venture. The development of Loretto mirrors Thring's Uppingham: on arrival Almond found twelve boys; by 1876 this had risen to eighty-eight; the 100 mark was reached two years later; and in 1882 Almond's self-imposed limit of 120 was attained.[2] Fame also brought many English staff to the school; they in turn took Almond's influence with them as they gained promotion to schools back in England. Harry McKenzie, who later became headmaster at Lancing College, Durham and then Uppingham, was one whose early teaching career included a spell under Almond.[3] Loretto's uniqueness lay in its headmaster. He created a school 'whose convention was unconventionality, and tradition independent of the past' – and, like Thring, he had at his fingertips a school ripe for experiment.[4] The foundation on which Almond built Loretto was physical education: to keep the body in the best possible condition became a point of conscience and a matter of religion.

Almond was interested in all boys, and perhaps even in the dullard more than the scholar: the training of character was his prime role. 'Loafers' and 'croakers' were never tolerated. The school was an amalgam of relaxed authority within a rigid hierarchy. There were no bolts on doors or bars on windows, no roll calls or bounds and plenty of free time. Dignity was abhorred: boys were called by their Christian names; masters went without caps and gowns; and games helped the social mixing of boys and masters so, it was claimed, their relationship was more akin to brothers than to masters and pupils.[5] Almond appointed prefects galore; boys stayed on to eighteen or nineteen to be school prefects. Seventeen-year-olds could be house prefects, heads of bedrooms, heads of school-rooms, heads of form, or heads of dining-halls.[6] Punishments allowed no 'humanitarian, softness'. Almond believed that boys 'needed' corporal punishment and that they preferred it to lines and the like that would keep them indoors. To Almond it was 'unmanly' to 'shrink from pain', and this even extended to a dislike of local anaesthetics in minor operations.[7] Corporal punishment came in two types – switching and caning. Switching was for serious offences, such as thieving, lying and bullying, and could only be administered by Almond. The more common caning could be applied by masters and prefects for petty school offences.[8]

Though H. B. Tristram, the historian of Loretto, is wrong in asserting that Almond was the 'first Headmaster who openly set himself to make the physical education of his boys part of the regular school system', the error is only one of magnitude.[9] Scholarship, music and the arts, crafts and hobbies, and even the chapel, all played minor roles when compared to physical education. His fanaticism on the subject was to match Herbert Spencer's, though he always maintained that he only came across Spencer's works much later in the century. Indeed Almond's paper on 'The Breed of Man', published in *Nineteenth Century* in 1900, could almost have been written by Spencer, so close are the affinities.[10]

The equation of life at Loretto was simple. Fresh air, personal cleanliness, careful diet, regular hours of sleep and study, physical exercise and sensible dress, combined to produce manliness.[11] The motto Almond chose for Loretto comes as no surprise – *Spartam nactus est: hanc exorna* ('You have won Sparta: adorn her') – and the school would lead the way in both physical education and health reforms. As Almond told the Royal Commission on Physical Training in Scotland:

> The laws of health are the laws of God, and we can be a great deal more certain of them than of many things about which people are a great deal more exercised. It is impossible for us to decide whether God prefers his Church on earth to be governed by bishops or presbyters, but we know

quite well that it is very bad for our health to work in a vitiated atmosphere, and anyone who does so wilfully is guilty of sin.[12]

Almond's campaign began his first year with the introduction of open-necked shirts, wide-opened windows in the dormitories at night and the rejection of suits and stiff collars. Flannel shirts, tweed shorts and the morning cold bath were introduced in 1864, soon followed by working in shirtsleeves in classrooms (1866), the banning of waistcoats (1868) and forbidding 'tuck' between meals (1869). The following years witnessed the end of school caps (1870), playing golf without coats (1871), the introduction of sensible 'anatomical' boots (1872), changing into flannels for games (1872) and the replacement of tweed by flannel for everyday wear (1874).[13] Many of the innovations may now seem commonplace but at the time they were all regarded as foolhardy. Almond in his later years extended the sartorial attack to the dress of soldiers and women; for the latter he felt that liberation from encumbering skirts, misshapen figures and deformed feet would do more than any women's rights association.[14] Almond built a small gymnasium and employed part-time staff from nearby Edinburgh to teach gymnastics. All boys were to attend for half-an-hour every day. By the 1870s Almond had appointed a resident ex-army sergeant to superintend the work.[15] In 1867 quarter-yearly bodily measurements were introduced for all boys, one of the earliest examples of such practice. With these, the physical development of each boy was traced and remedial action was taken where necessary.[16]

The playing of games was so important that Almond invented 'Loretto time', fifteen minutes ahead of Greenwich, so that more daylight was available to accommodate the two and a half hours allocated to them in the daily routine.[17] All games were 'moral agents' that helped in the formation of character, and in this respect football had the edge over cricket.[18] If it was too wet for games then cross-country runs, conducted on a basis of personal trust, were undertaken. This early version of the 'honour system', later to be developed by George Howson at Gresham's, soon became a Loretto hallmark. No matter what the weather, no matter how deep the snow, boys would still be off on their 'grinds'.[19] If games were to be moral agents, they had to be played by all, and not just by a few and watched by many. If a boy did watch a school match, he would have to take his own exercise afterwards.[20]

The athletic hero, colours, cups and competitions found no place at Loretto for Almond knew that they would bring professional attitudes to games, which in turn would lead to the watching of games rather than the playing.[21] Matches with other schools were important in that they imbued the spirit of chivalry, fairness and good temper – they tested 'the manly prowess of teams of schools'.[22] They also served as a means of advertising Almond's system. To foster both these aims, Almond inaugurated the 'Interscholastic Games' of Edinburgh in 1866, but the suspicion of other headmasters soon brought about their demise. A revived Games in 1880 fared little better.[23] Team spirit, or 'school patriotism', was induced through games. At the Interscholastic Games supporters would shout for the school and not the individual, and in Rugby football Almond developed the team play of the passing game. This latter development did not at first please the boys for they felt that the opposition would think that passing before a tackle was mere 'funking'.[24] Football was more esteemed than cricket, as here it did not matter who actually made the score, whereas in cricket the scorer's success could not be ignored.[25] Golf, the boys' favourite game on Almond's arrival, did not inspire 'school patriotism' and was soon replaced by football and cricket.[26] Almond was also an avid supporter of sportsmanship in all games. He felt that cricket was most open to lapses: here the time wasting of batsmen failing to cross after a wicket fell, and teams preferring a draw to a chance of victory, were two items singled out for attack.[27]

Success in games was a means of demonstrating the value of Arnold's system:

> As for the collective success of the School, it is natural that I should be keen. It is natural that I should desire to prove by results the soundness of the system of physical training I am trying to work out. How else but by success against larger numbers could I teach boys to believe that many things which are irksome to them at the time are tending to turn them out into the world stronger, more active, and more high-spirited men than they would otherwise be?[28]

Athletic successes indeed brought both Almond and the methods he applied at Loretto to the nation's attention. In 1873 the first Loretto boys entered Oxford; in 1878 some were in the Rugby football XV; in 1880 Loretto fielded five Oxford blues; in 1881 eight out of nine former pupils up played for the university and ultimately won blues; and in 1884 eleven of twelve were full blues at some sport, with seven playing in the Varsity Rugby football match. From this period until the end of the century there were generally three or so Old Lorettonians in the Oxford and Cambridge XVs.[29] Then in 1900, as the *Public School Magazine* reported, came 'The Triumph of Loretto': both captains had been at Loretto together.[30]

Games were vitally important to Almond:

> I would not care to face the responsibility of conducting a school were there not rooted in it as, I hope, an imperishable tradition, an enthusiastic love of football.[31]

Yet games were always a means to an end. Kipling's *The Islanders*, with the parody of the 'flannelled fool' and the 'muddied oaf', incensed him. The playing of games might now be an end in itself at English schools, but at Loretto it was only the means to a moral purpose. The professional approach to games much in evidence at the turn of the century disgusted Almond and nearly undermined faith in his own creed: 'I consider competitive "athletics" (though I thought otherwise) to be nearly as great an evil as competitive scholarship.'[32]

At John Skrine's Glenalmond, the second Anglicised public school in Scotland, the cadet corps was reckoned more important than games, but at Loretto there was no corps. Almond, like Thring, probably did not wish to subjugate his own authority to that of an outside body; in addition there was the question of dress. Almond had for many years argued against the senseless uniform then worn by soldiers, including tight collars. As David McNair suspected, if Almond had lived a few more years then Loretto would probably have supported Baden-Powell's developments in scouting.[33]

Almond's ideal of manliness combined the physical qualities of muscular Christianity with the scientific and rational spirit of the age as embodied in the philosophies of Herbert Spencer. At no time was there a trace of Platonic or Romantic influence. He preferred tangible, concrete realities to sentimental, artistic 'vapourings'; Homer's *Odyssey* was more to his taste.[34] To be manly meant to be physically able, and through physical activity the virtues of courage and temperance could be fostered and the sense of *esprit de corps* felt.[35] This was a Spartan-Christian ideal of manliness, one exemplified in Almond's sermon on 'the consecration of the body':

> It was in the spirit of the soldier, and not the monk, that Paul offered up his body as a living sacrifice to God. He . . . simply kept it in the best possible condition for the work he had to do, and then utilised it in fighting his good fight. He no more shirked pain, or disfigurement, or mutilation, or death, in fighting the battles of his Kind, than any of you would do if you found yourself with a rifle in your hands, face to face with an invader.
>
> Which of you would then reckon the speed of the runner, or the strength of the gymnast, or the honours won between the wickets and goals, or the glowing satisfaction of facing some wild storm on our bleak uplands, or the possession of healthy, hardy bodies – enabling you to enjoy life as only healthy men can do – as the supreme end of an athletic training? [. . .]
>
> Why, oh why, cannot there be a holy alliance between the athlete and the Christian – an alliance against the common enemies of both: against intemperance, and indolence, and dissipation, and effeminacy, and aesthetic voluptuousness, and heartless cynicism, and all the unnatural and demoralising elements in our social life? Why will some take so narrow a view of the true aims of physical training that they bound their horizon by the vision of prizes and athletic honours, not seeing that in themselves and by themselves these things are as worldly and worthless as unsanctified wealth, or knowledge, or literature, or art? Why will others . . . not regard sedentary habits, and softness of living, and feebleness that might have been strength, and delicacy that might have been hardihood, as physical *sins*?[36]

In many ways the *Public School Magazine* correctly traced the line from Uppingham to Loretto, for indeed Thring and Almond had much in common. Both were practising teachers rather than idealistic theorists, and for both their memorials are the schools they created. As with Thring and Uppingham, many parents sent their boys to Loretto just to be under Almond, and both headmasters shared a dislike and mistrust of examinations.[37] On the other hand, Almond's practice was much narrower than Thring's for he restricted his interest to one straightforward aim. With Thring it was character and intellect, but with Almond it was character rather than intellect: discipline, chastity, manliness and mercy were, in the view of his biographer, R. J. Mackenzie, far more important to Almond than scholarship.[38] However, Almond lived until 1903 and had to face problems that loomed in the decades either side of the new century, problems that Thring was spared by his premature death but which proved the undoing of his successor. In this respect Robert Bruce Lockhart's view that Loretto at this time was 'the cleanest and sweetest school in Britain' clearly places Almond as one of the most important headmasters in the history of the ideal of manliness, and supports Bruce Lockhart's claim that Almond was the greatest Scottish headmaster ever.[39] His legacy lived on in most of Scotland's boarding schools, at Sedbergh just over the border in the West Riding of Yorkshire and, with some modifications for a day school, at Edinburgh Academy where Mackenzie served as rector from 1889 to 1902.[40]

V Bowen: 'The tramp of twenty-two men'

'Harrow was a fine, manly place', wrote J. G. Cotton Minchin. 'There was nothing namby-pamby about Harrow boys.'[1] Such was the verdict on Harrow's manliness in 1898. The exemplar was the games player:

> Who then were the autocrats of Harrow, for our Hill was not likely to be the only spot on the world's surface without an aristocracy. This was an aristocracy of the finest cricketers and "footer" players that the School could for the time produce. No thinking man will blame us for idolising the athlete. The cricketer in his flannels was our hero, not the student immersed in his books. Can there be any question as to which is the more picturesque figure?[2]

Games at Harrow were played more gently fifty years earlier when the Hon. Frederick Ponsonby and the Hon. Robert Grimston began to help with the cricket XI.[3] The efforts of these two aristocrats, who were Old Boys of the school but not masters, soon bore fruit and gradually the playing of games began to impinge on Harrow life. By 1871 Grimston could

> claim for our cricket-ground and football field a share, and a very considerable share, too, in the formation of the character of an English gentleman. Our games require patience, good temper, perseverance, good pluck, and, above all, implicit obedience.[4]

Games became compulsory for all boys from the 1860s, they occupied as much time in the school's week as formal lessons, and absentees were caned by the monitors.[5] Spencer Gore reckoned that the 'object of every boy' was to get into the cricket XI, and the moment when he was 'given his flannels' would be 'the supreme moment of his life'.[6] The government of the boys was dominated by the athletes from 1869, the year when Montagu Butler, the Headmaster, permitted boys below the sixth-form to become monitors. Arthur Holt applauded:

> (the) brilliant cricketer and the sturdy footballer will always have authority. Make that authority constitutional and responsible, and you will at least escape a good deal of friction; while such boys, if they know that they are trusted, will often be found to exert an influence for good which does not always belong to brains.[7]

Others were not so sure, for by 1874 the rule of the 'bloods' had bred bullying and crushed individualism. Boys were made to conform to the consensual type and replicate the approved image of 'good form'. The wearing of spectacles, for example, was seen as unmanly; perversely, this prevented some boys from excelling at sport.[8]

The man who, more than anyone else at Harrow, moulded the course of this new cult of athleticism was Edward Bowen. As one of the most respected schoolmasters of the era, his influence was felt at many schools.[9] That it came from an assistant master, in an age dominated by headmasters, is remarkable and confirms the strength of his personality and his commitment to the cause. Bowen, the son of a Church of England clergyman, was born in Ireland in 1836. After schooling at Blackheath he followed the route of Frederic Farrar and Charles Kingsley to King's College, London and then Trinity College, Cambridge.[10] In 1860 he joined the common room at Harrow, remaining there until his death in 1901. When the Modern Side was created in 1869 to provide an alternative to the traditional classical curriculum, Bowen became its first Master and he only resigned that appointment in 1893 when the new headmaster, J. E. C. Welldon, began to use it as a sink for the least able boys.[11] In addition to the fame he gained through the Modern Side, Bowen was for thirty-seven years a well-respected bachelor housemaster. His influence was to be both deep and wide: his nephew and biographer had no doubts – 'As a source of moral inspiration he was scarcely second to Arnold. He had the vigour, the energy, the manly hardihood of Thring.'[12]

To his contemporaries Bowen was the walking embodiment of *mens sana in corpore sano*, a tag that suited him 'to a T'. He was always an avid walker and rambler. When an undergraduate he had walked the ninety miles from Cambridge to Oxford in less than twenty-four hours, and in later life he claimed to have walked all England's coastline and a goodly portion of the Alps.[13] At Cambridge he had been a keen footballer and there he played a small role in the formation of the Association rules. His fame at Harrow as a games-player was legendary, his enthusiasm was boundless and his caution negligible. Racquets, gymnastics, swimming and the corps were all present at Harrow in the 1860s, but they were of little account in the boys' eyes and none at all in Bowen's. They failed to inspire a sense of comradeship. Cricket and, above all else, football were second to none in 'fostering a healthy, manly, unselfish corporate life'.[14] To Bowen:

> It is not only the gain of doing in a manly way what others do, and sharing the common life, nor the health that comes to body and mind from mingled activity and sport, but on the football field the character is more revealed, for imitation or for blame, than at any other moment of the day.[15]

To enable games to do their work most effectively, Bowen believed that boys and masters should be of equal rank when on the playing-fields, and that due attention should be given to younger boys – he created teams for boys under fifteen and under sixteen, the Infants and Colts.[16] Masters were encouraged to play, indeed Bowen was still playing football until shortly before his death at the age of sixty-five, but they should take no part in the organisation or coaching. This attitude had the benefit of keeping professional attitudes at bay but, in passing all authority to senior boys, the masters effectively sanctified the rule of the bloods.[17] The dominance of games in the life of boys and many masters also retarded the intellectual and social development of both. Talk of games rather than intellectual pursuits was the staple of school conversation, school-work was seen as of secondary value, boys were kept as boys when they should have been becoming men, and the worship of the athlete slipped easily to the aesthetic delight in the beautiful body. Bowen may not have wished for what followed in later years, but his over-riding commitment to athleticism paved the way.[18]

Manliness was an ideal ever present in Bowen's personal influence as a housemaster: 'Stoicism and honour were the qualities it was mainly directed to form. Every boy was expected to show manliness and endurance, and to utter no complaint.'[19] The regime that he created was decidedly Spartan. Bowen adopted Christian codes and principles but he was an infrequent presence in chapel. Christianity did not contribute to his ideal of manliness and boys in his house could opt out of confirmation classes. Sparta was the model set before the boys. Bowen scorned luxury both for himself and for his boys; the house rule proclaimed that plain living was virtuous and luxury evil. Fresh air, vigour, hardihood and physical strain were preferable to armchairs, hot baths, early fires and daintily furnished studies. A pupil related to James Bryce that when Bowen learnt he was in the habit of taking two hot baths a week, the transgression was reproved with the words: 'Oh boy, that's like the later Romans, boy.'[20]

Bowen is best remembered today for his words to *Forty Years On*, that anthem for Harrovians. John Farmer, who joined the Harrow staff as music master in 1862, forged a memorable partnership with Bowen that produced over thirty

songs, mainly on games.[21] *Forty Years On* cemented love of the old school to
the cult of games, Harrow football in particular:

> Forty years on, when afar and asunder
> Parted are those who are singing today,
> When you look back, and forgetfully wonder
> What you were like in your work and your play,
> Then, it may be, there will often come o'er you,
> Glimpses of notes like the catch of a song –
> Visions of boyhood shall float them before you,
> Echoes of dreamland shall bear them along,
> *Follow up! Follow up! Follow up*
> *Follow up! Follow up*
> *Till the field ring again and again,*
> *With the tramp of the twenty-two men.*
> *Follow up! Follow up!*[22]

E. B. Castle, in his *Moral Education in Christian Times*, argued that Bowen
had no illusions about athleticism.[23] Certainly the superficial frivolity of his
essay on 'Games', published in the *Journal of Education* in 1884, lends support
to Castle's view. Here games are extolled for their aesthetic pleasure, male
companionship, and general social influence for good. There are even some
passing shots at the over-zealous games master. However, underlying that
frivolity is the thesis that games are the most important and most valuable of
all factors in the educational process. Games induced respect for command,
obedience, dignity and courtesy; in addition they corrected 'laziness, foppery
and man-of-the-worldness'. Bowen had no doubt that 'the best boys are, on
the whole, the players of games'.[24] If he had no illusions about athleticism, he
certainly did little to stem its tide, and the hero-worship epitomised by Cotton
Minchin's encomium was sympathetically received in Bowen's ear. Bowen's
philosophy was Spartanism, for the muscularity of muscular Christianity
had smothered the Christian foundations. 'There lies more soul in honest
play, believe me', wrote Bowen, 'than in half the hymn-books.' His favourite
maxim was 'Always play the game.'[25]

VI Games mania:
'A coloured cap was worth more than any prize'

E. C. Mack, the distinguished American historian of British public schools, saw
the years between 1870 and 1890 witnessing 'the greatest upsurge of passionate
adoration to which the schools had ever been subjected'. Much of the adoration
was centred on games:

> The passion for games, checked somewhat in the sixties, blossomed
> more fully under the influence of the increased competitive spirit of the

age, encouragement by the new plutocracy, and the more widespread interest in imperialism, until it assumed proportions undreamed of in the sixties.[1]

Inter-school matches steadily increased from the 1860s and school magazines logged the records of their rivals as well as their own. In 1875 the *Public School Magazine* was founded to distribute news of public-school sport and to raise 'a spirit of healthful rivalry between young Athletes of our several Schools': Uppingham was noticeably omitted from the first issue.[2] When *The Public Schools Year Book* was published in the following decade, nearly a third of it was given over to games at the various schools.[3]

The 1870s saw 'the height of the craze for games'. They were now commonly compulsory on three days a week; a youngster asked in *The Cliftonian* – 'I want to know why everything here is compulsory. I like football well enough, but when I am forced to play whether I feel inclined to or no it is not pleasant.'[4] Inter-school matches gained considerable status and large crowds would go to Lord's in London on the day of a public-school match. In the 1850s the Eton and Harrow match there attracted hardly any spectators; by 1864 it was necessary to rope off the playing area; in 1880 the match became so important that it affected the duration of the London social season.[5] The same period saw the large-scale publication of books on sport, including the renowned *Badminton Library*, and the expansion of the communication media. Edward Lyttelton, formerly a member of William Cory's coterie at Eton and now an assistant master at Wellington, observed:

> Nowadays, the (Boat Race) crowd assembled to see the practice of the crews equals the number of those who used to watch the actual race; moreover, the minutest facts connected with the play of each oarsman's muscles are anxiously picked up on the spot, form a paragraph in the daily papers, and are telegraphed to the Antipodes.[6]

Games were now generally accepted for their moral training. Clement Dukes was the school doctor at Rugby; in his view they taught self-reliance and self-control. Games also kept sexual temptations at bay for they taught a boy to respect his own body as 'the casket of his soul' and, as such, 'the thought even of defilement will not enter his mind, or if it enter will be indignantly repelled'. The morning cold bath, now the attendant of compulsory games, was advocated for the same reasons:

> the hot bath at bedtime, so commonly resorted to compulsorily, and so strongly advocated by many, is capable of serious harm to many a boy by suggesting ideas and feelings which lead to practices that otherwise might never have been originated.'[7]

Together games and the cold bath would produce a manliness with 'the utter absence of effeminacy.'[8]

It was not necessary for games to be played well or skilfully for the moral effects to be experienced: the knocks and bruises, bumped balls and dropped catches would nonetheless still come. This was one of the reasons why both Edward Thring and Edward Bowen opposed coaching by masters. The Public Schools Commissioners in the 1860s had suspected that the attentions of games masters and professional coaches would soon turn games into a 'science', and by the 1880s this was the case. The athletic means to a moral end were becoming the end.[9] In addition, the 'deification of success' and the 'worship of the athlete' brought problems in their wake, for the effects of games lasted far beyond the hours of play. Boys day-dreaming of their matches damaged the intellectual interests of the school, and the athletic hero and his worshippers seriously undermined the prefectorial system of government. Many schools now followed Harrow's example, choosing their prefects from the games-players rather than from the scholars. At Rugby, where the games-player did not officially rule, the bloods began to do so unofficially as the prefectorial system started to decay.[10]

To counteract this damaging individualistic trend, but to keep the important moral advantages of games, *esprit de corps* was raised as the supporting creed. Thomas Hughes in 1857 had suggested the alliance of team games and *esprit de corps* in *Tom Brown's Schooldays;* Leslie Stephen, William Cory and Edward Bowen in the 1860s and 1870s had claimed it as the new secular manliness; now in the 1880s this ideal received general acclaim. Edward Lyttelton was one spokesman:

> A boy is disciplined (by games) in two ways: by being forced to put the welfare of the common cause before selfish interests, to obey implicitly the word of command, and act in concert with the heterogeneous demands of the company he belongs to; and secondly, should it so turn out, he is disciplined by being raised to a post of command, where he feels the gravity of responsible office and the difficulty of making prompt decisions and securing a willing obedience.[11]

Now team spirit and training in leadership were added to the manly qualities instilled by games. The change involved other increases in the regimentation of school life: bounds and regulations proliferated; more time was given to studies and games and less to leisure; the freedom that every early Victorian headmaster thought vital, for personal recreation or to roam the countryside, was abolished.[12]

Great Public Schools was published in 1893 with portraits of the nine Clarendon schools, with the addition of Clifton, Marlborough and Haileybury. Uppingham is again conspicuous by its absence. Long chapters dealt with the games at Eton,

Harrow and Rugby, lovingly describing the dress, the colours, the rituals, and the language. The Rugby chapter by Lees Knowles now seems particularly asinine.[13] This period saw Rugby's brand of football revered as 'the most manly game on earth' and it was claimed that 'no Etonian worthy of the name fails to carry the memory of the Eton Playing-Fields with him to his grave'.[14] At Marlborough, games were compulsory daily, a practice that prevented 'loafing' and enabled the housemasters to know exactly where every boy was every minute of the day.[15] At humbler schools it was the same story: when Frederick Sanderson went to Oundle as headmaster in 1892, he found 'little except that vague hunted gregariousness known as *esprit de corps*, cricketing sentiment, and a gentlemanly habit of mind'.[16]

Games now played an enormous part in the life of a public-school boy, and to many the chief ambition on entering the school was to distinguish himself at games. Boys felt that 'the swiftest and surest way to eminence is through athletics'. The most prominent games-player was in practice head of school and his position was 'more absolute than the Pope's'. The veneration with which boys regarded their heroes was such that George Lyttelton, nephew of the brothers, could write:

> (the) body of the school are far more interested in the prowess of the school eleven than in playing the game themselves. For days before the principal school match, excitement is at fever heat; during the match itself all other games are left off, the whole school assemble round the protagonists to yell themselves hoarse with delight or dismay, and the excitement takes some time to settle down.[17]

Manliness for many was now acquired second-hand and by association.

The games master was both a product of the system and a prime factor in its continuance. The legend that a cricket blue, on completing his century in the Varsity match at Lord's, received five telegrams from headmasters offering him posts, may not have been true, but it was believable. H. J. Spenser pictured such a master as healthy, selfish, philistine and generally slack. He had neither professional zeal nor dignity and, as the attraction of schoolmastering faded, he invariably took Holy Orders and escaped to the Church.[18] Parents too not only supported the games ethos and lobbied headmasters for more matches and London tours, but they also worshipped the games-player.[19] A. H. Gilkes, the headmaster of Dulwich College, was once introduced to a great English bishop with − '"He is the father of P. T. S. − ", naming a youth well-known for his powers of cutting'. Gilkes also recalled dining with a parent

> who after dinner said to me, with some feeling in his tone, that he had that day taken his son for the first time to −, naming a great school, and that he had taken the opportunity given him by the parting to offer the boy the best advice in his power. I said that the occasion was well chosen . . . for

then his heart was soft and open, and thus he would receive and remember what was said. The father agreed with me, and said that the advice which he had given his boy was to take up bowling rather than batting as likely really to be of more service to him.[20]

Parents, staff and boys were agreed that games were a vital and central feature of school life. Further support was gained from A. F. L. Smith's examination of continental educational systems:

one cannot help noticing the contrasts afforded by the attempts made by France in the direction of a system of education more democratic in its scope and more purely intellectual in its aims. Its results are hardly such as an Englishman would be likely to appreciate. The absence of athletics inevitably involves more work, and more work generally means too much work. The nerves cannot stand the strain, and the result is an abnormal development of the morbid side of the character.[21]

E. C. Mack's conclusion is apt: 'the religion of athletics seems the perfect expression of a Philistine age.'[22]

With the general raising of the age of entry into public schools to thirteen, the later Victorian years saw the formation and expansion of preparatory schools as feeders to the public schools. These schools, with boys aged from eight to thirteen, diffused the public-school ethos to their charges. The curriculum, attitudes and morality were all those of the public schools. Religion to J. H. Simpson, who was at prep school in the 1890s, merely became a 'divine sanction' for an ethical code of 'dutiful, upright, sensible, industrious, reasonably well-to-do, upper middle-class Englishmen; in particular a sanction for honesty, patriotism, loyalty to one's school and order, and for a rather negative conception of purity'. The games and drill of public schools were wholly adopted, and no time was given to activities more suitable to the age group, such as creative movement or dance, for 'grace would have been suspect as unmanly'. Simpson and his contemporaries were encouraged to admire the outstanding games-player, and their heroes were the men of action, especially the soldier, sailor and explorer, whereas it was scarcely suggested that the world owed anything to artists, scientists and statesmen.[23]

The increase of the athletic ethos in the public and preparatory schools in the 1880s and 1890s took place against a growing national obsession for competitive sport. The public-school boys of the 1860s had taken their love of games with them to their urban parishes and northern factories and mills, and there they were instrumental in the formation of football and cricket clubs for their parishioners and workers. Most of these football clubs played the Association code, and during the 1880s the game drifted away from accepted public-school values and adopted working-men's ones instead. Professional players had now appeared. In 1883 the Old Etonians surrendered the Football Association Cup to Blackburn Rovers, and no public-school side ever again reached the final. A passion for league football developed, especially in the industrial towns of the north of England, and even Members of Parliament and the aristocracy were drawn into 'The New Football Mania'.[24] Professionalism in the game brought betting and corruption in its wake and the crowds and cup-tie atmosphere began to impinge on the public-school world. Soon gentlemen were to feel that they could only play football against other gentlemen to avoid the 'risk of plunging into the moral slough'.[25] Schools that played the Rugby code felt aloof from such contamination but some of the Association schools found the alliance embarrassing and actually changed codes.

The developments in cricket were not so traumatic, but here bigger crowds and more ardent support demanded outcomes that satisfied supporters, thus the object of the first-class game became the avoidance of defeat rather than striving for victory.[26] Three articles published in the *National Review* between 1898 and 1903 indicate how deep was the worry over the game. Reforms were advocated to increase scoring, stop time-wasting and prevent drawn games.[27] Of the traditional public-school games only rowing seemed to escape the tarnish of professionalism for the sport was not conducive to large crowds and so did not draw the all-powerful gate-money.[28] Track and field athletics did attract a large following, with over 6,000 at the inaugural meeting at Stamford Bridge in April 1877. The officers of London AC, the world's oldest athletics club, struggled over the succeeding years to cope with rigging of handicaps to gain unfair advantage, over-enthusiastic pot-hunting by ungentlemanly contestants, professional 'pedestrians' infiltrating all-amateur competitions, and bookmakers and gamblers fixing the outcome of races.[29] Gentlemen amateurs planned to maintain the public-school spirit of athletics in an 'Anglo-Saxon Olympiad' as part of an 1892 English-speaking festival, but they never materialised.[30] Baron de Coubertin's revived Olympic Games of 1896, however, did catch the imagination of others, and there they were pleased to see that the 'Anglo-Saxons' defeated foreigners in almost every event. Anglo-Saxon, it should be noted, included men from the British Dominions, the Unites States and Germany, with the Americans winning the bulk of the prizes.[31]

Games were now part of the culture for both the gentleman and the working-man. Special papers were published for the separate sports; the respected reviews contained summaries of the sporting seasons; and most men and boys immediately turned to the sports pages of their newspapers.[32] A cult of participation was becoming a cult of the spectator.[33] Sport even began to displace other news on the front page, as A. C. Benson noted:

> It is apt to disconcert the philosophical mind to find a leading evening paper displacing the war news (1900) for a column, introduced by prodigious headlines, recording the performance of an English team of cricketers in Australia.[34]

Against this background the defenders and opponents of games-playing in the public schools volleyed at one another in the national journals. Games were supported for their disciplinary role – games' fagging was a useful punishment and it prevented loafing and visits to the pastry-cook – and for their moral training.[35] E. M. Oakley agreed:

> It is almost unnecessary to remark that the system of compulsory games is in full swing at Clifton, to the enormous benefit of all, especially of the physically indolent and the morally soft, and certainly too in most cases of those precious tender plants, the boys of precocious intellect, who in the old dispensation used to be seen "on half-holidays walking round and round the school-close, arm-in-arm, discussing their mutual confidences, whilst the games went on".[36]

Hero-worship was also seen as being perfectly healthy and normal: 'Bodily prowess is to boys the most tangible and visible form of success, and, as such, will always be admired and emulated.'[37] Besides, such qualities made England great: 'The sportsman continually precedes the trader in new countries; and the trader the statesman. These qualities can be developed on our playing-fields.'[38] The interval of more than a decade had expanded Clement Dukes's list of qualities that games cultivated. They now generated not only a well-balanced mind and character but also instilled glowing spirits, quick obedience, good temper, fair play, self-reliance, endurance, confidence in comrades, ambition, quick judgement, unselfishness, courage and self-control. Games and the cold bath provided the best antidote to vice. Through manly games 'the foolish effeminacy' that might make a boy's study 'like a lady's boudoir' was avoided and the 'unmanly precocity of self-indulgence' was discouraged.[39] Many would have agreed with J. G. Cotton Minchin 'that the more athletics flourish in our public schools, the less vice will be found in them'.[40]

The opponents of the athletic ethos were in general not opposed to the games themselves, but rather to their excessive domination of school life and their acceptance as a cult. The writer of 'Old Eton and Modern Public Schools' in the *Edinburgh Review* of April 1897 was typical. He hoped that the day was far distant when a parliament was to be without cricketers, sportsmen and farmers, but the 'glorification of athletics' had gone too far when 'the attractions of the Eight and the Eleven are enormously exaggerated in boys' minds'.[41] The 'tyranny', 'idolatry' and 'superstition' of athletics were regularly exposed. Lessons were missed for matches and the intense pre-occupation in athletic matters destroyed the boys' interest in their work.[42] As the premier school match of each term drew near, so fewer boys played games and more began to watch. Several critics asked:

> How does it help the health of the school to have some few boys in violent exercise while several hundred lounge about and eat cherries, as the only occupation of the day?[43]

Pleas to cut down the number of matches, to prevent boys missing classes to play in them, and to ban the newspaper reporting of the contests, all went unheard. The oft-repeated call to bring in other leisure activities such as photography and natural history to redress the balance, or even to soften the games through the introduction of tennis or golf, were never heeded.[44]

The philosophy that enabled the supporters of games in the public schools to dominate the argument was the insistence that games inspired *esprit de corps*. It has already been shown how this ideal was first acclaimed in the 1880s; now in the closing years of the century its power went almost unchallenged and its virtues were universally applauded. Arthur Ponsonby, in *The Decline of the Aristocracy*, asked the reader to compare public-school team photographs of the 1850s and the 1900s. In the former the random grouping and the variety of hairstyle and dress suggest the carefree atmosphere of the period, whereas in the latter the sitters are precisely placed in stereotyped poses, and the dress and even the expressions look alike.[45] This is the projected image of *esprit de corps*, an ideal based on belonging to a group, the concealment of all emotions, and the 'stiff upper lip', and it was this that was extolled as the new manliness. Inasmuch as it made the least member of the school share identity with the cleverest boys gaining scholarships at Oxford and Cambridge and the athletic heroes winning school matches, it had its good points; but in the sublimation of the individual to the group norm, the fear of 'bad form', and the moulding of personality to the dominant types, the effect was stultifying. As games were chosen as the prime medium for inducing *esprit de corps*, it thus became natural for the talented games-players to be regarded as the exemplars. Thus, the reign of the 'blood' and the 'hearty' began in earnest. Even when the effect of this reign was seen in the undermining of discipline and the lowering of morality, the earlier reasons for encouraging athleticism, the ideal of *esprit de corps* remained intact. Such was its all-enveloping ethos.

If games were to inculcate *esprit de corps*, then they had to be planned accordingly. Individual activities such as tennis, gymnastics and golf would have no part.[46] Hockey, in these early days of play on football pitches, was hard to make a truly team game, so it too was regarded as effeminate and fit only for malingerers, or perhaps it was valuable 'just for a change'.[47] Cricket can hardly be described as a team game in the *esprit de corps* sense but its position in the public schools was long-standing and beyond reproach. It was thus left to football and rowing to produce the ideal. Rowing, as Leslie Stephen had proclaimed in the 1860s, was the perfect sport, with success dependent on the individual acting in concert with his fellows, but not all schools had the good fortune to stand beside suitable rivers. The status of Association football had dropped due to the professionalism in the game, though some of the oldest schools still fervently maintained the code, and it was thus seen to require less 'speed, endurance, courage or chivalry than its rival'. At most schools therefore, the mantle of *esprit de corps* fell on Rugby football. In the 1860s the aim of the individual player in the game, and in the numerous school versions of both football and hockey, had been to take the ball as far up-field as possible. Only when he was tackled did he try to pass the ball to a team-mate, and then he too would plough forward. It will be recalled that boys at Loretto were unhappy when Almond suggested that they should pass the ball before the tackle was made, for that would be both sharp practice and unmanly behaviour. Oxford teams developed 'the passing game' in the early 1880s and with it successfully defeated Cambridge for a number of years. This tactic was soon in use at schools.[48] As a true team game in which the success could depend on the weakest player and where much of the best work was done out of sight, and thus unsung, in the scrum, Rugby football was universally extolled for the inculcation of *esprit de corps*. Individual success in games might affect the character in undesirable ways but it could not happen in Rugby football.[49]

The house system common at most public schools was found to be almost purpose-made for *esprit de corps*. Now not only could a boy offer loyalty to his school, but a second and much narrower and more enforceable loyalty could also be given to his house.[50] This house spirit was almost wholly concerned with games and especially Rugby football. Housemasters commonly encouraged it, whilst at Marlborough their desire for victory in house matches was often seen to overpower all reason.[51] A spirit of 'sportsmanship' and a love of 'good form' were two happier side effects of *esprit de corps*. Clifton was renowned in the 1890s as 'the only school in England' that applauded its opponents when they played well as much as they cheered their own side.[52]

This then was *esprit de corps*, and games were the medium of its education. Throughout the late-Victorian years the standing of the ideal was unchallenged, and even foreigners as eminent as Baron de Coubertin, the founder of the modern Olympic Games, came to see it as the formula behind England's greatness.[53]

VII   Mitchell and Warre:
'A tyranny of athletics and an idolatry of athletes'

Eton was special. A thousand strong in the 1890s, it was twice the size of Butler's Harrow, three times larger than Thring's Uppingham, and it dwarfed the 120 at Almond's Loretto. Eton had long regarded itself as Britain's premier school, and with much justification; the royal foundation and strong aristocratic connections played their part.[1] One consequence of its size and prestige was the high number, rich quality, independent wealth and diverse opinions of its housemasters and assistant masters; educational fads and fashions might assault the masters' common room but never would they carry all before them. The reaction to the cult of athleticism proved no exception, for in the period between 1860 and 1900 Eton numbered amongst its masters not only the leading protagonists of the athletic movement but also some of its most articulate opponents. Their battle within the confines of the school echoed the struggle at large in the rest of the country.

By 1864, the year when the Public Schools Commission reported, games were well established at Eton. G. R. Dupuis, the son of the school's Vice-Provost, had been coaching cricket there since 1858, and by the time of the commissioners' visit the game's importance was enormous. They noted:

> The cult of cricket playing has now reached a pitch of perfection which demands of those who are ambitious of success in it, professional instruction and long and constant practice. Five hours a day, at least on half holidays (or twice a week), and two hours at least on the whole school days are considered by the boys necessary to get into the Eleven.[2]

R. A. H. Mitchell joined the school two years later and, with Dupuis, brought Eton cricket to a high plateau of success that was to last until his retirement in 1901. Harrow had stolen a march in the pursuit of athletic manliness, winning all but two of the matches at Lord's in the period 1850 to 1869, but now Mitchell would restore the balance.[3] His cricketing pedigree was faultless: he had played with distinction in the Eton XI for four years, captaining it in 1861, and the brilliance continued at Balliol where he was a four-year blue and captain of the side in all but his first year.

Back at Eton, Mitchell imposed his own style of play throughout the school, and he began directing school matches from the boundary. Matches at Lord's against Harrow gained such importance that Mitchell was not averse to spying on the opposition in the weeks before the game, nor to providing the opening batsmen with Dutch courage during the actual contests.[4] Mitchell's appointment, rather than Bowen's, set a trend that most schools would soon follow. Gilbert Coleridge recalled that 'He did not impress us in school as a profound scholar', but added that he was very popular with the boys – and known as Mike.[5] Mitchell was the first of the 'games masters', Oxford and Cambridge blues or those who had played sport for their country, who were appointed to the teaching staff of public schools primarily to coach games. Certainly Etonians knew which of studies or games ranked higher in Mike's eyes: 'Never talk to Mr. Mitchell on extraneous subjects, such as a General Election, during the progress of a Public School match when Eton is playing.'[6]

The developments in other school games matched those of cricket. Football, with the Wall and Field games peculiar to Eton, was purely an internal game and so it did not rank as highly as cricket. Rowing, as the Public Schools Commissioners found, did: 'The Captain of the Boats is the greatest man in the school, and next to him ranks the Captain of the Eleven.'[7] Competition on the river not only taught neatness of wrist, a sense of rhythm, acute feeling for balance, subtle variation of power, judgement, pluck and gallant effort to a stroke's command, but also gave 'the glorious sense of brotherhood which animates a crew in their united struggle for a common end, the unselfishness of the result, and, above all, the long, hard weeks of hopeful training. Good for the body and good for the soul'.[8]

The man behind the developments in rowing was another Old Etonian, Edmond Warre. Also a Balliol man, Warre returned to Eton in 1860. Poor eyesight had prevented his participation in ball games, so it was to the river that Warre had turned for sport. In his final year he was president of the University Boat Club, and on arrival at Eton he immediately took the rowing VIIIs into his charge.[9] Like Mitchell, Warre was not regarded by the boys as an inspiring teacher but, as the best rowing coach in England, his position in the school was supreme. Two decades later, and to the surprise of many, Warre succeeded James Hornby as headmaster. A critical letter in *The Times* greeted the news with dismay: he lacked scholarship, he was a poor preacher, he had written nothing of note, but he was known throughout England as an expert rowing coach and an able field officer in the cadet corps.[10] Even in his dress of straw hat, striped blazer and flannels, the sportsman generally overcame the don, and only when a lesson could be twisted towards Odysseus and the raft or the construction of an Athenian galley would Warre teach enthusiastically.[11] Athleticism flourished as Warre imposed an ideal of manliness that was boyish in conception: he was, in Percy Lubbock's view, a great schoolboy wanting to produce everlasting schoolboys.[12] E. C. Mack's assessment of his twenty-one-year reign at Eton was spot on: 'he was eminently fitted to create a model school for turning out athletic philistines, and that was, indeed, exactly the sort of school that he developed so effectively.'[13]

The schoolmaster critics ranged against the 'athletic philistines' were numerous but, with Warre as headmaster, their efforts were generally non-availing. The Spartans had been in the ascendant even before Warre's elevation. His predecessor, the keen cricketer Hornby, had dismissed Oscar Browning for his loud opposition to games whilst W. E. Jelf had complained in the 1860s that for nine-tenths of Etonians it was 'all play and no work' and that 'amusement is essence, work the accident, of daily life'.[14]

> When the muscular theory places the duty and perfection of man in athletic excellence, it is perhaps no wonder if the Eton boy follows suit, and embraces heartily the notion that amusement is as much his duty as work.[15]

Ralph Nevill of the Warre years agreed: 'An entire absorption in games to the exclusion of practically all other interests cannot be called a healthy feature of education.'[16] Lionel Ford complained that the 'tyranny of athletics and an idolatry of athletes' seriously undermined the role of games as character trainers.[17]

The most reasoned and articulate case against the cult of athletics was presented by A. C. Benson, the son of the former headmaster of Wellington. Benson was a senior housemaster throughout Warre's headmastership and in those two decades he witnessed the full onslaught of athleticism. That the dulling effects of the cult were eventually modified owed much to his well-publicised efforts. Benson was himself physically active and a member of the Alpine Club, but it saddened him that schoolmasters could

> send out from our public schools year after year many boys who hate knowledge and think books dreary, who are perfectly self-satisfied and entirely ignorant, and, what is more, not ignorant in a wholesome and humble manner, but arrogantly and contemptuously ignorant – not only satisfied to be so, but thinking it almost unmanly that a young man should be anything else.[18]

Manliness had become philistinism. Intellectual aims were low and schoolmasters sought merely to make boys morally good and physically healthy. In three books – *The Schoolmaster, The Upton Letters* and *From a College Window* – and in articles in the *National Review*, Benson wrote of the autocracy of games. Many schoolmasters were games players, for the presence of a blue on the staff gave parents confidence and provided an excellent advertisement, but these men, with their 'sense of complacent superiority, and a hardly disguised contempt for the people who do not play', supported athleticism to the detriment of the rest of school life.[19] Boys could

> find plenty of masters who are just as serious about games as they are themselves; who spend all their spare time in looking on at games, and discuss the athletic prospects of particular boys in a tone of perfectly unaffected seriousness.[20]

Parents were little better: 'For one parent who said anything about a boy's intellectual interests, there were ten whose preoccupation in the boy's athletics was deep and vital.'[21]

> It may safely be alleged that a very large percentage of parents of Eton boys would make no secret of the fact that they would rather that their boy was in the Eleven or the Eight than obtain any number of school prizes.[22]

To Benson the result was 'a pedantry, a priggishness, a solemnity about games which is simply deplorable' – the whole thing was 'distorted and out of proportion'.[23]

Benson agreed that games were a healthful occupation and that they could confer on boys certain manly qualities. They could also inspire serenity under defeat and sacrifice of self to the interests of the side, but this was not always the case.

> I once asked a good many boys to tell me candidly whether they would prefer to gain great distinction in a match and have their side beaten, or

that their side should win, but that they themselves should be discredited; and I can only say that very few indeed chose the latter alternative.

Benson also questioned the theory that games were valuable from a moral standpoint, and that they kept physical temptations at bay: here he believed the adoration of the athlete presented even greater sensual temptations.[24]

The danger of athleticism in Benson's view was that activities meant for recreation were taken far too seriously. Success in games became ardently desired and was identified with success in life. The pressure on boys was considerable: some would suffer in health and have sleepless nights when their game went off, and were deeply relieved when rain gave them a day free from the burden of anxiety. Benson's remedy was very Thringian: the importance of games should be diminished and other activities given equal opportunity for development. Masters should ensure that every boy had something he could do well.

> What I desire with all my heart to see is an increase of the intellectual spirit, a larger share of generous admiration for all effort, a true view of the end of physical prowess, and a stronger, healthier, more manly tone of morals; more simplicity, less conventionality; a bigger conception of duty, a larger view of patriotism.[25]

These could have been Thring's very words.

VIII Uppingham-by-the-Sea:
'Playgrounds – leagues on leagues of shore'

Uppingham was not immune to the mania for games. John Skrine had been a boy at the school from 1861 to 1867, serving as captain of school and playing in the football XV for his last two years. Six years later, after graduating from Merton College, Oxford and taking Holy Orders, he returned to the school as a master. He noticed that Uppingham had changed in the intervening years; it was larger, more prosperous, better provided and more confident. But, in Skrine's eyes, all was not well: 'Prosperity is the trial time of ideals, and it was so for ours.' The boys were no longer proud of the school's distinctiveness and a spirit of conventionalism was evident; the title 'Uppingham Grammar-School' had fallen out of favour and now the words 'public school' were in common usage. Discipline was less than perfect and the standard of morality lower. Along with this relaxation of the school's character went some weakening of Thring's own magnetism. Skrine's Oxford years had seen Thring fighting for the economic and political survival of the school as it faced the Schools Inquiry Commissioners, and he had devoted much time and energy to its agency of response, the Headmasters' Conference. With his attention drawn to external matters, changes occurred at the school without his real attention.[1]

Mention has already been made that Thring, in his tenth year at the school, had begun to delegate more responsibility to senior boys. Now, on the command of the captains of games, football and cricket were played daily in their seasons with compulsion operating once a week. Three separate playing-fields had been acquired, one each for the Upper, Middle and Lower hundreds. Colours were awarded to the heroes of the cricket XI and the football XV, a scarf or band being tied around the recipient's waist, and the committee of games gained hunting crops – to serve as a badge of office and to control spectators at matches.[2]

Calls to conform to the sporting culture found at other public schools increased in regularity and volume: gymnastics came under renewed scrutiny; boxing was introduced but did not last long; hockey was dropped altogether; fives lost its place in the house championships; and there were calls for a 'Rifle Corps'. The athletics sports remained in favour and the number of events increased to twenty, each with its own prizes.[3] Football transferred to a new field to the south of the town in 1864. The members of the XV had their names recorded for posterity on honours boards and shirkers were condemned; these were the 'unfortunate few, who cannot, and a contemptible few, who will not join the game'. The former were the sick; the latter the lazy, the swells, the gluttons and the funks. Charles Thring wanted Uppingham to join the new Football Association but his brother withdrew the application. That Uppingham still maintained its own code meant that no 'foreign' matches could be played, so it was left to Old Boys to challenge the school: the first match was played in February 1865. The boys won comfortably against a very scratch side, a pattern that was to continue until March 1868 when the Uppingham Football Club was founded at Cambridge, with branches in Oxford and London.[4]

C. E. Green was the Uppingham cricket captain who had issued the challenge to Rugby in 1863. Two years later, and now at Cambridge, he had bowled out Rugby's XI for twenty-eight runs. Thring was delighted:

> He was the captain they sent the insolent message to, offering to send a house eleven to play us. This has stuck in his mind ever since, and now he has wiped it off.[5]

Rugby, a Clarendon school, had not considered Uppingham a public school; now Uppingham dismissed the schools at Oakham and Oundle on the same grounds, preferring instead to play Rossall and Repton – undoubted public schools but neither, like Uppingham, of long-standing.[6] Green had also persuaded Thring to allow the boys to hire a cricket professional for a few weeks at the beginning of each season on alternate years, the first in 1864. William Earle's connection with the Essex club brought well-known coaches to the school – Fred Silcock, Roger Iddison and Edgar Wilsher twice – and they laid the foundations of Uppingham's subsequent fame.[7] Earle resigned his place in the XI in 1864 – Thring had withdrawn a few years before – and no master ever again played in it.[8] With these innovations and despite Thring's best intentions, cricket was becoming a 'science': statistics on matches were logged in the school magazine; boys were encouraged to review their summer's play during the winter months; a new ground just for cricket was rented to the east of the town; and the names of the XIs were recorded on panels in the newly-built pavilion.[9]

Charles Green's ambitions for cricket at his old school were far from exhausted. In the autumn of 1863, when still at school, he and two friends founded the Uppingham Rovers; only Aldenham School and Eton established Old Boys' cricket clubs earlier. At first all who had played in the XI were eligible for membership but within a year it became an exclusive club with one vote in twelve keeping out the unwanted.[10] The status of the game was increasing at the school too: members of the XI gained silk scarves that were worn about the school and not just on the cricket field; they usurped privileges formerly limited to praepostors; and, in an era of formal surnames, they went by their Christian names amongst their peers. In 1868 the whole school watched the two days of the XI's match against the Old Boys, and witnessed with increasing excitement the first win for the school.[11]

Green and fellow Old Uppinghamians up at Oxford and Cambridge were determined that their school should be placed alongside the great Clarendon schools, and they saw that the quickest and surest way to achieve this aim would be for the school to win national renown as a nursery of cricketers. They used their wealth, persuasive powers and school connections to bring this about. Expenditure on games rose from £192 in 1863 to £500 in 1873; a school shop selling sporting goods was established to raise other funds; and publicity was generated when the results of school matches in cricket and football were reported nationally in *The Field*, *The Sportsman* and *The Football Annual*. The consummation of Green's efforts was achieved in April 1872 when he persuaded Thring to allow him to pay the wages for a resident cricket professional for the whole of the season.[12] Green, either innocently or deliberately, knew how to flatter the headmaster – as a conversation recorded in Thring's diary later that year illustrates:

> I do not know that I ever in my life heard anything more inspiriting and touching than C. E. Green's statements in talking with me before this, "that the stupidest boy who went out of Uppingham knew and felt he had a mission in life" and much more to the same purpose. It is a glorious work of the Spirit of the living God when this living feeling of true life catches fast hold of men like him, – a feeling, a life, not a knowledge, power, or a school of thought, but a spirit of holy effort. Thank God for it.[13]

Green's 'mission in life' was cricket and he had already earmarked H. H. Stephenson as the man best fitted to bring cricketing glory to the school. They had met and talked during the match at Rossall in 1863 when Green was captaining the Uppingham XI and Stephenson was the Rossall professional. Now he had caught his man. Stephenson began work on 15 April and immediately offered to present a prize bat to the boy who gained the highest batting average in school matches. The bat would have come from his sports shop, one minute's walk from the school-room and chapel, and a favourite place for boys to mingle, examine memorabilia and photographs, and talk cricket. Stephenson had plenty to tell: in 1858 he took three wickets with three consecutive deliveries, the first recorded hat-trick; he was a member of the first English team to tour abroad, in 1859 to the Unites States and Canada; and in 1861 he led a party of twelve English professionals to Australia where they played matches against area teams. This was the first visit of a side to the colony and the forerunner of the modern Tests.[14]

Stephenson's work brought quick results: the *Cricket Annual* reported that 'cricket is in a flourishing condition at Uppingham, where H. H. Stephenson has taken up his quarters, and is teaching the boys some of that straight play for which he is so famous.' The writer concluded that Uppingham was 'not far removed from the first rank of Public School Elevens in 1872'.[15] Capitalising on this successful start, Green pressed Thring to allow the appointment to be permanent. Thring had his doubts but Green's advocacy and zeal eventually won the day. Thring confided to his diary:

> I must give way on the professional. It is better to make and control a movement than to be dragged by it. And not to have one has become equivalent to losing rank as a school, which would damage my rank with the boys immensely. So I mean to give way, and take it into our regular routine.[16]

Green had taken nine years to get his man, and his trust had not been misplaced; W. G. Grace regarded Stephenson as 'one of the best coaches of young players'.[17]

Between 1871 and 1876, Thring appointed several men to the teaching staff who had sporting interests: Willingham Rawnsley and Christopher Childs, like Skrine, were Old Boys of the school and all had played in the XI, the XV or both. W. C. Perry had captained the Sherborne School XI and represented the Gentlemen of Dorset; A. J. Tuck continued to play for the MCC; W. d'A. Barnard and C. W. Cobb joined the town's cricket club; and Sam Haslam was a keen player.[18] None of these were blues or games masters in the mould of Mitchell but their commitment to cricket must have raised its importance in the boys' eyes.

Stephenson's advice to the boys was that cricket was to 'be played, and not played with', and that each aspect of the game was to be 'worked at in a scholarly way'. Tips on batting, bowling and above all fielding filled many pages of the school magazine. Practice nets were erected on the Upper and Middle grounds to increase the effectiveness of the coaching sessions, and a professional 'bowler' was appointed each season to assist Stephenson's work. The 1873 season ended with a published analysis of the performance of each member of the XI, an initiative that was maintained annually.[19]

The 1873 *Cricketer's Companion* contained a gushing report on the standard of play of the Uppingham XI. Glamorous matches had been added to the fixture list: the MCC sent a strong team, and an elated school won by two runs in a two-day match; the Free Foresters were also entertained; and an invitation to play Surrey Club and Ground, Stephenson's old club, at the Oval was accepted. This last soon developed into a three-match London tour. After successive victories against Haileybury by over an innings, the members of the XI found laurel leaves in their plates at the Haileybury headmaster's farewell breakfast. Thring's thoughts, predictably, were devoted to fears of hero-worship and the spirits of the vanquished. The same year, at Green's instigation, a return match to play the MCC brought the school's first visit to Lord's.[20]

Old Boys continued these triumphs at the universities. Green had captained the Cambridge XI, played in four matches against Oxford and represented Essex, I Zingari and the Gentlemen of England; now a succession of Uppinghamians won blues in the Varsity match at Lord's – two in 1875, four in 1876 and five in 1877.[21] 1876 was Uppingham's year: in Cambridge's nine-wicket win A. P. Lucas contributed sixty-seven and twenty-three not out, D. Q. Steel twenty-four, W. S. Patterson 105 not out and seven wickets, and H. T. Luddington six runs and nine wickets.[22] The Uppingham Rovers' Dinner followed hard on this momentous occasion and a jolly evening found the 'Rhyming Rover' on particularly cheerful form:

> Who taught them this excellent cricket?
> Was the question of many that day,
> Who taught them to keep up their wicket,
> And to hit just as well as they play?
> Oh, who did these cricketers nourish?
> Who trained their eyes, nerves, and thews?
> 'Twas STEPHENSON! Long may he flourish!
> The coach of the Uppingham Blues![23]

The following year five Uppinghamians played for Cambridge, a record for one school, although this time Oxford won.[24] Here was an immediate return on Green's investment in Stephenson, and Uppingham continued to reap the dividend until his death in 1896. Small wonder then that E. W. Swanton would later describe him as the 'first of the great school coaches'.[25]

*****

Thring never quite claimed that what followed was divine intervention, but on 12 March 1876 he came close:

> One thing I feel more than I ever have felt, that a great shaping power is round about me, guiding, and ruling, and making, and moulding this fierce crucible work and fiery rush of evil and danger, and friendship, and help to

all about one, and that some strange birth of strange good and marvellous divine purpose is to come out of it all. Tomorrow I start for Liverpool, and on Tuesday for Borth and other places in North Wales.[26]

In 1875 an outbreak of scarlet fever caused two fatalities in the town of Uppingham. The drainage system was found to be primitive but, despite Thring's pleadings, the local Board of Guardians did nothing. Typhoid fever soon followed, and five boys of the school died; a local sanitary inspector still pronounced the town's wells pure. Thring was not convinced and, with the town persisting in its lethargy, he sent off a sample of water to London. Inspectors soon arrived and condemned the Uppingham drainage system. On 2 November Thring disbanded the school, ending the term a month early. The boys re-assembled on 28 January, but a further outbreak of disease enforced a second dispersal on 11 March. The future of the school was now at stake. Thring was strongly condemned in the press for keeping the school open and a mass withdrawal of boys was imminent. Thring looked for suggestions at a meeting of housemasters: one offered, 'Don't you think we ought to flit?' Thring agreed, and two days later he set off to inspect possible havens in North and Mid Wales. On 4 April the school reassembled at Borth, a few miles north of Aberystwyth. A whole year was spent on the Welsh coast, with the school housed in the Cambrian Hotel and some nearby cottages. On 4 May 1877 the school returned to a healthier Uppingham.[27]

These are the raw facts of a remarkable flight; the spirit is logged in the three much-annotated volumes of Thring's Bible.[28] The bookmark for the first volume still rests at Genesis XXVIII, verses 11–22, the text for Thring's last Borth Commemoration service on St Barnabas Day 1887. This chapter had a special connection with the Borth exodus: it was used for a sermon soon after the return and in several other commemoration sermons. Genesis XXVIII tells part of the life of Jacob, and Thring's interpretation gave meaning to the adventure. Jacob was seen as

> the father of all the toiling, striving men, who have to make their own way; the men who through many mistakes, and much suffering purge out the meaner views and mixed motives, and come out at last into the full Light of God, princes of God, no more Jacob, but Israel.[29]

Jacob had lived all his life in a wealthy and peaceful home where religion played an important part. In this secure atmosphere he had experienced all the usual minor vexations of life, but he was spared the real worries. Nothing in terms of religious doubt or personal trial came to test him. Jacob's life was simply too comfortable, everything was taken for granted. One day God called to Jacob and asked that he should relinquish all this security and follow Him. Without any clear motive Jacob made his decision, and chose to follow the call to foreign lands. Jacob bemoaned his plight, bitterly contrasting his former life as a rich man with his present state as one of the poorest of the poor. One night, as Jacob slept in some strange land, he experienced his now well-known dream, of a ladder stretching up to heaven, and at the top seeing not only angels but also God Himself. In this dream God revealed to Jacob that he was one of the chosen people and that his descendants would be forever blessed. On awakening, Jacob returned to his former home, forsaking his life as an outcast and for the rest of his years led a truly godly life.[30]

Uppingham was now an outcast in foreign lands; luxury was abandoned and sport had to improvise. Beisiegel's gymnasium was installed within the hotel's coach-house; the swimming instructor had four miles of good beach; the athletics sports were run on the roads about the town; and the heavy roller brought from the Upper flattened an area between the sand-dunes large enough for some cricket nets. A local land-owner, Sir Pryse Pryse, lent a meadow at Gogerddan for games and the Cambrian Railway provided a special on half-holidays to transport the boys. Most school matches continued, though those needing long journeys were cut, and geographically nearer Shrewsbury provided new opposition in both cricket and football – the latter the sole occasion in the nineteenth century when Uppingham played to an approximation of the Association rules.[31]

The year at Borth not only saved the school from 'the Valley of the Shadow of Death' but also rescued it from the cult of athleticism.[32] Team games could no longer dominate school life when 300 boys shared one proper pitch, and that four miles away. Artificial recreations lost their attraction among the cliffs and beaches, mountains and rolling surf on the Cardigan coast:

> Playgrounds – leagues on leagues of shore;
> Classrooms – all the sea-king's caves;
> We are touched by Ariel's power,
> Free of air, and earth, and waves.[33]

The reality of hare-hunting replaced the make-believe of the paper-chase; fishing in the Lery occupied both boys and masters; rambles were made to collect shells, seaweed and flora; and the exploration of ancient British camps provided hours of fun. Masters organised expeditions following rivers or up in to the mountains. Skrine particularly enjoyed 'the pleasant moments . . . spent on the beach at sunset, whither the School flocked down after tea for half-an-hour's leisure in the after-glow'. The boys played ducks and drakes or else chatted in small groups: it was Thring's favourite time of day.[34]

After the year at Borth, the school, like Jacob, returned home. Jacob had a mission, so too did Thring:

> Those, who have been saved by a great deliverance, have been saved for a great purpose: to give witness before Caesar, to stand out boldly, and fearlessly in the world, and maintain truth, and purity, and obedience,

self-government, and honour, in the face of the prevailing powers of the day, if need be, and fashionable idolatries. The being saved means this. I am sure, if you will quietly think over the fact, that for one whole year this school was in exile, and at any moment might have come to an end in that grim struggle for life, when more than once all seemed lost to those who really knew what was going on, a strong feeling will take possession of you, that a great debt is owed by the school to God, Who opened the way, when there seemed no way, and saved it through all. The school has a work to do in the world, or it would not have been saved.[35]

Thring was now revitalised to deal with 'the prevailing powers of the day' and the 'fashionable idolatries'. Old Boys bemoaned the fall in sporting interest and prowess, and blamed the unsettling move to Borth and the new timetable that Thring put into operation on return, but the reins were now back in Thring's hands. In his last Borth sermon, Thring reminded the school that the whole episode was far more than a pleasure excursion; indeed, the Borth year is a great divide in the history of the school. Thring saw the typhoid epidemic as an act of God sent to point out that the school had strayed from its true path and had taken the easier road of conventionalism. His identification with Jacob gave him the will to rediscover those earlier ideals and the energy to put them into practice, and once back at Uppingham this is indeed what Thring did.

Cricket was now just part of the whole Uppingham curriculum; no more powerful, and certainly no less powerful, than music, the classics or chapel. The tours to London were abandoned; Stephenson was encouraged to devote less time with the XI and give more to younger boys; housemasters were forbidden from directing play in house matches from the boundary, and a similar ruling applied to house captains for junior matches. Stephenson's influence reached the whole school in 1879 with the publication of the first of a long series of 'letters to the editor' of the school magazine; these were to build to a text-book of Uppingham cricket.[36]

Old Boys lobbied for the school to adopt one or other of the national football codes, Association or Rugby, so that Uppingham's new-found sporting fame could extend to the winter game, but in vain. This prevented foreign matches at football.[37] Annual expenditure on all games dropped to £350; repeated attempts to raise a cadet corps were rejected; and activities other than team games were encouraged.[38] Fives gained new courts; gymnastics classes continued; the athletic sports moved off the roads to a newly-acquired playing-field; and the countryside rambles rediscovered at Borth were maintained.[39] One concrete legacy of the town's new water supply came in 1883 with the building of an indoor swimming pool, the first at a British school. All boys were taught to swim and dive, and many received instruction in life-saving for the Royal Humane Society's medal.[40]

Thring often said that Borth provided the happiest time in his long career and, as Nigel Richardson judged, it confirmed much of his educational thinking and practice, and restored his belief in the essential goodness of human nature and the importance of trust. The repercussions of that year were as powerful and far-reaching as those of a deep geological fault that strikes across the face of the countryside, and they restored Thring's ideal of manliness. Never again in his life-time was it seriously challenged.[41]

IX The religion of athletics: 'That vague hunted gregariousness known as *esprit de corps*'[1]

The cult of athleticism made steady progress over the sixty years from 1830, beginning with the decision of public-school headmasters to clamp down on lawless recreations off the school site, to provide fields and facilities for play and to insist that boys stayed within bounds in their leisure time. The boys responded by adopting and adapting a range of activities to match their surroundings and the different seasons: cricket and rowing were already popular pastimes with established rules; football and fives, however, had to be modified to meet local needs. Most headmasters took no further interest and left the organisation to the boys – until George Butler at Harrow saw that it was easier to impose discipline if senior boys were given authority to compel their juniors to play. Games occupied free time.

Masters joined in the boys' games as the reformed schools accepted Thomas Arnold's lead that pastoral welfare was as important as classroom teaching. As Arnold's methods gained wider acceptance from the 1840s, so men who had worked under him at Rugby became the headmasters of the next generation, some at newly-founded schools and others at revived ancient ones. Charles Vaughan at Harrow and George Cotton at Marlborough needed to impose the new discipline on unwilling pupils, and both used games as one of the means. Vaughan gave senior boys authority to rule in the boarding houses and power to compel on the playing-fields; Cotton appointed young and athletic masters to do the job.

The Clarendon Commission of the 1860s had doubts about the quality of the teaching in public schools but only praise for the role that games played to improve boys' health, provide exercise and serve as moral trainers. As the public-school system expanded to meet the expectations of the increasingly ambitious middle classes, with even more new foundations and raised grammar schools, so the playing of games by boys and their masters was universally accepted as a standard component of school life. Headmasters and parents were sure of the benefits they would reap and were happy to accept what the boys wanted in return – status and symbols, cups and colours, professional coaches and foreign matches, more time for play and better facilities.

The muscular Christian messages of Thomas Hughes's *Tom Brown's Schooldays* and Charles Kingsley's *Westward Ho!* were eagerly bought and happily transmitted by the new public-school parents. Affection for schools and regard for their ability to inspire group loyalty reached levels never experienced before and soon, through the efforts of William Cory at Eton and nameless versifiers at other schools, love of school was extended to include love of the old school. Improved mail services and new-fangled telegrams, rapid trains and the invention of the weekend, all combined to encourage Old Boys to meet more often, dine together in London, enjoy reunions at school, and show the boys that they had not forgotten how to play their games.

Many of these Old Boys had taken their love of sport to the universities and there became instrumental in the codification of rules and the etiquette of competition. Young dons joined them at play and endeavoured to give it respectability and moral authority. Some, like Leslie Stephen, separated the muscular from the Christian. Now as graduates, many Old Boys worked to improve the sporting provision at their old schools, in part to raise each school's status, in part to boost their own social standing. Some returned as masters, others gave freely of their time as coaches, more made generous financial support. The period witnessed a massive expansion of inter-school sporting contests.

Loretto's whole-hearted commitment to character training and Spartan hardiness pushed the manliness ideal even further into the athletic sector, and two of H. H. Almond's legacies found special favour in English schools – the passing game in football and the cold bath. Edward Bowen also advocated Spartan living at Harrow and games were extolled as the best moral trainers. Bowen's insistence that senior boys, and not masters, should have all authority over games unwittingly passed much school management to the heroes of the XI and XV and the reign of bloods and hearties began in earnest.

The 1870s saw games become the most obvious feature of public-school life. Results of school matches filled the back pages of newspapers and journals, thus enabling proud fathers and loyal Old Boys to cheer their team from afar. Sport rather than religion defined and bound each school community and team spirit, or *esprit de corps*, was praised as the new manliness. Rugby football, rowing and, to a lesser extent, cricket were the vehicles for its inculcation. Eton had appointed the first games master in R. A. H. Mitchell, but he was not the last. No ambitious public school could afford to be without several blues and international players on the teaching staff. Some schools relinquished their city-centre sites and moved to the countryside to gain a healthier environment and to provide more room for playing-fields; these included Charterhouse, Christ's Hospital and Shrewsbury.[2] Sport's hold over the public schools was confirmed, even sanctified, in 1884 when Edmond Warre was appointed Headmaster of Eton. What was right for England's premier school must be right for all.

*****

The lesson of Borth had strengthened Thring's resolve to control athleticism and his thirty-four-year reign at Uppingham enhanced his power to maintain a sanity of outlook on sport and its trappings. He was present at the fourth annual meeting of the Headmasters' Conference, held at Winchester in 1873, when the increased importance of games warranted their first appearance as a topic for discussion. John Percival of Clifton complained that too much attention was given to games:

> It is not so much the amount of time ordinarily given to school games, as the amount of talk which follows upon the time and the impression the games make upon the boys' minds, which are absolutely ruinous, so far as many boys are concerned, to intellectual development.

Robert Henniker of Rossall responded:

> I contend that athletic exercise is good not only for the bodily but also the moral strength of a boy. I like every boy in my school to have so much exercise and fresh air that, when bedtime comes, he may soundly sleep till next morning without even dreaming.

Montagu Butler of Harrow argued that the cost of prizes for some games was becoming excessive, and he blamed the subscriptions from parents and 'injudicious friends' for bringing this about. George Blore of King's, Canterbury criticised the increased publicity given to school matches and vehemently condemned the self-advertisement of present society. Then, almost gingerly, William West from Epsom College volunteered a suggestion: 'I think we might judiciously introduce something like the German system of gymnastics, where every muscle is regularly brought into use and strengthened.' Thring could keep quiet no longer:

> It seems to me it is useless to talk, or to trust to personal influence unless you can find for every boy a place for the sole of his foot where he can distinctly feel that whatever he may be in other subjects, he has self-respect and is respected. I have in mind sundry boys, which in my judgement, the gymnasium has absolutely saved, and others who in the carpentry have found the place they wanted.

Perhaps they had heard before all about the 'great educational experiment'; perhaps, like Thring's own boys, they waited for the phrase 'True Life'; whatever the reasons, the words fell on deaf ears. Frederick Fanshawe of Bedford School got the meeting back to the real business in hand; 'I do not suppose that without games we should have any means at all of fostering *esprit de corps* amongst boys.' The discussion carried on in this vein, whilst Thring remained silent.[3]

Most public-school headmasters found it impossible to resist the march of games. Some, like Vaughan and Cotton, needed to impose discipline on a reluctant school. Most saw games as the one area of school life where boys and masters could congenially mix. Health was seen to improve, and the discomforts and hard knocks that are always part of games were believed to be good character-trainers. Teaching was in general dull and the classrooms cramped, so games brought some light relief, especially if little other amusement was provided. The adulation of the successful athlete might be unwanted, but then boys always did worship physical strength; besides if games sent the boys to bed dog-tired, there were no worries about immorality. In addition, sport was an aspect of school life that could be left to the boys as a training ground in management and the group loyalty inherent in team games was useful in the smooth running of boarding houses. Games also provided an area of the curriculum where competition was definitely acceptable, and even the dullard could play his part without embarrassment. As time went by, boys, Old Boys, masters, headmasters, governors and parents came to believe that all must be well in the religion of athletics.

For it was a religion. The original message of muscular Christianity had been sincere and its ethos came as a breath of fresh air after the mawkishness of Evangelicalism and the piety of the Tractarians. Sadly, as we have seen, the Christianity gradually became servant of the muscularity, and soon disappeared altogether. This was the pattern of the times. The erosion of belief had begun under the influence of the Utilitarians and then accelerated in the era of Darwinism. Science brought a chill to the very belief in orthodox religion, especially from 1862 to 1877 when the conflict was at its most bitter. By the 1880s church attendance was markedly down and the trend was accentuated by the increasing tendency of the Church to split into extremes of denomination. Then, with the Forster Act of 1870, came the inevitable separation of religion and education. As the century ended, so headmasters found it progressively more difficult to appoint professedly Christian masters, and then too came the lay headmaster.[4]

As the belief in true Christianity declined, so the ideal of *esprit de corps* rose in its stead as a secular sentiment. *Esprit de corps* had its good points. Some saw that it put down bullying, and it cannot be denied that to put the side before the individual can be a good thing, but in the forced concealment of all emotion and the suppression of individual character in order to create a uniform type, the effects were not attractive. Platonic Athens had given way to Sparta. At its worst this fostered a violent partisanship, and positive hatred was sown between groups of people artificially selected in the same world of schools. The Eton and Harrow matches, with up to 15,000 spectators crowded into Lord's, became a feud, almost a vendetta, and it was impossible to include the two teams in the same luncheon room. Corporate spirit was identified with athletic warfare.[5]

Chapter 4

Imperial manliness

I Imperial federation: 'The greatness of the moral work our race has yet to do'

> To the philosopher of any nation (not excluding our own) the spectacle of the Englishman going through the world with rifle in one hand and Bible in the other is laughable; but to Englishmen, who are neither logicians nor idealists, it is not. . . . If asked what our muscular Christianity has done, we point to the British Empire. Our Empire would never have been built by a nation of idealists and logicians.[1]

Such was the opinion of J. G. Cotton Minchin, formerly Britain's Consul-General in Serbia, in the 1901 publication *Our Public Schools*. It has been shown already how the ideal of manliness had evolved by way of muscular Christianity to a cult of athleticism; this chapter will examine how the same ideal developed under the auspices of what J. A. Hobson termed 'Imperial Christianity' into militarism.[2]

During the middle years of the century a series of nationalist uprisings occurred in a number of European countries, notably in Holland, Poland, Belgium, Norway and the Balkans. English nationalism was raised by the excitement of the Crimean War of 1853–56 and by the imperial designs of Napoleon III in 1858–59, but these only fanned the flames of an already kindled fire. At an early meeting of the Christian Socialists in 1849, some Chartists began to hiss as the National Anthem was about to be played; Thomas Hughes sprang on to a chair and announced that the first man who hissed the Queen's name would have to settle the account personally with him.[3] When volunteer movements of militia were formed in 1859, Hughes was one of the first fifty or so to enlist, and he soon raised two companies at the Working Men's College.[4] Hughes's enthusiasm was matched by others. At Cambridge Leslie Stephen formed a small company and trained it at his college; the Oxford corps originated in Edmond Warre's rooms. Both corps had drilling as the main activity but soon rifle shooting was added; in 1859 Warre was a founder member of the National Rifle Association.[5]

One of the first signs of imperialist spirit was seen in the love of the glories of Queen Elizabeth's reign. Just as early Victorian England felt a kinship with Athens, so the mid-Victorians drew support from the adventures of Drake and Raleigh. The bond spanning the centuries was fear of the anti-national power of the Church of Rome. Tennyson's *Revenge* and Kingsley's *Westward Ho!* caught the spirit of the times. *Westward Ho!* not only preached the creed of nationalism and attacked the influence of Roman Catholicism, but it also taught a larger view of England's mission to civilise the world. The benefits to be gained from Protestant Christian Socialism should not be restricted to England; rather they should be diffused everywhere. Charles Dilke expressed this social imperialism through the concept of a 'Greater Britain': the home countries together with America, Australia, Canada, India, New Zealand, South Africa and half the habitable globe. Dilke's view, first expressed in 1869, soon saw fruition in Benjamin Disraeli's expansionist policies:

> The aim which in all the length of my travels has been at once my fellow and my guide . . . is a conception, however imperfect, of the grandeur of our race, already girdling the earth, which it is destined, perhaps, to overspread.[6]

A correspondent in the *Dublin Review* observed this growing English nationalism with a mixture of amused scorn and fearful horror. Englishmen now regarded themselves as the finest people in the world and perpetually prided themselves on their courage, pluck, nerve, daring, 'bottom' and 'stubborn, unflinching, dogged, perseverance'.[7]

In 1860 a meeting was held in London under the chairmanship of Lord Elcho to discuss the establishment of cadet corps in public schools; several schools formed contingents later that year. The first was at Rossall, where two companies were raised as part of the Lancashire Regiment, and Eton, Rugby, Marlborough, Winchester and Harrow followed in quick succession. The number soon reached between twenty and thirty, and then remained steady until the end of the century. At Rossall and Bradfield College elements of drill were taught to all boys, and not just those in the corps, but in general the corps was voluntary.[8] Each corps was commanded and officered by masters at the school and each had the professional assistance of one or more 'sergeants'. These men, the school sergeant (or porter), gymnasium sergeant, and corps sergeant, joined schools on leaving the army and were responsible for the day-to-day running of the corps as well as other activities such as boxing and fencing.

Drilling, camping and shooting were the main activities in these new corps. Drilling might be dull so it quickly acquired character-training overtones to confirm its usefulness to boys: 'It gives them an upright carriage, expands the chest, removes the slouch, and trains them to be attentive to the word of command and quick in obeying it.'[9] Summer holiday camps were more popular but shooting drew most support from the boys. Shooting could be run on the lines of a game, with house matches and school matches, and soon Rifle Corps were more numerous than Cadet Corps. The establishment of the National Rifle Association's Wimbledon (later Bisley) competitions for the Ashburton Shield in 1860 did much to enhance shooting; in general, however, its status was much below that of other games, and drill did not rate at all. An Old Boy described the hierarchy at Clifton:

> Football and cricket really counted. Gym and athletic sports came next, a very bad second, swimming an even worse third, while the Rifle Corps, O. T. C. as it is now, not only did not count, but proficiency in it, even gaining the shooting colours, labelled a boy an outsider.[10]

Eton was one school where the corps was important. Warre, a friend of Lord Elcho, formed a contingent in his first year in the school, 1860; by 1878 it was 318 strong.[11] Etonians also had the vociferous support of William Cory whose patriotic poems caught the imagination of many boys. Ever since the time of the Duke of Wellington, and perhaps earlier, Eton had maintained a strong connection with the military; now newer schools were forging such links. From early in their foundation Cheltenham and Marlborough were quick to prepare boys for the military colleges at Sandhurst and Woolwich, and by the 1880s Clifton and Wellington were prominent too. Haileybury and the Imperial Services College at Westward Ho! were in effect service foundations with almost all their boys the sons of serving officers, whilst Glenalmond in Scotland was gaining a similar reputation as a 'military caste' school. The military ethos at all was paramount: strong corps, plenty of shooting and most leavers joining the Army. These schools, however, were few in number; most at this time were untouched by the seed of militarism.

The reason for the small number of schools with a military ethos is seen in the comments of the Old Cliftonian: the corps was of little importance when compared with games. In that Clifton resisted the formation of a corps until 1875 because it was felt that it would lower the standard of the cricket and encourage loafing, it is perhaps typical.[12] Almond never permitted the introduction of a corps at Loretto. Problems over the uniform clashed with his own theories of dress but more important was Almond's belief that games could do everything that a corps could, and much more besides. Uppingham in Thring's time was another school that had no corps. A 'Rifle Corps was an institution common in every other public school' wrote 'A Volunteer' to the school magazine in 1863 and, perhaps in consequence, a weekly 'drilling class' was introduced for a while in 1864.[13] An Old Boy questioned this need for a corps: '"deportment", "exercise" and "amusement" can be secured . . . from the good old games and the Gymnasium' and its introduction would 'sap much of the interest in these true Englishman-making games'. He hoped to see Uppingham at Lord's one day but this would never happen if a boy was 'playing at soldiers in a fine uniform . . . when he ought to be learning to catch a ball'.[14]

That Uppingham consistently did not adopt a corps must have been at Thring's insistence. Thring's position would seem to be three-fold: first, the acceptance of a corps would make the school answerable to an authority outside his own control, and that was unacceptable; second, the corps could add nothing to Thring's interpretation of the ideal of manliness; and third, Thring's views on Empire did not match those of the militarists.

To see this last point in context, we must go back from 1885 to the years that follow Disraeli's 1867 Second Reform Bill. Disraeli gathered together the various threads of imperialism, most noticeably those of Charles Dilke, and wove them into a national policy that was received sympathetically by the newly-enlarged electorate. The years 1874 to 1880, Disraeli's second term in office, witnessed the growth of this imperial idea; an ideal based not on imperial aggression but on imperial federation, an ideal best seen as an extension of the Christian Socialist philosophy beyond the confines of England.[15] Thring had been a supporter of this imperial vision for more than a decade, telling his boys at the opening of the school-room in 1863 that he expected generations of Uppinghamians to 'pass out into the great English empire as a band of brothers'.[16] The leading force on imperial federation was a Canadian educationalist, George Parkin. Whilst on a visit to England in 1873 to examine the English school system, Parkin was directed to Thring as the leading educationalist in the country. The two men were to have much in common and a natural affinity quickly developed; when Parkin returned to Canada, they corresponded much on educational and other matters.[17]

Parkin and Thring shared Dilke's fundamental belief that England, as the most civilised nation, had a duty to civilise the world. Thring challenged his boys to accept this duty in a sermon preached in 1881:

> England is confessedly the leading country in the world in enterprise and colonizing. And equally certain is it that the great schools ultimately are the leading power in England. You by position stand already in the first rank of the leaders of the world. You stand first in the chance given to each and every boy here, be he clever or stupid, to do something, and make the most of himself. O leaders of the world in what will you take lead? Is it useless to set up the standard of trust, honour, truth?[18]

Of the 950 boys who joined Uppingham in that decade, 144 – or 15% – forged civilian careers in the Empire or in countries strongly linked to it.[19] Most went to South Africa, India, Australia or Canada. Old Uppinghamians who joined the army added to the imperial experience, for most soldiers would have received a posting to India, Africa or the Orient at some stage in their careers.[20] Many who went to Alberta in Canada became successful settlers, developing a strong sense of fraternity and known to the locals as a 'high class corps of cowboys'.[21]

As Britain and the colonies were part of the same great body, Thring and Parkin believed that it was essential that they should combine in federation so that the civilising influence would be the greater. As Thring wrote to Parkin in 1885, 'The English-speaking race is by nature master of the world, especially when combined with the only other colonizing power, Germany, its kinsfolk.'[22] Remembering the strong German links at Uppingham, the inclusion of the country within Thring's concept of federation is not surprising – and he was not alone in promoting it. Relations between Britain and Germany had been friendly for most of the nineteenth century: the two royal families were closely linked; the countries were important trading partners; both were Protestant powers; and there were strong cultural ties through music and literature. It was not until after the deaths of Kaiser Wilhelm I and his son, Frederick III, both in 1888, that cooperation slowly changed to conflict as Wilhelm II saw it as his duty to make Germany a world power.[23] Thring too was now dead.[24]

That increased trade, commerce and defence would follow from imperial federation were all beneficial, but they were wholly secondary to the main ideal. This Pan-Britannic Empire was to be fostered through arts and sports as well as by commerce; aggressive, bullying imperialism would play no part. England, according to Parkin's *Imperial Federation*, should learn two things from history: the small Greek republics, centred on Athens, would have survived the onslaughts of Rome if they had combined in federation; and the 1776 breakaway of the American colonies, with its disruptive effect on the Anglo-Saxon alliance, must not be allowed to happen again.[25] Together, the new colonies and the old country could civilise the world and spread the Christian gospel:

> If we really have faith in our own social and Christian progress as a nation; if we believe that our race, on the whole, and in spite of many failures, can be trusted better than others, to use power with moderation, self-restraint, and a deep sense of moral responsibility; if we believe that the wide area of our possession may be made a solid factor in the world's politics, which will always throw the weight of its influence on the side of a righteous peace, then it cannot be inconsistent with devotion to all the highest interests of humanity to wish and strive for a consolidation of British power. It is because I believe that in all the noblest and truest British people there is this strong faith in our national integrity, and in the greatness of the moral work our race has yet to do, that I anticipate that the whole weight of Christian and philanthropic sentiment will ultimately be thrown on the side of national unity, as opening up the widest possible career of usefulness for us in the future; inasmuch as it will give us the security which is necessary for working out our great national purposes.[26]

This political philosophy is an extension of Thring's ideal of manliness. When the politicians from across the Empire met at Queen Victoria's Golden Jubilee in 1887, this ideal of federation was giving way to preferential trade through a customs union and then to the scramble to gain more colonies. That was not the fault of Parkin; like Thring, he lived to see his ideals distorted.[27]

II Imperial fever: 'What will be the next great European temptation and tempter?'

W. B. Yeats, in a letter to Henry Newbolt, defined two types of patriotism: 'that which lays burdens on men, and that which takes them off'.[1] The imperialism associated with Disraeli is an example of the former, whereas that of the age of Gladstone matches the latter.[2]

As a consequence of the new power of the united Germany in the wake of its resounding victory in the Franco–Prussian War of 1870–71 and the emerging industrial strength of the United States as the new country recovered from its Civil War of 1861–65, Britain in the late 1880s was seen by many observers to lose some of its lead over other world powers. This, together with Gordon's martyrdom in Khartoum in 1885 and the subsequent denting of British pride, led directly to an era of aggressive imperialism in the scramble for colonies. Africa became the main attraction: under a cover of doctrines on national destiny and civilising mission that were crudely married to policies of materialistic greed, the continent was carved up by Britain and the other world powers. Soon the Far East and the Pacific brought new acquisitions for the British Empire. All the pure and elevated adjuncts of imperialism as propounded by Parkin and the federationists were kept to the fore, but the real purpose was conquest, colonisation and commerce. Imperial Christianity was born and the Englishman with a rifle in one hand and the Bible in the other was to be found wherever the map was turning red. India was the pay-chest for thousands of Englishmen and a colonial caste of planters, merchants and adventurers, both abroad and in retirement at home, supported this new imperialism. Soon, too, so many British incomes were to depend on the Empire that any idealistic philosophies of mission were totally out of the question.

What Thring had feared fifteen years earlier had now happened. With his strong links with Germany, Thring had kept a close interest in the progress of the Franco–Prussian War. He made no public pronouncements but his diary reveals his support for the German cause.[3] He also noted that the application of new technologies to military purposes had not only changed the way that wars were being fought but had also influenced the international outlook of spectating non-combatant nations. Trains moved armies quickly; balloonists tracked enemy deployment; the telegraph provided rapid communication; and machine guns and fast-loading rifles strengthened defences.[4] On 27 August 1870, he wrote:

> It is a strange epoch. The dead French nation is now being shattered, and standing armies are doomed. For they cannot stand against armed nations as the German system is. . . . The modern epoch which railways have made possible is by this war thoroughly begun, and a new world, though as yet people little suspect it.[5]

As the war drew to a close, Thring returned to his theme of 'a new world' on
29 October:

> The news of the fall of Metz yesterday.... (T)he great French bubble which
> for two hundred years has been a fear and a glitter in Europe has burst;
> that strange compound of cleverness, vanity, lies, lust, blood, and robbery
> is come to an end. What will be the next great European temptation and
> tempter; is it England, with its greed of gain and money self-worship?
> A new page is turned – what is that page going to be?[6]

'What is that page going to be?'[7] At Queen Victoria's accession in 1837 hardly
a thought had been given to the Empire; at the 1887 Golden Jubilee the emphasis
was on civilising mission and paternalistic duty; the Diamond Jubilee of 1897
was an orgy of self-congratulation and national assertion. Crude, rumbustious,
imperial fever intoxicated the nation in the last decade of the century and this
sentiment carried all shades of political and religious opinion and all classes
of people in its wake. Whether trumpeted by the newly-founded *Daily Mail*
(1896), imbibed in the verse of Henry Newbolt and Rudyard Kipling, or sung
in such patriotic songs as *Another Little Patch of Red* or *Soldiers of the Queen*, the
hysteria of imperialism swept the country. To ensure that the nation would both
vote for and pay for these imperial policies, the country was subjected to crude
appeals to hero-worship and sensational glory, and to adventure and sporting
spirit. Current history was falsified in coarse, glaring colours for the direct
stimulation of the combative instincts of stay-at-home adventurers. This was
'jingoism': sham glories of military heroism and exaggerated claims of empire-
building engendered a narrow patriotism built on the lust of the spectator, a lust
devoid of all personal risk, effort and sacrifice. The result was a blind passion of
aggression and assertion, and a stage set for militarism.

Soon the lands that were good only for grabbing by the adventurer and
subduing by the soldier began to grow. By 1899 the area of the British Empire
was equivalent to four Europes; its population was about 400 million; and
it provided half the world's seaborne trade. Nationalism can only grow into
imperialism through military might, and the Empire needed its million men in
the armed services.[8] As the century drew to a close, so the national expenditure
on the Army and Royal Navy burgeoned: £22.7 million in 1870; £32.8 million
in 1890; £35.9 million in 1895; and £69.4 in 1900. The following year
witnessed the peak of £121.0 million, with £67.2 million drained by the Boer
War.[9] Imperialism masquerading as patriotism was extolled in schools and the
army was pictured as the ultimate in *esprit de corps*.[10] This linking of the school
corps and the ideal of *esprit de corps*, the philosophy previously attached to team
games, proved remarkably successful: soon fighting for one's country was seen
as playing in the ultimate team.

The bond between games and matters military was supported by the findings
of A. H. H. Maclean's *Public Schools and the War in South Africa*, an attempt

to justify the privileges accorded to public schools by their contribution – Maclean used the term 'results' – in the Boer War. The expected schools sent most soldiers (Eton, Harrow, Wellington and Cheltenham) and 'rank for rank, and man for man, the public schools were much superior to other schools.'[11] A look down the list of comments on individual schools shows the constant use of games language: 'The Charterhouse results are throughout disappointing'; 'The Scotch schools were only moderately successful';'the day schools . . . made but a poor show'.[12]

The climax of this association of school, sport and war is found in H. A. Vachell's *The Hill*.[13] For much of this 'Romance of Friendship' at Harrow, Vachell portrayed a philistine and athletic school where intense loyalty and house feeling culminated in sporting triumphs. The last chapters, however, witness the approach and declaration of the Boer War: 'War is an alchemist', Vachell proclaims, 'the discipline of the camp will transmute the bad metal into gold.'[14] The hero is the athlete–soldier, Henry 'Caesar' Desmond, who dies whilst courageously attempting to capture an enemy position. When the news of his death reaches the school, the headmaster addresses the boys in chapel:

> Henry Desmond . . . died so gloriously that the shadow of our loss, dark as it seemed to us at first, is already melting in the radiance of his gain. To die young, clean, ardent; to die swiftly, in perfect health; to die saving others from death, or worse disgrace – to die scaling heights, to die and to carry with you into the fuller ampler life beyond, untainted hopes and aspirations, unembittered memories, all the freshness and gladness of May – is not that cause for joy rather than sorrow? . . . I would sooner see any of you struck down in the flower of his youth than living on to lose, long before death comes, all that makes life worth the living. Better death, a thousand times, than gradual decay of mind and spirit; better death than faithlessness, indifference, and uncleanness.[15]

'Better death . . . better death': to die young, in perfect health, fighting for queen and country, leading the attack on an imperial battlefield, such was the glamorised fate for the exemplar of the ideal of manliness at the turn of the century.

The cadet corps rose from the very bottom of the status ladder in schools in the first decade or so of the new century and climbed right to the top; now a 'military caste' replaced the older 'athletic caste'.[16] In 1900 Warre, still headmaster at Eton, persuaded a committee of the Headmasters' Conference unanimously to pass a resolution that 'all persons in *statu pupillari* at the Universities or the Public Schools above fifteen years of age, able ('and, willing' was later inserted) to bear arms, should be enrolled for the purposes of drill and manoeuvre and the use of arms'.[17] A total of eighty-three of the 102 schools represented agreed to take action immediately: dormant corps were revived and enlarged and, where there were none, new corps were created. The increased numbers were matched with more time in the day for corps activities and greater keenness on behalf of the boys. The Navy League and the National Service League, two bodies promoting national conscription, were quick to catch on to this new enthusiasm and each sent representatives to the schools to lecture on military topics and to inspect the corps. Here Lord Roberts, the hero of South Africa, proved the National Service League's greatest advocate:

> Peace, not war, is my aim and earnest desire; defence, not offence . . . and therefore what I do well to stir up, to foster and develop, is a more manly and patriotic spirit in the nation – spirit which shall induce our youth to realise that they must be not only ready but prepared to guard the heritage handed down to them.[18]

To Roberts, 'the right to be taught to defend your country' was a fundamental principle and he toured the schools to champion the cause.[19] Up and down the country Roberts presented prizes, reviewed corps, and opened Boer War memorials: everywhere the military message was preached, and everywhere it seemed to be well received.

In the fifty years between 1850 and 1900, patriotism, the love of country, evolved into imperialism, the love of more country: at the same time militarism developed to foster and maintain this expansion. Patriotism, imperialism and militarism are thus inextricably intertwined. The dangers inherent in this triangle had earlier been identified by Thring; now they were recognised by Herbert Spencer, the pacifist and liberal of the old Victorian school, but in 1900 his views carried little weight.[20] Everywhere he saw 'this diffusion of military ideas, military sentiments, military organizations, military discipline': it pervaded all life; religion, literature, education, journalism, art and even sport.[21] The growing sacerdotalism of the Church and its doctrine of authority were both in accord with the increased militarism; like Sparta, an air of zealous warring brought a decline in the arts, letters and philosophy; oligarchy and bureaucracy soon became the natural supports of imperial militarism; and the government became blind to the social needs both at home and in the colonies.[22] Perhaps worst of all were the effects of jingoism: 'No one', wrote Esmé Wingfield-Stratford, 'who remembers the outburst of vulgarity which made the patriotism of the non-combatant populace the laughing-stock of Europe during the South African War, will be at a loss for an example'.[23] Many, in retrospect, blamed the whole phenomenon of imperialism and militarism on the emerging *nouveau riche*, a materialistic class who measured pleasure by its cost and who sought through it to identify with the governing classes. Wingfield-Stratford continued:

> The last twenty years of the nineteenth century saw the rapid break-up of (the) old order. The bourgeoisie had attained a position of such importance that their dignity as a class had been undermined; the very word "middle" had a savour of inferiority, and instead of being and breeding respectable citizens, they hankered after the status of "ladies and gentlemen".[24]

But the real danger in imperialism lies in the inevitable war when two imperialist regimes clash. Ardent imperialism may have been stifled by the national shame brought about by the Boer War, but the perpetual European disquiet held sway in the new century, and the gloom of 1914 loomed ahead. It was then, and only then, that it was seen by all that the end of the soldier was not, as was previously proclaimed, to die for his country but to kill for it. In as far as he dies he is a failure, and the militaristic ideal of manliness died with him in the fields of Flanders and France.

III Newbolt: 'Play up! play up! and play the game!'

Beyond the book his teaching sped,
He left on whom he taught the trace
Of kinship with the deathless race,
And faith in all the Island Race.
He passed: his life a tangle seemed,
His age from fame and power was far;
But his heart was high to the end, and dreamed
Of the sound and splendour of England's war.[1]

These closing lines from *Ionicus* in praise of William Cory come from *The Island Race*, a collection of poems composed by Henry Newbolt in the years between 1892 and 1898. That Newbolt should be inspired by Cory is fitting: Cory eulogised games and patriotism in his verse; Newbolt linked them through war. He basked in both popular and critical acclaim: a sermon delivered by the Bishop of London from the pulpit of St Paul's in the presence of King Edward included quotations from Newbolt; Ministers in the House of Commons used extracts in their speeches; Old Boys roared *Drake's Drum* and *The Fighting Temeraire* again and again at their re-unions; and Sir Charles Stanford's magnificent settings for *The Old Superb* and other poems took the message to a still larger audience.[2]

Newbolt was a true patriot of the conservative order. It is in his novel *The Old Country*, published in 1906 and set against the magical power of the English landscape, that Newbolt showed how the same English character had reacted over the centuries to the same national difficulties and dangers.

"I love this Country," Aubrey said; "I love it as I love nothing else in life. It is to me everything that men have ever loved – a mother, a nurse, a queen, a lover, and something greater and more sacred still. There is not one look of it that I shall ever forget or cease to long for, and I would as kill a friend as change the name of the smallest of its fields."

"I understand," he said; "but I had almost forgotten that patriotism could be so intense and yet so local."

"If you forget that," she replied, "you forget all. Patriotism has its own high spiritual thoughts, but it has a body too – very earth of very earth, born of time and the land, and never to be found or made: it is as human as our other passions, instinctive and deep and unreasonable, and as hot as the blood by which we live."[3]

This appeal to intense local patriotism as the vital foundation of the larger national patriotism was naturally and sympathetically received in the public schools for it implied that the narrow patriotism of school life, or *esprit de corps*, was in itself part of that foundation.

Newbolt also successfully revived the interest in chivalry and easily wedded it to the ideal of patriotism. Homer's *Odyssey*, the *Song of Roland*, tales of Richard Coeur de Lion or the Black Prince, they all thrilled Newbolt by their 'heroic vitality'; he in turn, in stories like *The Book of the Happy Warrior*, passed on this enthusiasm to the younger generation.[4] Further tales for boys about more modern heroism on sea and on land were vividly and, at times, horrifically portrayed in such books as *The Book of the Blue Sea* and *The Book of the Thin Red Line*. The introduction to the latter read:

> My dear Man,
>   I have written you another Christmas book – this year it is a book about soldiers. You are hardly ready to serve your country in that way yet, but I take it for certain that you are thinking of such things. I take it for certain too that when you read about war you want real battles and real people, not imaginary ones. Well, in this book everyone is real, every page is true, and as accurate as I could make it.[5]

At times Newbolt's love of chivalry became quite fanciful. The Navy – 'These great ships are very like medieval castles, warlike and comfortably unluxurious, and solid as rock' – and the public schools were both chivalric institutions.[6] In short, to Newbolt 'chivalry was a plan of life, a conscious ideal' and, as the boy at Clifton who was nearest to Percival's ideal of the balance of work, games and service, he was to many the embodiment of his own philosophy.[7]

No poet was more closely associated with his old school than Newbolt and Clifton. Numerous poems allude to the school, one is dedicated to its chapel, and a novel, *The Twymans*, is effectively an autobiographical school tale. At Clifton Newbolt was a success: he was a good scholar and prefect, and he captained the school corps and the shooting VIII; but it was the fellowship of school and house feeling that were to leave the deepest impression:

> I knew what glory meant, for in my time at Clifton we had an extraordinary succession of victories and our champions were almost as well known to the public as to ourselves. It was not for them only but for us that the light of what I have called Glory lit up the horizon: we went about our work and play in a proud obscurity, content to know that we belonged to a great and famous fellowship.[8]

Clifton as portrayed in *The Twymans* was no mere school but a society 'complete with nations, senates, battlefields, crimes and seats of justice'.[9] Games were viewed as a 'compulsory military service, a duty to the state', and through them the players were trained in the sacrifice of selfish interests to the ideal of fellowship and the future of the race.[10] Newbolt pictured the exemplar:

> To be in all things decent, orderly, self-mastering: in action to follow up the coolest common-sense with the most unflinching endurance: in public affairs to be devoted as a matter of course, self-sacrificing without any appearance of enthusiasm: on all social occasions except at the regular saturnalia to play the Horatian man of the world, the gentleman after the high Roman fashion, making a fine art, almost a religion, of stoicism.
>
> (The taboos of this tribe included) To show emotion in public, or indeed to show emotion at all; to make any sound at a match, beyond a hand-clap, to applaud at the fall of an opponent's wicket or the failure of his kick at goal; to wear, even in holidays, any but a black or undistinguished dress.[11]

G. M. Trevelyan noted that in the years around the turn of the century there 'was the close connection of poetry and politics, when poetry could serve the purposes of pamphleteering'.[12] *Drake's Drum*, for example, worked as a rallying cry for rearmament as the Kaiser built up the German fleet in the late 1890s.[13] Some of Newbolt's poems, including *The Best School of All*, which portrays the return of an Old Boy to his school, do no more than follow conventional lines, but others of far greater significance link schools and their games with patriotism and war. It is these poems that best 'serve the purposes of pamphleteering'. *The Schoolfellow* – 'He led the line that broke the foe' – and *The School at War* – 'We . . . cheered the dead undying names' – sing the praise of Old Boys fighting on the front line in South Africa.[14] Another, *He Fell among Thieves*, tells of the dying soldier dreaming of his old school:

> He saw the School Close, sunny and green,
> The Runner beside him, the stand by the parapet wall,
> The distant tape, and the crowd roaring between
> His own name overall.[15]

More important, and more revealing even, are two poems: *Clifton Chapel*, written just after the Boer War, and the famous, or notorious, *Vitaï Lampada*. In the former we mourn the dead who, having learned how to serve and fight at school, have given their lives for their country.

> Here in a day that is not far,
> You too may speak with noble ghosts
> Of manhood and the vows of war
> You made before the Lord of Hosts.
>
> To set the cause above renown,
> To love the game beyond the prize,

To honour, while you strike him down,
The foe that comes with fearless eyes;
To count the life of battle good,
And dear the land that gave you birth,
And dearer yet the brotherhood
That binds the brave of all the earth. . . .

God send you fortune: yet be sure,
Among the lights that gleam and pass,
You'll live to follow none more pure
Than that which glows on yonder brass:
'*Qui procul hinc*,' the legend's writ, –
The frontier-grave is far away –
'*Qui ante diem periit:
Sed miles, sed pro patria.*'[16]

The Latin phrase – 'He who died so far from home, died before his time: but he was a soldier, and it was for his country he died' – is Newbolt's own variation on Horace's *Dulce et decorum est pro patria mori* – 'A sweet and pleasant thing it is to die for your country'.

In *Vitaï Lampada*, written in 1892 after Newbolt met an Omdurman veteran at an Old Cliftonians' reunion, there is no attempt to mask the link between school games, *esprit de corps*, and death on the battlefield: the militaristic ideal of manliness is complete.[17]

There's a breathless hush in the Close tonight –
Ten to make and the match to win –
A bumping pitch and a blinding light,
An hour to play and the last man in.
And it's not for the sake of a ribbonned coat,
Or the selfish hope of a season's fame,
But his Captain's hand on his shoulder smote
"Play up! play up! and play the game!"

The sand of the desert is sodden red, –
Red with the wreck of a square that broke; –
The Gatling's jammed and the Colonel's dead,
And the regiment blind with dust and smoke.
The river of death has brimmed his banks,
And England's far, and Honour a name,
But the voice of a schoolboy rallies the ranks:
"Play up! play up! and play the game!"

This is the word that year by year,
While in her place the School is set,

Every one of her sons must hear,
And none that hears it dares forget.
This they all with a joyful mind
Bear through life like a torch in flame,
And falling fling to the host behind
"Play up! play up! and play the game!"[18]

The bungling of the Boer War, where civilian guerrillas inflicted embarrassing defeats on the British professional army, and the consequent loss of national honour and denting of British pride, raised concerns about the military attributes of Old Boys from the public schools and, in particular, questioned the theory that school games were a suitable preparation for war.[19] Newbolt leapt to the defence of the schools in an article on 'Public Schools and their Critics' but he had shifted his ground slightly: games inculcated the ideal of the warrior, but the mere mechanics of soldiering had to be added later.

> The typical virtue of the playing field is the habit of trained faculty of putting the game first and self last, of refusing under all temptation . . . to do that which is harmful to the player's own side or unchivalrous to his opponents.[20]

But

> If our games are to be a thorough training for war, they must include throwing the bomb as well as the cricket ball.[21]

Before the Boer War tempered idealism with reality, Henry Newbolt portrayed the climax of the athletic-militaristic ideal of manliness, an ideal best seen in the preference for a noble death rather than an ignoble peace, or a glorious youthful adventure on the battlefield rather than a safe life at home. The ideal was proclaimed by a 'brotherhood of manliness' and claimed for its exemplars strong institutional loyalty, conformist belief, ardent patriotism, unstinting acceptance of service and duty, and natural command.[22] Others saw also a delight in worldly success, philistinism in artistic taste and a mild sense of homosexuality.[23]

IV Kipling: 'The flannelled fools at the wicket'

Newbolt may have developed doubts about the effectiveness of team sports at school as training for future officers in the armed forces but the man who most articulately questioned that games were a suitable preparation for the warrior was Rudyard Kipling. His poems and novels of the decades on either side of the new century proved as effective as Newbolt's political pamphlets, but their tone was less respectful of the established order and more critical of its leaders. Newbolt – Clifton, Cambridge and Lincoln's Inn – was an insider; Kipling – India, United Services College, and Lahore's *Civil and Military Gazette* – was not.

If Britain were to save her Empire, Kipling was certain that the nation would have to learn *The Lesson* of the Boer War. His report of current failure, and warning of worse that might come, was published in 1901 – with the war still in progress:

> We have had no end of a lesson, it will do us no end of good!
> It was our fault, and our very great fault – and now we must turn it to use.
> We have forty million reasons for failure, but not a single excuse.
> So the more we work and the less we talk the better results we shall get –
> We have had an Imperial lesson; it may make us an Empire yet![1]

In *The Islanders* of the following year, and the war eventually won, Kipling pointed the lesson explicitly. The nation had 'set your leisure before their toil', had been satisfied with 'witless learning and your beasts of warren and chase', and had 'grudged your sons to their service and your fields for their camping place'. Inevitably the country's 'shame' was revealed 'at the hands of the little people'. Only with the help of the 'Younger Nations' of the colonies had England defeated the Boers, and had then

> returned to your trinkets; then ye contented your souls
> With the flannelled fools at the wicket or the muddied oafs at the goals.

Before it was too late, all this had to change. All men must give 'a year of service to the lordliest life on earth' and receive a training for war:

> Soberly and by custom taken and trained for the same;
> Each man born in the Island entered at youth to the game –
> As if it were almost cricket, not to be mastered in haste,
> But after trial and labour, by temperance, living chaste.
> As it were almost cricket – as it were even your play.

A return to the old methods could only bring disaster:

> Will ye pitch some white pavilion, and lustily even the odds,
> With nets and hoops and mallets, with rackets and bats and rods?
> Will the rabbit war with your foemen – the red deer horn them for hire?
> Your kept cock-pheasant keep you? – he is master of many a shire.
> Arid, aloof, incurious, unthinking, unthanking, gelt,
> Will ye loose your schools to flout them till their brow-beat columns melt?
> Will ye pray them or preach them, or print them, or ballot them back
>   from your shore?[2]

Newbolt was the amateur, games-playing idealist, whereas Kipling was the serious professional realist. But if their means differed, the ends were the same: both had a firm belief in the mission of Empire. And if the means did differ, they at least agreed that the medium for producing the product was the public schools. Newbolt was a traditional apologist – but Kipling was of the new age. The difference between these two poets of imperialism is largely due to their respective backgrounds: Newbolt was of true English stock and had been educated at a top public school; Kipling, on the other hand, was of a colonial background. He was born in Bombay, today's Mumbai, and spent the first five years of his life with his parents in India before being sent without them to England for his schooling; first in a series of private lodgings and then from the age of thirteen at the narrow, non-traditional United Services College at Westward Ho!. He returned to India in 1882 and was appointed assistant editor of a small local newspaper. Four years later he published his first volume of verse, *Departmental Ditties*.

Kipling enjoyed his schooldays at Westward Ho! on the north Devon coast as much as Newbolt did at Clifton but the influences were different. The United Services College was a new foundation, promoted by army officers for the cheap education of their sons. It was, in Kipling's terminology, a 'caste school' where 70% of the boys were born outside England and from which most hoped to join the Army.[3] Though military in concept, it was not military in outlook: there were no parades, no uniform, no flags and no corps. As a modern foundation, the curriculum was based on the requirements of the military colleges at Sandhurst and Woolwich rather than on the traditional classics for the universities, and it was a secular school. The headmaster, Cormell Price, was not in Holy Orders; there was no chapel and no religious enthusiasm, and Kipling left it owing nothing to religion. Though the school was as ardent on games as any other, this influence too Kipling did not receive, for poor eyesight debarred his sporting proficiency despite his strong physique. In comparison with Clifton, then, Westward Ho! was Spartan, secular, small, cheap and more intensely army orientated. Kipling also maintained that it was a 'clean' and 'healthy' school; one of Price's aims was to send the boys to bed dog-tired.[4]

It is from this background that Kipling drew his school tales. The first, 'Slaves of the Lamp', was published in *Cosmopolis* in April 1897, soon followed by 'In Ambush' in *McClure's Magazine* for August 1898, but most appeared in the 1899 novel *Stalky and Co.* On a first reading the tales seem the very antithesis of public-school life. The heroes deride cricket, 'even house-matches'; they sneer at those who say '"Yes, sir," an' "No, sir"'; and episode after episode sees Stalky and Co. challenging the authority of masters and prefects.[5] To generations used to *Tom Brown's Schooldays* and *Eric,* the novel came as a real shock: George Sampson, author of *The Concise Cambridge History of English Literature*, judged it 'an unpleasant book about unpleasant boys in an unpleasant school'.[6] Literary giants rushed to condemn Kipling: H. G. Wells called the boys 'mucky little sadists'; Henry James thought the book 'deplorable'; and Somerset Maugham declared it an 'odious picture of school life'.[7]

By the end of the book, however, their judgement has to be modified for now Stalky, along with 'Cheltenham and Haileybury and Marlborough chaps' is serving the Empire like any true-blooded public-school Old Boy.[8] The modern reader now realises that this hilarious novel is a serious text in which Stalky is Kipling's ideal boy and that he, rather than the athlete, ought to be the exemplar of the public-school system. In essence, Stalky is a return to the ideal of schoolmasters before 1850. He is healthily extrovert, brave, resourceful, ingenious and above all, practical; but, and this is the difference, he is also entirely free of Christian ethics and wholly untroubled by an *Eric*-like morality. As Kipling explained in the first Stalky tale: '"Stalky", in their school vocabulary, meant clever, well-considered, and wily, as applied to plans of action.'[9] It is not that Stalky and Kipling loathed games but that they saw them for their limited worth and that they rejected their moral trappings. It is not that Stalky was unpatriotic but that the school corps was only 'playing at soldiers' whereas Old Boys from Westward Ho! would eventually be the real thing. It is not that *Stalky and Co.* was an anti-public-school novel; rather it was an appeal to return to the simplicities of earlier Victorian times. It was also an appeal to beware the complacent view that games produced effective army officers, a view that was horridly exposed in the Boer War, two years after the book's publication.[10]

First and foremost, Kipling was the inspired propagandist of the imperial idea. He was the last of the Victorian romantics: his heroes were not the merchants and millionaires of the materialistic Empire, but the small men sharing 'The White Man's Burden', his own phrase, in far-flung corners of the globe. Through his poems Kipling opened up to his readers new worlds to the east and south, and always the flag of England stood for service and sacrifice. Civilising the world was a worthwhile task, though always it was likely to be thankless. Kipling also broadcast a romanticised vision of Empire to a nationwide audience. This drum-and-trumpet history vividly brought the Empire within the compass of the moderately educated and the lower classes: in effect he became the people's laureate. 'I have done my best', wrote Kipling in 1907, 'to make all the men of the sister nations within the Empire interested in each other.'[11]

Kipling was convinced that an ideal of manliness formed from his experiences as a boy at Westward Ho! and developed by what he had learnt as a man in India would serve the home country and the Empire far better than the public-school athletic model. His exemplar would invigorate a jaded British manhood and a jaded nation.

The school in *Stalky and Co.* promoted a strand of late-Victorian educational thinking that insisted that the aggressive and boisterous instincts of boys should not be tamed, civilised or eliminated but rather harnessed for imperial purposes. Stalky, for example, used some of the tricks that he learnt at school to good effect when he and his friends were re-united on colonial service.[12] The under-civilised and untamed colonial servant or army subaltern would thus be ready to understand, combat and eventually rule the untamed and uneducated natives of the Empire. The encouragement of this 'barbarism', a quality admired by Cecil Rhodes, led to the challenge for present-day Englishmen to live up to the heroic examples of the primitive past, a theme that had been explored a decade earlier in H. Rider Haggard's *King Solomon's Mine* (1885). Kipling thus permits the school's headmaster, its chaplain, Stalky, and his friends to act outside the law and in contrary to accepted moral codes in order to secure the desired ends. All parties, for example, are complicit in the savage and prolonged torture that the boys inflict on a gang of bullies.[13] H. G. Wells was not alone when he condemned this tacit conspiracy of authority and illegal violence, together with the implication that modern soldiers must adopt the brutality of the ancients and the ways of savages if Britain's hold on the Empire was to be maintained.[14]

Kipling saw competition between nations as competition between men and, therefore, as competition between different ideals of manliness. In his poem *The English Flag* of 1891, he challenged the complacency of the nation's leaders: 'what should they know of England who only England know?'[15] Convinced that other races had ideals of manliness worthy of examination, Kipling turned to the East to illustrate that an Indian could instruct an Englishman on its acquisition. In *Gunga Din* of the following year, the eponymous hero is a lowly water-carrier in the period immediately after the Indian Mutiny of 1857. He shares the demands of courage and the expectations of danger with the British soldiers he serves and gradually wins their respect and admiration to such an extent that the poem's soldier-narrator concludes – 'By the livin' Gawd that made you, You're a better man than I am, Gunga Din!'[16] Kipling used *Gunga Din* to introduce imperial duties and virtues to a stay-at-home and metropolitan readership, and to encourage Homer-like respect for worthy warriors, whether allies or adversaries.[17]

Despite Kipling's firm convictions to the contrary, soldiers inspired by *Gunga Din* and *Stalky and Co.* fared little better in the Boer War than the typical public-school product. In addition, the morally dubious and potentially illegal British response to the guerrilla tactics of the Boer farmers, a response that matched the barbarism admired by Rhodes, may have been effective in bringing the war to a close but it also earned sustained condemnation from many nations.[18] It was in the wake of these setbacks that Kipling composed *The Lesson* and *The Islanders*. He now saw that a Stalky-like education was not enough and, like Newbolt, that the nation must also be trained in the mechanics of modern warfare. Kipling soon founded a Rifle Club in his own village and then lent his weight to Lord Roberts's National Service League and the call for national conscription.[19]

The poet who delighted most in studies of soldiers and sailors was enthusiastically received by the militarists. 'The White Man's burden' implied the cult of a 'Master Race' and of 'lesser breeds' as much as it did imperial service, whilst his involvement in the 'sahib' class of India brought to mind many analogies with the Roman Empire. As the novelist and critic Frank Swinnerton remarked: 'He had seen the Empire, and the Empire filled his dreams.'[20]

V Selwyn:
'To fear God, to speak the truth, and to shoot straight'

Edward Thring died at Uppingham on 22 October 1887 and was buried in the parish church's cemetery. The school's trustees acted speedily to find his successor: applications were received by 1 December and a fortnight later the appointment was made. Edward Carus Selwyn began his headmastership at the start of the following term.

Selwyn was born on 25 November 1853, two months after Thring began his life's work at Uppingham, at Blackheath in south-east London where his father was principal of the local proprietary school. He was an excellent scholar: at Eton he gained the treasured Newcastle Scholarship, then at King's College, Cambridge, he won numerous awards. With the exception of one year's curacy at Jarrow-on-Tyne, the interval between his ordination in 1876 and his appointment to the headmastership of Liverpool College in 1882 was spent as fellow, lecturer and then dean at King's College. Selwyn was a brilliant theologian and he continued his scholarship at Uppingham. He became a doctor of divinity in 1900 and he published a number of texts on the New Testament.[1] Selwyn's connections, as much as his qualifications, must have impressed the Uppingham trustees: on his own side he could list the Bishop of Lichfield, whilst his wife was the grand-daughter of Thomas Arnold.

A new broom had arrived. Demand to get into Uppingham had long been high but Thring had maintained his limit of 300: now Selwyn relaxed this veto and soon the numbers climbed over the 400 mark. An extra boarding house was acquired, housemasters admitted more boys, and shared studies became common. The curriculum was reformed: compulsory Greek was dropped, and special army and engineering classes were introduced for the Sandhurst and Woolwich examinations. With the loss of many of the 'extra' subjects of Thring's time, the curriculum for most boys was dominated by the classics.[2] Selwyn was a respected teacher of the sixth-form but no other boys were taught by him; a gulf grew between headmaster and boys and most regarded him in awe from afar. H. W. Bothamley, who never reached the sixth-form, told the school's historian that he hated Selwyn.[3] He was, however, generally popular with the staff, although in the early years men who were especially loyal to Thring's ideals did not readily accept Selwyn's innovations.[4] His relationship with the Thring family was predictably strained: the Thring daughters never liked Selwyn, and his elder son, Gale, recorded that the 'changes which upset his father's cherished aims were hard to bear'.[5]

Three other aspects of school life quickly felt the passing of Thring: school uniform, football and the cadet corps. School praepostors had worn white straw boaters in Thring's last years; now speckled ones replaced the German-style caps for all other boys.[6] Junior boys dressed in Eton collars and short black jackets, older ones wore striped trousers, and praepostors could wear winged collars with their black tail-coats. The last also gained umbrellas as badges of office. Harold Howitt, later an eminent accountant, recalled that all trouser pockets were sewn up, in part to prevent slouching but also to discourage masturbation.[7]

The Uppingham football game was exchanged for Rugby football in 1889; the acceptance of a national football code was probably both inevitable and sensible.[8] Such a change had nearly happened in 1876, only then it would have been Association football: now the conversion was made to the recognised public-school code. School games became compulsory three days a week and house games might take another two.[9] A league system of house matches was introduced; tasselled caps were awarded to the XV; and fixtures were arranged with college and school sides, and with London Rugby football clubs.[10] Selwyn was a keen supporter at matches:

> One remembers him, in his silk hat and clerical overcoat, walking up and down in the rear of the boys massed on the side-lines of the Leicester ground, using his gold-headed stick on any part of their lower anatomies and exhorting them to "Shout, boys, shout!" Quite oblivious – or was he? – of the fact that as his mild castigation drove the line forward, it was driven back by the hunting-crops of the praepostors keeping the touch-line clear.[11]

Despite the increased status of football, cricket was still Uppingham's main game. The 1890s saw the return of the glories of the early 1870s.[12] Stephenson now had an assistant professional and, as he confessed to the headmaster of the visiting Haileybury team, even greater influence:

> "Well, between you and I," he said in answer to a question as to the age of a very powerful eleven of boys, "I tell you what I does. If one of these 'ere parents wants to take one of these boys away, I just writes him a letter and so keep them."[13]

The fixture list saw the return of the London matches and the arrival of new school opponents: in 1897 for the Jubilee Day match at Rugby the whole school travelled to watch the game.[14] Other school sports increased in due proportion; expenditure on games was more than doubled; athletic adornment proliferated both on and off the field of play; and sports day heats served merely to clear out the incompetent.[15]

The cadet corps was formed in April 1889: membership was voluntary, and at the end of its first term the roll numbered a third of the school.[16] Thring had consistently rejected the creation of a cadet corps but he would have found little to oppose whilst William Vale-Bagshawe and then Sam Haslam, both loyal and long-serving colleagues, was commanding officer. Activities included drilling and skirmishes in local woods; a band was formed and given its own 'Marching Song'; and a thousand-yard rifle range was constructed two miles west of the town.[17]

From 1898 there was an injection of military spirit in the school through Selwyn's appointment of C. H. Jones, aged thirty-three, to teach the Army Class and take over command of the corps from the fifty-two-year-old Haslam.[18] Herbert Jones, a professional soldier at heart, was an outstanding commander and under his powerful influence Uppingham leapt to national renown. Jones agreed with Field Marshal Sir Evelyn Wood, Adjutant-General to the Armed Forces, that the country would eventually decide on compulsory military service but that in the interval 'the sons of the upper classes should give more time and attention to rendering themselves capable of defending their country in case of need'.[19] The Uppingham corps quickly expanded to a battalion and gained additional officers; a house drilling competition was inaugurated; the shooting VIII shot with success at the Bisley meetings; and from 1899 a detachment attended the newly-founded Public Schools Camp at Aldershot.[20]

At the start of the first term of the new century, and in the midst of the Boer War, Selwyn made an announcement that placed Uppingham at the forefront of public-school militarism: all boys, whether in the corps or not, were required to pass a shooting test, and no boy would be allowed to take part in any inter-house athletic or sporting contest, nor accept a school prize, until he had passed that test. Selwyn argued that this 'glorious innovation into a Public School curriculum' was based on a lesson learnt from the Boers' tactics, 'that any body of men who are not cowards and can shoot straight, even with little or no drill, are an extremely formidable element in the defence of their country'.[21]

In February 1900, Jones left for active service in the Boer War as a lieutenant in a volunteer battalion; Selwyn, in his Speech Day address, reckoned that he was probably the only public-school master serving at the front.[22] His exploits in South Africa were reported in the school magazine in graphic detail: 'We hear that Mr. Jones has killed five Boers single-handed. We congratulate him heartily on the exploit and hope he will dispose of many more.' In June 1901 Jones, now a captain, returned to a hero's welcome.[23] James Elroy Flecker, the future poet, who was at the school at this time, recorded the scene in a letter to his parents:

> On Saturday the conquering hero, Captain Jones, came. By a stretch of unparalleled generosity we were let off school an hour and a half on Monday. The Rifle Corps parade in vast solemnity down to the station; our drummer looks resplendent in his leopard skin. You will find him somewhere beneath the big drum. The fifes give a little squeak rather out of tune. The civilians line the palings, the élite of Uppingham keep the other side of the road discreetly. Punctual for once in its eventful and irregular

life, the smoke is seen half a mile away. Someone suggests a luggage-train and we groan. But it is the proper sort after all. In ten minutes the half-mile is covered, and five astounding pop-guns proclaim its momentous arrival.

A long wait in the station; we hope for the sake of the corps that it is the wrong train. But no, a slim figure in khaki emerges and a rather erratic wave of cheering arises. Captain H (Haslam?), after a soldierly embrace, gets him to walk at the head of the corps.

Then again the boom and squeak, and to the school march the glorious vermillion crowd, followed by a vast and seething throng of smart-clothed civilians. The masters assemble on the green in the quad. The chief robes himself in a great hood like a red ensign fluttering in the wind. The corps form an inner circle, we an outer. Sedgwick bawls forth his peroration – rather spoilt by a babe belonging to the élite who formed the inevitable rear. Captain Jones also bawls forth some soldierly words apropos of the corps, and there are more cheers, and one side sings *God Save the King*, and the other doesn't, and the solemn and impressive ceremony ends.[24]

Jones's 'soldierly words' predicted 'great days, and greater days still in store for Public School Corps'.[25] Back in harness as a schoolmaster, Jones kept the school informed of progress in the war, told of his own experiences, and reviewed military novels for the school magazine.[26]

Selwyn usually invited senior soldiers to present the prizes at the annual Speech Day; in 1906 this duty fell to General Sir Charles Brunt, a family friend. Brunt had recently served as British attaché to the Japanese army during the Russo-Japanese campaign.[27] His speech to the assembled boys and their parents was recorded in full in the school magazine: his theme was 'Patriotism'.

I have just come from a country – Japan – where patriotism is a religion, where every man, woman and child puts duty to the country to the forefront, irrespective of everything else, even of life itself. One day in Manchuria, talking to General Nogi, I happened to remark that what struck me most since I had been there was the enthusiasm of the Army and the patriotism of the nation. He said, "It is a very extraordinary thing you should mention that this morning, because only a short time ago I received a letter from the mother of one of my soldiers, in which she says, "Your Excellency, every day of my life in my village I hear of women who have lost their husbands, women who have lost their sons, women who have lost relations of all sorts, and yet of my son I hear nothing. I only hope that he is doing his duty; if he is not, please have him placed in the most dangerous position you can find, and have him killed if necessary." A Spartan mother, you will say, and rightly so too . . . Is it not a very high and very noble ideal, and one worth more than a passing remark? (Applause)

You will know England entered late in the race for Empire, for mastery of the sea, and for commercial supremacy . . . now Greater Britain stands out as the most powerful and largest Empire the world has ever seen. (Applause) That, my boys, is your inheritance . . . it has been founded, built up, and cemented by the blood of your ancestors, shed liberally on land and sea by all classes of the community . . . that your nation might be great and able to play its proper part in guiding the destinies of the world. (Applause) The burning question of the moment is, Is this Empire of ours going to last? The answer to that question, I submit, rests with the rising generation, with their fathers, with their mothers, and with their instructors. . . . Play by all manner of means; enjoy yourselves certainly; but in the midst of all your amusements remember the duty you owe to your King, to your country, and to yourselves. . . . If there is one thing more certain than another, it is that the nation with the biggest reserves will win the next big war, and the question is, where are we to get these reserves from? . . . I think I see the dawn of a national army which will give us all the reserves we want if it is only properly carried out, and surely it is a far higher and a far nobler ideal to see the citizens of a great country of their own free will preparing themselves to defend their rights, and the rights of their country, as opposed to any system founded on compulsion. (Hear, hear.) In this respect, Uppingham School has set a noble example, and I am quite convinced that when history comes to be written, not only will the fact not be overlooked, but I am sure it will meet with favourable comment.

I preach the doctrine of preparation. (Loud applause) I should like to remind everybody here that there is such a thing as paying even too high a price for peace, with all its blessings, and I think I am only voicing the opinion of everyone in this room when I say that the bloodiest war ever fought yet is preferable to a disgraceful and disastrous peace. (Applause) We all know Rob Roy's motto, "The good old rule, the simple plan – Let him take who has power, and let him keep who can." . . . I urge preparation, for surely as preparation means peace, so surely does want of preparation and neglect mean war. (Loud continued applause)

Selwyn responded that the 'words would sink into their hearts, into the parents' hearts, the boys' hearts, and the masters' hearts, and that they would bring forth fruit in due season. (Applause)'.[28]

In the early years of the new century, about half the school was in the corps and by 1905 over 1,000 cadets had passed the Uppingham 'Recruit Drill and Fire Exercise'. To Selwyn the corps was 'one of the glories of the school'; to the visiting Lord Roberts, Uppingham's lead was an example to all public schools. Speaking in 1905 at the opening of Uppingham's South African War Memorial, a combined gymnasium and concert hall, Roberts congratulated the school on its 'very satisfactory results' in the war; 222 Old Uppinghamians fought in South Africa, nine lost their lives.[29] Roberts hoped that other schools would follow Uppingham's lead in making shooting compulsory.[30] Rear-Admiral W. F. S. Mann of the National Service League echoed this praise in the same year, when he presented the school with the League's medal for patriotic service.[31] The Navy League also found Selwyn an enthusiastic ally.[32]

The introduction of punishment drills for minor school offences on Jones's arrival in 1898 undermined Beisiegel's educational approach to gymnastics.[33] This drill was held early in the day and meant that the offenders often missed breakfast.[34] Beisiegel refused to take this drill, leaving it to the corps sergeant, but responsibility was passed back to the ex-army gym instructor who succeeded Beisiegel on his retirement in 1902. Gymnastics had already lost its coveted place in the scoring system for the athletics championship; now Beisiegel was allowed to slip away with the briefest of farewells:

> Mr Beisiegel has been here for 42 years, and during that time, alike in the Music-room and in the Gymnasium, he has done useful work, and been a valued friend to many boys.[35]

Jones took charge of the gymnasium and the swimming pool, supervised the work of the ex-service instructors and added boxing to the curriculum.[36]

The *vale* on Selwyn's retirement in 1907 recorded: 'We (Uppingham) were still very much in the rough, and to him fell the task of smoothing out that roughness.'[37] If this meant that he turned Thring's unique school into a conventional and conservative public school, then Selwyn did indeed smooth out that roughness. No matter what criterion was applied, Uppingham was now on that elite list. But the price paid was high: Charles Paget Wade, later a renowned architect, labelled the school the 'Tiny World of Limited Vision'.[38] Athleticism swelled, militarism flourished, morality slipped and the Thringian ideal of manliness became the Selwyn ideal 'to fear God, to speak the truth, and to shoot straight'.[39] The rapid growth of the school was a prime cause of the change in ethos, reaching a peak of 440 after 1900, and the type of boy changed too. No longer were most parents from professional backgrounds, attracted to the school by Thring's reputation, but many were 'the newly rich from Yorkshire and Lancashire' who sought any public-school education for their sons.[40] The relationship between boys and masters became more formal: Paget Wade noted it – 'An impossible icy gulf was placed between the Masters and the Boys and no speech passed between them outside the classroom'.[41] The housemasters had changed too: by 1901 only three of the thirteen had been appointed by Thring, just six were in Holy Orders and three were bachelors. Where once housemasters' families had several young children adding to the family atmosphere, now there were few and the old homeliness had gone.[42] The Sunday liberty, so vital to Thring's philosophy, was replaced with chapel morning and afternoon, and 'Sunday Questions' for the spare moments.[43] C. R. W. Nevinson, later the celebrated war artist, was a boy in the school immediately after the Boer War; he 'attended endless divine services; listened to strange sermons by doctors of divinity in which Englishmen were confused with God, Nelson with Jesus Christ, Lady Hamilton with the Virgin Mary'.[44]

The habit of roaming the countryside disappeared on what Flecker termed 'about the busiest day in the whole week'.[45]

The cult of athleticism joined forces with new militarism and the virtues of Tom Brown were extolled to the boys alongside those of Lords Roberts and Kitchener. Nevinson recalled that 'the main object of the boys ... undoubtedly was cricket and perhaps rugby football', and he witnessed the school bathed in 'appalling jingoism'.[46] Boys in their house XI or XV were excused fagging, and only rarely did other than the talented games-player reach the rank of praepostor. The Captain of Games became the post of real authority and even masters were seen to judge a boy's ability solely on his athletic prowess.[47] Charles Raven, later an eminent Cambridge theologian, recalled how moral goodness was equated exactly with games prowess; Christianity was at a low ebb in the school; and 'good form' became the all-pervading ethos.[48] Flecker looked back on his Uppingham experiences in *The Grecians: A Dialogue on Education*. He noted that games coaching was limited to the star players while the 'athletic dullards' like himself played out interminable games without guidance merely as occupation, or spent whole afternoons watching school matches by compulsion. Physical education had been 'perverted'.[49]

Selwyn showed no interest in his pastoral responsibilities, nor did he seek to influence the policy in the houses; he even proposed that the headmastership and the housemastership of School House should be separate offices – but this suggestion was rejected by the trustees.[50] The baize-covered door between the private side and the boys' side in each of the boarding houses was closed and the reign of the 'swell' and the 'hearty' began.[51] Paget Wade recalled: 'I was imprisoned in LORNE HOUSE' – 'a loathsome murder-hole atmosphere hung about it'.[52] It still had the reputation of being the unruliest house a decade later.[53] Praepostors would beat boys for not cheering at football matches; and from their bicycles would whip dawdlers on house runs. Boys were bullied, coerced and tortured for the diversion of the 'swells'.[54] Nevinson, next door in the headmaster's house, was 'kicked, hounded, caned, flogged, hairbrushed, morning, noon and night'.[55] If two boys of unequal ages and different houses were seen speaking, immorality was taken for granted; sexuality was driven underground, passion became distorted, and there grew a 'dirty delight in illicit acts'.[56] Nevinson reckoned he possessed a more extensive knowledge of 'sexual manifestations' than any voyeur, and the later sex life of Flecker owed much to his Uppingham years.[57] On one occasion Selwyn must have suspected that all was not well, for both Flecker and Howitt remembered the headmaster calling a meeting of house captains at which a resolution was passed to 'stop the immorality in the school'. The result was that each house captain was sent to address his house and Selwyn preached a 'vehement sermon' on 'The Happy Husband' in a chapel with all but masters and boys excluded.[58]

The inscription over the Tudor school-room at Uppingham reads, in a translation of the Latin, 'let no foul word or sight approach a house which holds a boy'. H. W. Bothamley, a historian of the school, believed that this sentence 'ought to have been in front of the H–M and his staff in blazing letters'.[59] Bothamley was at Uppingham from 1897 to 1902, the same period as Flecker, Nevinson, Howitt, Paget Wade and Raven. Three others – H. L. Lyon, J. C. Gibson and F. Savery – were also at the school at this time and their observations match those already cited.[60] Paget Wade thought that the school's motto should have been 'Boys are the lowest form of animal life.'[61] These nine Old Boys span five houses and fifteen years, so the laxity in morals was not restricted to 'a bad house in a bad time'. The statistics in the school roll and the entries in the register of scholars make unhappy reading. To take one term for example: of the thirty-four boys who came in January 1903, seventeen left in three years and under, and nine of them left within two years of arrival. Of the twenty-one boys who came the same term exactly fifty years later, none left in the same spans. Obviously there are various possible reasons for the early departures, but boys do not usually leave after a year or two unless the circumstances are special.[62] The register shows that between 1900 and 1905, seventeen boys were expelled, three were withdrawn on Selwyn's request, five ran away and a further four entries have their withdrawal reasons noted in Selwyn's curious Dog Latin.[63]

A rot had set in and soon numbers in the school began to fall. From 1899 onwards, the trustees and Selwyn were increasingly at loggerheads: Selwyn was reprimanded over the school's accounts; there was talk of withholding his salary; the shooting edict was not welcomed unanimously; and then there was question of the housemastership of School House. Breaking point was reached in March 1906 when the trustees were appalled at the nature of Selwyn's punishment of a boy and incensed by his desire to withhold the facts. His resignation was demanded; in 1907 Selwyn retired to Hindhead to follow his theological studies. [64]

Selwyn's eldest son, also Edward, felt that his father should never have become a headmaster, and that he should have remained at Cambridge as a theological scholar. Bothamley, Flecker, Nevinson, Howitt, Raven, Paget Wade, Lyon, Gibson and Savery would surely have wished that it was so.[65]

VI Following the fashion: 'Conform or be kicked'

Many of Thring's cherished aims were abandoned during his successor's tenure at Uppingham and in those first years of the new century Thring would have found little to connect the Uppingham of the so-called 'Golden Age' of public schools with the school he had created fifty years before.[1] But is it fair to denigrate Selwyn when perhaps all he did was conform to the standards of his time? Thring came to Uppingham in a period ripe for educational innovation, and in mid-Victorian England a headmaster as strong as Thring could, and did, set his own course without much reference to the accepted public schools. In that isolated market town in the heart of the Rutland countryside, it was perhaps relatively easy for Thring to fashion his own school, and then to set and attain his own ideal of manliness.

Selwyn had to face problems in late-Victorian and Edwardian England that Thring would have been glad to have been spared. The country was now brash, noisy and materialistic. As the creed of imperialism rose, so the mid-Victorian confidence in Christianity fell. With 30,000 boys in the public schools of 1900, there were more boys than ever; but the schools were bigger and more numerous so the pressure to fill them was consequently greater. Schools had to be more business-like in their operation and the rise or fall in numbers did much to reflect parental popularity; a sharp but prolonged drop in numbers could settle the fate of the unsuccessful headmaster. The competition may have made a headmaster's position more precarious, but the boom brought the schools comparative immunity from outside criticism. They were confident in their purpose and of their ability to realise it, and this confidence was not shaken until the later Edwardian years when the economic depression after the Boer War and the impact of the new industrial strength of Germany brought about a liberal onslaught on these conservative bastions of privilege. But before these factors took their toll, this was the greatest time for public schools; so, in an age of crushing conformity, perhaps Selwyn did no more than conform.[2]

Certainly Selwyn conformed to the accepted pattern of the public-school headmaster, a pattern seen both in fiction and in reality. In *Good-bye Mr Chips*, Ralston, the new young headmaster, is efficient, ruthless and ambitious; as he glides around the school in his rustling silk gown – a sartorial necessity for fictional headmasters – he exudes confidence with a pontifical air. The status of the school rises under Ralston's leadership and there are long waiting-lists.[3] H. A. James was headmaster at Rugby at the turn of the century, and regarded by a boy of the period as 'outwardly an impressive figure in the fashion of his time'. James's punishments were remembered as 'quite primitive'.[4] Welldon, headmaster of Harrow from 1885 to 1898, flogged an average of a hundred boys each year.[5] The most memorable picture of a headmaster of this period was drawn by Harold Nicolson: Bertram Pollock, who was appointed headmaster of Wellington at the age of twenty-nine in 1893 and ruled until 1910, was twice vividly portrayed by his former pupil: first in the essay 'J. D. Marstock' from *Some People*, and later in his preface to Pollock's autobiography, published just after the subject's death. Nicolson recalled:

> my feelings in regard to him were a mixture of fearful curiosity and religious awe: there was something emotionally magnificent about him, something theocratic. His tall slim figure billowed in a silken gown as he glided rapidly through the cloisters, leaving behind a faint but pleasant smell of hair-wash, an impression of something rich and luxurious and mundane: a striking contrast to the drab penury of our existence: a touch of the great coloured world beyond.[6]

Pollock was worshipped by his sixth-form but feared by the rest of the school, and perhaps by the staff. To the smaller boys, Nicolson remembered, he appeared as a distant and majestic figure; robed in silk, it was said, to make a visible distinction between himself and his subordinates.[7] Punishments were severe, and years later Pollock could still recall with sadistic pleasure what he had set for a boy who misbehaved at the end of a term:

> A boy would be sent for to see me after breakfast and I would then tell him I was busy for the morning and he would come back before lunch. The other boys had left at 7 a. m., and he had a very dull and desolate morning.[8]

Pollock was at his grandest on ceremonial occasions when, decked in his doctor's red robes, and surrounded by the royalty whose special favour he enjoyed, he could turn a speech day into a social event to rival Ascot.[9]

If the headmasters had changed since mid-Victorian times, so too had the boys and their parents. Thring may have attracted parents from the professional classes who were in sympathy with his educational experiment, but now new classes were sending their sons to the public schools. From about 1900, boys from homes of the *nouveaux riches* arrived in droves to make fashionable friends and to become gentlemen. Compared to his predecessor, the public-school boy of 1900 was pampered in terms of food and clothing, furniture and fittings, and, above all, in pocket money. Dressiness and an over-appreciation of sartorial splendour became commonplace in the schools.[10]

Religion was changing too. Welldon was certain that the British Empire was 'divinely ordained' to civilise the world; his mix of Christianity, crude imperialism and mawkish sentimentality was shared by many other headmasters. He was one of the first public-school headmasters to become a Freemason; he was not the last to capitalise on this institutional male camaraderie, and a new conservative force entered the world of schools.[11] The chapel was still officially the heart of each school but it was the scene for grand ceremonies and the sound of hearty singing of popular hymns rather than the setting for religious worship and moral guidance. Schools might publish their own hymn-books, and headmasters their sermons, but there was a hollow ring about the whole proceedings. To some there was no real morality: Arthur Ponsonby, later Lord Bessborough, found 'no setting up of an ideal, suggestions for moral training, no guidance for conduct, no aim for growing hopes and aspirations'.[12] Muscular Christianity certainly had its short-comings, but it did aim at moral education. Imperial Christianity, as a correspondent to *The Nation* explained, was merely an endorsement for a way of life:

> The average parent understands by religious training something which will provide a sanction for the commercial spirit and the existing social order. In a vague way he wishes his boy to realise that wealth is blessed

and poverty slightly discreditable, and that the British Empire is a sounder and more practical ideal than the Kingdom of Heaven. If a boy must be righteous it is desirable that his righteousness should not exceed that of the Scribes and the Pharisees; whatsoever is more than this comes of Socialism or some other evil thing.[13]

The growing regimentation of school life and the attendant erosion of a boy's individuality, factors noted in the late-Victorian public school, continued in the new century. Still more time was given to studies, to games, and to other organised activities, and less time was available for a boy's own disposal. At Rugby, the whole town was out of bounds, including places of worship, and mid-afternoon call-overs ensured that no boy could wander too far. Sunday afternoon chapel prevented long country walks, and for some its retention was a bastion of morality. Prudery was such that the Rugby *Rule Book* insisted that games shorts should be tied below the knee and, when showering, a boy needed two towels; one for drying himself, the other to preserve modesty. As housemasters relinquished the pastoral role that had been the norm in the past, and now rarely penetrated the boys' part of the house beyond the dining hall, so the general running of the school fell on the prefects.[14] New boys at Harrow were forced to box to amuse their elders; pretty boys were in high demand as fags; and violent initiation rites were rife.[15] In many schools this prefectorial power evolved into an absolute monarchy with, as at Harrow and Wellington, positive encouragement from the headmaster: the rule of the bloods was in earnest. The individual average boy, as Nicolson recalled, nearly sank without trace:

> At Wellington … one ceased to be an individual, to have any but a corporate identity, that the question scarcely arose whether one might or might not be odd. One was just a name, or rather a number on the list. The authorities in their desire to deprive us of all occasion for illicit intercourse deprived us of all occasion for any intercourse at all. We were not allowed to consort with boys not in our own house: a house consisted of thirty boys of whom ten at least were too old and ten too young for friendship; and thus during those four years my training in human relationships was confined to the ten boys who happened more or less to be my contemporaries. In addition, one was deprived of all initiative of action or occupation. The masters took pride in feeling that not only did they know what any given boy should be doing at that particular moment, but that they knew exactly what the said boy would be doing at 3.30 p.m. six weeks hence. We thus had no privacy and no leisure, there was never open to us the choice between two possible alternatives.[16]

Games continued to be an important part of the process of occupation and regimentation.[17] As the new century progressed, so more time was given to games and matters athletic dominated schoolboy thought, as Robert Bruce

Lockhart remembered: 'Everyone *still* talked sport; in fact, talked more sport than ever.'[18] Little had changed in the purpose of school sport: in 1885 Lord Harris wrote of the qualities of command and leadership that games instilled; fifteen years later, and now President of the MCC, he expounded in the same manner at a Dulwich speech day. In Harris's view, the public school had two aims: first, to make a boy a good citizen so that he might maintain England's honour and uphold the dignity of the British flag; second, to ensure that each boy got as much exercise as possible.[19] In this period of relative immunity from criticism, games as an institution went untroubled.[20] Kipling's outburst in *The Islanders* on 'muddied oafs' and 'flannelled fools' had not been universally well-received, for it was read as an affront to values which were widely shared, but one cannot but smile at Harold Nicolson's picture of such a hero:

> A tall figure, he seemed, in his black and orange jersey striped as a wasp. Upon his carefully oiled hair was stuck a little velvet cap with a gold tassel; he would walk away from the field, his large red hands pendant, a little mud upon his large red knees. He would pause for a moment and speak to a group of lower boys. "Yes, Marstock, – no, Marstock", they would answer, and then he would smile democratically, and walk on – a slight lilt in his gait betraying that he was not unconscious of how much he was observed.
>
> How clean he was, how straight, how manly! How proud we were of him, how modest he was about himself. And then those eyes – those frank and honest eyes. "One can see," my tutor said, "that Marstock has never had a mean or nasty thought" . . . It took me six years to realise that Marstock, although stuffed with opinions, had never had a thought at all.[21]

Edmond Warre's call in 1900 to the Headmasters' Conference to establish cadet corps in all public schools was answered swiftly. In the late 1890s only 12% of all public-school boys were in the corps, but soon it was to grow to more than a half.[22] Many advocated that all boys should be taught the rudiments of rifle mechanics and should learn how to shoot, and in quick succession Harrow, Rossall, Glenalmond, Repton, Dover and Wellington followed Uppingham's universal call to arms.[23] At first the corps rated poorly when compared to games:

> A father would feel it a grievance if his son, on leaving for good, were not a skilled proficient in some game, probably in more than one. . . . But he is usually quite indifferent if his boy is unable to hit a target at five hundred yards, or even if he is ignorant of how to load a rifle.[24]

But gradually the corps gained status and time, and by 1905 it rated as highly as any game. The Boer War helped to change attitudes but much of the credit was due to the skilful propaganda of the advocates – headmasters such as Warre at Eton, Cyril Norwood at Bristol Grammar School (and later Marlborough and Harrow) and John Way at Rossall – all of whom had actually commanded school corps. The cries of militarism were stifled with strong protestations of peaceful intent and of service to the community; more importantly, the corps was offered to the boys and parents in the manner that Kipling advocated, as if it were a game. Character-training overtones that had earlier been the preserve of games were readily attached to corps activities.[25] It comes as no surprise to find the term 'manly' attached to them:

> The voluntary submission to a sound military training, as a duty, for the good of their country, and the defence of those near and dear, may indeed be said to lay a sound foundation for the finest type of Christian manliness.[26]

In the conservative public-school world, where there is no house like *the* house, and no school like *the* school, the narrow, local patriotism of *esprit de corps* was easily extended to the corps.

The first years of the new century saw the public schools at the peak of their popularity. They were full; they were respected; they educated royalty as never before; they were relatively free of criticism. Their speech days were magnificent, their ceremonials were grand. They were the very picture of conservative, imperialist, Edwardian England. But, as David Newsome found when writing on the Pollock period at Wellington, appearances were deceptive: the life of the average boy was not as glowing as painted; and the gloss and glamour hid the true health of the school. The Golden Age was less solid gold and more a thin film. Newsome's predicament over Pollock can legitimately be extended to many headmasters. It is indeed hard to distinguish between 'true ideals and cant', between 'honesty and insincerity' and between 'real values and sham'.[27] The early and mid-Victorian headmasters seem sincere, simple and worthy when compared to the shadowy figures of their late-Victorian and Edwardian successors. Perhaps, as the President of the Council at Marlborough asserted, they were honest in their attempt to produce 'a manly, straightforward character, a scorn for lying and meanness, habits of obedience and command, and fearless courage', but the evidence does not support them. The Edwardian headmaster may have given his school a bit of polish and a grace of manner, the *gravitas* of a leisured gentleman and the *dignitas* in outward appearance to match it, but beneath the surface all was not well. 'Conform or be kicked', Arnold Lunn declared in *The Harrovians*, was the command that should have been written over the portals of every public school.[28] These years saw the destruction of the individual boy and his absorption into the group type. Behaviour was governed by 'good form', and characters were moulded to the new ideal of manliness – a healthy, good mannered type, but philistine in taste and without moral strength; religion was totally unimportant. These same years saw the acceptance of the materialism and snobbery of the *nouveaux riches*, the peak in athleticism and the noisy rattle of militaristic imperialism. Then too, the homosexuality that had been kept in bounds by the earlier freedom and moral zeal now sprouted in the atmosphere of regimented manliness.

Selwyn and Uppingham were perhaps no more than a typical headmaster and a typical school, but the contrast with the Thring years is stark.[29]

VII Democratic manliness: 'Be Prepared'

All schooling in the British Isles was independent of the state before the implementation of William Forster's Elementary Education Act in 1870 and Arthur Balfour's Secondary Education Act of 1902. Free education for all children up to the age of eleven was introduced in 1891; in 1899 the school-leaving age was raised to twelve years and then to fourteen in 1918. The evolution of the ideal of manliness was thus the preserve of the public schools until at least the turn of the century, and perhaps beyond. The public-school Old Boys may have taken their games to their parishes and factories, but these activities were more for the recreation of their parishioners and workers rather than for their education. Not until the 1880s did it seem proper to provide wider aspects of education to the lower classes.

The first influences came through The Young Men's Christian Association, or YMCA, with its aim of Christian brotherhood, and with the efforts of various national recreation societies. Octavia Hill and Lord Brabazon were two of many who endeavoured to provide gymnasia, playgrounds, parks and open spaces for working-class children, while George Fletcher was one of a group of public-school medical officers who sought to bring physical education into the curriculum of the public elementary school.[1] By the 1890s physical training and drill were being introduced under the insistence of Lord Meath's National Physical Recreation Society. Its members were appalled by the poor physical state of working-class men, women and children, and by the high rejection rate of working-class recruits for the Army, and they sought to gain the benefits that Sweden and Germany had found from their state-sponsored gymnastic programmes.[2] By the turn of the century, the militarists were advocating the formation of cadet corps for working-class children and drill classes in the elementary schools to complement the public-school corps.[3] The last were providing the officers, now attention should be given to the other ranks.[4]

The work of all these groups was only marginally involved with the propagation of the ideal of manliness but for two others, the Boys' Brigade and the Boy Scouts, it was a central aim. Through these enormously popular boys' organisations, the public-school ideal of manliness reached hundreds of thousands of boys who never attended these schools, and eventually it infused the whole system of state-provided secondary education.

The Boys' Brigade was founded by William Smith in 1883. Smith, a Scot born in 1854, came from an army background and as a young man in Glasgow his main interests were the Church, the YMCA and the Militia. The Boys' Brigade was based on the idea of using militia volunteer methods in Sunday schools,

schools created by churches and chapels from the 1780s to provide education to working children on their one day of release from the factory, field or mine. Smith felt that these schools would be more exciting, and thus more able to hold on to their boys, if they instilled 'discipline and *esprit de corps*' – but he had no plans for the girls. The first Brigade was launched from the Free College Church Mission in Glasgow and it numbered three officers and twenty-eight boys: three years later there were four companies with nearly 2000 boys, and by the 1890s the movement was nationwide. The Brigade was restricted to boys over twelve, whilst Old Boys were encouraged to return as leaders. Through activities such as elementary drill with dummy rifles, physical exercises, team games and camping – the Boys' Brigade was one of the pioneers of camping – Smith endeavoured to inculcate 'that *esprit de corps* which public school boys acquire as a matter of course'.[5]

> Our aim was to band the boys together and create an *esprit de corps* that would make them proud of their company, jealous of the honour, ashamed to do anything to disgrace it, and prepared to make any sacrifice rather than be dismissed from it.[6]

A Christian, moral education was an integral part of Smith's plan and, unlike later lads' brigades, the Boys' Brigade was undenominational in nature. As Smith explained:

> By associating Christianity with all that is most noble and manly in a boy's sight, they would be going a long way to disabuse his mind of the far too prevalent idea that there is something essentially feminine about it, and that, while it is all right for girls, it is something alien to the nature of high spirited boys.[7]

All Brigades were thus attached to churches or church missions, and bible-reading classes formed a compulsory part of the programme. Manliness was the central Christian ideal: 'All a boy's aspirations are towards manliness, however mistaken his ideas may be as to what true manliness means.' Smith's stated 'Object' in the Boys' Brigade was more specific: 'The Advancement of Christ's Kingdom among boys, and the promotion of habits of Reverence, Discipline, Self-Respect, and all that tends towards a true Christian Manliness'.[8]

The Boys' Brigades did magnificent work throughout the country and soon various offspring groups, all owing much to Smith's ideals, were founded. Many of the new brigades were associated with particular religious denominations – the Anglican Church Lads' Brigade, the Catholic Boys' Brigade and the Jewish Lads' Brigade. The Boys' Life Brigade, founded in 1899 and later to amalgamate with the original, also included the phrase 'manly Christian character' in its aims. As the brigades expanded, so support came from figures as varied as the Archbishop of Canterbury and the military Lords Methuen, Wolseley, Roberts and Kitchener. By the turn of the century, Methuen, wanting the brigades to be in step with the public schools, was advocating that all the lads should be taught to shoot.[9]

Robert Baden-Powell's Boy Scouts' movement was, however, the most popular and most influential of the offspring of the Boys' Brigade. Baden-Powell's background contrasts vividly with Smith's, and much of the difference between the two movements can be traced back to their respective founders. Whilst Smith was the quiet Scot from a humble background who came to the Boys' Brigade from Sunday schools, Baden-Powell was a public-school Old Boy, a dashing army officer and, through his exploits at Mafeking in the Boer War, a national hero.[10] Born in 1857, educated at Charterhouse and then straight into the Army, Baden-Powell possessed all the late-Victorian public-school attributes. He felt that he had gained nothing at all in the classroom at school, for he believed 'the main point in Public School Training is that it supplies Commonsense, Manners and Guts, even if it does not supply knowledge'. Team games prepared the player 'for the greater game of life', and they promoted discipline in obedience to rules and to the captain, fair play, and playing for one's side and not for personal glory.[11] The Army brought new sports – polo, hunting and pig-sticking. And then there was the adventure and the fighting, with all their appeal to 'any red-blooded man'.[12]

When he was serving in India in 1899, Baden-Powell wrote a small book, *Aids to Scouting*, for his fellow soldiers. The book was produced cheaply so that even privates could afford it and, as it was published at the time of the author's Mafeking exploits, the sales were enormous. Though the book is outwardly a military text, in effect it is bound up with the training of a scout's character: the good scout needed pluck, self-reliance, confidence and discretion. Baden-Powell pioneered straightforward, colloquial and readable writing for boys; the book was a folksy collection of yarns with much exotic vocabulary – posse, jamboree and the like.[13] On his return to England after the Boer War, Baden-Powell found that this book was being used by various boys' groups, including the Boys' Brigade, and that the editor of *Boys of the Empire* had serialised the contents under the heading 'Boy Scout'.[14] Then in 1905, after being invited by Smith to inspect the Glasgow Boys' Brigades on the twenty-fifth anniversary of their founding, he decided to form his own boys' movement.[15] In 1907 the Boys Scouts were created, and in 1910 the founder retired from the Army to devote all his energies to the new venture. The first camp was held in 1907 on Brownsea Island in Poole Harbour. The party of twenty comprised ten public-school boys and ten working-class members of the Boys' Brigade: this social mixing was important, for through his Scouts Baden-Powell hoped to break down class prejudice.[16]

Baden-Powell thought that city life was eroding national values and character, that the popular press was steering young men to hedonism and that these would undermine the fitness of the nation.[17] Baden-Powell grafted new ideas on to the established practice of the Boys' Brigade, ideas gleaned from his years as a soldier and from his experiences with the famed Mafeking Cadet Corps, boys who were trained to support the troops, carry messages and help in the hospital throughout the duration of the siege. The well-known scout uniform was adopted from the khaki shorts and shirt, plus the wide-brimmed hat, of the Mafeking boys with other touches borrowed from the South African Constabulary. Drilling was rejected as being too conformist; boyhood gangs were transformed into scout patrols; and an emphasis on outdoor life was stressed far more than by any comparable organisation.[18] In effect the Scouts were a realisation of Kipling's ideals of *Stalky and Co.*, and indeed Kipling's tales of Kim and of India were adopted as part of scouting mythology.[19]

The fundamental purpose of the Scouts was the character-training of the nation's youth: it was to be an education in manliness.[20] Initially only boys aged eleven to fifteen could join; by 1916 younger boys aged eight to eleven were admitted; and soon older boys were drawn in as Rovers.[21] The Wolf Cubs, the organisation for the younger boys, drew heavily on Kipling's *The Jungle Book* and the adventures of the man-cub Mowgli.[22] The games mania of the public schools, in Baden-Powell's opinion, created a boyish, immature product whereas he sought to fashion a more adult version. Boys, he argued, always aimed to grow up; only men harked back to childhood games. The emphasis in the Scouts would therefore be on adult, manly pursuits, and field sports were preferred to team games.[23] The adult theme was reinforced as Baden-Powell drew on chivalry for the basic scouting code of conduct. From this foundation Baden-Powell framed the Scout 'Promise' to do one's duty to God and the King; to do a good turn every day; and to obey the ten components of the Scout Law:

1   A Scout's Honour is to be trusted.
2   A Scout is Loyal.
3   A Scout's Duty is to be useful.
4   A Scout is a friend to all.
5   A Scout is courteous.
6   A Scout is a friend to animals.
7   A Scout obeys orders.
8   A Scout smiles and whistles under all difficulties.
9   A Scout is thrifty.
10 A Scout is clean in thought, word and deed.[24]

The promise and the laws were the most exact formula of the contemporary ideal of manliness; all the ingredients were included. Through obedience to these laws, and through the various scouting activities, Baden-Powell determined that the ideal of manliness would be inculcated into the youth of the country; what the ordinary school curriculum could not provide, scouting would; and the qualities of observation, endurance, courage, patience, resourcefulness, self-reliance, nerve, a love of nature and comradeship would no longer be the preserve of the public-school boy but would be available to all.[25] Boys were also afforded a degree of autonomy, and the absolute conformity found in other youth organisations and in the public schools was absent. Here Baden-Powell adopted ingredients of working-class manliness with its stress on being able to 'look after yourself'; indeed, 'Be Prepared', borrowed from the South African Constabulary, was the Scout's motto.[26]

The Boys' Brigade was primarily a movement for the working classes whereas the Boy Scouts had a wider appeal. Of the 14,000 scouts enrolled in 1913, a large proportion was from middle-class backgrounds and many of the troops were attached to grammar schools.[27] During the last quarter of the nineteenth century and in the first years of the new one, increased attention was paid to the state secondary education programme. Old grammar school foundations were revived, and new ones created to give an education based on public-school lines to intelligent middle- and lower-class children. The Scout troops attached to these schools did much to inculcate public-school ideals; many more aims and methods, practices and philosophies, principles and prejudices were adopted straight from the original models. The new grammar schools had a strong religious tone, with assemblies each morning instead of the public-school chapel, and most of the headmasters were in Holy Orders. Many of the masters were public-school Old Boys; a strong emphasis was placed on sixth-form scholarship; and prefectorial systems were universally adopted. Almost all were wholly day-schools, yet the boys were split into four to six houses, though the only expression of house feeling in most schools was limited to sporting competitions. Public-school games and their attendant fashion accessories were taken on with enthusiasm: rowing generally proved too expensive, and so Rugby football proved the staple diet − it certainly could not be the working-class game of Association football. Education for leadership became the aim of the schools and soon the airs and graces of their second-hand public-school image brought out all the worst in social snobbery in towns and cities throughout the country. Sixty years later and the grammar-school pattern had hardly changed at all: the ideal of manliness had spread well beyond the confines of the public-school cloisters.

VIII Henty and Co.: 'The glory of battle and adventure'

The ideal of manliness gained even broader circulation in much of the popular literature of the period. The 1880s and 1890s witnessed a flourish of historical adventure novels for boys, all plotting the exploits of their manly heroes; then the years after 1900 saw the heyday of the public-school novel for men and the public-school story for boys, each portraying the ideal of manliness in action. Such literature not only broadened the horizons of the ideal but also helped to sustain it. These tales of adventure and public-school stories were avidly read by the very boys who would go to those schools at the age of eleven or thirteen;

thus each new boy had a picture of the code of conduct he ought to employ before setting a foot over the threshold.

Of all the countless writers for boys of the late-Victorian years, it is G. A. Henty who was the most popular and most widely read. Between 1868 and the turn of the century, Henty produced over a hundred books at a rate of three a year. More than 150,000 copies of each book were sold and serialisation in journals broadened the market further. At his death in 1902, the usually staid *London Sketch* felt that 'by the death of George Henty, the boys of England lose one of the best friends they ever had'.[1]

Henty in real life was almost as large as his heroes were in fiction. Born in 1832 and educated at Westminster, Henty went up to Caius College, Cambridge. There he was pictured as a true muscular Christian – 'a big, robust, heavy, manly looking Englishman' – who spent most of his time boxing, wrestling, rowing, fencing and on fifty-mile-a-day walks about the countryside.[2] Whilst at Cambridge, Henty's imagination was fired by the excitement of the Crimean War and he left the university without taking his degree in order to enlist and play his part. He was appointed to the Commissariat Department of the army and set off to the battlefield. This post, however, did not bring him close enough to the action so he transferred to become a war correspondent for a London newspaper, the *Morning Advertiser*. He went on to cover the 1868 British expedition to Abyssinia, the Franco-Prussian War, the Ashanti War in West Africa, the Carlist Rebellion in Spain and the Turco-Serbian War. He also witnessed the opening of the Suez Canal, followed Garibaldi's progress through Italy, and travelled to Palestine, Russia and India. Many of his later tales were drawn from his own adventures.[3]

Henty prided himself on the historical accuracy of his books and he added a sense of 'I was there' reality to bring the stress of war right into the reader's home.[4] Henty inserted heroic boys into a succession of true historical events and, by this personalised approach, he persuaded young boys to identify with real adult heroes.[5] Whether it was with Clive in India, Wellington in the Peninsula, Roberts in Kandahar, or Buller in Natal, Henty was always able to take the boy reader right to the heart of the action. To aid the process, the hero was generally a 'fighting boy', 'very manly, full, as he termed it, of pluck'. He had well-developed muscles and a Stalky-like eye for the main chance; he believed in fair play but rarely displayed his inner feelings.[6] And there was nothing 'namby-pamby' about Henty's writings: he once ventured to allow a boy of twelve to kiss a girl of eleven, but he received so many indignant letters that he never allowed the lapse to be repeated. Like Baden-Powell, Henty believed that a boy's one 'aim is to become a man and read what men do and have done'.[7] The novels exuded an English nationalistic pride in the race that had peopled North America, Australia and the south of Africa, held possession of India and stood forth as the greatest civiliser in the world; practical patriotism displaced muscular Christianity.[8]

In the wake of Henty's success, the late-Victorian years saw a spate of nationalistic boys' journals hit the newsagents and the railway-station bookstalls.[9] Each had a manly title – *Pluck, Captain, Vanguard* and more – and all were full of tales in the style of the master.[10] Their heroes, labelled 'Tom Brown's Imperialist Sons' by Louis James, reflected the jingoistic attitude of the nation.[11] The stories abound in racial stereotypes, with the English always uppermost: the Russians are treacherous and loutish; the Spaniards are cruel; the Chinese are wily; and dark skins can only be savages, and thus can be killed without compunction.[12]

Literature from a higher plane was presented to boys in a similar manner and became an essential disciplinary aspect of the imperial project: in 1891 the poet William Henley compiled 'a fighting book' of verse for boys.[13] Its purpose was to

> set forth, as only art can, the beauty and the joy of living, the beauty and the blessedness of death, the glory of battle and adventure, the nobility of devotion – to a cause, an ideal, a passion even – the dignity of resistance, the sacred quality of patriotism, this is my ambition here.[14]

Henley held the view that working-class young men of the period did not match their fathers in terms of patriotism, determination and courage: public-school boys learnt of self-sacrifice in the nation's cause from their study of the classics; boys at the elementary schools needed something similar.[15] These *Lyra Heroica* – Tennyson's 'The Heavy Brigade', Cory's 'The Two Captains', Kipling's 'The Flag of England', Austin's 'Is Life Worth Living?' and a host more – proved immensely popular and were still being given as school prizes thirty years later.

The successors to Henty's tales of adventure and excitement in the new century, with manly heroes who always started the day with a cold bath, came from the pens of Captain F. S. Brereton, Herbert Strang, Percy Westerman, E. W. Hornung, Arthur Conan Doyle and, above all, John Buchan.[16] Buchan was the very epitome of the whole-man ideal and talented enough to be listed in *Who's Who* when still an Oxford undergraduate. Buchan's manliness credentials were pure: a confirmed Platonist; a lover of Wordsworth's pantheistic poetry; a biographer of Walter Scott; and an enthusiast for Kingsley's stories of Devonian seamen in Elizabethan times. Though not a public-school boy and no games-player, Buchan exuded all the best qualities of the ideal. Indeed, his lack of a public-school and games-playing background may have aided his manliness for it is of an earlier age, almost mid-Victorian in its roundedness. Like Parkin, Buchan was a convinced imperial federationist, dreaming of a world-wide brotherhood with a common background of race and creed, and consecrated to the service of peace.[17] Buchan dedicated his life to service: first as secretary to Lord Milner, another federationist, in South Africa; back home as a Member of Parliament; then courageous service in the Great War; and finally as Governor-General of Canada.

Buchan wrote his first tale of manly exploits in 1910; the result was *Prester John*.[18] It tells the story of a young Scotsman – David Crawfurd – and his adventures in South Africa at the time of a Zulu uprising. In quick succession other adventure stories followed, including the famed Richard Hannay series, notably *The Thirty-Nine Steps*. Though the books were written in a nationalistic age and on an imperial background, there is no mock patriotism.[19] All his books sold widely, and from them the boys at school in the years before the Great War gained some insight into a purer ideal of manliness.

The hugely popular boys' magazines that flourished in the years either side of 1900, with sales totalling a million each week, not only carried tales of adventure but, as a regular ingredient, also contained accounts of public-school life. Both genre were filled with rousing plots, an imperial outlook, and character training – and little religion or virtue.[20] Talbot Baines Reed, the king of *Boy's Own Paper* writers, penned their first school tale in 1879, but it was not until the turn of the century that every issue of the magazine had to contain such a story to satisfy its readership.[21] These tales kept alive the public-school legend, passed it on to the new generation and spread the public-school ideal to thousands of boys who would never come near such a school.[22] A historian as eminent as E. C. Mack felt sure that in this way the *Boy's Own Paper* influenced in no small way the course of public-school history.[23] The formula for these tales was fairly standard, almost *Tom Brown's Schooldays* but without the seriousness and idealism. Manliness for the masses was equated with patriotism, sturdiness, steadfastness, and sound common-sense: the readers of *Boy's Own Paper* were to be trained to follow their public-school leaders and so would not need the higher qualities of the elite model.[24] The picture they portray of public-school life was remarkably realistic, especially when few of the writers had attended these schools themselves. Countless longer public-school stories were published in book form, often for only a few pence. The advertisement for Walter C. Rhoades's *Our Fellow at St. Mark's* indicated that it managed to roll all the excitement of *Tom Brown* and *Eric* into one:

> It concerns the adventures of Grayson and his friends at St. Mark's School. All the elements which go to make up a good school story are here: exciting school sports, cricket and football matches, the thrashing of a bully, narrow escapes and brave rescues, an adventure at sea, and a host of other important things.[25]

Through these myriad tales, public-school practice and a simple manliness built on conventional courage were presented to generations of boys.

Stories of public-school life were not reserved for boys alone. The 1899 publication of Kipling's *Stalky and Co.* released a barrage of public-school novels for adult readers. They were avidly read, especially in the Edwardian years, in an atmosphere that some contemporary observers felt was 'child worship' or a 'cult of childhood.'[26] The most notable works in a long line of titles were Vachell's *The Hill* (1905), Portman's *Hugh Rendall* (1905), Gilkes's *A Day at Dulwich* (1905), Newbolt's *The Twymans* (1911), Walpole's *Mr. Perrin and Mr. Traill* (1911) and Hornung's *Fathers of Men* (1912).[27] With the exception of *Mr. Perrin and Mr. Traill*, a story about masters rather than boys, the novels have a basic formula not too different from that of the tales for younger readers. The new boy enters the school with a mixture of fearful apprehension and determined ambition; he has usually read about Tom Brown or Eric or both; at first he suffers from loneliness and the rigours of fagging; then comes the regimentation of games and the harshness of masters; he makes a few friends as he moves up the school; and he becomes free, mischievous and leads a rebellious life. Eventually he learns true manliness, becomes a loyal prefect and helps put down bullying, the excesses of athleticism or both; finally, as he leaves the school with regret, he is soundly placed on the path of a successful life. Most of the novels owe their lineage to Tom Brown rather than to Eric or Stalky: in the last the individual is everything and the school nothing; in the Edwardian successors, it is the school that plays the role of alchemist, transmuting the base metal of childhood into the purity of manhood.

The Hill, with its snobbishness and its ardent Imperial Christianity, we have already met; so too we have examined the conservative patriotism of *The Twymans*. Lionel Portman's *Hugh Rendall* was set at Wellington in Pollock's headmastership. It pictured a school seeking aristocratic favours; bursting with 'manly' games; striving for *esprit de corps*; and ridden with mild homosexuality. Portman supported the athletic ideal of manliness so that boys might 'absorb some of the indefinable elements that constitute an English gentleman':

> To judge one's fellows mainly by their muscles and power of using them in a certain way may seem ludicrous enough to older eyes. But the idea, if primitive, is undeniably sound. Apart from the other and more obvious advantages, games have this above all – that they create a corporate life, an absorbing common interest which would not otherwise exist. And so the boy who will not play his part in that corporate life is generally tabooed; while of him that thinks of little else the world can reasonably expect the soundest citizenship when he grows up.[28]

A Day at Dulwich was one of several novels on the school written by A. H. Gilkes, at that time its headmaster. The hero is a manly boy, and the role of the school is the inculcation of manliness:

> The aim may be described with much precision. The qualities which make a man are truthfulness, cleanness, courage, public spirit, kindness, with an understanding quickened in all directions, and most of all in the direction of that Unseen power which rules us all; these qualities, together with a healthy body, seem to us schoolmasters to be those at the production of which we should aim.[29]

This, then, was the vein of the Edwardian public-school novel; and it was not until the liberal attacks on the schools in the years before the Great War that the tone changed. For the present, the athletic-imperialist ideal of manliness was secure.

IX Bachelor boys: 'The flight from domesticity'

Edward Thring encouraged his masters to marry young and to waste no time before raising children. All his housemasters were married men and many had large families: Thring led by example with five children, a total matched by Hodgkinson, Walter Earle, Hesketh Williams, Mullins and Vale-Bagshawe. William Earle raised four and Mathias just three; but ahead of them were Candler's family of seven, Haslam's eight and the prolific Campbell with ten.[1] Women and girls comprised a significant part of the school community and their presence was appreciated by boys and their parents.[2] In an era when the wives of professional men did not have their own careers, all the housemasters' wives served as help-meets, a very Victorian term, to their husbands. Sophia Haslam's role as mother to one sons and seven daughters did not prevent her from supporting her husband by supervising the house in his absence, dining with the boys, tending the sick and spectating at sporting contests; and she was a housemaster's wife for thirty-seven years.[3] None of the housemasters' daughters attended Uppingham as pupils and most, like the Thring daughters, were probably taught at home by governesses.[4] It is likely that their education did not contain the rigour of the boys' curriculum.

The role of Uppingham's mothers and daughters matched that of mothers and daughters from middle-class families throughout mid-Victorian Britain: they were no threat to the status of their fathers and brothers; nor did they compete for their university places or jobs. Change, however, was in the air. The few schools for girls that existed before 1850 deliberately neglected academic subjects and physical exercise in favour of stylish accomplishments; by the 1860s, however, many middle-class parents wanted to do better by their daughters. They were supported by the findings of the 1868 Taunton Commission: in a side effect of the examination of endowed grammar schools for boys, the commissioners were highly critical of girls' education. The result was that new day schools for girls were founded to provide a rigorous academic education – beginning in London and then extending to most major cities. The first was North London Collegiate School, founded in 1850 by Frances Mary Buss; the term 'collegiate' was used to distinguish the schooling from that provided by 'home-based' governesses. The first girls' boarding school, Cheltenham Ladies' College, followed three years later; Dorothea Beale became its principal in 1858.

A select few women were able to receive a university education, if not university degrees, with the foundation of Girton and Newnham Colleges at Cambridge (1869 and 1871) and Lady Margaret Hall and Somerville College at Oxford (1878 and 1879). In 1878 the University of London was the first to accept women on equal terms with men and to award degrees to female students. Teaching was one of the few professions open to women, though their status was much lower than that for their male counterparts, and in the following decades the new girls' public schools appointed young mistresses from the universities, many of whom had enjoyed sports. These 'Lady Blues' carried their love of learning and enthusiasm for games with them, and shared them with the next generation of girls. Girls' public schools emulated much that was happening in boys' schools, but they avoided imperial jingoism, and athleticism never became a cult. Sport was primarily used for health and moral education purposes, but it was also associated with freedom and thus played its part in the push for women's progress in education and in society.

Following the lead of Thring, who invited the Association of Headmistresses to bring their annual conference to Uppingham in 1887, the girls' schools adopted a comprehensive physical education programme well before the majority of games-mad boys' schools. Gymnastics, swimming and games were all on the curriculum: North London Collegiate built a gymnasium in 1879; taught swimming in the 1880s; and acquired playing-fields in 1885. Physical education and games at Cheltenham Ladies' were taught solely by a team of specialist teachers, the start of a female tradition that was not to be rivalled by the men until the 1940s. Newly-adapted or imported female-only games such as rounders, netball and lacrosse were adopted to avoid taints of masculinity. The 30-plus members of the Girls' Public Day Schools Company maintained this progress with a physical education specialist in every school and an overall inspector for the subject. The boarding schools at St Leonards and Roedean placed even more emphasis on physical education: the former introducing Swedish gymnastics in 1891, the latter appointing three graduates of what was to become the Bergman-Österberg Physical Training College. This, the first of a string of women's colleges founded in the 1890s, espoused the Swedish tradition whilst the rival Chelsea College, as it was later known, looked to Germany for its gymnastics. Together they created a new career path for middle-class girls.[5]

The boost in the educational and career opportunities for women, their newly-won right to control their own wealth and finances, and their liberation from compulsory domesticity did not go unnoticed by public-school men.[6] Many saw a threat to the patriarchal *status quo* and feared increased competition for jobs. Some felt enervated and challenged by the new female confidence; others saw it as evidence that Britain was becoming over-civilised and going soft; many feared being henpecked at home.[7] Male responses were many and varied, and they lasted until the Great War. The age of first marriage for professional men rose to thirty in 1885.[8]

The domestic bliss of wife and family had been central to middle-class masculine identity, a haven for the hard-working professional man to return to after a long day at the office. The regular companionship with his wife reminded him of goodness and virtue; home was a morally wholesome environment; and a large family provided potent evidence of his manly virility.[9] Now some women of this class chose to follow careers rather than marry; more opted to delay marriage to a time of their choice; still more chose to have smaller families. The average upper- and middle-class family dropped from 6.4 children in the 1850s to 3.5 in the 1880s.

The relationship between husband and wife changed too. Many men distanced themselves from all domestic matters and consequently showed less affection for their wives and interest in their children. They might stay at work longer and perhaps go on to their clubs in the evening; a London-based professional might even remain in the city all week, only returning home for the weekend. A man who stayed at home too long might be viewed by his peers as unmanly.[10]

The public schools were not immune to the cultural shift. From 1853 until 1901 almost all housemasters at Uppingham were married men; ten years later a third were bachelors. Anecdotal evidence suggests that this pattern was replicated, even expanded, in most public schools.[11] H. Lionel Rogers, a master at Edwardian Radley College, agreed: 'In most public schools the assistant masters lead a life which is essentially monastic.' Rossall in 1909 had just two married men on the staff, one the headmaster.[12] A Mr Elstow, writing in *The Spectator* in 1902, was fearful: 'We should soon have feminine influence totally excluded from our public schools, with disastrous results.'[13] A. C. Benson, a bachelor housemaster at Eton, made a strong case for what he termed the 'celibate housemaster': he was free from domestic cares; did not need to make a large profit to support his family; and could devote all his evenings and weekends to his boys. Then, when the holidays came, he would be refreshed on foreign jaunts with his bachelor friends, whereas the married housemaster had to try and pick up the threads of a 'broken domestic life'.[14] In this wholly masculine world boys' studies became less homely with few family mementos on display; mothers and sisters were rarely mentioned; calling boys by their Christian names was viewed as cissy; whilst Lyttelton banned plays at Haileybury that needed boys to play girls' roles. All this was part of the hardening process of a public school.[15] The boy, who in previous generations was seen as 'the angel in the house' for the care he showed to the weak, was now more likely to be shunned as 'the degenerate in the cupboard'. Close friendships between boys were judged morally undesirable and the physical contact of hugs and holding hands became taboo.[16]

The adult world became more masculine too. University colleges continued the regime of the public school, new monastic religious foundations were created, East London settlements attracted male artists and writers, and the number of men-only clubs in London and all provincial cities rapidly increased.[17] Some clubs were founded to support academic and cultural interests; more were socially exclusive havens for masonic rituals or luxurious recreation; still more provided opportunities for sport.[18] Sport, newly popular golf and mountaineering included, provided more excuses why men need not be at home at the weekends and contributed to the decline in church attendance. The turn of the century was the best of times for clubs and for London's clubland in particular.[19] The fictional life enjoyed by A. J. Raffles in

Hornung's tales – an apartment in Piccadilly's Albany and membership of the Old Bohemians – reflected the reality for thousands of full-time and part-time *fin de siècle* bachelors.

Bachelorhood was a voluntary life-style for middle-class men living in Britain, but it was a necessity for those serving in the Empire. Few women travelled from the home country to the colonies – the heyday of the 'fishing fleet' lay in the future – and racially-based imperial orders discouraged mixed-race marriages for the men stationed there. The Empire thus became a play-ground for perpetual adolescents, acting out buccaneering lives in the manner of Boy Scouts or Stalkies – lives that were legitimised in countless imperial novels. Baden-Powell, Milner, Rhodes, Kitchener, Gordon, Lawrence and many more imperial heroes were the real-life exemplars: all were confirmed bachelors or married late in life.[20] As John Tosh wrote: 'Empire was man's business.'[21]

Both at home and abroad, a new hegemonic masculinity exerted great influence in the decades either side of the new century. Its members rejected family life and domesticity – Tosh coined the much-borrowed phrase 'flight from domesticity' – and chose competition as the way to manhood, honour and glory as the prize, and recognition by peers as the sole means of validation. Manly appearance was important: the Army had long compelled soldiers to grow moustaches to present a more fearsome impression and to suggest an aura of command; now the custom was adopted by most professional men.[22] Other prized manly qualities included raw strength, courage, aggression and a loyal commitment to other members of the tribe.[23] This tribe revelled in the seamless homosocial world of public-school boarding houses, university colleges, the Army, the London professions, clubland, sports clubs and the Empire.[24]

The mid-Victorian public-school boy had been encouraged to keep himself chaste, saving himself for eventual marriage to a woman of his own race and class; religious appeal was the medium for the message, usually by headmasters. The concern that masturbation would lead to debility was no longer accepted in the succeeding decades; purity thus became the watchword from the 1880s, and a major concern for parents and schools. Such purity was synonymous with manliness and its opposite was homosexuality. This manliness was also the ideal of the members of the homosocial hegemony but it may not always have been realised in practice.[25]

The attractions of homoerotic and aesthetic decadence proved too great a temptation for some – at least until the trial and conviction of Oscar Wilde in 1895 for gross indecency with other men.[26] Others sought alternative means to sublimate or satisfy their sexual demands. Native women in the Empire presented no challenge to an Englishman's authority and, despite official disapproval but unofficial blind-eyes, many men sought their pleasure in far-off lands.[27] Wealthy men in the home country could turn to art for their satisfaction. The late-Victorian period witnessed an obsession with sexually-charged paintings of idealised representations of near-naked adolescent girls, all set in classical or exotic landscapes. The girls' poses and outward gazes were seductive to the male viewer, but also threatening.[28] Throughout the 1880s and 1890s, the London galleries were filled with works of this nature by Lawrence Alma-Tadema, Edward Poynter, Frederic Leighton, John Waterhouse, Albert Moore, John Godward and a host of imitators. Their sweet imagery blurred the distinction between woman as a saint, angel in the house, or siren on the street. Many of these classically-set portrayals were, like Sextus Propertius's *Monobiblos* and Homer's story of Circe and Odysseus, from well-known public-school texts. In all these paintings, female sexual desire was seen as a threat to male security and solidarity.[29]

X Turning the tide: 'Go and practise what you have learned in the hard unsympathetic world'

A. C. Benson and others continued to direct their fire at the conservatism of the public schools and on the tyranny of games in particular; as the new century unfolded, so the voice of liberalism grew louder. A radical political swing to the left in 1906 had allowed a Liberal government led by Henry Campbell-Bannerman to succeed Arthur Balfour's ardently imperialist Conservatives, with a landslide victory over all other parties. The new government's reforms placed great emphasis on social improvements at home at the expense of imperial and military budgets; a liberal change was in the air. That change came slowly to the schools, and it had neither dug deep nor expanded far before the declaration of the Great War, but a change had indeed begun. It can be traced in the public-school novels of the period and in the schools themselves.

Two novels particularly reflect the new liberalism; G. F. Bradby's *The Lanchester Tradition* and Arnold Lunn's *The Harrovians*, both published in 1913.[1] Bradby was a much respected housemaster at Rugby, and one who was intolerant of 'the militarists, the athletocrat, the sacerdotalist, the precious highbrow, the educational faddist'.[2] He was never an enemy of new ideas, but he was wary of endangering the unity of a school's moral purpose. In *The Lanchester Tradition*, Bradby used gentle sarcasm to report how the principles and practices set by a great former headmaster, Dr Lanchester, are imbedded in whole fabric of the school but that they mean different things to different groups. Old Boys, masters and governors interpret the inheritance to suit their own purposes. Chandler is the personification of the athletic housemaster 'who finds it easier to be chivalrous to a vanquished foe than fair to a victorious one'. A triumph in a house-match

did not mean merely that his boys, by superior will or skill, had scored one goal more than the boys of another house. It meant, somehow, that the Lanchester tradition had been vindicated; that all that was best and noblest in the place, all that had made the past glorious and the present fulfilled, had, in the face of tremendous odds, asserted itself in a supreme and convincing manner. He was glad that his house had taken the field with two of their best players away, glad that le Willows had sprained his ankle and that the referee had been blatantly unfair. All things had worked together for good, and misfortunes which looked like irretrievable disasters had only served to enhance the moral sublimity of the victory.[3]

Football, the school's own brand, was the sole means of engendering manliness; the only impressive thing about the chapel was the singing of popular hymns, and that was noisy rather than reverent. The school, Bradby recorded, exuded all the most important virtues of the public-school traditions – loyalty, discipline, gentlemanly behaviour and a subordination of the individual will to the interests of the community. *The Lanchester Tradition* is, of course, a parody of the legacy of Thomas Arnold, a legacy that countless public schools now claimed as their own; what is perhaps surprising is that it should have come from a conservative housemaster at the school Arnold made famous. When a new headmaster is appointed to Bradby's fictional school, he tries to limit athleticism and improve the moral tone; in the process he comes up against that Lanchester tradition. Then one of the masters discovers some old papers belonging to the great man and the false premises on which the tradition had been built become clear to all.[4]

In contrast to Bradby's scholarly cynicism, Arnold Lunn produced the first realistic school novel; it was based on a diary he kept at school between 1902 and 1907. Lunn set out to show as sham the sentimentality of that earlier Harrow novel, *The Hill. The Harrovians* caused immediate outrage and indignation, and Lunn was forced to resign from his five London clubs.[5] Lunn's fictional housemaster, Dent, matches Bradby's Chandler as a sportsman, and games are again seen to dominate school life; but the whole tone of the book is more biting than in *The Lanchester Tradition*. Youngsters are bullied in the houses and harassed at their games; always it is the 'swell' and the 'autocracy of muscle' that do the hounding. Even the prefects are 'of little importance compared with the XI'. Lunn set the novel in his own school years; he was pleased to note that matters had started to improve by the time of its publication in 1913.[6]

Turning from fiction to reality, the headmaster who gained most support and encouragement from the intellectual radicals of the age, including George Bernard Shaw and H. G. Wells, was Frederick Sanderson. Sanderson's achievements at Oundle bear some comparison with Thring's at Uppingham, for under his leadership the school rose 'from comparative obscurity to a position of eminence among English public schools'.[7] Many of Sanderson's innovations were no more than those found forty years earlier at Uppingham but in other important ways Sanderson tackled problems peculiar to his own age. He greatly reformed the academic curriculum, raising science and engineering to important levels; yet, like Thring, his aim was not so much the mere acquisition of knowledge but that it should be directed towards the training of creative instincts, almost as a moral education.[8] The athletic ethos of the school was rigorously challenged: Sanderson's own physical interests were centred on country pursuits and adventure activities in the Lake District. Reading parties of boys came too, whereas the 'aristocracy of athletes' gained little favour. Richard Palmer has shown how Sanderson continued to encourage games, athletics, gymnastics and swimming, but he never allowed their position in the school to be dominant. Cooperation and not competition was the Sanderson philosophy.[9]

Changes were also occurring in the established public schools, and usually in reaction to the athletic and militaristic excesses of recent years. When William Vaughan succeeded Pollock at Wellington in 1910, he instigated a remarkable about-turn. The importance of games diminished, bogus intellectuality was discouraged, prefectorial power declined and much of the exotic splendour of dress and ceremony was curtailed. The cultivation of publicity and the impressive window-dressing that had been so successful in the Edwardian years ceased abruptly; an era of change had come. [10]

Edward Lyttelton was appointed headmaster of Haileybury in 1885 at the age of thirty-five. He had been one of England's best cricketers during the 1870s, he was a keen admirer of Frederick Maurice, and he knew of Thring's work from his occasional visits to Uppingham for the annual cricket match between the two schools. Like Thring, Lyttelton was a keen imperial federationist and in 1893 he invited George Parkin to speak to the school on the theme.[11] In the same period, Lyttelton produced a small book, *Mothers and Sons*, so that mothers might at home foster the ideal of 'true Christian manliness' during their sons' earliest and most formative years.[12]

Changes came at Eton too. When Warre retired in 1905 after twenty-one years as headmaster, he was succeeded by Lyttelton. Lyttelton at once worked to check the craze in games, he broadened the curriculum to include handicrafts, and he reduced the aura of militarism. Games were important to Lyttelton but he regarded the education they provided, both morally and physically, as lopsided. Games did nothing to feed the minds: 'Bowen of Harrow', Lyttelton wrote, 'stated boldly that games furnish the boys' minds with something to think about. So they do, but it is thin fare, and if the mental anaemia is combined with a full-blooded physique, complications set in.'[13] Nor did games fully develop the body: in 1910 Lyttelton built a gymnasium on the Swedish pattern, made the boys' attendance compulsory, and appointed masters to put into practice that physical education was more than just games and gymnastics but also included health education and remedial exercise. One of the masters, Reginald Roper, had read classics at Owen College, now Manchester University, and studied gymnastics in Sweden. Lyttelton and Roper argued that drill and games taught by untrained instructors and games masters provided a poor physical education; they replaced drill with three half-hour physical education classes every week. These lessons were taught by teachers trained in 'scientific physical education', including compensatory exercises to counter the debilitating effects of boys sitting at their desks for up to eight hours each day.[14] Many of Lyttelton's and Roper's innovations were abandoned in the years of the Great War – and they departed with the two men. In the spring of 1915 Lyttelton, perhaps unwisely, preached at St Margaret's Church in Westminster on the moral aspects of war; in the frenzied atmosphere of the first year of hostilities, his comments that the whole German nation should not be condemned were blown large by the press. As a consequence, and 'in deference to a view of his patriotism entirely inconceivable to anyone who knows him', Lyttelton tendered his resignation. Roper, a pacifist, had already left.[15]

William Temple was headmaster at Repton from 1910 until 1914. Son of the mid-Victorian headmaster of Rugby and later Archbishop of Canterbury, Temple was destined to follow his father's footsteps to that same See. Temple preached the new creed of liberal Christianity that opposed the 'self-aggrandisement' of Empire at the expense of smaller nations, seeing it as false patriotism: 'We shall value Empire, not as the satisfaction of a futile pride, but as the opportunity of influencing human history, and guiding it according to the laws of God, by whom the opportunity is given.'[16] He saw national patriotism as the culmination of devotion to family, school and university, and 'the more complete our loyalty in the narrower sphere, the more effective will our patriotism be'. The King was portrayed as the outward and visible sacrament of this patriotic religion, and the ultimate test of a school rested on its ability to serve the nation. School affection was a training ground in citizenship, and the boys were encouraged to 'go and practise what you have learned in the hard unsympathetic world'.[17] The ethos had returned to the quiet and modest bearing of the White Man's Burden.

Harry McKenzie succeeded Selwyn as headmaster of Uppingham in 1908; the events surrounding his Speech Day address of July 1914 were recounted in the Prologue. He came with a reputation for good management: within a year the pupil numbers reached the 400 mark again, and by 1911 they were back to the earlier pattern of 440.[18] Uppingham's position in the public-school world was re-established and, when The Public Schools Club was founded in 1909, the school was one of just twenty-six on the list.[19] E. W. Hornung, the popular novelist and poet, celebrated with the 'Old Boy's Song':

Eton may rest on her Field and her River.
Harrow has songs that she knows how to sing.
Winchester slang makes the sensitive shiver.
Rugby had Arnold, but never had Thring!
Repton can put up as good an Eleven.
Marlborough men are the fear of the foe.
All that I wish to remark is thank Heaven
I was at Uppingham ages ago![20]

Known as 'the Man', and a 'resolute, sure muscular Christian', McKenzie absorbed into the prefectorial body the talented athletes who had run amok in the last Selwyn years, and the brutal self-appointed privileges of the swell and the hearty ceased.[21] The reign of terror came to an end, as did the horrific accounts from Old Boys of bullying and worse. Life was still hard, but now it was largely fair. Ronald Browne recalled that his house-captain's strong arm kept the house in such good order that the appearance of the housemaster in the boys' studies and dormitories was resented.[22] Cecil Hodson's housemaster, known as the hardest hitter on the staff, did his own beating with a cane that was the length of a walking-stick.[23]

Though McKenzie did curtail the excesses of athleticism there was little change in the games organisation or the athletic outlook; more than three-quarters of school magazine content was devoted to match reports. Brian Horrocks, the future general, felt he was typical of many boys of the period: 'I was a games addict, and did as little work as possible – my whole life was devoted to sport.'[24] More school matches were introduced in this period, and second team matches became more general: a large increase in the playing-fields is one of the material legacies of the McKenzie years. The corps continued to flourish and the number of boys choosing the Army as a career doubled to an average of thirteen a year.[25] Jones was now a major and soon a lieutenant-colonel.[26] McKenzie supported his efforts keenly, telling the boys that such service taught discipline, submission and eventually command. It made, in McKenzie's words, a boy 'manly'.[27] He would have given headmasterly approval to the publication in the school magazine of July 1912 of Lord Roberts's 'Message To Boys Leaving School':

> As you know, some of our fellow-countryman across the seas have already adopted the principle that it is the duty of every man to be trained in the use of arms; believe me, boys, you can give no greater service to your country than by doing your utmost to procure the adoption of the same noble principle in the Motherland.[28]

Vera Brittain, author of the acclaimed *Testament of Youth*, came to Uppingham for her brother's last Speech Day in the idyllic summer of 1914. She liked this stern man, almost an intimidating figure, for he knew his boys well and always recognised their parents. She remembered too the closing words of McKenzie's speech that day: Count Nogi's fourteenth and final precept – 'If a man cannot be useful to his country, he is better dead.'[29]

XI The age of heroes: 'Who wants an easy victory?'

Whatever the dispute about which career a gentleman could or could not follow, one was always suitable – fighting. The causes of this military ideal of manliness, an ideal that flourished in the twenty years before the Great War, are several. We have seen how since the 1850s the temper of the country became increasingly nationalistic; 'we were the best breed in the universe'.[1] As the second half of the nineteenth century unfolded, the demands made on the home country were raised to support an Empire that had spread to cover a quarter of the globe. A spirited foreign policy was a necessary adjunct of imperialism; so too a large army and navy were essential if what had been gained was to be held. The need to breed an 'Imperial race' was seen to be vital, and the armed forces rose to the top of the career league for public-school boys.[2]

Other influences helped to shape the new ideal, for British society was changing rapidly. As the crown passed from Victoria, 'a respected, puritan granny', to Edward, 'the jolly old uncle of Liberty Hall', so a reaction to the Victorian era set in and, even though Edward VII died in 1910, the new age lasted four more years under his successor, George V. The changes began in the 1870s, when Edward was Prince of Wales; by the 1890s 'the Corinthian manner was more in vogue than the Attic' and by 1905 some feared that the Empire was dying at its heart.[3] The 'naughty nineties' gave way to a 'vulgarity and worship of wealth' in the new century; 'Smart Society' hungered for excitement and amusement, and sought it where it could. The mid-Victorians had idolised 'scholarship and manliness', now the Edwardians worshipped 'manliness and good breeding'.[4] The newly rich acquired their good breeding second-hand through successful marriage into landed families, and strived to imitate those who inherited old money by aping their fashions, their mode of life and their interests. Matthew Arnold's 'Philistines' sought to became 'Barbarians'.[5]

The idea of a gentleman was vitally important in Victorian and Edwardian society; it was hard to define, but one gentleman would immediately recognise another. The elusive definition was changing too: a mid-Victorian was suspicious of the religion of wealth, his Edwardian successor worshipped it.[6] True religion became even more identified with ethics, church attendance slipped further and spiritual doubt increased. The surface of Edwardian life was both brilliant and glamorous, and indeed there was a superficial code of strict decorum, but below the surface morality was lax. Hypocrisy was rife: prostitution was both illegal and violently condemned yet its pleasures were regularly enjoyed by many gentlemen.[7]

The code of the gentleman rather than Christian principles became the dominant ethos in the public schools. As laymen headmasters and housemasters replaced men in Holy Orders, so the religious teaching evolved into a code of ethics to support the commercial needs of the nation and the British Empire was promoted as a greater reality than the Kingdom of Heaven.[8] There were new powers in the public schools too. The reforms of the mid-Victorian headmasters had been consolidated by their successors and spread throughout the public-school system. In the process two institutions were created to support efficient organisation and management: houses and prefects. Housemasters, often bachelors, owned their houses; their income came from the boarding fees; the more boys the better; and tenures of thirty years and more brought great profit.[9] Headmasters were often one of the youngest men on the staff and many were persuaded to leave the day-to-day running of the boys' lives to the men who knew them best. Few headmasters could exert Thring's influence over their staff, especially as the schools became larger, and gradually housemasters assumed extraordinary powers. The houses became baronial castles; independent, self-regulated and conformist. It was the same pattern within the houses; the longer a housemaster remained in residence, the more he delegated day-to-day power to his prefects. Unsupervised prefectorial rule permitted increased fagging by youngsters and sanctioned punishment beatings for all. Most boys got their turn at the top, so Old Boys generally agreed that all was well.[10] As headmasters surrendered their right to innovate to the conservative intentions of housemasters and prefects, public schools began to petrify.

Norman Dixon, a military historian, defined 'militarism' as 'an ever-increasing web of rules, restrictions and constraints, presided over by an elite, one of whose motives was to preserve the status quo'.[11] This describes the Edwardian public school. Boys were squeezed into identical moulds; devotion to house and school by boys and Old Boys was blind and passionate; friendships were limited to the ten boys of the same age-group in same house; individual hobbies and pursuits were surrendered to house interests; emotions and all individuality were buried deep.[12] School society became intolerant; whether of Jews, day-boys, *parvenu* masters or anything out of the ordinary mould.[13] Games-playing and *esprit de corps* were an educational mystique, still praised for the reasons listed at the end of the previous chapter; the obsession with compulsory games ever grew. An educational moratorium would be declared during important matches; success and failure were vital, whether to school or house; and a row of silver cups became the visible and tangible evidence of a united will.[14] Standards of sportsmanship fell. There was the scandalous university cricket match when C. M. Wells, at the Cambridge captain's request, bowled five wides to the boundary to prevent Oxford following on;[15] when Mitchell retired as cricket master at Eton, Wells was his successor. The cadet corps in Victorian times was little more than a game, and a minor one at that, but in the new century it climbed in status to the very top. A new 'military caste' replaced the older 'athletic caste'. Great importance was attached to outward signs of maleness and, for example, hair length rapidly decreased to the 'short back and sides'. Field Marshall Lord Wolseley, one of the champions of the cadet corps, gave the reason: 'It is very difficult to make our Englishman at any time look like a soldier. He is fond of longish hair ... hair is the glory of a woman but the shame of a man'.[16]

Boys were told that life was a game. E. W. Hornung, author of the best-selling Raffles stories, was a popular preacher on his occasional visits to his old school, Uppingham.[17]

> It is a very old comparison that likens Life to a game; so old indeed that there is very little in these days that we cannot, and do not habitually, express in terms of cricket, for example. Thus, when you want anybody to try hard at anything – to make an effort – you tell him to "play up". When you find it hard to do the right thing, hard to be quite straight about something, you say to yourself "I must 'play the game' – because", you may

add, "because what I'm tempted to do is 'not cricket'." If it be a case of doing our share in some way to help another, we call that "keeping our end up"; and if only one good word could be said for us by our friends, and by the world, and if it were for us to choose that one good word, what do you think it would be? I believe we should one and all, man and boy, love to be known above all else as "sportsmen" – simply because the word "sportsman", as we use it among ourselves, has come to signify every virtue which is dearest to our hearts. Courage, honesty, unselfishness, chivalry, you can't be a sportsman without all these; and if you *have* all of those, you, *must* be a good man.

Who wants an easy victory? Who wants a life of full pitches to leg? Do you think the Great Scorer is going to give you four runs every time for those? I believe with all my heart and soul that in this splendidly difficult Game of Life it is just the cheap and easy triumphs which will be written in water on the score sheet. And the way we played for our side, in the bad light, on the difficult pitch, the way we backed up and ran the other man's runs; our courage and unselfishness, not our skill or our success; our brave failures, our hidden disappointments, the will to bear our friends' infirmities, and the grit to fight our own: surely, surely, it is these things above all other that will count, when the innings is over, in the Pavilion of Heaven.[18]

Hornung and his fellow preachers might tell boys that life was a game, but for the younger ones, life in the boarding houses was more a battle. Boys in the 1890s had complained of 'low and nasty ways', but the conviction and imprisonment of Oscar Wilde in 1895 for homosexual practices brought a jubilant proclamation from public-school Old Boys that all was well in the philistine camp: only aesthetes could be immoral.[19] As we have seen, the excesses at Uppingham and elsewhere had gradually gained public attention: nonetheless, in 1910 'A Public School Boy' could still complain to the *National Review*.

The state of affairs in the Public Schools on moral matters is of the gravest kind, (he asserted) from my own experience, as well as from what I have heard from many in diversities of schools, things are done which are hardly mentionable, which would make many respectable parents jump in their chairs. There is often an absolute tolerance and indifference to the most shocking immorality. Young lives are ruined, incurable habits are contracted, disgusting and horrible cases are brought to light.[20]

A heated debate followed. 'An Undergraduate' felt that the case had been over-dramatised but 'A Parent' supported the original thesis. In May the following year 'An Ex-Assistant Master' replied that such things only happened in a bad house, in a bad school, in a bad time. 'A Public School Boy' was not to be silenced and in June he re-stated his original remarks; this time adding the experiences of many who had written to him.[21] By now reforms had started to come.

Imperial manliness was the last English romantic ideal. Christianity had been found wanting; Aestheticism was discredited with the downfall of Oscar Wilde; and the early public-school ideals became a dead-weight Lanchester-like tradition. At its best the spirit of The White Man's Burden was a high ideal that was nobly sought. Many public-school boys decided that they would 'never go into an office' but would go out into distant lands to uphold the honour of Englishmen and play, on a wider scale, the role of a prefect.

The ideal was not, however, always seen at its best. Most public-school boys were narrow in knowledge, outlook, social conscience and responsibility. They were well-bodied, well-mannered and well-meaning, keen at their games and devoted to their schools, but they were ignorant of life about them and contemptuous of all outside their own caste. At best, most would become efficient administrative cogs in the political and social system of the Empire.[22] This then might be the average. Richard Aldington, in his biting novel *Death of a Hero*, portrayed the worst aspect of imperial manliness. Aldington's hero, George, goes to a public school which aims to turn out 'thoroughly manly fellows'. The pride of the school is its excellent games record, and there is a cadet corps where boys compulsorily learn 'to take up arms' for their country. The whole school exudes manliness – 'manly' corps, 'manly' games, 'manly' prefects, even 'manly' beatings and 'manly' bullying. George's contemporaries all seek to be approved, and to be 'healthy barbarians' cultivating 'a little smut on the sly'. On leaving school each will go to some minor and unpleasant post in an unhealthy colony where 'a thoroughly manly fellow' was still appreciated. George is, of course, bad at games, keen on painting, and thoroughly 'unmanly'. He is beaten by the headmaster, who then kneels with him to pray that he might become 'a manly fellow'. The headmaster is both corps commander and chaplain; in the corps he stresses: 'It is so important to learn how to kill. Indeed, unless you know how to kill you cannot possibly be a Man, still less a Gentleman.' In chapel he preaches the moral 'prepare to meet thy God and avoid smut' – 'Within ten years one half of you boys will be DEAD!'[23]

The spirit of Christianity and the legacy of the Romantics no longer held sway in the schools but the emphasis on the classics was as strong as ever. They were still the core of the curriculum. Eighty years earlier Thomas Arnold had made them a means of moral education and, through a concentration on the works of Plato and Thucydides, this tradition had strengthened in the mid-Victorian public schools. The classics still provided intellectual support in the Edwardian era but Plato was almost unread and Homer was the fashionable author. R. M. Ogilvie, in his study *Latin and Greek*, noted how swiftly the change occurred. By the turn of the century all schools read Homer; men as diverse as Edmond Warre, Arthur Ponsonby and T. E. Lawrence were all enthusiasts.[24] It was an age of real heroes – Gordon, Kitchener, Roberts and more – thus it was perhaps inevitable that Homer should be chosen to give their exploits substance and identity. The writings of Henty, Vachell, Newbolt, Kipling, Buchan and Hornung all resound to the adventures of heroes ready to risk all, death included. Current history was a heyday of English heroism: David Livingstone and Richard Burton were exploring Africa and the Middle East, and the Boer War was packed with heroic excitement.[25]

The eighth-century BC poems of Homer recorded the legends and myths of the Greek heroic age, one that lasted for about four generations and ended in the battle of Troy.[26] The *Odyssey* and the *Iliad* were almost exclusively concerned with the deeds of aristocrats, for the main function of the ordinary man was to be killed by his superiors. The Homeric hero fought for his own glory, and only in later Spartan times did the worthy cause displace personal honour as the prime-mover. Homeric *arête* was equivalent to honour, but such honour bore little resemblance to its Christian and chivalric successors. Honour came with the evidence of the hero's worth, which in turn stemmed from how much glory he had won, and was reflected in his demeanour, his manners, and his dress. The Greek for hero originally meant a warrior, and the hero's status depended on the quality of his opponents, his manner of fighting and the result of the contest. The heroic qualities thus included high courage, modesty and courtesy; prizes gained were lasting evidence of glory and were to be displayed on all appropriate occasions; and grand ceremonies would proclaim the hero's virtues.[27] The Edwardians found many parallels between the heyday of the British Empire and the Homeric legends of the past, and saw their own society as the new heroic age. Edward Thring's mid-Victorian ideal of manliness had been coarsened in the era of athletic heartiness and *esprit de corps*; now it was wholly perverted to produce a warrior race.

Heroes are trained for war, and here too the classics brought support – acting like the medieval rules of chivalry to elevate warfare for its moral worth and to make some sense of death. The Greek model of the warrior nation was held up for example; its ideals were seen as fit for emulation; youthful heroes were adopted as objects of worship; and the anodyne notion that young death was swift, sweet and painless was seriously purveyed. Death lost its sting as emasculated and prettified versions of Homer provided a precedent for what was happening in South Africa and other warlike corners of the Empire.[28] The Greek age of heroes had died quickly, for when the community became settled the hero was tamed – a domesticated hero is a contradiction in terms.[29] The Edwardian age of heroes died quickly too, but not in the same manner.

Chapter 5

The survival of true manliness

I The Great War: 'Now, God be thanked Who has matched us with His hour'

When war was declared against Germany on 4 August 1914, it was almost as if Providence had set a test by which the public schools might prove their worth. War – with its call to self-sacrifice, to duty and to honour – was seen by many as the realisation of a hope. The Homeric hero was first and foremost a warrior and in his eyes valour alone justified life. Only in battle could he fully realise himself; only in battle could he be put to the greatest test of all.

The schools and their Old Boys answered the call to arms in the most glorious and dramatic of ways: young masters and senior boys set to return for the autumn term said quick farewells to their schools and volunteered almost to a man to go to the front; boys left behind at school hoped that the war would not be over before they too had the chance to 'do their bit'; Old Boys at the universities and in the professions left lectures and careers to hunt for commissions in the regiments that would be the first to go to Belgium and France.[1]

The public-school subalterns did well at the front, remarkably so when we remember that they had only a few weeks of training in England prior to embarkation, and we realise how young and inexperienced they were. Their cheerful humanity in difficult conditions, ready acceptance of leadership by example, easy comradeship and mucking in, concern for men under their command, determination to succeed, hardiness amidst all the deprivations of war, and, above all, their simple open courage, soon won the respect of the professional soldiers under their command. Junior officers were the first 'over the top', leading their men into battle, and the last to return, shepherding laggards back to the safety of the trench: they were thus most at risk from enemy fire. Then too, their distinctive uniform of tapered riding breeches and Sam Brown belts made them easy targets for enemy snipers.[2] The legion tales of selfless devotion and unstinting heroism are still famous today and the literature of the period constantly reminds us 'lest we forget': perhaps Ernest Raymond's *Tell England* is the most sincere and wonderful example of all that is best in public-school service, honour and manliness.[3]

British armed forces suffered nearly one million deaths in the First World War, nearly double the total for its successor. One in ten who fought died. The toll was even more horrific for the public-school Old Boys; here one in five perished. Almost all had served in the army; most were junior officers; most were very young. A third held the lowest commissioned rank, second lieutenant, and a quarter never reached the age of adulthood, twenty-one. Boarding schools suffered heavier losses than day schools, with totals larger than their 1914 school lists.[4] The Uppingham dead numbered 450: almost every other name in the *School Roll* for the years 1907 to 1909 has the words 'killed in action' appended to its entry. The average lifetime at the front, whether in the trenches or in the air, was six weeks; sailors had a slightly greater chance of survival.[5] Never did a generation go to war so willingly and so idealistically, and never did so few return.

In this most literary of wars, it seems that every army officer from the most junior to the most senior was a soldier-poet: Roland Leighton, just out of Uppingham and now with the Worcestershire Regiment in France, sent poems to his fiancée, Vera Brittain; General Sir Ian Hamilton, sailing to command at Gallipoli, wrote to clear his mind and put events into perspective.[6] Rupert Brooke, however, was the soldier-poet *par excellence*; the voice of his generation and the inspiration for his peers. With his good looks, boyish enthusiasm, society connections and effortless success at Rugby and Cambridge, Brooke was a young Apollo. His war sonnets of 1914 were soon on everyone lips:

> Now, God be thanked Who has matched us with His hour,
> And caught our youth, and wakened us from sleeping.[7]

On 4 April 1915, William Inge, Dean of St Paul's Cathedral in London, included Brooke's *The Soldier* in his Easter Day sermon.[8] The sonnet had been composed at Christmas and published in *The Times Literary Supplement* on 11 March:

> If I should die, think only this of me:
> That there's some corner of a foreign field
> That is for ever England. There shall be
> In that rich earth a richer dust concealed;
> A dust whom England bore, shaped, made aware,
> Gave, once, her flowers to love, her ways to roam,
> A body of England's, breathing English air,
> Washed by the rivers, blest by suns of home.
>
> And think, this heart, all evil shed away,
> A pulse in the eternal mind, no less
> Gives somewhere back the thoughts by England given;
> Her sights and sounds; dreams happy as her day;

And laughter, learnt of friends; and gentleness,
In hearts at peace, under an English heaven.[9]

Dean Inge told his congregation that 'the enthusiasm of a pure and elevated patriotism, free from hate, bitterness, and fear, had never found a nobler expression'. The nation agreed – and the belief that the death of a young soldier was swift, clean, sweet and heroic sustained many grieving families.

Nine months earlier, on the first Sunday of the war, the Bishop of London, Arthur Winnington-Ingram, had preached on the same theme in the same cathedral. 'The supreme test of the manhood of the British race had arrived', he said, yet

> death was not the supreme disaster. There was one thing at least far worse than death, and that was dishonour. If a heathen poet with only a vague belief in another world could say "A sweet and pleasant thing it is to die for your country," with how much more conviction should a Christian parent say the same.[10]

The Bishop's quotation came from the Roman lyrical poet Horace's *Odes* (III.2.13) – *Dulce et decorum est pro patria mori*. It gained widespread acceptance as an epitaph on the graves of soldiers and as a text on memorials.[11]

Throughout the autumn of 1914, when the war was only going to last a few months, the idealism of the public-school officer was high. Many, like Siegfried Sassoon, endlessly prepared for the cavalry break-through that never came.[12] Lieutenant-Colonel David Campbell felt honoured that he had the good fortune to lead two troops of the 9th Lancers in the last lance-on-lance cavalry action of the war, on 7 September 1914. Campbell, who had won the 1896 Grand National, was wounded during the charge and had to dismount. He was treated for 'a revolver wound in his leg, a lance wound in his shoulder, and a sword wound in his arm'. Despite this, the colonel told the doctor: 'I've just had the best quarter of an hour I've ever had in my life!'[13]

The war became steeped with ritual, myth and romance. Memories abound of combatants gaining inspiration from the medieval quests of Roland and King Arthur.[14] London's *Evening News* published a story in which the ghosts of the English bowmen at Agincourt came to the assistance of their countrymen fighting just a few miles to the east.[15] The pilots of the Royal Flying Corps pictured themselves as knights of a twentieth-century chivalric order and, like Richard Coeur de Lion before them, young officers captured as prisoners of war felt honour-bound to escape and re-enter the conflict.[16]

Paul Fussell has recorded how the letters, diaries and other writings of these young men are littered with a raised, almost medieval language that they had absorbed from their boyhood reading. A friend was a 'comrade' and a horse became a 'steed', whilst the enemy was the 'foe' and the front became the 'field'.

A soldier was a 'warrior'; actions were 'deeds'; danger was 'peril'; the brave were 'gallant'; and to conquer was to 'vanquish'. The possibility of death was one's 'fate'; to die was to 'perish'; the dead were the 'fallen'; and dead bodies were 'dust'. The whole war became a noble 'strife'.[17] After Lieutenant-Colonel Ernest Brown was killed when leading a charge at Gallipoli in August 1915, a brother officer wrote to his widow: 'After all it is a glorious thing to die for one's country and loved ones.'[18]

'It's all great fun', Rupert Brooke wrote home.[19] Julian Grenfell, another soldier-poet, but from Eton and Oxford, agreed: 'I adore war. It is like a big picnic without the objectlessness of a picnic. I've never been so well or so happy.'[20] It was almost like being at school still. A senior officer complained that subalterns were arriving at the front with enough kit to equip a boarding house study: camp furniture, crockery and soft furnishings.[21] Officers had batmen to serve them, just as 'fags' had waited upon prefects. The proximity of England meant that mail and hampers of 'tuck' from Fortnum and Mason's or Harrods came often; leave was regularly given for officers to go back to England, as if on *exeat*; the caste status of regiments, from the Guards at the top to the Territorials at the bottom, reflected school structure; indeed, the senior regiments expected the position of honour in any assault of the enemy.[22]

The athletic ethos came too. The battle for the Belgian sea-ports quickly gained the title 'The Race to the Sea', with its overtones of a sporting event; the German use of chlorine gas was felt to be 'illustrative of the Prussian idea of playing the game'; the Gallipoli campaign was seen as an 'away game of rugby'; and a craze developed for kicking footballs towards the enemy line during an attack. This feat was first performed at Loos early in 1915, but it soon spread throughout the Western and Middle Eastern Fronts.[23] Christmas 1914 saw the declaration of an informal truce and at various points in Belgium and France soldiers from the opposing armies met in No Man's Land; gifts were exchanged and knockabout games of football were played. Arthur Harrison, a keen member of Rosslyn Park Rugby Football Club and an England international, likened leading the charge to the enemy lines to a forwards' rush in a match.[24] When Second Lieutenant Fredrick Key was killed on the Somme in July 1915, it was discovered that he had prepared a 'Cricketer's Farewell' for his parents: 'If you receive this you will know that I have been bowled out, middle peg. You can be sure however that I batted well.'[25]

The first year of the war saw the publication of a mass of games-playing verse, for Newbolt had many imitators.[26] E. W. Hornung's *Lord's Leave* (1915) is just one example:

No Lord's this year, no silken lawn on which
A dignified and dainty throng meanders,
The Schools take guard upon a fiercer pitch
Somewhere in Flanders.
Bigger the cricket here; yet some who tried

> In vain to earn a Colour while at Eton
> Have found a place upon an England side
> That can't be beaten!

And so on for another seven verses.[27]

This was no mere jingoism: when Hornung's own son, Oscar, was killed at the Second Battle of Ypres on 6 July 1915, aged just twenty; the grieving father composed *Last Post* in his memory. Its jaunty tone matches that in *Lord's Leave*. The title, *Last Post*, has civilian and military overtones: it refers to the contents of Oscar's last letter home and to its arrival in the evening delivery; as well as to the bugle call sounded at the end of a battle to guide wounded or lost soldiers to safety, and at funerals as a final farewell to a dead soldier.

> Still merry in a dubious trench
> They've taken over from the French;
> Still making light of duty done;
> Still full of Tommy, Fritz, and fun!
>
> Still finding War of games the cream,
> And his platoon a priceless team –
> Still running it by sportsman's rule,
> Just as he ran his house at school.
>
> He said those weeks of blood and tears
> Were worth his score of radiant years.
> He said he had not lived before
> Our boy who never dreamt of War!
>
> He gave us of his own dear glow,
> Last summer, centuries ago.
> Bronzed leaves still cling to every bough.
> I don't waylay the postman now.
>
> Doubtless upon his nightly beat
> He still comes twinkling down our street.
> I am not there with straining eye
> A whistling imp could tell you why.[28]

Old Boys in the armed services made frequent visits to their schools, parading in their new uniforms before embarkation and telling of their exploits when home on leave. Many corresponded with teachers or sent articles for the school 'mag'. Headmasters and housemasters wrote to their former charges at the front and organised memorial services for those who would never return. Old Boys' reunions were even held in France, made possible by the close relationship between regiments and certain schools. Winchester's headmaster attended one such dinner.[29]

At the schools, the cadet corps became compulsory overnight; often, as at Charterhouse, through direct action on the boys' part.[30] Uppingham's corps climbed from 335 in July 1914 to 414 in October.[31] Corps parades at school were suddenly meaningful and war exercises full of realism; all too soon these cadets would be joining their seniors in the crusade against German imperialism. The pre-war Monday parade was maintained at Repton and joined by a second on Friday, military lectures on Tuesday and Saturday, and 'field operations' on Wednesday. At Oundle there were three or four parades each week, several Field Days each term and regular practice at digging trenches and bayonet fighting.[32]

October's *Uppingham School Magazine* contained the first list of Old Boys in the armed services, the first casualty list, the first letter from the front and the first war poem by a boy – based on the Roman legend of Horatio holding the bridge. It also noted that Lieutenant-Colonel Herbert Jones, five more masters, the corps sergeant-major and two other school employees had left for military service.

School facilities and boy-power contributed to the war effort: room was found for military accommodation, hospitals, and Belgian refugees; cadets served as sentries at power stations and helped to guard prisoner-of-war camps. Boys working in the Uppingham metalwork shop made war materials including shell cases, cartridge punches and plunger bolts for mines; those in the carpentry shop made splints, bed tables and lockers for hospitals.[33] Oundle's workshops delivered 12,000 parts to a Peterborough munitions firm, sent 32,000 tools to Woolwich Arsenal and made over 1,000 large horse-shoes.[34] The Cheltenham Ladies' College established a Voluntary Aid Detachment hospital in one of its boarding houses, overseen by teachers and pupils past and present.[35]

In an era when children's deaths through illness and disease were not uncommon, public schools had long learnt to cope with bereavement – but not on this new scale. Parents and teachers felt the strain more than the boys: when Lieutenant Albert Harris was killed, his schoolboy brother at Chigwell wrote in his diary – 'Rice pudding today, but Bert was killed'. Headmasters and masters of boarding houses had to deal with multiple tragedies as well as running schools without their youngest and most vigorous teachers. They were now at the front, with at least five winning the Victoria Cross for gallantry. More than a quarter of these public-school masters died in the conflict, a higher proportion than their pupils.[36]

When a second front was opened at Gallipoli in the Eastern Mediterranean during the spring of 1915, Rupert Brooke was not alone when he expressed his delight at the prospect of battle in Homeric lands:

> It's too wonderful for belief . . . I had not imagined that Fate could be so
> kind . . . Will Hero's tower crumble under the 15-inch guns? Will the sea be

polyphloisbic and wine-dark and unvintageable? . . . Shall we be a Turning Point in History? . . . I've never been quite so happy in my life.[37]

Compton Mackenzie was also caught up in the excitement of war in the Dardanelles: here Xerxes had built his bridge of boats, and Leander had swum by night from Abydos to Sestos.[38] Nowell Oxland, Durham School and Oxford, wrote to his parents on the voyage out: 'Our destiny lies across the straits from Troy, and I dream that we may finish our business in short order and cross the Hellespont to walk on her ancient stones.'[39] Legend became fact when two thousand soldiers were hidden in an innocent-looking collier, the *River Clyde*, that was slipped like the Trojan Horse onto a Turkish beach.[40] This tactic, and indeed the whole Gallipoli campaign, proved to be disastrous but Brooke did not bear witness. He died on a French hospital ship moored at the nearby island of Skyros, suffering from sunstroke and blood poisoning, just two days before he was due to go ashore with the first wave of the invasion force. Winston Churchill, First Lord of the Admiralty and the instigator of the Gallipoli campaign, composed Brooke's obituary as he waited for news of the campaign:

> During the last few months of his life, months of preparation in gallant comradeship and open air, the poet-soldier told with all the simple force of genius the sorrow of youth about to die, and the sure triumphant consolations of a sincere and valiant spirit. He expected to die; he was willing to die for the dear England whose beauty and majesty he knew; and he advanced towards the brink in perfect serenity, with absolute conviction of the rightness of his country's cause and a heart devoid of hate for fellow-men.
>
> . . . Joyous, fearless, versatile, deeply instructed, with classic symmetry of mind and body, ruled by high undoubting purpose, he was all that one would wish England's noblest sons to be in days when no sacrifice but the most precious is acceptable, and the most precious is that which is most freely proffered.[41]

It was published in *The Times* on the day of the Gallipoli landings. As Philip Larkin was to write fifty years later: 'Never such innocence again.'[42]

II *Dis aliter visum*:[1] 'We will remember them'

The ideal of imperial manliness sustained the new heroes while the war was fought in this Homeric atmosphere but the arrival of entrenchment saw the start of its demise. By December 1914, just five months into the war, the Western Front was deadlocked. The British and French armies occupied their trenches to the west of No Man's Land, facing the German army in its trenches just a few hundred yards to the east. Eventually the whole trench system stretched more than 400 miles from the North Sea to the Swiss border. On the ninety miles that British troops defended, some 7000 officers and men were killed and wounded every day, even in the quietest times.[2]

There was stalemate too in Gallipoli. On 25 April 1915, British and French troops had landed on five beaches at the southern end of the peninsula, and more from Australia and New Zealand on one beach further north, but they made hardly any progress inland against the Turks despite horrendous losses.[3] In combat reminiscent of medieval warfare, steel on steel, the Allies were assaulted by repeated waves of bayonet charges. The British and French advanced just two miles before they were brought to a halt on the Eski Line; the ANZACs, after initial gains, were driven back to their beachhead. Eventually, after over eight months of attrition and more than 34,000 British dead, the campaign was abandoned.[4]

The failure to break through on the Western Front in the spring of 1915, where the huge loss of life for no gain at the Battle of Aubers Ridge set the pattern for the next three years, and the catastrophic events in Gallipoli led to a change in government in London; on 26 May the Liberals gave way to a coalition and the war effort gained new impetus. The loss of the *Lusitania* that had thrust civilians into the war and the enemy's first use of poison gas also stiffened national resolve: Germans were now hated.[5] Two million men volunteered for Kitchener's New Army over the course of the next year to replace the regular soldiers who had died; then, in March 1916, conscription was introduced; but neither led to significant advances against the enemy. All efforts were then placed on a break-through on the Somme – a battle that lasted from 1 July 1916 until mid-November – but the plans went wrong right from the start and no territorial gains were made. Of the 150,000 men who participated on the first day of the battle, 19,240 were killed and 38,230 were wounded or missing: it was the greatest tragedy in British military history. A thousand junior officers died that day, most had recently left school. The Battle of the Somme proved to be the costliest of the war: 419,654 British and Empire casualties, 95,675 of them dead.[6] After this terrible ordeal and the simultaneous death at sea of Kitchener, the talismanic Secretary of State for War, many felt that the war would never end.[7] The Somme had a profound effect on the nation and it made a deep impact on the public schools: 90% of the officers and many in the ranks who fought there were public-school Old Boys.[8]

War was no longer Homeric. There was nothing chivalrous about chlorine gas; there was nothing heroic in dying under bombardment from an invisible enemy; there was no valour in being mown down by machine-gun fire; there was nothing idealistic in inhuman mechanistic trench warfare. Fate and luck overruled personal decision-making and individual acts: every soldier knew that if his name was on the bullet, he would die.[9] As the mode of warfare moved from the nineteenth to the twentieth century, as the tactics of rapid movement were replaced by static attrition and as initiative gave way to collective team-work, so the public-school officer met his limit and the imperial ideal of manliness met its end.[10] The young officers still led as well, still fought heroically and bore all with a stoical reticence that could turn the worst disaster into something that was merely 'darned unpleasant'. Their leadership is credited with maintaining morale until the war's end; unlike the French and German armies, there were no mutinies.[11] The soldier-author Ian Hay was certain that second lieutenants won the war.[12] The bonding with men under their command and in their care grew stronger as conditions worsened and their comradeship of shared experiences was to last well after the war was won.[13] Now however the short-comings of their military training were becoming evident and, more importantly, the war had moved away from a level where individual action was vital to one where the individual was lost in an army of millions. The war that was to be the awakening of the ideal of manliness instead witnessed its death in the slaughter of countless battles; the war that would be over in months was now a protracted fight to the finish.[14]

That the war was no longer Homeric also hit public-school headmasters hard. Many had proclaimed the ideal of imperial manliness in their schools; many had echoed the sentiments of Rupert Brooke's sonnets; many had included Horace's *Dulce et decorum est pro patria mori* in their sermons. W. H. Auden and Christopher Isherwood, together as young boys at St Edmund's School in Hindhead, are just two who recalled their headmaster giving 'rousing speeches about the honourable actions going on in Europe'.[15] After Gallipoli and the Somme, after longer and longer casualty lists, after more and more names read out in chapel, it was inevitable that many headmasters would feel the strain. It was not meant to be like this.[16]

Harry McKenzie's collapse and early retirement were described in the Prologue. Alfred Cooke, headmaster at Aldenham, was 'struck to the heart' when his second son, Alan, was posted missing. Day after day he sat waiting for the postman but the longed-for good news never came.[17] He stepped down in 1920. Bingham Dixon Turner, who retired as headmaster of Loughborough Grammar School the same year, also lost a son. Roger had interrupted his studies at Cambridge to gain a commission; he survived Gallipoli only to die aged twenty of wounds received in the Mesopotamian campaign.[18] Roy, the eldest son of Frederick Sanderson of Oundle, died of wounds after the Battle of the Lys in April 1918. Loss after loss of Old Boys and masters' sons had already greatly distressed the headmaster but this culminating blow brought him low. Sanderson's spirit had been broken, he suffered a nervous breakdown, and he died in 1922.[19] Nowell Smith, headmaster at Sherborne, was deeply shaken both physically and spiritually by the cataclysm of the war. He felt unable to preside over a school whose life was centred on its chapel and resigned in 1927.[20] Perpetual bad news of Old Boys of Gresham's undermined the health of its headmaster, George Howson; he was ill for several months in 1917, again a year later, and he died shortly after the war's end – aged fifty-eight.[21] Frank

Fletcher, formerly headmaster at Marlborough and now at Charterhouse, was assailed with bad news from both schools. Worse than that:

> For more than four years, day after day, I had looked round the School Chapel, with the knowledge that of the 600 faces before me many would before long be looking upon the sordid horrors of war, silently asking myself how many, before a year was passed, might be lying dead on the battlefield.[22]

Fletcher kept a wartime scrapbook with sepia photographs of young men in uniform, letters telling him of their deaths, and black-edged letters from their parents in reply to his condolences.[23] Many more headmasters suffered just as severely: Anthony Seldon and David Walsh have recorded several harrowing accounts in their recent study, *Public Schools and the Great War*.[24]

It was the same story for the boys in the schools. In 1914 the atmosphere had been vigorous and idealistic; games were seen as unimportant 'in the presence of the real thing'; cadet corps absorbed all energy and interest; school magazine editorials were devoted to the war; and playing-fields were turned over by boy labour for the growing of vegetables.[25] The lists read out in chapel of 'Those who have laid down their lives for their Country' brought the reality of war back to the schools, yet a greater impression was usually made by the visit of a newly-decorated Old Boy:

> "Who is the one with the empty sleeve?"
> "Some sport who was in the swim."
> "And the one with the ribbon who's home on leave?"
> "Good Lord! I remember him!
> A hulking fool, low down in the school,
> And no good at games was he –
> All fingers and thumbs – and very few chums.
> (I wish he'd shake hands with me!)"[26]

By the summer of 1915 excitement was on the decline and by January 1916, according to S. P. B. Mais who went back to teach at Sherborne, all was back to normal as if August 1914 had not happened.[27] As the war dragged on after the Somme, as the lists read in chapel grew ever longer, as the returning heroes became less idealistic, so the schools shrunk away from the reality of war and looked back to the halcyon Edwardian days.[28] School activities at Repton continued in an 'atmosphere of mingled enthusiasm, misgiving and despondency'.[29] The school's corps activities slipped into a dull routine for Richard Cripps and the rain that cancelled parades was greeted with joy.[30] Games suddenly increased in importance again at all schools and, once more, they dominated editorials in school magazines – as Vera Brittain noted at Uppingham. The obituaries of Old Boys killed at the front made slight reading beside the biographies of the XV and XI.[31] Apart from lists of the dead and the names of the newly enlisted, the war disappeared from school magazine content at both Repton and Uppingham from the spring of 1916 until the Armistice. As if to dull the senses of boys before they too were slaughtered in France and Belgium, the schools turned their backs on the war and sought to live in a world of peace. 'Business as usual' was the cry; the ideal of imperial manliness had evaporated.[32]

Critics noted that this harking back brought about the return of all the Edwardian public-school problems. H. E. Luxmore witnessed the games cult as strong as ever at Eton, with masters advocating its virtues as in the past.[33] Ian Hay wrote of the dulling effects of compulsory games, the conformities of public-school life and the moulding of personality to a stereotype.[34] Arnold Lunn's *Loose Ends* pictured a school where everything was athletic from the housemaster, 'one of that breed of professional-cricket-schoolmasters', to the displays on the annual speech day. The school of the tale, Hornborough, taught only two things: cricket and *esprit de corps*.[35]

When Harry McKenzie retired early from Uppingham in December 1915, the school's trustees opted for youth over experience in their appointment of twenty-eight-year-old Reginald Owen as his successor. He did not have an easy start. In a period when women presented white feathers to men who might be shirking their patriotic duty, many boys and masters felt that a young bachelor and former Oxford rowing blue, able to play Rugby football and cricket with the XV and XI, should not limit his military service to the school's cadet corps. Owen never explained – and he was judged a coward. Owen then compounded matters in 1917 by taking Holy Orders, at a time when several bishops refused to ordain men of military age.[36] Many young masters were now in the armed forces: their replacements were often elderly, some in their eighties; others already on the staff had been persuaded to delay retirement; discipline began to slip. Boys reckoned that three long-serving housemasters were incompetent and it was known that a fourth housemaster had agreed to keep to the private side if the boys behaved.[37] It took Owen four years to impose order.

The author Adrian Bell was at the school from 1915 to 1919 – it was 'not in good shape'. He had been given a copy of *Tom Brown's Schooldays* by an aunt to prepare him for his new life and he found many similarities to Rugby of the 1820s. Life in his house, not one of the five already mentioned, was barbaric and 'self-preservation was our chief pre-occupation': bullying was rife, youngsters ran the nightly gauntlet of knotted wet towels, and senior boys were periodically expelled.[38] After one episode, five of the thirty boys in the house were sent home. Praepostors, always the games hearties, 'flogged hard and often', so too did his housemaster, and so did Owen. Bell was beaten for shirking, having a 'bum-slit' in his jacket, and for walking on the wrong side of the street. House beatings were carried out on Saturday evenings after prayers when the praepostors caught up on the week's wrong-doers. Punishment continued even on twelve-mile cross-country runs as junior boys were whipped by seniors wielding hunting-crops. Bell labelled his housemaster a 'dreamer': when a boy complained to him about the bullying, he replied that he would not interfere for that would only make matters worse. In Bell's opinion, Uppingham was a 'totalitarian police state'. He did not know it, but the school had reverted to the days of Selwyn ten years earlier.[39]

It fell to the 1917 publication of Alec Waugh's *The Loom of Youth* to bring the public schools back into the headlines – and the news caused a stir. The novel had been written in the spring of 1916 when Waugh was seventeen. He had recently left Sherborne where he had been happy and successful, gaining colours in both cricket and Rugby football and he had just enlisted in the army for war service. Waugh later saw the book as 'a realistic but romantic story of healthy adolescence set against the background of an average English Public School', and pictured it as an attempt to expose the sham of the 'cornerstone of the Empire' philosophy that was prevalent.[40] In a way that no other book had done before, *The Loom of Youth* portrayed a contemporary school and revealed all its brutality, its rigidity, and its conventionality. Athletic gods reigned supreme and to be athletic meant that anything else might be forgiven; life in the boarding houses was barbaric, with homosexual relationships pictured as absolutely usual; true religion did not exist but was merely equated with 'good form' and 'playing the game'.[41] In short, Waugh in one adolescent novel exposed all that other writers since the turn of the century had merely hinted.

Waugh produced a storm of reaction that was to last until the end of the war. Conservative feelings were well represented by the writer in the *Contemporary Review* who found the book 'uniformly dull, occasionally unpleasant, and almost wholly untrue', and the same feelings saw fruition in an answering novel, *A Dream of Youth*, by another recent public-school boy.[42] Despite the furore and his name erased from the Sherborne Old Boys' list, Waugh stuck to his guns: in *The English Review* and in *Public School Life* he maintained that what he had written was true from his own experiences and that it was also, so he was informed, true for most other public schools.[43] Numerous writers, notably Sir Francis Fletcher Vane, supported Waugh's revelations and J. Howard Whitehouse commissioned a fact-finding review, published in 1919 as *The English Public School*.[44] Here the weakness of public-school religion, the games mania, the militarism, and the lack of freedom were all aired once more but now with greater objectivity and authority than in any previous denunciation.[45]

Other voices were also speaking out against earlier ideals. After the war's bloody mid-point at the Somme, the tone of the soldier-poets changed from naive expressions of the 'pure and elevated patriotism, free from hate, bitterness, and fear' that Dean Inge had found in Rupert Brooke's sonnets to the irony of Isaac Rosenberg, Siegfried Sassoon and Wilfred Owen.[46] With Rosenberg, who was killed near Arras in April 1918, the irony in *Break of Day in the Trenches* was gentle, using the conventions of pastoral poetry to describe the wanderings of a trench-rat:

> It seems you inwardly grin as you pass
> Strong eyes, fine limbs, haughty athletes,

Less chanced than you for life,
Bonds to the whims of murder,
Sprawled in the bowels of the earth,
The torn fields of France.[47]

Sassoon's irony had a satirical edge, as in *The Hero*:

"Jack fell as he'd have wished," the Mother said,
And folded up the letter that she'd read.
"The Colonel writes so nicely." Something broke
In the tired voice that quavered to a choke.
She half looked up. "We mothers are so proud
Of our dead soldiers." Then her face was bowed.

Quietly the Brother Officer went out.
He'd told the poor old dear some gallant lies
That she would nourish all her days, no doubt.
For while he coughed and mumbled, her weak eyes
Had shone with gentle triumph, brimmed with joy,
Because he'd been so brave, her glorious boy.[48]

Sassoon survived the war, but Owen was killed by machine-gun fire on 4 November 1918 during an unsuccessful British attempt to bridge the Sambre Canal, exactly one week before the signing of the Armistice. In the biting irony of *Dulce et Decorum Est*, composed in November 1917, Owen contrasted the horrors of the death of a young soldier from a gas attack with the quotation used by the Bishop of London on the first Sunday of the war – 'a sweet and pleasant thing it is to die for your country':

If in some smothering dreams, you too could pace
Behind the wagon that we flung him in,
And watch the white eyes writhing in his face,
His hanging face, like a devil's sick of sin;
If you could hear, at every jolt, the blood
Come gargling from the froth-corrupted lungs,
Obscene as cancer, bitter as the cud
Of vile, incurable sores on innocent tongues, –
My friend, you would not tell with such high zest
To children ardent for some desperate glory,
The old Lie: *Dulce et decorum est
Pro patria mori*.[49]

After the Armistice the voices of the mass of returning soldiers who were not poets also had their say. Many families and communities throughout Britain who had lost sons in the war had previously created private and civic memorials whose design was based on chivalric themes – St George and the dragon, a knight in armour kneeling in vigil and a bare-headed saintly Arthurian knight, these are examples found by Anthony Fletcher – but those who fought had witnessed at first hand that modern warfare was no longer chivalrous. When it came to the design of national memorials of commemoration and for the countless war cemeteries across the world, the tone was quite different – no romanticism, no triumphalism.[50] Edwin Lutyens caught the mood of national bereavement in his simple design for the Cenotaph in London's Whitehall; first a temporary structure for the march-past of the victorious armies in July 1919, then a permanent memorial for the first Remembrance Day on 11 November 1920. That year the Imperial War Graves Commission decided that officers and men should be buried side by side in the new cemeteries, thus seeking to erase the memory of Edwardian class consciousness, and that all should have the standard tablet-shaped headstone. There was no public-school privilege in death. Lutyens's Stone of Remembrance, inscribed with Kipling's words 'Their name Liveth for Evermore,' and Reginald Bloomfield's Christian Cross of Sacrifice were placed in every cemetery.[51] Civic, church, university and school memorials throughout the country followed this lead: quotations in Latin and Greek were inappropriate; the plain English of Laurence Binyon's words better expressed the nation's feelings.[52]

We will remember them.

III The New Age: 'The classical training in public schools is for the average boy a deplorable waste of most valuable time'

The New Age began with the end of an ideal and the virtual extinction of a word.[1] The noun 'manliness', and its adjective 'manly', dropped suddenly from current usage. The word that in 1914 had been in countless fathers' letters and every headmaster's sermon was now quietly and without ceremony buried with the dead; 1918 marked the end of a myth.[2] The pre–war generation of public-school Old Boys had strived to live the life of heroes but the war had not been noble; a whole generation had been slaughtered; and most had died without glory or honour.[3] The make-believe of Homeric times ceased in the egalitarian years of post-war Britain as heroic qualities went out of fashion: the ideal of imperial manliness was discredited. Britain in the New Age needed new ideas and new means to realise them – and so too did the public schools.

The liberal assault on the public schools that had continued unabated throughout the war was maintained in the first years of peace. Most criticism was directed at the perceived poor leadership and management of the war, particularly by the Army. The great majority of its officers, from the most junior to the most senior, had been educated at public schools and so these schools bore their share of the blame. It was generally appreciated that junior officers had performed well in terms of courage, determination and care for the men under their command, but the war had revealed that they lacked military knowledge and skills: they were amateur soldiers. The senior officers were subjected to more scathing criticism: they were the professional soldiers who had been charged with the direction of strategy and tactics, with the overall leadership of men, and with the management of resources. These generals, brigadiers and colonels were seen as remote, aloof, uncaring and incompetent.

The selection criteria for men deemed officer material and the training of junior officers thus came under rigorous scrutiny. Both before and during the war, army officers had been chosen on their physical attributes and for their gentlemanly qualities. Stature, strength and prowess at games together with upper-class breeding and a public-school education were paramount whereas little or no attention had been paid to intelligence, educational attainment, resistance to stress, or moral courage. The result was that although these officers had led well and served gallantly, they had exhibited little curiosity, they disliked innovation, they were over self-confident, they were totally obedient to the rule book, and they were bound by an inflexible principle of honour. The ethic of honour and fair-play, so admirable in itself, could lead to disastrous results when espionage was regarded as 'not cricket' or when matched against an enemy who 'plays the game' to a different set of rules.[4]

A survey conducted in the three years before the war found that 95% of army officers had never read a military book of any kind. Army leadership, with some notable exceptions, was amateur, anti-intellectual, intolerant of change and incapable of original thought. Thus, men who had seen the effectiveness of the Maxim gun at Omdurman in 1898 nevertheless rejected the machine gun as a useful weapon in 1914. Furthermore, the rifle was seen as less effective than the bayonet for infantryman and second best to 'the speed of the horse, the magnetism of the charge and the terror of cold steel' for the cavalry. Douglas Haig, the Commander-in-Chief, had been one of Kitchener's staff officers at Omdurman, yet in 1916 he limited the use of machine guns on the Western Front in case their presence dampened his soldiers' offensive spirit. He also resisted the introduction of steel helmets for the same reason, even though their effectiveness in reducing head injuries was well known.[5] The debate on whether or not to relax King's Regulation 1695, which stipulated that all soldiers should have a moustache to project that offensive spirit, was deemed more important.[6] Later analysis showed that 'cold steel' accounted for less than 1% of casualties, whereas rifle and machine-gun fire brought down a third of the dead and wounded, and heavy weapons the remainder.[7]

Other critics broadened the assault on public-school leadership training to include business, industry and government. They argued that the narrow curriculum and the sense of conformity stunted ability and ambition: the schools did not prepare boys for the adult world; they inoculated them against it.[8] The way that public schools taught and what they taught had to change.

In 5 June 1916 *The Times* published a letter from the Admiral of the Fleet, Lord Jellicoe, and seven other signatories:

> In view of the grave crisis through which we are passing, we venture to ask you to join us in a demand that the boys at the public schools should be properly trained in subjects essential for our national life. We consider a mastery of science and of modern languages is necessary to fit our sons to take their proper places in modern life whether in science, commerce, or the Forces of the Crown. [. . .]
>
> The wonderful efficiency of the Germans, both in science and languages, points to the fact that their schools and universities answer these two vital requirements better than do ours. [. . .]
>
> We wish to point out that the classical training in public schools is for the average boy a deplorable waste of most valuable time . . . while real essentials for our national success are dangerously neglected.

The Prime Minister, Herbert Asquith, responded by setting up two committees: one on science chaired by J. J. Thomson, a Nobel laureate; the other on modern languages, led by a civil servant, Stanley Leaves.[9]

Both committees reported their findings in 1918. Thomson discovered that the curriculum at prep schools and public schools steered the ablest boys to the classics and so few clever boys studied science at university. The result was that ignorance of science was a badge of status amongst the cleverest public-school men.[10] Leathes found that modern languages were taught 'like the dead languages and the results were very poor' and that no importance was placed on conversational ability.[11] These two heavyweight condemnations gave added impetus to the curricular reform that had begun at the end of the previous century, but progress was slow. The universities of Oxford and Cambridge made a start when in 1919 they abandoned Greek as a requirement for entry.[12]

The state-funded grammar schools, founded in the last quarter of the nineteenth century and in the first years of the new one, increased the pressure on the public schools to modernise. These schools already devoted more time in the curriculum to science and modern languages than to classics and, after calls by the professorial staff of London's Imperial College of Science and Technology in June 1916, the government allocated £500,000 so that more boys might stay on at these schools until eighteen before going on to study science at the universities.[13] The grammar-school Old Boys had also served with distinction in the war. The high casualty rates on the Somme and the expansion that came with conscription saw the public schools lose their monopoly of the officer corps. Men were promoted from the ranks to fill the gaps and then sent on crash courses that included lessons in social etiquette and much playing of team sports. These 'temporary gentlemen', like Second Lieutenant Trotter in R. C. Sherriff's *Journey's End*, proved brave and capable soldiers.[14]

Classics may have just survived the war, but the pendulum had swung back to the Latin sector. Greek had ruled as the thinking-man's mode of expression ever since Thomas Arnold's time at Rugby; now Latin was the staple diet. Homer was no longer read, no longer cited in headmaster's speeches and no longer quoted except in college and school senior common rooms.[15] Chivalry also fell out of favour – no more Gothic chapels, no more images of knights in armour and no more equestrian statues.[16]

Religion was taking a battering too. It was a difficult time for the Church, for the war had demolished much of what remained of post-Victorian confidence. Church attendance in all traditions surged for a few weeks at the outset of the war but, as military casualties and domestic sacrifices mounted, regular attendance fell away. Disillusionment with the Churches for failing to prevent or shorten the war and a search for alternative forms of expression, not least Spiritualism, maintained the decline after 1918.[17]

Religion at the public schools mirrored that in the country as a whole: it was in decline, though still powerful. Far fewer headmasters were in Holy Orders than in Victorian times.[18] Faithless, institutional, ceremonial religion was presented to the boys and it rarely touched their souls. All too often the visiting preacher would resort to athletic cant to capture the boys' attention: 'St Paul was no Mug but a bit of a boxer, in fact a regular Sportsman – yes, the Apostles were all Sportsmen.'[19] The playing-fields rather than the chapel thus became the spiritual centre for many schools.

The waging of the Great War had placed enormous expectations upon able-bodied men to serve in the military and upon women to contribute to the war effort in addition to maintaining their domestic roles. Many women after the war wished to preserve their increased independence – whether through education and a career, having shorter hair and wearing shorter skirts or even trousers, or fighting for universal suffrage – but most from the professional classes still wanted to marry and to raise a family, and were willing to relinquish or reduce their wartime employment to ease the men's return.[20] The pool of potential husbands had shrunk as a result of four years of carnage but the men who had survived were keen to forsake the homosocial world of the trench, mess and regiment for the joys of marriage and family life.[21] Marriage rates increased, the age of first marriage dropped, and the proportion of single-to-married women was lower in 1921 than it had been in 1911; a baby boom followed.[22]

This 'return to domesticity' by ex-army officers added pressure on the public schools to tackle the romantic and sexual relationships of their boys. Despite the scandal of the Oscar Wilde trial in 1895, it was only now that the innocence of intense male friendships was questioned by popular psychology.[23] G. H. Rendall, the headmaster of Charterhouse, told a conference just before the war that his boys were 'amorous but seldom erotic', but he nonetheless insisted that junior masters should patrol the dormitories at night to ensure that the boys stayed in their own beds. Walter Barton, headmaster at Epsom, installed electric light for ease of nocturnal inspection.[24] In his magisterial study of the literature of the Great War, Paul Fussell asked: 'Do the British have a special talent for such passion?'[25] Such desires found plenty of eminent men to enjoy them in the late nineteenth and early twentieth centuries: Tennyson, Cory, Vaughan, Flecker, A. C. Benson, Newbolt, Buchan, Lawrence, Burton and others mentioned in this study have all been cited in one place or another as possessing homoerotic tendencies. Much literature of the period is permeated with its spirit; some detect it in the muscular Christians, Kingsley and Hughes; and others in the Tractarians, Newman and Froude.[26] No twentieth-century public-school memoir seems complete without some observation on the author's homosexual experiences, whether overt or otherwise, and the possible couplings of master and boy, don and undergraduate, officer and soldier, scoutmaster and scout, choirmaster and chorister, have become absorbed in British culture.

Edward Lyttelton believed that 'the special evil' was unknown at the public schools in the 1820s, for it was checked by the hardness of life, but that by the 1870s 'decadence' had set in.[27] Its existence was publicly acknowledged in 1881 by J. M. Wilson, headmaster of Clifton, in his presidential address to the Education Society.[28] H. Havelock Ellis in the 1890s recorded many examples of homoerotic practice amongst public-school boys; the situation at Uppingham in the Selwyn years has already been described; J. R. Ackerley, Robert Graves, A. J. Ayer, and T. C. Worsley are just four of many authors who recorded their experiences from Rossall in the 1900s to Wellington in the 1930s.[29] Homoeroticism, whether in romantic friendships or homosexual acts, was an integral part of the public-school system.

Various reasons were put forward for its growth: the monastic all-male environment; the 'untouchable' image of pure Victorian womanhood; corporal punishment exciting sexual precocity; or submission as an antidote to Victorian and Edwardian manliness.[30] In this pre-Freudian era masturbation and homosexuality were seen as wholly physiological in origin and so the main line of attack came through the physical: mechanical contrivances were invented, cold baths were prescribed, and the exhaustive efforts on the games-field were sure to send the boys to sleep. The whole cult of games seemed planned to extend boyhood into early manhood so that the adolescent phase might be missed altogether. Religious fervour and emotional fear were two other weapons. The former had little influence, but the picturing of those who gave in to temptation as weak, stunted, underdeveloped, sluggish, secretive and nervous must have had some effect – unforeseen or otherwise.[31]

Paul Fussell judged that the British homoerotic tradition reached its peak in the Great War – and amongst the young men who had been taught the classics at their public schools. Greek philosophy had long been an alibi for the idealisation of the male nude and for male desire; as Simon Goldhill judged, 'Hellenism and homosexuality went together like a horse and cart.'[32] The army served as an extension of school life and the prefect-fag or master-boy relationship could easily transform to an officer-soldier one. Moreover, war is a well-practised destroyer of codes of sexual morality: memoirs of the Great War, for example, contain quasi-erotic vignettes of nude soldiers bathing and poems use a vocabulary of increasing erotic heat that transformed 'men' to 'boys' and then to 'lads'.[33]

An earlier civilisation, ancient Greece, had a homoerotic tradition: all games were performed naked and in front of admiring spectators; most gymnasia had a statue of Eros; and it was at the foot of his statue at the Academy that Plato discoursed to his pupils. Greek homoeroticism began as a high ideal and the partnership of young and old lovers became the very foundation of Greek education. Love affairs also provided opportunities for noble rivalry and eternal comradeship, the basis of Homeric honour. Such high-mindedness, however, was not always maintained and paedophilia might descend to pederasty.[34] It is ironic that the age that sought the Homeric virtues should succumb to the Homeric vice.

> How curious it was that, day in and day out, we should be soaking ourselves in the literature which glorified that addiction without its ever coming into the open. If the Greece we read of was really so glorious, weren't the passions they cultivated no less glorious, too?[35]

IV Public-school spirit: 'Reggiemented'

The public schools now faced many challenges: leadership in the New Age; the classics, modern languages and science; the decline in religion; school-boy romances and homoerotic practices; and the rise of the grammar schools. But there was no need for haste for the schools were full. Repton was one of many schools that benefited from a rapid rise in numbers after 1917 when the War Office ordered that boys who were likely to make efficient army officers should remain at school until eighteen and a half.[1] Eton, Harrow and Oundle all increased; Lancing doubled in size in the decade after the war; and Durham outdid that. Several new schools were founded to meet the demand for places, including Canford School and Stowe School in 1923 and Bryanston School in 1928. As Cyril Norwood, headmaster at Harrow from 1926 until 1934, proclaimed: 'The boarding-schools of the country are at the present time enjoying a period of unexampled prosperity.'[2]

The public schools might have prospered but the optimism of the New Age did not last long. Unemployment soared from 300,000 to over a million in the three winter months of 1920–21, the post-war economic boom had ended, and the gold had run out. The same years saw the rapid decline of the splintered Liberal party: it suffered disastrous results at the 1918 and 1924 General Elections, thus leaving the political arena to the Conservatives and the newly-emerged Labour Party. In an atmosphere of political polarisation, the gap between the upper classes and the working classes opened, with each side closing ranks and each adopting fixed ideological positions. This, and the recent revolution in Russia, threw the upper classes firmly to the political right and all overtures to liberalism were hastily withdrawn. The General Strike of 1926 and the Wall Street Crash of 1929 added to the gloom and the separation of the classes.

The public schools, as bastions of the upper-class system, immediately changed tack: reforms that seemed ready for implementation were dropped; policies that were politically safe were adopted; and all that was conventional and conservative was re-discovered and re-emphasised. The liberal reformers had made great advances in the years before 1914, the war swung the debate their way, and then a shift in the economic climate brought about total rejection. So entrenched and so conservative did the public schools now become that to criticise them was seen as unpatriotic. The twentieth century had lost its spring with a vengeance and it was all too easy to point to the public-school statistics of the war and make propaganda out of the dead.[3] The return to Edwardian ways at Harrow was seen as a corporate tribute to the fallen.[4]

No study has been made of the homecoming of masters who had served in the war, other than that in two later novels – James Hilton's *Good-bye Mr Chips* and R. L. Delderfield's *To Serve Them All My Days*.[5] The shattering events that these men had witnessed at first hand must have left their legacy. All schools had such men; many were badly scarred by the war, both physically and emotionally.[6] They went back to their schools and stayed there, rarely moving on to headmasterships or to other professions. Many became housemasters; many were still there in the 1950s. How the atmosphere of the jazz age and the glitter of night clubs must have stung them.[7] How did they react to the pacifist spirit so evident in the late 1920s; what did they think of the concept of a League of Nations? It is impossible to answer these questions but the attitude of returning masters to these and similar changes may well explain the reactionary, unadventurous, and narrow lives they followed in their schools. Of course, some of the returning masters brought back liberal ideas with them, together with a determination to seek for a brighter future, but many more concentrated on their teaching, the house, school politics and games, and failed to maintain interests outside the world of school. These men became progressively out of step with the times, ever looking back to the past, ever preventing change and ever suspicious of innovation. They can only have had a conservative effect on their schools.[8]

Many of the long-standing headmasters who had sent their Old Boys off to the war, and suffered greatly from their deaths, stayed on at their schools and reinforced the conservative outlook. The long reigns of the headmasters of seven of the nine Clarendon schools are typical: until 1924 for Montague Rendall at Winchester; 1925 for Harrow's Lionel Ford; 1927 for Albert Hillard at St Paul's and John Nairn at Merchant Taylors'; 1932 for Shrewsbury's Harold Sawyer; 1933 for Cyril Alington at Eton; and 1935 for Frank Fletcher at Charterhouse. It is likely that these men, and the many more among the other hundred or so public-school headmasters, looked to the past for security rather than embrace the liberal challenge for the future – once more, no study has been made on this question.[9]

The public schools of the 1920s and early 1930s exuded an air of conventionalism.[10] Each school became a small conservative world, protecting its charges from the bustle of the surrounding turmoil. Only safe politics were discussed; *The Times* and *Punch* formed the staple reading for the boys; there were no radios or gramophones; sermons of the 'Cross and Union Jack' variety were delivered regularly from chapel pulpits; and Navy League lecturers once more flew the banner of military imperialism.[11] Despite the passing of compulsory Greek at Oxford and Cambridge, all schools still based their curriculum firmly on the classical languages whereas the inclusion of 'material' and 'commercial' subjects was resisted strongly. A public-school education was to be a training of the mind was the oft-heard cry and all attempts to broaden the curriculum or to let boys specialise in modern subjects were seen as undermining this principle.[12] Art and music were now more commonly taught in these schools, and handicrafts were starting to come in, but in general they were regarded as extra-curricular, voluntary and of little importance. The belief that such aesthetic training could have a moral value was viewed with great suspicion.[13]

Games were compulsory and games still reflected the status of a school: a 'rugger' school was decidedly one up on a 'soccer' one – Harrow was one of several schools that changed codes – and to be classed a 'Lord's school' was the supreme epithet.[14] At most schools, as at Repton, it was the long-standing housemasters who 'were the high priests of the cult of athletics'.[15] The time given to games, the compulsion and the values derived from their play were exactly as in pre-war schools – and the virtues were confirmed by the example of those who had fought in Flanders and Gallipoli.[16] Rugby football, rowing and cricket were still the major games, major in terms of their character-training facilities, whereas hockey and soccer were acceptable merely as a change, and running was good for the 'stick to it' attitude. On the other hand, golf, tennis and racquets were hardly fit to be school games for 'they were not painful enough'.[17] If the character-training effects were to work on all boys, games had to be compulsory and, in like manner, the compulsory watching of school matches encouraged *esprit de corps*.[18]

The games were as competitive as ever; school magazines were filled with sporting exploits; the national press was keenly interested in the progress of school matches; and *The Times* still published portraits of the Eton and Harrow XIs on the eve of their match at Lord's. The cult of athleticism continued unabated, but with two new aspects that were not present before the war. First, it was now the masters and the parents, as much as the boys, who encouraged the playing of games; and secondly, there was no underlying ideal to be promoted through their play. Games were now used to 'occupy' boys, a popular term of the period, as well as to keep them from mischief and to send them to bed too tired for sexual irregularities, both long-established purposes.[19] The talented games-players continued to rule over other boys: members of the Philathletic

Club at Harrow had the right to wear distinctive grey waistcoats and bow-ties, and to walk arm-in-arm down the middle of the road – until motor cars became popular![20]

The cadet corps was compulsory too, if not by actual headmasterly statement then with the assistance of prefectorial and peer pressures. Every school with public-school ambitions had its own corps; at Harrow it became the central feature of school life and all masters were expected to join.[21] A corps' training was seen by most headmasters as a means to prepare boys for the needs of their country by awakening a patriotism that was greater than narrow school loyalty. A. H. Ashcroft, the headmaster of Fettes, was unusual when he voiced the opinion, more often heard in private than in public, that service in the corps was a preparation for national defence and that this formed an integral part of a public-school education. In Ashcroft's opinion, this was religion in a most practical form.[22]

Although life might be a little softer than in Spartan times – Ashcroft thought there was too much coddling – although masters were on friendlier terms with boys, and although boys were certainly on better terms with their seniors and juniors, in general 'the green baize door which led to the boys' side of the house' was still closed and rarely did the housemaster penetrate the far side. In this under-supervised boy world, it was all too simple in 'a bad house, in a bad school, in a bad time' for homosexuality to rear its head. The evidence that homosexual acts were common in public schools, that they were practised for amusement, and that they were openly tolerated, is huge.[23] The age-old belief that games – 'part of the discipline by which Satan is prevented from providing mischief', according to Norwood – could keep such irregularities at bay has a particularly hollow ring.[24]

At first glance there is little then to distinguish a public school of the 1920s and early 1930s from a school of the Golden Age – beyond a slight tightening of the economic belt. The Edwardian school, however, looked forward: buoyed by its confidence in Imperial Christianity it sought to inculcate a Homeric ideal of manliness. The post-war school, however, looked back at the past, found support in the substance of the pre-war school but could not believe in its Christianity, nor in its manliness. Religion now taught safe civic virtues and chaplains, more pastoral leaders than schoolmaster-priests, found it difficult to encourage inner spiritual life.[25] It had been hard to distinguish between sham and idealism in the Edwardian school, but at least there was some idealism; now the post-war school was in danger of becoming a means without an end. Headmasters recognised that there was a need to reassert the old manliness in a new guise, one fit for a society undergoing rapid change.[26] To fill that vacuum, 'Englishness' became the creed and 'public-school spirit' was raised as the ideal.[27] The search for 'That Something' occupied headmasters and Old Boys from 1924 to 1928 with articles and correspondence filling the reviews. Eventually the components of public-school spirit were agreed: total trust, cheerful obedience, ability to get on with others, honour and service to one's country. It was *esprit de corps* in new clothing. Life in the boarding houses and games on the playing-fields were seen as the formative influences, but how short this falls of an ideal of manliness. 'Good form' was a poor substitute for Christianity; 'play the game' was a weak maxim for a hero; to be a 'sport' was hardly a fitting life's ambition.[28] Manliness had become chappishness.[29] Yet in the post-war public-school world, life was indeed a game: games were the main form of school service; athletic goals provided the ultimate ambitions; fair play was the rule of life.[30] A British plot to assassinate Hitler during the 1930s was turned down as 'not cricket', the very words used by the government of the day.[31]

Reginald Owen got Uppingham under control a year after the end of the war. Adrian Bell, who had suffered in Owen's first years, noticed the improved 'tone' and there was now 'daylight at the end of the tunnel'.[32] The appointment of new housemasters to seven of the thirteen houses helped, so too did the retirement of four masters and the return of five after war service.[33] In addition, fifteen new masters were appointed between 1919 and 1922 to accommodate the increased pupil numbers: 418 boys in 1918 rose to 501 in 1926. Owen believed that the school was resting too firmly on the reputation of a once great past; now he sought to increase the boys' endeavours in both work and games. Owen was tireless and his whole energy was devoted to the school. He was never absent overnight in term-time, he taught a hefty timetable, he regularly played games with the boys and through weekly meetings with the praepostors he had a firm hand on the pulse of the school. Derek Patmore, the later playwright, met little bullying when he arrived in 1922.[34]

Owen reputedly knew the name of every boy but personal relationships – whether between headmaster and masters, or both and the boys – were not to be encouraged. Young boys could not address their seniors unless they were spoken to first; few boys managed friendships outside the narrow circle of their house contemporaries.[35] Old Boys remembered Owen arousing more fear than affection, even in the praepostors who might have expected 'something warmer than an official relationship'. His edict to the masters was clear: 'However friendly the relations between master and boy and they ought to be friendly – it is not healthy for the element of fear to be absent entirely.'[36] Owen was a stern disciplinarian and could look incredibly severe. An Old Boy remembered: 'If a boy strayed from the straight and narrow, punishment was merciless and administered personally, and on busy sessions reported to be as painful to the recipient at the tail of the queue as it had been to the first victim.' A dilapidated straw hat, a hair-style without a parting, and irregularities of dress were not 'tolerated'.[37] Owen's grip extended to the masters and their wives; any laxity in appearance or smoking in the wrong place would produce a written reprimand.[38] Praepostors matched the headmaster's methods, maintaining house discipline through corporal punishment.[39] In a play on Owen's Christian name, the boys declared that they were 'reggiemented'.[40]

There were some on the staff who feared that such rigid rule might restrict the full development of the individual boy, but to Owen the aim was the subordination of self to the needs of the community. 'Service' was Owen's call, and his magnificently organised and well-functioning school produced it.[41] Service was always the theme of Owen's brisk sermons and his addresses on Speech Day. It was a puritanical service too: games results, no matter how good, were never praised on Speech Day, nor were they published in the national press. Owen's version of service could be realised in just two ways, the corps and games; his insistence on the school's insularity prevented exploration of other options.[42]

Jones was still commander of the Uppingham corps; he was the only master Owen could not dominate.[43] The corps was not compulsory but in the words of Uppingham's annual entry in the *Public Schools Year Book*, 'almost all boys were in it'.[44] The compulsory shooting test that Selwyn had instituted in 1900 was maintained until at least 1932.[45] Company Sergeant Major Bacovitch was appointed gymnasium instructor in 1919 and he served in this capacity until 1952. Swedish drill supplanted Beisiegel's German gymnastics: boys were instructed in serried ranks to perform a prescribed sequence of free-standing exercises in unison and to Bacovitch's commands. The object was to improve breathing, muscle tone and flexibility.[46] Gymnastics was now a team sport and able to contribute its part to the inculcation of *esprit de corps*. Bacovitch also supervised 'breathers': summoned by a bugle call, the whole school assembled in the quadrangles at morning break, removed their jackets, and performed free-standing exercises under the command of praepostors and Bacovitch's watchful eye.[47]

'Games were a fetish', recalled Derek Patmore.[48] Uppingham XIs and XVs played them extremely well whereas the less talented endured interminable house league games with little or no instruction.[49] As a near-*haiku* in the 1928 school magazine recorded: 'Dreams / Mere puff and bluff! / 'Tis teams / Both rough and tough / The School esteems/Enough.'[50] The cricket under Frank Gilligan and the Rugby football under Alastair Smallwood were in the highest rank of public-school sport, and no school won more blues in the latter during this period.[51] Owen intended his school to be narrow in outlook, insulated from the outside influences and philistine – and that is what he made. The arts, he decided, 'were a dangerous waste of time'.[52]

V Skrine:
'The truth has found a champion to carry it on'

The public-school ideal of imperial manliness died in the Great War and the words 'manly' and 'manliness' fell quietly from the vocabulary of a nation – a silent memorial to a lost generation. That ideal was indeed dead but the seeds that were responsible for the final flowering also gave root to a second strain. This growth was slower yet steadier than its more colourful cousin and it did not come to full bloom until almost a century after the seeds were sown. In order to follow its evolution, we must return to Thring's Uppingham.

Thring's diary for 13 March 1861 noted the arrival of a new boy in School House: 'Little Skrine came last night with his elder brother, such a bright innocent looking little fellow. I quite loved him as I looked on him.'[1] It was not usual for the headmaster to record the arrival of every new boy; this one made a strong first impression. Headmaster and boy were close for the six years of John Huntley Skrine's schooling. In 1865 he succeeded Lewis Nettleship as captain of school and served in that capacity for two years. He won a scholarship to Corpus Christi College, Oxford and was elected a fellow of Merton College after a successful undergraduate career. Skrine was a competent poet, winning the Newdigate prize and publishing several volumes of verse. In the summer of 1873 Thring offered Skrine a mastership at Uppingham; his diary of 2 June records – 'Received his acceptance this morning to my great comfort. These two lines very little represent the longing, and prayers and trust that I might have God's blessing on him and me in this, or the relief and strength of heart I feel at his coming.'[2] Thring was clearly preparing Skrine for great things.

In October 1874 Skrine was offered the headmastership of the Liverpool Institution. He consulted Thring and received the advice that he needed a few more years' experience before seeking an independent command. Then Thring spoke plainly to Skrine, telling him that he 'looked to him some day being a leading headmaster, and it was good he should have my experience'.[3] Hardly a day now passed which did not see Skrine and Thring walking together about the school or in the countryside, heads locked in conversation.[4] By May 1875 Thring was using the epithet 'disciple' in relation to Skrine, and this indeed was the relationship for the next twelve years.

Skrine was Thring's trusted lieutenant during the Borth exodus and he later recorded the life of the school there in *Uppingham-by-the-Sea*. He wrote a splendid thanks-giving hymn, set to music by Paul David, which has been sung at every Borth Commemoration Service from 1880 onwards. The same partnership later presented Thring with hymns for use at the beginning and end of term.[5] 1880 also witnessed Skrine's total acceptance of Thring's philosophy of 'True Life': the moment is recorded in Thring's diary of 10 November:

> Skrine preached, and took for his sermon the faith of Abraham offering Isaac, pointing that up to then Abraham's trials had all had some admixture of earthly gain in them, but this was utter overthrow of everything excepting faith in God. Then he drew a short parallel, of the boy and young man's life, in which all the hardships are connected with personal gain; but a time comes when the demand is to give up all the personal dreams, and he ended with the noble sentence, "Let not the holder of the promise think he can lose it by too much obedience, knowing that God is able to raise it up even from the dead". I knew he had made his choice. And my own heart swelled, and was comforted.[6]

Skrine had accepted the true gospel of Thring's ideal of manliness.

Cormac Rigby noted how Thring believed that no 'great public work' should be attempted before the age of thirty, and the lives of Joseph, David,

John the Baptist and Christ Himself gave support to his belief.[7] This was why Skrine needed that long apprenticeship under Thring. Skrine, however, had attained the age of thirty in 1878. Was he being groomed to take over from Thring at Uppingham? This was certainly the view of a contributor to the *Journal of Education* and, after Borth, Skrine assumed responsibility for much of the routine running of the school.[8]

On Thring's death in October 1887 the trustees appointed William Campbell, the senior housemaster, as acting headmaster; then in January 1888 Selwyn came to succeed Thring. Why did the trustees overlook Skrine? No answers are recorded but one can surmise. First, Thring had been at odds with the trustees throughout his life at Uppingham. The example of the Borth year, when they washed their hands of the school, is one of countless clashes that one could cite. Would they be willing to appoint a second Thring? Second, many of the Old Boys and parents may have wanted other than Skrine, perhaps seeking an outside appointment of a new broom who would lead the school to accepted public-school status. Whatever the reasons, Selwyn came and Skrine went – to Glenalmond in Scotland.

As Warden at Glenalmond, Skrine was true to his apprenticeship under Thring. He raised a struggling school to a position of security, with a reputation in Scotland second only to Almond's Loretto. He wrote a touching *Memory of Edward Thring* that is the best of the early Thring biographies, and when he came to write of his own teaching experiences in *Pastor Agnorum*, the work was inevitably dedicated to Thring – 'Shepherd, the tender and strong, Giver of Life for the sheep.'[9] *Pastor Agnorum* exudes an Arthurian code of manliness with games as the 'tilt yard' of school life, and this was to be the pattern of most of his writings – a Glenalmond boy's progress from fag to prefect matched that of page to knight in chivalric times.[10] School life became a 'Romance' in the best traditions of the knightly ideal:

> Is our chivalry of the school a true phase of the world-old conflict of "Soul out now with sense"? Is the public school a fortress held for the ideal against earthliness of money, fashion, luxury, selfish competition, sloth, cowardice, dread of pain, and all other forms of materialism? Are we rearing there a knight errantry fit to keep the marches of an empire, and to purge the land nearer home of wrong, violence, lust?[11]

Here indeed is the soul of the Thringian ideal of manliness but much of the body was lost in Skrine's emphasis on spirituality; it is no wonder that the boys at Glenalmond found his sermons too transcendental.[12] Skrine's ideal of manliness was no match for the hearty athleticism on show at Almond's Loretto.

In the view of Norman Whatley, the headmaster of Clifton in the 1930s, the period in which he had taught in public schools had witnessed many good headmasters, and indeed the average may never have been higher, but there were no great ones. The headmaster of a late-Victorian and Edwardian public school had become an administrator rather than a prophet; he followed rather than led.[13] Here Whatley hits the nail right on the head: if there had been an Arnold or a Thring (or a Temple, a Benson, a . . .) then the ideal of manliness might have endured in the public schools. But there was not, and it did not – thus one must look outside the established ranks of public schools for the survival of Thring's ideal. Skrine, despite his training, was not the man.

VI Reddie and Badley: 'We now recognise more clearly that education is concerned with the whole human-being'

The Schools Inquiry Commission of the late 1860s, led by Lord Taunton, examined all the secondary schools that lay between the great public schools and those which educated children from the labouring classes. The Endowed Schools Act of August 1869 that resulted from the Taunton Commission's recommendations was then applied to all schools that were wholly or partly maintained by means of any endowment, except for the Clarendon Nine. Many headmasters of the new public schools were outraged that the older foundations were receiving special treatment and their agitation led to the foundation of the Headmasters' Conference. Twelve of the thirty-seven headmasters invited by Thring assembled for its first meeting at Uppingham in December that year. No invitations had been sent to the headmasters of the Clarendon Nine.[1]

Thring explained his stance in a letter to Hugo Harper, the headmaster of Sherborne:

> For my part I desire to separate my lot entirely from the fashionable schools, and to cast it in, come weal come woe, with the earnest working men, and smaller schools, which one may hope to see doing honest work.[2]

The exclusion of the Nine was raised at the Uppingham conference. Thring's diary records:

> Dr. _____ wished to make concession to try and bring in the great schools, and tack us on to them. I laid down plainly that I thought it was simple death to do so; we rested on our vitality and work, they on their prestige and false glory: if they would meet us on common ground, well and good; if not, not.[3]

The minutes of the meeting identify Steuart Pears of Repton as the Doctor and they record more on Thring's objections:

> Our schools depend entirely on the vitality of progressive work. . . . Eton . . . has wonderful powers of a certain kind and earnest men using that power; but (in) progressive work, we stand better than they; more alive to the

necessity of it; comparatively unfettered in carrying out our discoveries, and we do carry them out more effectively.[4]

Pears did not press the point and the matter was dropped.[5]

Thring's commitment to progressive schooling continued for the remainder of his life and in the 1880s he was called upon to expand on his ideas and methods to trainee teachers, practising teachers and teacher trainers: he addressed conferences, wrote articles and produced a celebrated book. The last, *Theory and Practice of Teaching*, was first published in 1883, ran to seventeen reprints by 1912 and reached readers in Canada, Germany, Hungary and the United States. Then, in 1885, he invited the Association of Headmistresses to hold its 1887 gathering at Uppingham. The ladies came, but not before Thring had issued a challenge to Frances Buss and Dorothea Beale, headmistresses of North London Collegiate School and Cheltenham Ladies' College respectively, to 'do something to reform our wretched Education (so called)'.[6]

It is surely more than mere coincidence that the birth of what came to be called 'the progressive school movement' occurred in the late 1880s, and almost in Thring's lifetime. Abbotsholme, the first progressive school, was founded in 1889, less than two years after Thring's death. Like Uppingham in the early Thring years, Abbotsholme and its direct and indirect successors, were innovatory schools, created in protest against the conformity of the traditional public schools.

Cecil Reddie, the founder of Abbotsholme, was the first of a new generation of educational radicals. There are many similarities between Reddie and Thring. Both had a deep belief in the Platonic whole-man concept of education, both admired Ruskin, and both were much influenced by German educational thought; after schooling at Fettes and graduation from Edinburgh University in 1878, Reddie gained a doctorate in chemistry at Göttingen University six years later.[7] Both were autocrats, both had battles with their masters and their governing bodies (or partners in Reddie's case), and both tolerated no outside influence. Like Thring, Reddie hated sophisticated luxury, loathed a slovenly posture, and enjoyed long rambles in the countryside. He was seen by many as the embodiment of *mens sana in corpora sano*.[8]

The New School at Abbotsholme was founded as a protest against what Reddie viewed as the rapid degeneration of England; the remedy was to lie in the abandoning of all that was cramping and conformist in the public-school curriculum that he had encountered when teaching back at Fettes and later at Clifton, and the adoption of all that could be individualistic and aesthetic. As Thring had done before him, Reddie likened education at the public schools to a meteorological phenomenon:

> All were the outcome of English fog and insularity, want of ideas and social co-operation. All bore the stamp of selfish individualism, and all preached mental and social chaos to the wearied beholder.[9]

Two immediate targets were classics and games. Classics were to go and a modern curriculum based on history, modern languages, mathematics, science, hygiene, social study and, above all, English literature, art and music was constructed in its place. Cooperation rather than competition was to be the emphasis in the classroom, for Reddie judged that only games in the public schools inspired team spirit. This approach inevitably brought in its wake a Thringian distrust of examinations and prizes.[10] The attack on games was also Thringian in concept: games were to be limited to two afternoons a week, compulsory watching of matches was denounced and other interests were brought in to destroy athletic 'shop' as the only talk between boys.[11] The other interests reflected the strong influence of Ruskin's thought on Reddie's practice. Manual labour – building, hay-making and general estate work – was a compulsory afternoon activity and much time in the curriculum was devoted to craft activities.[12] Further evidence of Ruskin's and Thring's belief in an aesthetic education is seen in the importance Reddie attached to a freedom to roam the surrounding Derbyshire countryside and on the care he bestowed on the architecture of school buildings and on the decoration of the chapel and classrooms.[13] His concern for physical health and hygiene was even stronger than Thring's and owed more to the influence of Almond: a wholesome diet, a ban on tuck and the adoption of 'sensible' clothing all show the Loretto trademark. Hygiene was taught in class; there was a carefully conceived physical education programme in which every boy's weight and height were logged; and the encouragement of positive health rather than just responding to illness and injury prevailed.[14]

Not all public-school traditions were rejected. The chapel was the centre of Abbotsholme life but with the difference that Reddie tailor-made the means of worship to match his own religious and educational support for the concept of the whole man. Reddie wrote his own prayers and modified much of the *Book of Common Prayer* and the Bible to suit the needs of his school. As a preacher, Reddie veered away from the contemporary custom of moral exhortation and returned to the approach favoured by Arnold and Thring, using the sermon to explain the school's role in the development of each boy's life. Like these predecessors, Reddie persuaded his pupils to accept that their school was odd when compared to its neighbours.[15] Abbotsholme also aimed to teach leadership but Reddie sought to do this in a less hierarchical way than in the traditional public school. As at Almond's Loretto, there were countless offices to give as many boys as possible a position of responsibility. Service to the community was vitally important and duties for all replaced the normal prefect and fag system.[16] Abbotsholme also differed from the traditional public school in two other important ways. First, Reddie incorporated sex education within his curriculum, convinced that this would prevent homosexuality; and second, he believed in a slow and unforced maturation through puberty, for only in later adolescence was it possible to form the physical, moral and mental individuality that he sought.[17]

Many ingredients of Thring's ideal of manliness were thus to be found at Reddie's Abbotsholme. When H. Courthope Bowen, a Cambridge University lecturer on the theory of education and an ardent admirer of Thring's work, inspected the school in 1895 he reported that

> I know of no other school in which the predominant aim is so markedly the development of the boy's whole nature, moral, physical, and intellectual, and none in which the effort to bring his knowledge, power and skill into harmonious inter-relation is so carefully maintained.[18]

Abbotsholme might have won greater renown and gained financial security but for events linked to Reddie's autocratic manner. His two partners quit at the end of the first term and rebellions by masters in 1900, 1904 and 1907 brought pupil numbers to a low ebb.[19] Despite this setback, Reddie's hope of giving birth to The New School Movement was realised and his influence was to be felt at schools across Europe and in America. Abbotsholme eventually found long-term stability but in its insecure interval the progressive education torch passed to Abbotsholme's more famous English descendant, Bedales. Its success was also Reddie's greatest disappointment.

One of Reddie's first appointments to the staff of Abbotsholme was J. H. Badley. Badley had been a boy at Rugby in the 1880s and there felt the full brunt of its philistine education. After graduating in 1889 with a first in classics at Trinity College, Cambridge, Badley determined to do his best to remedy the traditional public-school educational malaise. He heard about Abbotsholme from Goldie Dickinson, the future political scientist, whilst at Cambridge. He visited the school, was impressed by all that he saw and joined Reddie's staff.[20] Badley was in sympathy with almost all Reddie's philosophy, and he worked hard for the success of the new school, but there was one marked disagreement: the female sex. Badley wished to get married, but Reddie could not abide women; the engaged couple wanted the school to become co-educational, Reddie would not tolerate the arrival of girls. The result was that Badley left Abbotsholme in 1892 and the following year opened his own school, Bedales, in Sussex with just three boys.[21] Two more of Reddie's masters followed in 1902.[22]

At first Bedales just took boys but in 1898 it admitted girls and thus became one of the first co-educational boarding schools in Britain.[23] By 1900 the school had grown to 240 and this necessitated a move to new premises in Petersfield in Hampshire to allow for further expansion. Although anti-feminism was Badley's main objection to Reddie's practice, there were other differences of opinion. Badley felt that Reddie was too autocratic, too authoritarian; his ideals were too Prussian in their application and his dislike of examinations undermined intellectual attainment.[24] Bedales was however true to Abbotsholme's fundamental principles, and then Badley added to them ingredients taken from the educational theories of Maria Montessori and Friedrich Froebel, and from the practice of Baden-Powell's Boy Scouts.[25] In addition, through the early appointment of Oswald Powell to his staff, Badley gained direct contact with Thring's Uppingham – Oswald Powell had been a boy in Thring's last years, 1881 to 1886. After Cambridge and a spell teaching at Manchester Grammar School, Powell had 'cast about to find some school that might be putting into practice the ideas Thring had in mind when he founded Uppingham without being frustrated, as he was, by the medieval layout and traditions of the Public School'.[26] Powell's eye fell on Bedales and together as headmaster and second-master, Badley and Powell served their lives' work at Bedales.[27]

Bedales was firmly founded on the whole-man philosophy:

> Scholarship, good breeding, and leadership no longer form the whole of our educational idea. We now recognise more clearly that education is concerned with the whole human-being, on every side of his nature, and cannot neglect any of his activities and needs.[28]

The Ruskin influences were there: many of the school's facilities were built by the pupils and estate work was tackled by all. Craft-work, art, music and drama all flourished as part of the curriculum – and here Badley cited Thring's influence – and not just as extra-curricular activities.[29] Rambling in the countryside was encouraged and camps modelled on Baden-Powell's practice were introduced in the early 1900s to facilitate this union with nature. Badley was one of the first headmasters to bring the wider possibilities of outdoor activities into the regular curriculum.[30]

Badley visited Loretto and on his return to Bedales adopted several of Almond's principles: the introduction of a wholesome diet; a ban on tuck; and the wearing of 'sensible' forms of dress. He recognised that games were not enjoyed by all and so a variety of physical activities was introduced together with many non-sporting alternatives. Games were held on two afternoons a week, with two more given to outdoor manual work.[31] Gymnastics was to have an important role and, through the appointment of Reginald Roper in 1914, Badley made the greatest contribution to curricular physical education since Thring's appointment of Georg Beisiegel in 1860.[32] Roper had spent two years at the Royal Central Gymnastic Institute in Stockholm. On his return to England he taught at Edward Lyttelton's Eton for a few years; then, on the headmaster's fall from grace and after appearing before three tribunals for his pacifism, Roper arrived at Bedales during the early stages of the Great War.[33] With Badley's encouragement, Roper put into practice the philosophy that physical education was not just games and gymnastics but also all those aspects that would later be known as 'health education'. Diet, clothing, hours of rest, and so on all came under Roper's supervision. Weights and measures were regularly logged, checks were made on posture and feet, and remedial exercises were prescribed for those in need. Roper was convinced that Platonic 'gymnastic' was one of the two ingredients of life – a view expounded in his 1917 publication *Physical Education in Relation to School Life*.[34]

And the whole-man philosophy included girls: in 1914 the school numbered 125 boys and seventy-five girls aged from seven to nineteen.[35] Badley argued that boys gained an academic stimulus from co-education because girls matured physically and mentally more rapidly than boys. In addition, he saw nothing but good if

> a boy is induced by a girl's example to find a pleasure in other than merely muscular activity, to admit other kinds of interest, to talk French and to enjoy poetry, perhaps even not to be ashamed of making it.

The gains for each girl were, he maintained, just as real:

> a sense of greater freedom and an enlargement of her horizons such as otherwise she only gets if one of a large family of brothers and sisters. . . . The common life together provides the natural corrective for the pettiness and sentimentality rife amongst girls when always thrown upon themselves and their own interests alone.

He concluded:

> Each has something to give to the other that it needs, and cannot otherwise get. If the boy needs civilizing by the girl, so, no less, though in another way, is the girl's nature made fuller and more human by daily contact with the boy.[36]

Then too, and here Thring would applaud, there were the advantages to be gained by living in a boarding community that was led by adults of both sexes and surrounded by the family life of the spouses and children of members of staff.[37]

> Our aim . . . (is) to develope (sic) the habit of self-government, both in the individual and the community, and, in due course, the power of leadership; and to maintain the moral conditions of family life, by letting different ages and sexes mix freely together, and ourselves sharing all parts of their life.[38]

Other practice at Bedales saw a relaxation of Abbotsholme's example. Badley delegated responsibilities; teachers did not wear cap and gown; Latin was taught; school rules and conventions were reduced; the militaristic spirit was replaced by quiet pacifism; and the religious ethos, though the same as Abbotsholme's, was portrayed without the aid of chapel and chaplain or adherence to any particular Christian doctrine.[39] Badley's aim was religion through education:

> To many, no doubt, a school which does not teach the doctrines or enforce the forms of any Church may seem to have no religion. But if there is a

growing sense of something beyond self and its immediate desires, and of a purpose in life that is worthwhile, and if in the whole school life of the community there is a spirit of comradeship and joy and freedom, there is something of real religion in the school.[40]

This is the crowning aim of education . . . to help all, the stupid with the clever, to learn to live lives worth living, to use all their powers, great and small, to the service of God and man.[41]

Thus, the ingredients of Thring's ideal of manliness entered the twentieth century under the banner of The New School Movement. Though it is highly unlikely that Thring would ever have contemplated admitting girls to Uppingham, he would have been pleased that their education at Bedales matched that of the boys and that they too experienced an education of the whole man. What the old public schools no longer valued, the new progressive schools adopted wholeheartedly.

VII Howson: 'Fresh Air and Morality'

A second direct line from Thring's Uppingham can be traced to Gresham's School at Holt in Norfolk. G. W. S. Howson joined the Uppingham staff in 1886 specifically to be under Thring but he was granted just one year before the headmaster's death.[1] He stayed on under Selwyn, finding as time elapsed that his position became increasingly uncomfortable. He felt very much the odd man out: the only Oxonian in a common room dominated by Cambridge men; a scientist in a non-scientific atmosphere; and a poor games-player in a school where such prowess now meant so much. Life at Uppingham brought Howson no pleasure: science was given little scope in the curriculum, he disliked the sharp boundary that had developed between boys and masters, he feared the growth of athleticism, and he felt that boys were left far too much to their own devices in the boarding houses.[2] When the Gresham's headmastership became vacant in 1900, he left to make a fresh start in a school that had no adverse traditions to hamper him.

George Howson's move to Gresham's was a fortunate one. Like Uppingham, the school was an Elizabethan grammar school and on his arrival it still occupied the original buildings and had no more pupils than at its foundation in 1555. Three years later, after the trustees had negotiated vastly increased income from the renewal of farm leases, the school moved to purpose-built accommodation on the outskirts of Holt and pupil numbers began to rise. In 1900 there were forty-four boys and four staff; three years later the boys numbered 103; and by the time of Howson's death in 1919 the figure had reached 240.[3] Howson was also fortunate in the geographical location of the school: not only was there ample countryside and bracing air on the east coast of Norfolk but, more importantly, the school was remote from the influences of other public schools. In this setting Howson was able to start a school from scratch, just as Thring, Almond, Reddie and Badley had done in their turn.

Many of Thring's best principles and practices went with Howson to Gresham's. Both shared the belief that 'a school chapel is the heart of a school'; Gresham's got its heart when the newly-built chapel was consecrated in 1916.[4] Pupil numbers were kept low enough so that the headmaster would know every boy and, against the pattern of many schools, Howson made himself a housemaster so that School House would be the model for others to emulate.[5] Boys had individual studies as at Uppingham; the barriers that existed between the boys' side and the private side in the boarding houses were largely destroyed; the relationship between boys and masters became less formal and more friendly; Howson invited boys to join him on holiday fishing trips in Wharfedale; and facilities and expert teaching were available across a broad curriculum.[6] Intellectual training was important but Howson gave most attention to moral education; here his belief that 'in comparison with moral worth, intellectual excellence counted for little' coincides exactly with Thring's judgement.[7] Howson knew that his methods were a departure from the public-school norm and that their standards were not Gresham's standards, but he was careful not to align himself with the New School Movement. Gresham's aimed to be a public school and so had to avoid being labelled cranky or progressive. 'This is not the kind of school where, if a boy is not good at arithmetic, he is allowed to keep rabbits instead', Howson once told his biographer, J. H. Simpson.[8]

Howson set out at Gresham's to create the conditions necessary to foster the moral aims he sought; in this, as in all respects, the life of the school was centred on his own personality. 'Fresh Air and Morality' could well have been Gresham's motto.[9] The attractive site of the school gave easy access to the surrounding countryside and no locked doors, barred windows or unreasonable limits to the bounds curtailed the boys' liberty to roam. There were no printed school rules and the freedom of the Sunday afternoon was restored. Hobbies and the arts flourished, and each boy was encouraged to develop his own particular interests. Howson introduced outdoor performances of Shakespeare's plays.[10] All boys were expected to be hardy, active and free of minor ailments.[11] Howson was also a bitter foe of athleticism: games were regarded as healthy and agreeable exercise that promoted proper moral behaviour, and nothing more. Howson's biographer recalled a discussion:

> I remember being asked, with some of my colleagues, to meet at dinner a rather distinguished visitor to the School House. "Bad news from Australia, isn't it?" had begun the latter in a harmless attempt to make conversation, when he was brought up short by Howson's blank expression. It would be difficult to say which was the more surprised, the guest at finding a public schoolmaster who did not know that a Test Match was in progress, or his host at the idea of anyone of intelligence sparing a thought for so trivial a matter.[12]

Games at Gresham's were played keenly and well but with a non-devotional attitude. Any factors that smacked of professionalism were banned: there were no cups, no school matches, no scrum caps or starter's pistol and spectators could clap but not cheer at matches. The result was that athletic idolatry dropped, prowess as a games-player counted little in the appointment of prefects, and the less athletic boys and masters felt that they too could join in and enjoy games without receiving the impression that their efforts were absurd.[13] Howson's impact on these matters was so strong that even after his death these policies were maintained by his successors and it was not until the 1930s that Gresham's met another school at sport – a hockey match with Kurt Hahn's Schule Schloss Salem. The Germans came to play at Gresham's in 1930 and then the English school returned the visit in 1933.[14] In this same period a comprehensive programme of physical education – including timetabled lessons for all, remedial gymnastics and postural measures – had been introduced by Philip Smithells, who as a boy at Bedales had been strongly influenced by Reginald Roper.[15]

Howson's most original contribution to educational philosophy and practice rested on the 'Honour System', though there are similarities between the Gresham's and Loretto models. Howson believed that everything should be geared to the good of the community and, underpinning that aim, that this goodness could only be realised if every pupil attained self-respect and acquired a sense of responsibility. The system depended on a private compact between Howson and each boy. One advantage, as Howson saw it, was that prefects were now released from a policing role and could concentrate on leadership. Each new boy on arrival in the school was interviewed by Howson and asked not to indulge in 'smoking, swearing and indecency', and also positively to discourage his fellows from succumbing to such temptations. The boy was then to report this conversation to his housemaster who, in turn, would talk freely about morality, including sex. A boy was expected to own up if he lapsed in any way and, in general, the malefactors did. In the view of Howson's biographer, trust truly became the basis of school life.[16]

Many of Thring's ideals lived on at Howson's Gresham's but, by the very modest nature of this modest school, their successes were not broadcast to the public schools at large. Nonetheless, the life-line was there.

VIII Jacks and Coade: *'Total Education'*

The whole-man philosophy of education was brought to light once more in the late 1920s and early 1930s through the widely received views of L. P. Jacks, professor of philosophy and theology at Manchester College, Oxford.[1] In various journals and newspapers, at schoolmasters' conferences, and in two books – *The Education of the Whole Man* and *Education through Recreation* – Jacks expressed his plea for a new spirit in education.

> The training of the whole man in the skilful achievement of excellence within the bounds of a socially valuable vocation – such is the general

formula of education when viewed in the social perspective. . . . Much emphasis will be laid on the *whole man*. To achieve his education in the wholeness of his personality, the conception of man as a patchwork partnership of mind and body, in which the mind alone, as the celestial partner, falls within the province of education, while the body, as the terrestrial, is left to hygienists and medical practitioners – an evil inheritance from the past which still dominates our educational methods . . . – will have to be abandoned. In place of it our plans must be laid for a vigorous co-education of mind and body regarded as an inseparable unity in every stage of their development.[2]

Jacks mistrusted the fragmentary nature of a traditional public-school education in which the mind was 'educated' by teachers in the classroom and the body was 'trained' by instructors in the gymnasium. Jacks sought to combine the two extremes and then infuse them with a Christianity that was not restricted to the chapel but went with the boy to playgrounds, the classrooms and the workshops.[3] Jacks felt that the current imbalance of the whole-man ideal was primarily at the physical extreme of the spectrum; he thus devoted most attention to what he termed 'the wider possibilities of physical culture'. Here, using colourful phrases to illustrate his points, Jacks asserted that 'man is a skill hungry animal', yet a majority of the population were 'physical illiterates'.

I regard a trained body – trained to be master of its movements as a whole and not in fragments – as the necessary foundation for all kinds of creative activity, just as reading and writing are the necessary foundation for the acquisition of knowledge.[4]

Thus, in this most Thringian of concepts, Jacks asserted that physical education was the core of all creative activity. To realise his aim, physical education needed to be given due importance in schools and its teaching had to be by men and women who were as qualified as the other members of the teaching staff. He knew of such a school and was able to report that with good modern physical education the composition of Latin prose had improved – a sentiment close to Thring's heart.[5] The school was Mill Hill, and its young headmaster was his son, M. L. Jacks.

Not only was M. L. Jacks the active propagator of his father's theories but he was also a keen disciple of Thring. One of his staff, Gerald Murray, related to me how frequently Jacks mentioned Thring's pioneering work and his books contain many Thring quotations.[6] Jacks referred to the whole-man ideal of education as *Total Education*, the title of the book that expounded his views in detail, seeing it as the synthesis of all aspects of schooling.[7] On his appointment as headmaster in 1922 at the age of twenty-eight, Jacks was encouraged by the governors to reform and develop the school. Jacks sought to build a Christian-Platonic community in which service to one's fellows was implicit in every aspect of its life. Education was no more than an apprenticeship for citizenship;

this would later be seen in active involvement by Old Boys in local politics, charities, youth organisations and the like.[8] Following his Ruskinian beliefs, Jacks gave much time in the curriculum to leisure activities and he put his father's ideals for physical education into practice. Health was seen as being a positive sense of well-being and not merely the absence of disease. Jacks believed that the athletic balance and outlook were all wrong at the traditional public schools, with too much emphasis placed on team games and on the talented players.[9] To remedy this situation, Jacks appointed Gerald Hedley to his staff as 'director of physical education' with the brief 'to cover promotion of the physical development of every boy in the school, especially the less skilful, the weak and the unstable, and liaison with the school doctor, the formmasters and the house masters'.[10] Both Hedley and his successor, Gerald Murray, were ardent disciples of Reginald Roper. Hedley and Murray, together with Philip Smithells of Gresham's, were instrumental in the development of the Secondary Schoolmasters' Physical Education Association which, through its conferences at Mill Hill and by means of various publications, disseminated these modern ideas on physical education to all who would listen.[11] In 1937 Jacks left Mill Hill to become director of the Department of Education at Oxford University; there he argued the case for every school to have a physical education department whose status, and that of its director, should be on par with every other subject area.[12]

One of the outlets of L. P. Jacks's philosophy of education was the Harrow Conferences for Young Schoolmasters, and these same gatherings heard papers on physical education delivered by Smithells and Murray.[13] These conferences were founded in 1931 by a Harrow schoolmaster, Thorold Coade, and after the Second World War were reconstituted by him as the Oxford Conference for Schoolmasters. When, in 1932, the headmastership of Bryanston, the new Dorset public school, surprisingly became vacant only four years after its foundation, Coade was appointed its headmaster and remained in that office until his retirement in 1959. Bryanston's first headmaster was an Australian graduate of Melbourne and Oxford, J. G. Jeffreys, who set out to create a school where boys would 'become honest, manly, and Christian citizens of the British Empire'.[14] The venture was a success: the twenty-three boys at the opening of the school in January 1928 quickly rose to 250 by 1932. Jeffreys developed Bryanston on two principles that were departures from general public-school practice. First, he brought with him the Dalton Plan of learning in which the boys worked on an organised system of personal study guided by one or more tutors and, secondly, he advocated an Almond-like code of health. Life at Bryanston was to be simple: no servants would wait on the boys, the school uniform was to be of the shorts and open-necked shirts variety, and all corporal punishment was banned.[15] When Coade arrived, he thus found a new, lively and receptive school, one in which he could put into operation his own germinating educational plans.

Thorold Coade was born in 1896, the son of a clergyman. Much of his early life was spent in the Lincolnshire countryside where, as he later saw it, he imbibed a belief in Nature as an educator. At preparatory school in Norfolk, where he was shocked by the innate cruelty of under-supervised small boys, and at Harrow, where he experienced all the limitations of such a school at the turn of the century, his simple faith received a bruising. His disillusionment with the public-school system was reinforced by what he saw when he went to Sandhurst in 1915. Here the cream of public-school youth appeared smart and orderly on the parade ground but off-duty all was chaos and licence – and no-one in authority seemed to mind. Coade was horrified at the naked barbarism and the stark philistinism of the behaviour of his fellow cadets. Even when allowance had been made for the war-time environment, and the fact that many of them were soon to die, the impression was scarcely softened. The war was an accident, and their schools had prepared them for a glorious life, yet the public-school Old Boys were a disgrace.[16] He vowed that, if he survived the war, he would endeavour to remedy that situation – and it is here with Coade at Bryanston that Thring's ideal of manliness found its most enthusiastic advocate.

After his wartime service and four years at Christ Church, Oxford, Coade went back to Harrow as an assistant master. He found that little had changed since his own pre-war schooldays.[17] Not until Cyril Norwood's appointment as headmaster in 1926 did things begin to move forward again. Coade was part of an able group of young men who brought liberal ideas to the school. With Norwood's encouragement, these survivors of the Great War created a Young Masters Club to discuss educational and political issues, occasionally led by visiting speakers, which in 1931 became the Harrow Conferences.[18] Coade had a fundamental belief in the public-school system of education but he felt that it was now anachronistic in terms of its curriculum, its attitude and its product. He set out to build a school that was a balance between the old-fashioned Victorian autocracy and the ultra-modern free school – a school at the progressive end of the public-school spectrum. Bryanston was to be 'the place of the Individual in the Community'.[19] Coade aimed at strong teacher-parent liaison and he sought to develop a relationship between master and boy built on mutual education and mutual respect, and to do this through common interests. He had a Thringian mistrust of examinations and prizes; he regarded M. L. Jacks's *Total Education* as a teaching philosophy of great significance; and he became a close friend of the German educationalist, Kurt Hahn.[20] Their friendship began in 1929: some boys from Bryanston exchanged with boys from the Schule Schloss Salem for some weeks in 1932; and when Hahn was exiled to Britain in 1933, Bryanston was his first resting-place.[21] Coade greatly appreciated Hahn's notion of the *grande passion* – every boy must do something well was Thring's equivalent – and his stress on physical achievement other than through team games.[22]

Coade placed great emphasis on what other schools labelled 'extra-curricular activities', providing more than fifty clubs and societies for the boys to choose from.[23] He felt that too many schools were satisfied with just the occupation of the boys' leisure-time and accepted low involvement provided the boys were amused and kept out of mischief. To Coade these activities were 'when most of our significant and creative thinking takes place', thus they should be of vital importance to educators and should be brought into the mainstream of the curriculum. He did not believe that this would reduce the level of academic or sporting success for, if the proportions were right, the general enrichment of life would be reflected in higher standards at everything. Arts, crafts and, most notably, drama were brought into the curriculum for all; skilled instruction was provided; ample facilities and materials were made available; and due recognition was given to the boys' achievements.[24] Such creative work was an article of faith to Coade:

> The effect of introducing creative and corporate activity into the curriculum is to break up and fertilize the ground, to prepare the way, by awakening in the young an alert sensitiveness, awareness, responsiveness to beauty, to truth and to the needs of others. Into a life so lived in childhood and adolescence, the Christian religion comes sooner or later as a comprehensive, illuminating and energizing revelation of the meaning of life; and it will carry us on with a greater confidence and a surer faith than we have now into the unpredictable future that lies ahead.[25]

The corporate activity came through various forms of community service; these also formed a significant part of Coade's conception of a school. The Pioneers were instituted in 1933 as a liberal alternative to the cadet corps; here Bryanston blazed the trail of community action that many schools were to adopt in the 1960s and which led indirectly to the founding of Community Service Volunteers (CSV) and Voluntary Service Overseas (VSO). Group projects could be hut building, outdoor manual work and the building of an open-air theatre, whilst pioneer holidays included exploration expeditions and visits to Outward Bound Schools.[26] As Coade told the 1939 Harrow Conference for Young Schoolmasters shortly before the Second World War, the importance of the individual's service to the community was paramount:

> What we need in this country is to awaken in youth the same enthusiasm and readiness for service as we find in totalitarian states, but enable them to relate it to the Christian ideal and the Christian way of life. That we cannot do until we have begun to find that way and live that life ourselves.[27]

All aspects of physical education fitted into the framework of creative and corporate activity. Games were encouraged, and there was a broad spectrum of choice, but compulsion was limited to a boy's first three years. Individual sports such as canoeing and climbing were keenly followed.[28] As W. David Smith remarked, 'in its breadth of approach and variety of activities Bryanston anticipated by many years what has since become standard physical education practice'.[29]

The philosophy and practice of the ideal of manliness stood out from every aspect of the curriculum at Bryanston. 'Religion is Education and Education is Religion' was Coade's guideline. By religion he meant a relationship with God, and education was the process by which each individual became aware of it. Education was not just moral, intellectual and physical – but also spiritual; and spiritual education could only be realised in the Platonic manner through music, arts, crafts and literature. The object was the awakening of the whole personality and harnessing that energy to the purposes of God; the method was through the 'sense of purposeful creative joy in all that (a boy) does, in his games, in his physical training, in all his leisure activities and in his work'; the aim was the 'wholeness of man' or, its Coade equivalent, 'the holiness of spirit'.[30] Here indeed is Thring's ideal of manliness.

IX Hahn: 'A moral equivalent of war'

Coade put his ideals into practice at Bryanston quietly and with very little publicity. His friend Kurt Hahn ran his school at Gordonstoun in Morayshire on many of the same principles, including the Dalton Plan, but here Hahn's undoubted gifts as a publicist brought the work to world-wide attention and his efforts were to contribute much to developments in various sectors of British education.[1] Hahn was born in Germany in 1886 of Jewish parents. He was educated first in Berlin and then from 1904 at Christ Church, Oxford. By this time he was an avid Platonist; his years at Oxford made him an admirer of Thomas Arnold and brought about an abiding affection for Britain.[2] He was introduced to Reddie's ideas and methods when he met a party of Abbotsholme boys on an expedition in the Alps.[3]

In the years immediately after the Great War Hahn served as private secretary to Prince Maximilian of Baden, the last Imperial Chancellor of Germany, and he was closely involved with the measures thought necessary to restore a defeated nation's confidence. Prince Max settled on education as the most likely means of bringing this about and, in 1920, he founded Schule Schloss Salem in Bavaria, a boarding school for boys and girls aged ten to eighteen. Hahn was appointed headmaster. At Salem Hahn was particularly concerned with physical fitness and moral independence, and powerful emphasis was placed on the character-training qualities that appropriately chosen physical activities could inculcate. As Hahn admitted, nothing at Salem was original: ideas were borrowed from Plato, Arnold's Rugby, Eton, Abbotsholme and a host more schools and educationalists; and other features were rejected, including the public-school shortcomings of arrogance, privilege, entitlement and games-worship.[4] It was the mixture that was unique. The school was already internationally famous – with the future Duke of Edinburgh as one of his pupils – when in 1932 Hahn's denunciation of the Nazis led to his imprisonment and then, in July 1933, his exile to Britain.[5] Encouraged by Geoffrey Winthrop-Young and William Arnold-Forster and with the help of influential friends – including Archbishop William Temple, the historian Sir George Trevelyan and John Buchan, now Lord Tweedsmuir – Hahn secured Gordonstoun as the setting for his British continuation of the Salem scheme.[6] The first boys arrived in 1934, mainly the sons of German refugees known to Hahn and attracted by his philosophies; others were the misfits and failures from British public schools.[7] Numbers climbed to 135 by 1939, but Salem's practice of admitting girls had to wait until 1972.[8]

To Hahn there were three types of education: the Ionian was individualistic, free and totally disregarded the community; the Spartan devoted everything to the community, while the individual counted for nothing; and the Platonic, in which 'the individual becomes a cripple . . . if he is not qualified by education to serve the community'.[9] There were many Platonic parallels at Gordonstoun: the terms 'Guardian' and 'Helper' were adopted for school officers; *paideia*, defined by Hahn as the development of energetic participation, became the central ideal; and the morally responsible person, and not the scholar, artist or games-player, became the educational exemplar of the school.[10] To cut down on nationalism and to harness all energies in the cause of peace, Hahn sought for 'a moral equivalent of war'; here community service, sports and arduous training activities were to play their part.[11] The aim was to inculcate in the individual the ability to recognise right – despite hardships, despite dangers, despite inner scepticism, despite boredom, despite mockery from the world, despite emotion of the moment – and its test became the risking of all in the service of one's fellow men.[12]

The plan at Gordonstoun was precise. Each boy was responsible for his own physical fitness and had to tick off his daily routine on a chart: this was the basis of the school's 'Trust System'. School uniform included shorts and sweater; the day started with a run and a cold bath; a mid-morning athletic break was designed to sharpen the senses; and no tuck was allowed.[13] The physical education programme was based on individual skills – running, jumping, throwing and the like. Team games were played, and were both keenly contested and successfully performed, but they were not allowed to dominate the programme. A broad spectrum of art and craft activities was introduced and compulsorily followed by all boys: here the aim was to find one activity for each boy that would be his *grande passion*.[14] Hahn insisted, like Thring, that

> Every boy could do something well and that it was the task of the schoolmaster to find out what that was.[15]

Vigorous and arduous outdoor activities, such as sailing, climbing and canoeing were included for the hazards they presented to boys in order that they would learn to triumph over defeat. Service to the community was encouraged through activities including life-saving, manning a coastguard station, running the local fire-service, practical estate work and mountain rescue patrols: here a reality of useful service was the keynote.[16] In order to give the boys time for contemplation – the need for 'aloneness' – Hahn insisted that they walked unaccompanied and in silence on their daily progress to chapel.[17]

Encouraged by his undeniable success at Gordonstoun, Hahn set out to extend his influence. He hoped to open more schools for boys from poor homes but he was hampered by a lack of funds; instead he inaugurated the Gordonstoun Badge in 1936 so that boys in the surrounding area could benefit from some of Gordonstoun's principles.[18] The badge was earned through fitness tests, life-saving drills and cross-country expeditions. During Gordonstoun's wartime evacuation to North Wales, Hahn in 1940 set up a summer school to demonstrate his methods and the following year the Outward Bound Sea School was founded at Aberdovey. Here was Hahn's 'war equivalent' in action. In his address at the launching ceremony for the school's schooner *Garibaldi*, Sir George Trevelyan voiced the Hahn creed: 'If ever youth loses the thirst for adventure, any civilisation, however enlightened, and any state, however well ordered, must wither and dry up.'[19]

Within a decade this first Outward Bound School was followed by five more in Britain, and a score were established world-wide. It is through Hahn's work that outdoor activities soon formed an integral part of the physical education programmes at public and state schools, and his Outward Bound Schools spawned countless outdoor activity centres where, if only for a limited period, the benefits of a boarding-school life, together with those of an arduous training programme of activities, were experienced by the nation's youth. In 1956 the Duke of Edinburgh Award Scheme was launched as a nationwide successor to the Gordonstoun Badge: at first it was for boys only but soon the scheme was widened to include girls. Under the vigorous sponsorship of the Duke of Edinburgh, who had been a boy under Hahn at both Salem and Gordonstoun, thousands of youngsters were attracted to a scheme built on physical fitness, community service, outdoor pursuits and expedition training. The declared aim to promote useful citizenship ensured that the scheme was widely adopted by schools and youth organisations and in industry. Each participant received this challenge:

> Face the days that lie ahead with a spirit of adventure, compassion, honesty and confidence. Brave the stormy seas that are bound to confront you, determined to sail your ship on to the quiet waters that lie ahead. Help those whom you may find in trouble and steer clear of the whirlpools of destruction which you will meet on your voyage through life. Be not afraid of who you are, what you are or where you are, but cling implicitly to the Truth as taught in the religion of your following. If you do all these things, you will be "of service". If you are "of service" you will make others happy, and you will be happy too.[20]

Hahn's main contribution to the survival of the ideal of manliness was as the publicist *par excellence*. Coade may have been truer to Thring's original concept – for surely Gordonstoun is just a shade too hardy – but Hahn drew the nation's attention to its benefits. Since his early days as Prince Max's private secretary, Hahn had the knack of getting influential people on his side. These men all saw the value of Hahn's passion and inspiration, and they were able to temper his innovations to meet British needs. The result was the widest possible audience for the ideal of manliness. By the 1950s and 1960s, most public schools had assimilated many of Hahn's ideas, even if they took only those that they regarded as acceptable or those that could be fashioned into their own traditional mould.

X Turning points: 'The age of assumed and assured privilege is over'

Cyril Norwood, headmaster at Harrow, boasted in 1929 that the public schools were enjoying a period of great prosperity:

> Applicants crowd to their doors, and parents sue humbly for the admission of their sons. They house themselves in buildings of increasing convenience and splendour, and lay out playing-fields with an elaboration which would astonish our immediate forerunners.[1]

It did not last long. The world economies plunged into the Great Depression as Norwood wrote these words and its effects were to last a decade. Unemployment in Britain soared to 20% of the workforce; heavy manufacturing industry collapsed; the value of exports halved; and the country was hit by a series of hunger marches. The incomes of the rich plummeted and school fees were out of reach for many. Pupil rolls for some schools in the north of England fell to 40% of capacity. Repton, in the Midlands, closed a boarding house, made several masters redundant, and reduced the salaries of the remainder. Even Harrow, in wealthy London, closed a house.[2]

The economic worries coincided with a questioning of the purpose of the public-school system. The belief in Empire was wavering and the schools realised that soon there would be little left to send out boys to. A growth of liberalism in political conscience, but not of the Liberal Party, meant that increased emphasis was placed on moral responsibility both at home and abroad. It was no longer acceptable that public-school service should be restricted to supporting a ruling class when the nation needed a greater sense of compassion as well as sensitivity to the plight of the poor. The heroic image of the Great War subaltern had faded; the ostentatious flaunting of privilege was unacceptable; and the schools' very existence became a matter of controversy.[3] Graham Greene, the editor of a collection of essays by liberal-minded public-school Old Boys, forecast that the schools were doomed.[4] The pacifist movement, including the League of Nations Union and Pledge for Peace group, made the regimented character of the public schools and the militaristic ethos of their cadet corps out of keeping with the times. These three factors, the decline in Empire, liberalism in political conscience and the rejection of militarism gradually undermined public-school confidence.

There were hard facts to be faced. As the century had progressed so the state provision of secondary education had improved. Through the innovation of the School Certificate examinations in 1917 and the introduction of State Scholarships to universities in 1920, a steadily increasing stream of grammar-school boys and girls was gaining graduate status for entry to the professions. These grammar schools were closely modelled on public-school practice, though usually they were a shade more progressive, and now they were seen to produce a rival product at no or little cost. The effects were two-fold: the public schools had to work harder on academic attainment – and harder work meant less time for games; and the public-school market became competitive – thus the schools had to fight for custom, and at a time when the boys of the birth-rate bulge after the Great War were already in the system and lower entries were forecast for the 1940s.[5] It was against this background that reform came and, as so often in the past and in the future, it was the reaction of the public schools to the accumulation of pressure that brought it about.

That change had to come was obvious to all public-school headmasters but the process of bringing it about was sporadic, seemingly radiating out from London and the Home Counties at so many miles a year. But for the intervention of the Second World War, it is probable that reform would have reached all schools by the 1940s. A change in the attitude to games also cast doubt on the value of 'team spirit' and the role games played in its inculcation.[6] Calls were made for the inclusion of individual sports such as golf and tennis to supplement the traditional diet.[7] In addition, games alone were seen as insufficient for the whole physical well-being of a boy and – through the efforts of Smithells, Hedley and Murray – the Roperian view of physical education gained wider acceptance. The desire for better practice, however, was limited by the shortage of qualified male physical education teachers. Relief eventually came with the founding of physical training colleges for men at Leeds Carnegie in 1933 and Loughborough in 1937 but the reforms that many headmasters wanted could not be achieved until these teachers were available.[8] Nonetheless, the intention that schools should adopt a broad approach to physical education had been signalled and, in 1942, the Headmasters' Conference recommended that all public schools should appoint a qualified director of physical education.[9] The weakening of the over-riding belief in the values of athleticism and team spirit had begun. The movement was not consistent, with some schools attaining in the 1970s what others had accepted in the 1930s, but the momentum had been generated; it could be resisted but not checked.

Owen retired from Uppingham at Easter 1934 and, in time, was appointed Archbishop of New Zealand. He was succeeded by the twenty-seven-year-old John Wolfenden; he would also find fame in later life as vice-chancellor of Reading University and chairman of two influential government reports.[10]

The Uppingham trustees had made a brave appointment, and not just because of the headmaster's youth. The first day of the summer term was a multiple first for Wolfenden – at a public school, at a boarding school, as a housemaster and as a schoolmaster. He had proceeded as a scholar from Queen Elizabeth Grammar School in Wakefield to Queen's College, Oxford; there his lack of pedigree was outshone by his achievements – a first in *Literae Humaniores*, election as fellow and tutor in philosophy to Magdalen College, and hockey goal-keeper for both Oxford and England. He had married a year earlier; soon School House echoed to the voices of four young children, one fewer than in Thring's time.[11]

Wolfenden had only five years to implement changes at Uppingham before the declaration of the Second World War checked his efforts but they were five years of reform. He started gently, abolishing the custom of giving boys with the same surname the distinguishing suffix of *ma, mi* or *min*, instead permitting the use of initials – thus ending forever the Woosterish progression of Smith *octavius* to Smith *major* over a five-year school career.[12] Life in School House became homely – the Owens had no children – and Wolfenden relaxed much of Owen's regimentation to allow the boys some say in what they might or might not do. And he questioned the amount of time and energy that were devoted to games in a memorandum to housemasters:

> In comparison with other schools in our class we are, on the whole, better at games than they are; but are we as much better than they are at games as they are better than we are at other things? What are we sacrificing for our athletic success? Do we encourage our boys to think too highly of athletic success to the exclusion of some other things? Is it not our job as Housemasters to correct anything that is wrong in our values?[13]

Wolfenden set out to raise academic attainment by abolishing the system by which stupid or lazy boys never climbed up the forms and in its stead he instituted annual progression and streamed sets. Jones's Army Class was replaced with the Commercial Sixth, with teaching better suited to the majority of older boys who would enter business, industry and non-graduate professions. The cleverest were encouraged to work hard for the School Certificate, Wolfenden telling them that is was 'a necessary qualification without which you have little chance of entering a university'.[14]

William Temple, the former headmaster of Repton and now Archbishop of York, illustrated the changes that Wolfenden had wrought when he spoke at Uppingham's 1938 Speech Day. He still preached the ideal that games were the school manifestation of service to the community, but now new means had been found. With the encouragement of an Old Boy who was a director of the steelmakers Stewarts & Lloyds, Wolfenden set up the Uppingham-Corby Boys Club in 1939 to bring together young workers from the nearby steel town and his own pupils. Each evening twelve Uppinghamians and a master would go over to the club-room in Corby and join in the various activities under the leadership of Cecil and Ruth Colyer; more would spend most of the weekend there.[15] Expeditions, outings and visits to Uppingham were all part of this twentieth-century equivalent of Thring's mission at North Woolwich.[16]

But reforms came to an early halt on 3 September 1939 with the declaration of the Second World War. First Wolfenden had to prepare the school for the rigours of life in war-time. In addition, 270 boys evacuated from Kingswood School in Bath were due to arrive for the start of the autumn term and had to be accommodated in the town for the war's duration.[17] Then in December 1940 Wolfenden was summoned to the Air Ministry in London and offered the post of Director of Pre-Entry Air Training for the RAF. He accepted and was absent from school for the whole of 1941. Finally, Wolfenden had stated in 1934 that he would stay at Uppingham for just ten years. That decision, and the difficulties associated with running a school in wartime, saw his energies in the remaining two years devoted to the school's survival rather than to its development.[18] An indication that Wolfenden had hoped to give Uppingham a broader cultural outlook, a balanced curriculum, a stronger sense of community and a commitment to holistic ideals can be found in the address that he delivered on his return to the school in 1953 at the time of the Thring centenary celebrations. In this most succinct summary of his predecessor's theory and practice, Wolfenden drew out the three strands that made Thring a revolutionary. Two were principles, the third was a method, and all three had relevance for the modern public school. They were that individual attention should be given to every pupil; that teaching should be directed to the education of the whole man; and that every school should create a system to ensure that the two principles were realised.[19] The accident of war had denied Wolfenden the realisation of his ambitions.

Reforms at Uppingham and in other schools may have stalled in 1939 but the pressure for change was now even greater. Pupil numbers were in free-fall; in part, and contrary to experience in the Great War, because boys were leaving school early in order to serve in the armed forces.[20] There had been 510 boys in the school when Wolfenden arrived in 1934; now in 1942 the total had dropped sharply to 406. One boarding house, Redgate, was closed – the first reduction in Thring's 'Almighty Wall'.[21] It was a similar story across the public-school system. The governors at both Mill Hill and Liverpool College debated the chances of survival after the war; numbers at Repton fell from 393 in 1937 to 276 five years later, necessitating the shutting of a second house; and Harrow came close to financial ruin.[22] Between 1938 and 1942 the Harrow governors shut several houses, warned masters of likely redundancies, and in 1940 made a two-year internal appointment as headmaster in case the school collapsed completely.[23] One effect of the war in all schools was that clothes rationing necessitated a reduction in athletic decoration and exotic varieties of school uniform. Tailcoats and the speckled straw hat became voluntary at Uppingham and striped trousers were replaced by grey flannels, except on Sundays.[24]

With the looming danger of the collapse of the public-school system, headmasters revisited a scheme that had been proposed by Frank Fletcher, the headmaster of Charterhouse, in the early 1920s. The financial threat at that time was caused by the implementation of the School Teachers Superannuation Act and the recommendations of the Burnham Committee's Report on teachers' pay; both improved conditions for teachers in state schools and the public schools were forced to respond. This was costly. Fletcher and headmasters of other leading schools proposed to the Board of Education that their schools should give free places to boys from elementary schools in exchange for state funding of pensions. The board rejected the offer on the grounds that, as Fletcher recalled, 'there was no demand for places in our schools for ex-elementary schoolboys'.[25]

Cyril Norwood, now President of St John's College at Oxford, told the Board of Education in 1938 of the public schools' difficulties and that in exchange for training the nation's leaders they should receive some government funding. His proposal that 10% of places at public schools should go to pupils from elementary schools, with the government paying the fees but not interfering with the schools' independence, was incorporated in the *Norwood Report on Secondary School Education* in 1943 and again a year later in the *Fleming Report on The Public Schools and the General Educational System*.[26] The recommendations of the latter included that places at public schools should be made available to 'boys and girls capable of profiting thereby, irrespective of the income of their parents'; that they would be paid for by the state; and that boarding education should be more widely available.[27] The public schools had embraced the principle of equality of opportunity – if only to survive.

But the war-time desire for social equity and national unity did not persist. By the time of the report's publication, and to the amazement of public-school headmasters, the demand for fee-paying places had risen sharply and the schools were now financially secure. There was no need to trade independence for cash. In addition, the election of the Labour Party to government in 1945 ensured that Norwood's other proposal that state secondary schools should adopt the ethos of public schools had become unattractive, if not incendiary, and that Fleming's recommendations were never revived.[28] One element of equality of opportunity did survive however, when the Butler Education Act of 1944 granted 179 grammar schools a degree of state funding in exchange for accepting a quarter of their pupils from state primary schools; these were soon known as direct grant schools.

The public-school reforms set for adoption in 1939 had hardly made inroads before war was declared and the six-year wait saw much of the enthusiasm for the cause evaporate, especially when many of the men who would have implemented the changes did not return to schoolmastering. The pressures, however, were still there. The academic demands were greater than ever for, as Ralph Moore, the new headmaster of Harrow complained, 'the age of assumed and assured privilege is over' now that the 'subsidised and specialised second rate' from the grammar schools was squeezing out the more versatile public-school boy in the chase for places at Oxford and Cambridge.[29] The number of competitors attending state secondary schools had doubled between 1944 and 1955, and throughout the 1960s examination results of public-school leavers were below the national average.[30] Team games thus began to lose some of their strangle-hold on a boy's time, energy and interest as the new physical education departments at Marlborough in 1938, at Worksop from 1947, and elsewhere thereafter introduced more individual sports. The liberal revolution did not always move purposefully but rather leapt randomly when new headmaster succeeded old headmaster. As Tony Mangan discovered, Harrovians only began to challenge compulsory team games in the 1970s when Marlburians had won that battle before the war.[31] As late as 1966, Eton had just one physical education teacher for the thousand or so boys in the school, compared to the thirty-two masters needed to teach classics.[32]

John Wolfenden left Uppingham in 1944 to become headmaster of Shrewsbury and was succeeded by Martin Lloyd – aged thirty-five, married and soon to raise a young family. Educated at Marlborough and with a first in modern languages from Gonville and Caius College, Cambridge, Lloyd had taught at Rugby before the war. On arrival at Uppingham he instituted the practice, already common at many schools, of limiting an incoming housemaster's tenure to fifteen years. This opened promotion prospects for young men and curtailed the athletic influence of housemasters who had presided for thirty years or more. Nonetheless, team games continued to 'occupy' a boy's time five afternoons a week, even though the new General Certificate of Education (GCE) examinations at Ordinary and Advanced levels had raised the importance of academic attainment.[33] Some of the two-day cricket matches had been abandoned in 1945 but boys still might be let out of lessons early to attend batting practice in the nets.[34]

In 1948 there was a call from some boys for more individual sports such as tennis, athletics and swimming but an apologia on the virtues of *esprit de corps* by the captain of games signalled that the time was not yet ripe.[35] A team from His Majesty's Inspectorate visited the school for five days in 1949: the inspectors were impressed by the pleasant buildings and the life in the boarding houses but not by what they found in the classrooms – academic standards were 'not as high as the reputation of the School would lead one to expect'.[36] All might have been well with parents and Old Boys if the school's traditional prowess at Rugby football and cricket had remained high but standards there were falling. In the five-year period from 1955, just two-fifths of matches for the XV and one-fifth for the XI resulted in Uppingham victories.[37] The XI won just six inter-school matches in the period 1950 to 1962, and lost twenty-one.[38] Old Boys were dismayed, the school's trustees were concerned, and Lloyd was ordered to prepare a report on the lack of success and to propose remedies. He concluded that talented boys were going to rival schools, few masters were expert coaches, and not enough attention was given to boys in the lower teams and to younger boys. Changes were needed.[39]

Some were already underway. The PTI appointed by Owen in 1919 retired in 1952 and his successor, John Hall, had gained PT periods with the younger boys. With his encouragement the athletic sports were enlarged to include throwing events, clubs for fencing and badminton were added in 1958, and inter-school matches in athletics and tennis were introduced in 1960 and 1961 respectively.[40] 1959 witnessed a turning point when an editorial in the school magazine was permitted to voice objection to the dominance of school life by compulsory games and the authority of the committee of games to enforce attendance, with a beating if necessary. The editor noted that to be in the XV meant instant popularity and that few praepostors were other than games-players. Clever boys were dismissed as 'weeds' and 'the swots' whilst 'rugger chaps' and 'hockey types' were the real heroes. The appeal for a broader sporting programme and more recreational activities was objectively stated.[41] Compulsory team games lasted a few more years but 'breathers', drill competitions and boxing soon went, and basketball and soccer came in as optional activities.[42]

The music tradition in the school was as strong as ever, now under the direction of Douglas Guest, and concerts no longer had to include the hearty singing of a Newbolt song.[43] Much good drama, a little poetry, woodwork and art became increasingly popular. Academic standards had risen too, as the return visit of Her Majesty's Inspectorate in 1960 acknowledged, and there was a record haul of university awards in both 1962 and 1964.[44] When Lloyd retired in March 1965, his *vale* recalled the liberal innovations he had made – an increased freedom on Sundays, a reduction in personal fagging, and the broadening of the games programme were the three examples cited. But that was not enough and pupil numbers had begun to slide: 591 boys in 1962 but only 550 were promised for 1965.[45]

All public schools were now faced with the problem of restless teenagers wanting greater say in their appearance and dress, in the music they listened to and the films and television programmes they watched, in how they spent their leisure time, and how they could secure a reduction in the number of activities they were compelled to attend. In 1963 Lloyd reported to the trustees that Uppinghamians were content with their lot; a year later he admitted that hair-styles and clothing rules were areas of conflict, that the value of compulsory team games and compulsory chapel services was being questioned, and that praepostors had decided unilaterally that they would no longer beat miscreants.[46] There had also been an example of collective indiscipline in chapel, the first since Owen's stare had quelled disruption at a concert thirty-three years earlier.[47]

It was time for another turning point.

XI Full circle: 'True Life is to be found in true worth'

The post-war public schools had enjoyed fifteen years of prosperity and complacency, and suffered five years of discomfort; now they were to be threatened from without and challenged from within. Public schools were subject to compulsory inspections from 1957 and in 1965 the Labour government signalled its intent to integrate them within the state system by appointing a Public Schools Commission chaired by Sir John Newsom; its main recommendations, however, were never implemented. Five years later a second commission, headed by Professor David Donnison, led to the demise of the direct grant schools. To the government's surprise, 118 of the 179 schools opted for complete independence from the state and, as a consequence, forced the public schools to respond to the new competition. Parents and pupils demanded better teaching to fend off the newcomers in the race for higher education places and the spotlight moved from the most able trying for Oxford and Cambridge to the average seeking admission to civic redbrick and new plate-glass universities. Boys and girls now needed to work harder and so they rebelled against compulsion and conformity, restrictions and rules, conventions and corporal punishment.[1]

With the Empire gone and the state-school competition getting stronger, the public schools needed new objectives: training in leadership gave way to social responsibility; academic standards had to rise; a well-rounded education guaranteed secure employment; parents demanded greater accountability; and there was the need to see off the fast-improving state schools. A different and better product was required; modernisation was signalled with the sector's rebranding as 'independent schools'.[2]

John Dancy, Master of Marlborough, was quickest off the mark:

> The public schools of Great Britain will only survive if they cater for the whole man: his intellectual, cultural, technological, physical, emotional, and spiritual growth and understanding.[3]

Girls' schools were less alert, with many still devoting more time to social accomplishments than to academic attainment, and several boys' schools tempted their brightest and best to join their sixth forms. Marlborough led the way in 1968, quickly followed by Wellington and Charterhouse, and then a rush of many more in the 1970s. The presence of the girls boosted A-level results, raised the importance of the arts, made the communities more caring, improved living conditions in boarding houses, softened much of the athletic heartiness and discouraged homoeroticism. The girls mocked silly rules and privileges, hated the fagging system, ridiculed prefectorial beatings and tolerated no slipping back. The all-pervading masculinity of the boys' schools was further diluted with more women on the staff and married couples with young children running boarding houses. Co-education brought the ideal of the family into the classroom and domestic ties were strengthened with the introduction of weekend exeats and half-term breaks, and through the encouragement of regular visits by parents for concerts, plays, matches and the innovation of parent-teacher meetings.[4]

It fell to John Royds to bring about change at Uppingham, not least because Oakham School, just six miles to the north, was shedding its direct-grant status and beginning its evolution as Britain's largest independent co-educational day and boarding school.[5] If a school praepostor of 1898 or 1925 – the middle years of the headmasterships of Selwyn and Owen – had walked along Uppingham's High Street in 1966, he would have caused hardly a ripple of surprise. But for the puzzled expression on his face as he met the fashions associated with the Beatles and the Rolling Stones, his appearance was identical to that of his successor of Royds's first year: white straw hat, black tailcoat, black waistcoat, white shirt with detachable starched collar, black tie, striped trousers, dark socks and black shoes, and a rolled umbrella. He illustrated how little the school had altered in seventy years.[6]

Royds's life before Uppingham had been rich and varied; he was not afraid of change and innovation. Born on 23 September 1920, he was the third son of the headmaster of Milton Abbey School in Dorset. He attended Monkton Combe School in Bath, where he was head prefect and captain of cricket, before going up to Queens' College, Cambridge in 1939 to read history. When war intervened he enlisted in the ranks of the Royal Artillery before transferring to the Indian Army, serving in the Far East and attaining the rank of major. He was captured by the Japanese and incarcerated as a prisoner-of-war. On repatriation he resumed his studies, graduated with an upper-second in 1947, and joined the teaching staff at Bryanston. There he served as head of history, master-in-charge of cricket and housemaster. A keen actor, his roles spanned King Lear, Sherlock Holmes and a Babe in the Wood, and as housemaster he was remembered for 'his insight into the character and needs of boys, his sympathetic approach to their problems and his powerful natural discipline not requiring any external props'. In 1961 Royds was appointed headmaster of the General Wingate School in Ethiopia. His ability to raise funds to enable talented boys from poor homes to receive the same education as sons of the country's elite brought him both gratitude and renown. Among the gifts Royds received when he returned to England in 1965 were a spear, a shield and a lion's mane, items traditionally presented to Ethiopian heroes.[7]

The Uppingham trustees recognised that Royds was a visionary. His unconventional career brought unconventional ideas and methods to Uppingham; or, rather, brought them back to Uppingham. Twelve years as a master under Coade at Bryanston had given Royds an apprenticeship at the school where the theory and practice in every aspect of the curriculum most closely represented the legacy of Thring's ideal of manliness. The wheel had turned full circle. That everything Royds initiated in his ten-year headmastership quickly became commonplace in all schools bears testament to the clarity of his vision and his determination to bring it to reality.

Change began at the end of Royds's first year with the appointment of fifteen new members of staff, nearly a third of the common room. Seven of the fifteen had graduated from universities other than Oxford and Cambridge – they joined just one other already on the staff – and several had attended state schools.[8] Some taught subjects new to the timetable – Christopher Richardson led in design and drama, and Myles Sewter in computing, electronics and technology – or, in the case of physical education, now gaining common-room status.[9] These subjects needed appropriate facilities so Royds set about appealing to Old Boys and other friends of the school to fund an explosion of new buildings and conversions of old ones: a centre for design, electronics and technology – named the Thring Centre; a sports centre incorporating the 1883 swimming pool alongside a gymnasium and sports hall; an extension to the science school; a theatre in place of the 1902 gymnasium; a language laboratory and a computer room; three squash courts; a motor workshop; the horizontal division of the assembly hall to accommodate a sixth-form centre, complete with a bar; and an all-weather hockey pitch. The Bryanston-inspired Pioneers were established some thirty years after the original to offer outdoor manual labour and estate work as an arduous alternative to the cadet corps. When volunteer numbers in the corps stabilised, the Pioneers gave way to Community Service – whether service to the school or to the town and county.

Royds acknowledged Thring's principle that a 'headmaster is only headmaster of boys he knows' and made it his business to take an interest in every pupil, in part through interviews on or near their birthdays.[10] This innovation was not well received by some housemasters who saw it as spying on how they performed their roles and undermining their authority, yet they complained when he asked them to be responsible for punishment. The introduction of tutors for sixth-formers, to add academic stimulus and enhance pastoral care, was also regarded with much suspicion.

Tailcoats and starched collars went, as did striped trousers for chapel on Sundays, so too the sewing up of trouser pockets. Compulsory watching of school matches ceased, quickly consigning the crowd-controlling hunting crops to the dustbins of history; attendance at concerts and plays became voluntary but one service each Sunday remained compulsory. Here Royds took the trouble to explain his decision in a series of open letters in the school magazine.

Many of the young men appointed by Royds were keen sportsmen and the results for the school's traditional sports steadily improved. The decade from 1966 saw the Rugby football XV under the leadership of Malcolm Bussey and Michael Gavins hold its own against other schools, as did the cricket XI when Garth Wheatley gained assistance from Maurice Hallam. Peter Colville's hockey XI won the majority of its matches.[11] New or upgraded sports did even better: tennis, cross-country and athletics, led by Ashley Dawe, Michael Tolkien and Malcolm Tozer respectively, won most of their matches whilst the shooters coached by Simon Pattinson took the school to national renown, winning the Ashburton Shield five times in thirteen years.[12] Good coaching was not the whole story. Royds had introduced timetabled lessons in physical education for all in the first two years, appointed a team of five specialist teachers who also taught another subject up to sixth-form level, and initiated both remedial and rehabilitation gymnastics. Boys in their first year played Rugby football and hockey out of step with the rest of the school so that they could be taught by the best coaches and, when a year older, many were permitted to opt instead for activities in the sports centre. This allowed teams in badminton, basketball, fencing, squash, swimming and water polo to flourish, and soccer became a popular Sunday recreation. Canoeing, climbing, life-saving and sailing broadened the choice still further. Only Thring's beloved Eton fives languished.[13]

Royds was an inspiring teacher and, like Thring, especially so in religious studies. Newly-appointed subject heads were often the youngest in the department and were given the task of rejuvenating the old hands. Young masters were encouraged to work in foreign schools for a year to broaden their experience and to bring back new ideas; sixth-form leavers were challenged to do social work abroad before starting at university. Boys from Ethiopia and Hong Kong brought the outside world to Uppingham. Academic attainment rose and A-level pass-rates climbed. Music found Royds a keen supporter, concerts large and small saw him in the audience, and he asked the department to take its message beyond the talented and classically-trained.[14] Pop groups were not only allowed but also given a stage. Wolfenden's Uppingham-Corby Boys Club had ceased to function as a partnership in 1960; in its place Royds created the Action Group which raised funds for a host of causes through an array of initiatives under Peter de Voil's leadership.

The greatest leap of faith came in September 1973 when Barbara Matthews, the eldest daughter of the Second Master, was admitted to School House as a day pupil.[15] She was joined in the school the following year by the daughter of another master and the sisters of three boys at the school; the last boarded with masters' families. Then in 1975 Pat and Tony Land, members of the 1966 new wave, opened the first house for girls at Fairfield in the grounds of Thring's aviary. The full complement of fifty was reached the following year. The Royds revolution was now complete and school numbers were the highest ever. Uppingham was both successful and full.

Attention to the individual child was once more stressed; academic standards rose; music, art and drama were no longer viewed as purely effeminate activities; the cadet corps was voluntary; community service and charitable support were important; choice of leisure-time activities was permitted; team games no longer served merely to occupy time; athleticism had mellowed. A balance returned, both to the total educational experience and to its physical education content. Thring would have been pleased to see PE lessons on the timetable and qualified staff to teach them. He would also have liked the broad programme of games and sports, the enthusiasm of those who ran them, and the excellence of the new facilities. The increased provision of recreational opportunities and the attention given to remedial gymnastics were both sympathetic to his principles. The weekend and holiday expeditions in outdoor activities were merely a modern extension of Thring's rambles in the Rutland countryside. Seventy years had been lost but not Thring's 'True-life'.

The novelist E. W. Hornung remembered Thring best for his sermons in chapel; Nigel Richardson, when preparing his address for Royds's memorial service, found that many of his former pupils recalled how powerfully their headmaster commanded the pulpit, whether challenging them to think about the existence of God or to spell out how the stronger members of the community had a duty to protect the weak and eccentric.[16] Royds told them how fortunate they were and how they must capitalise on that good fortune:

> Rotten boarding schools are the rottenest of schools, but the best ones offer unrivalled opportunities for co-operation – for doing things together; games and good music, arts and crafts, the visiting of handicapped and old people; adventurous training and field studies in term-time and holidays.[17]

> Go out to meet life. On your first day at Uppingham, I urged you to make the most of the great opportunities here. Now I say it again. Don't come to the end of your life wishing you had been more adventurous, or had made better use of your opportunities. Always volunteer; always be ready to chance your arm, to accept responsibility. Your privilege lies in actually being able (more or less) to choose your work in life. Most of your fellow human beings have no such choice. Remember the other 99% and be generous in giving yourself to others.[18]

Bryan Matthews, his Second Master and an Old Boy of the school, appreciated that Royds shared Thring's belief in the value of 'True Life', and he recalled these words from Royds's final sermon, delivered shortly before he left to take Holy Orders:

> True life is to be found in true worth, where the common wealth, the common weal, the common good are the concern of all.[19]

In one of his first sermons at the school, Royds had warned parents and staff in the congregation:

> Gigantic changes are afoot . . . we need special wisdom in helping young people steer a course between dangerous extremes . . . individuality is precious, but so is unselfish service to the community.[20]

Royds had that special wisdom; from 1965 to 1974 he guided Uppingham through the turbulent years of political and social unrest, outrage at home and abroad, student rebellions and public-school demonstrations, long hair and loud music, and brought it safely to the calmer decades ahead.[21] He had managed more change in ten years than his predecessors had in thirty – or perhaps even seventy – and he brought the school full circle to rediscover its Thringian inheritance.[22] [23]

Epilogue

A few months before the events described in the Prologue, the editor of the *Uppingham School Magazine* published a letter he had received from a boy in the school:

December 1913

Dear Sir

I wish to draw attention to the fact that the statue of Edward Thring, at the West end of the Chapel, is, and has been for a long time, covered with cobwebs and dust.

Would it not be possible for this statue to be kept clean, in view both of the excellence of the sculpture and the greatness of the subject represented? A little water is all that is required.

Yours, etc.
Quidam[1]

It is indeed one of Sir Thomas Brock's finest works. When the chapel was enlarged in 1965, the statue was moved to a portico outside the new entrance. Thring now sits at the heart of the school he made, watching over his 'soldiers of Christ'. It is a happy coincidence that his elevation from dust-covered relic to revered revolutionary occurred in the same year as the school's rediscovery of the principles and practice of True Life.

The economic, social and political conditions of the 1960s made possible the changes Royds sought: Napoleon looked for lucky generals; Uppingham got a lucky headmaster. His successors of the late twentieth century did not share his good fortune but the school was well set for the future; steady development rather than still more revolution was needed. The exhilarating decade was also exhausting and a period of calm was required. Coll Macdonald pushed forward the academic reforms but otherwise relaxed the pace of change; Nicholas Bomford valued pupils as individuals, delegated to good effect, managed a smooth-running school, gave great support to the music and arts, created a second girls' house and led a harmonious community; Stephen Winkley took the school to full co-education; and, in the new century, Richard Harman oversaw an extensive building programme.[2] Harman was Chairman of the Headmasters' and Headmistresses' Conference (HMC) in 2014, the first Uppingham headmaster to hold this position since Thring in 1869.[3]

Royds was a private and modest man. He concentrated all his efforts on Uppingham: he published nothing, shunned publicity, rarely attended conferences and avoided other headmasters. It is doubtful that he had influence beyond his school but, nonetheless, the last quarter of the twentieth century witnessed the revival of the whole-man ideal across the independent sector. M. L. Jacks and Thorold Coade were the likely sources of inspiration.[4]

David Newsome, Master at Wellington from 1979 to 1989, built his career on spiritual values, transforming a military and games-playing school to one with greater academic focus, stronger appreciation of the arts, and religion at the heart of the community. In an address to the Headmasters' Conference in 1972, when Headmaster of Christ's Hospital, he asked his fellow headmasters 'to imagine the rebuilding of a school after some dreadful catastrophe': his theme was that the heart of the school would not beat if the chapel was left to last.[5] Not all his listeners agreed but Newsome later got his chance, constructing the Crypt Chapel of The Epiphany at Wellington, not after a catastrophe but for private prayer and meditation.[6] Ian Beer, Headmaster at Harrow from 1981 to 1991, also subscribed to the whole-man ethos.[7] He was judged by the school's historian to have 'refashioned the ideals of Christian manliness' through 'his enthusiasm for holistic education'. Beer insisted that Harrow

> must be seen to be producing from the School pupils who will become men of integrity to manage our own country and its institutions, and also pupils who are motivated by the power of the spirit to go out into the world to work for the service of others.[8]

Thring would have approved.

The education of the whole man and attention to the individual child are the two central legacies of Thring's Uppingham; the principles and practices he established in the mid-Victorian years can be found in most independent schools of the twenty-first century. Attractive surroundings and a homely atmosphere; Christian teaching and moral guidance; pastoral care and concern for well-being; intellectual training and a broad general knowledge; a well-planned physical education programme and real attention to the arts and music; a sense of communal responsibility and charity to the less fortunate; the joy of childhood and preparation for adult citizenship; and a spirit of individual freedom – all these comprised an education in manliness. The current concern for character, happiness, emotional health, determination, resilience and perseverance whilst maintaining high attainment in all areas of the curriculum matches Thring's striving for a balance of the Platonic virtues of truth, courage and self-control.

Today's independent schools teach more pupils and are more successful than at any previous period in their long histories. The 1,301 in membership of the Independent Schools Council in 2017 educate nearly 7% of the school population – up from 4.5% in 1978 – produce the highest academic standards, send 90% of their boys and girls to university and prepare them for careers well beyond the traditional professions. Entrepreneurship and the internet, opera and popular music, literature and journalism, acting on both stage and screen, art and architecture, design and technology, Olympic medals and international caps, all see an over-representation by their former pupils and serve as testaments to the whole-man ideal. British independent schools have a world-wide reputation for excellence: children from more than thirty countries come to study in them and a network of foreign outposts has exported the brand across Europe, the Middle East and Asia. The legacy of Edward Thring's ideal of manliness has appeal across the globe.[9]

Richard Maloney has been Headmaster of Uppingham since 2016. It is proper that he should have the final word.

> Thring's legacy remains an inspiration to those who live and breathe Uppingham. Undeniably, he was a man ahead of his time. His foresight and uncompromising desire to put the whole person at the heart of education has only been adopted as guiding wisdom within the British educational system a century after his death. Happily, whilst other Victorian heads have historically hogged the literary limelight, Thring's contribution to education is now being re-appraised for its perceptive enlightenedness.
>
> As Thring's inheritors, our task is to reinterpret his legacy for a world that is moving through periods of change with unprecedented rapidity. The future world today's pupils will join is dynamic, faster-paced, ever-changing and global. The growth of digitalisation means almost every job will become technologically-related. Future work will become much more interconnected: different professions, working flexibly, collaborating and working virtually – across increasingly arbitrary geo-political borders – will become the norm. Innovation and creativity will matter more. Employment will be more flexible – the concept of a 'job for life' will disappear. Personal agility, resilience and risk-taking will be essential. In future, a highly-skilled minority of people will have the greatest bargaining power and those people who have strong creative, analytical, problem-solving and communication skills will thrive.
>
> Ultimately this means schools too have to be creative. Just as Thring recognised nineteenth-century schools were failing to respond to pupils' evolving needs during the transformational Victorian era, today's generation of educators are duty-bound to ensure that schools in the twenty-first century do more to address children's future needs. We have to understand the flexibility of work as it becomes less location-specific, more

network-oriented, project-based and increasingly technology-intensive. The next generation will have to take greater personal responsibility for acquiring and continuously updating their skills. They need to know how to take advantage of new and different approaches to learning and technology. Today's young people must be empowered to be courageous so that they can jump across specialist knowledge boundaries as technologies and work disciplines converge.

Uppingham, through its connections and networks, has to provide a global perspective and access to future-facing opportunities for its pupils. Most importantly, and just as Thring did in his era, the whole community must be inspired to think differently and change the world for the better, but without misplacing the very thing – Thring's philosophy – that gives Uppingham its soul.[10]

Publications

Some of the material in this book was originally published elsewhere:

1 *Physical Education at Thring's Uppingham*, Uppingham School, Uppingham, 1976.
2 The Lesson of Borth, in G. E. Frowde (ed) *The Borth Centenary Magazine*, Uppingham School, Uppingham, July 1977, pp. 29–30.
3 From Muscular Christianity to Esprit de Corps: Games in the Victorian Public Schools of England, *Stadion*, vol. 7, no. 1, Winter 1981, pp. 117–130.
4 Charles Kingsley and the Muscular Christian Ideal of Manliness, *Physical Education Review*, vol. 8, no. 1, Summer 1985, pp. 35–40.
5 Thring at Uppingham-by-the-Sea: The Lesson of the Borth Sermons, *History of Education Society Bulletin*, no. 36, Autumn 1985, pp. 39–44.
6 The Consecration of the Body: Physical Education at Almond's Loretto, *Physical Education Review*, vol. 8, no. 2, Winter 1985, pp. 84–89.
7 Education in Manliness: Idealist, Ideal and Exemplar – A Centenary Essay: Edward Thring, 1821–87, *Religion*, vol. 17, January 1987, pp. 63–80.★
8 The Joy of Strength and Movement: A Centennial Appreciation of Edward Thring, *Physical Education Review*, vol. 10, no. 1, Spring 1987, pp. 58–63.
9 Education for True Life: A Review of Thring's Educational Aims and Methods, *History of Education Society Bulletin*, no. 39, Spring 1987, pp. 24–31.
10 Safer to Trust Much Than to Trust Little: Moral Education at Thring's Uppingham, *The Journal of Moral Education*, vol. 16, no. 2, May 1987, pp. 131–138.★
11 Happy Gains: Edward Thring's Obligations to Literature – A Centenary Essay, *Journal of Education Administration and History*, vol. 19, no. 2, July 1987, pp. 26–35.★
12 Edward Thring, 1821–1887: The Most Christian Man of His Generation, *Education Research and Perspective*, vol. 15, no. 2, December 1988, pp. 3–15.
13 Thomas Hughes: Tom Brown Versus True Manliness, *Physical Education Review*, vol. 12, no. 1, Spring 1989, pp. 44–48.
14 Cricket, School and Empire: E. W. Hornung and His Young Guard, *International Journal of the History of Sport*, vol. 6, no. 2, September 1989, pp. 156–171.★
15 The Readiest Hand and the Most Open Heart: Uppingham's First Missions to the Poor, *History of Education*, vol. 18, no. 4, December 1989, pp. 323–332.★
16 The Great Educational Experiment: Edward Thring at Uppingham School, *Rutland Record*, no. 12, 1992, pp. 58–65.
17 To the Glory That Was Greece: Classical Images in Public School Athleticism, in Tom Winnifrith and Cyril Barratt (eds) *Leisure in Art and Literature*, Palgrave Macmillan, London, 1992, pp. 109–129.

18 To the Glory That Was Greece: Classical Images of Athleticism in the Public Schools of Victorian and Edwardian England, in Fritz-Peter Hager (ed) *Aspects of Antiquity in the History of Education*, Bildung and Wissenschaft, Hannover, 1992, pp. 213–226.

19 A Sacred Trinity – Cricket, School and Empire: E. W. Hornung and His Young Guard, in J. A. Mangan (ed) *The Cultural Bond: Sport, Empire and Society*, Frank Cass, London, 1992, pp. 11–26.

20 That Humpty Dumpty Word: Manliness in the Victorian Era, *Physical Education Review*, vol. 16, no. 2, Autumn 1993, pp. 131–135.

21 H. H. Stephenson: The First of the Great School Coaches, *The Journal of the Cricket Society*, vol. 17, no. 1, Autumn 1994, pp. 15–20.

22 Genial Solvents: German Influences at a Victorian English Public School, *History of Education Society Bulletin*, no. 54, Autumn 1994, pp. 21–28.

23 H. H. Stephenson: The First of the Great School Coaches, *The Sports Historian*, no. 15, May 1995, pp. 54–64.★

24 A Perfect Pattern of Manly Power: Coming to Manhood at Mid-Victorian Uppingham School, *Rutland Record*, no. 32, 2012, pp. 79–85.

    ★ Available on-line from the Taylor & Francis website: www.tandfonline.com/

Permission to reuse material has been granted by: 1 & 2 – Uppingham School; 3 & 18 – Academia Verlag GmbH; 4, 6, 8, 13 & 20 – Sage Publications, Inc.; 5, 9, 15 & 22 – History of Education Society; 7, 10, 11, 12, 14, 19 & 23 – Taylor & Francis; 16 & 24 – Rutland Record Society; 17 – Palgrave Macmillan; 21 – Cricket Society.

Index